Practicing Professional Ethics in Economics and Public Policy

Elizabeth A.M. Searing • Donald R. Searing
Editors

Practicing Professional Ethics in Economics and Public Policy

Editors
Elizabeth A.M. Searing
Department of Public Administration and Policy
Rockefeller College of Public Affairs and Policy
University at Albany – State University of New York
Albany, New York, USA

Donald R. Searing
Syncere Systems
Altamont, NY, USA

ISBN 978-94-017-7305-8 ISBN 978-94-017-7306-5 (eBook)
DOI 10.1007/978-94-017-7306-5

Library of Congress Control Number: 2015960200

Springer Dordrecht Heidelberg New York London

Printed on acid-free paper

Springer Science+Business Media B.V. Dordrecht is part of Springer Science+Business Media (www.springer.com)

This book is dedicated to the late
Woods Bowman,
A scholar, friend, and inspiration
to all who knew him

Preface

As I write this, I am sitting at an inn in Chitipa, Malawi. Chitipa is the northernmost district in this African country, sharing borders with both Tanzania and Zambia; citizens here endure higher levels of poverty and restricted access to basic services even compared to the rest of Malawi, which ranked 171 out of 187 countries in the Human Development Index in 2011 (United Nations Development Programme, 2011). I am here working with a nonprofit that was formed when a large INGO pulled out after a completed project, leaving an extensive network of over 300 churches to deliver a wide swath of human services. Since then, the churches have mobilized within their own NGO and expanded the original scope beyond even the boundaries of the original project, motivated by the knowledge that they are improving their own families and neighbors.

The electricity has gone out, as it is wont to do. The generator will kick in soon, which is a luxury here, but a necessary business expense for an establishment that houses *mzungu* (non-Africans). I am waiting for dinner, which will include *nsima* or white rice with a standard set of accompaniments (never all set out at once in a normal household – again, a luxury of being foreign). I mull the implications of what appears to be a successful devaluation of the Malawi *kwacha* on the people in and around this town. Since the devaluation and the ascendance to power of the most recent president, there is fuel available for the first time in years, and the road to the town is being paved. But the food stalls and goods vendors in the market are the closest thing to perfect competition I have ever seen, and there is no discernible margin for the sellers. Life can be very hard here for my new associates.

There is no shortage of ethical and moral questions in the practice of economics and public policy and anyone in those fields have had to address them, whether they admit it or whether they cling to the myth of positivist objectivity. Resources are scarce, and this is evident in the distribution of wealth, intellectual capital, disease prevalence, and so on in the world around you. There are static questions (what is the scenario?) and dynamic questions (how did the scenario become this, and how will it progress?). Inherent in the social sciences, however, are two elements: human behavior and normative elements. There are some that will insist that the place of economics is to describe the scenario and then project, dispassionately, how things would progress given a certain set of assumptions. The assumption which is overlooked, however, is that upon discovering such information, there is an inherent decision about whether such a situation should perpetuate. Unless our job involves explicit capacity for giving advice, we tend to comfort ourselves that we are there simply there to conduct the measurement, without regard to context or potential impacts. This is false. If we insist that our fields are sciences, we must be concerned with causal issues. If we are concerned with causal issues, we aspire to some degree of predictive power. Predictive power gives us the capacity to render aid – we cannot claim one without the other. Therefore, claiming the mantle of objectivity does not excuse us from making a normative judgment on preference – the abstention from a decision is still a decision. As numerous writers have opined, "[o]n the Plains of Hesitation bleach the bones of countless millions, who, at the Dawn of Victory, sat down to wait, and waiting died" (Cecil, 1923). The additional complication for public policy is that, based on our advice, many others may inadvertently sit down with us. The fact that we are uneasy with that does not excuse us from it.

Most of us realize this and have taken up the mantle of an applied social science because we have elected to spend your time attempting to improve this process in some way. The decision to spend money on school nurses or teacher raises or the recommendation of austerity measures or quantitative easing (or both) will now at least in part be up to you.

As I finish writing this piece, I am on the beach at Chintheche, also in Malawi. I ordered off a menu for dinner – chicken with feta and basil, gammon with honey-glazed sweet potatoes, or vegetable lasagna. The prices here are still low compared to the USA (about 50 cents for a bottle of Coke), but not as low as in Chitipa. Here at Chintheche, there are still people willing to trade a beautiful woodcarving for a pair of shorts on the other side of the resort gate, and there are children who wait in the reeds along the beach and shout "give me money" or "sweeties" in hopes of the candy they've learned *mzungu* will bring. Am I heartless that I give no candy? Or would I be heartless if I did? Or am I heartless for not spending all of my *kwacha* in Chitipa? What about the owners of this inn; who are located here out of a love for the community and the environment?

This book isn't going to tell you how to be a moral professional – you have other books, trainings, and experiences which are all a part of that. But it will clarify your thinking regarding how to implement ethics in your work. You may feel like a new *mzungu* in Chitipa – you feel as if you have no ability to communicate, no tools, and no knowledge of the ethical terrain. But take a good look around – you'll find that the formal tools of philosophers will become less intimidating and the practice of professional ethics more natural (and, as a note, that many Chitipans will speak English as clearly as you). It is time to apply rigorous and methodological thinking not only to our work but into how we work. Chitipa, and the rest of the world, will be the better for it.

Chitipa, Malawi
August 6, 2012

Elizabeth A.M. Searing

References

Cecil, G. W. (1923). Advertisement for international correspondence schools. *The American Magazine*, p. 87.

United Nations Development Programme. (2011). *Human development report 2011: Malawi.*

Contents

Part I
The Role of Ethics

Émile's knowledge is confined to nature and things. The very name of history is unknown to him, along with metaphysics and morals.
He knows the essential relations between men and things, but nothing of the moral relations between man and man.
He has little power of generalisation, he has no skill in abstraction.
He perceives that certain qualities are common to certain things, without reasoning about these qualities themselves.
He is acquainted with the abstract idea of space by the help of his geometrical figures; he is acquainted with the abstract idea of quantity by the help of his algebraical symbols.
These figures and signs are the supports on which these ideas may be said to rest, the supports on which his senses repose.
He does not attempt to know the nature of things, but only to know things in so far as they affect himself.
He only judges what is outside himself in relation to himself, and his judgment is exact and certain. Caprice and prejudice have no part in it.
He values most the things which are of use to himself, and as he never departs from this standard of values, he owes nothing to prejudice. . .
In a word Emile is possessed of all that portion of virtue which concerns himself.
To acquire the social virtues he only needs a knowledge of the relations which make those virtues necessary; he only lacks knowledge which he is quite ready to receive.

-Jean-Jacques Rousseau, *Émile, Or Treatise on Education,* 1899

Chapter 1
Why Am I Reading This?

Elizabeth A.M. Searing and Donald R. Searing

Abstract This chapter provides a brief introduction to the text, as well as the motivation behind the development of such a book. The difference between the use of normative elements in public policy analysis and the practice of professional ethics is discussed, with additional resources mentioned. The authors emphasize the need for an accessible ethical vocabulary and how the components of the manual – brief philosopher summaries, a decision methodology based on statistical tests, and the inclusion of personal essays from ethical exemplars in the field – advance the field of professional ethics in the policy sciences.

Keywords Ethics • Economics • Public policy • Professional ethics

1.1 Judgment Day

On June 7 of 2010, Alan Greenspan was called before a Congressional committee to explain the role of the Federal Reserve and his own judgment in the financial crisis. A great deal of the political discussion was along party lines: 2 years prior, Republicans held Fannie and Freddie to blame, while Democrats were more apt to hold Mr. Greenspan himself personally accountable (Andrews, 2008). Greenspan pointed the finger primarily at Wall Street, claiming that regulators are hopelessly outgunned by the complexities of the financial markets and the institutions that manipulate the market (Nasiripour & McCarthy, 2010).

Following this heated public inquiry of Greenspan came a steady parade of actors, both literally and figuratively. Congress called Alan Greenspan several more times, as well as other Federal Reserve officials such as Ben Bernanke. Other members of the government were also called, such as Geithner from the Treasury and

E.A.M. Searing, PhD (✉)
Assistant Professor, Department of Public Administration and Policy, Rockefeller College of Public Affairs and Policy, University at Albany – State University of New York, 305 Milne Hall, 135 Western Avenue, Albany, New York, USA
e-mail: esearing@albany.edu

D.R. Searing, PhD
CEO and Principal Scientist, Syncere Systems, Altamont, NY, USA
e-mail: dsearing@synceresystems.com

E.A.M. Searing, D.R. Searing (eds.), *Practicing Professional Ethics in Economics and Public Policy*, DOI 10.1007/978-94-017-7306-5_1

several members of the Securities and Exchange Commission. Members of government-sponsored or – owned corporations such as Fannie Mae and the FDOC were called. Corporate leaders and analysts such as AIG, Lehman, and former Citigroup executives gave testimony, often to a more hostile reception than even Greenspan received; the most notorious moment of the testimony was when the Vice Chairman of the Financial Crisis Inquiry Commission asked the Citigroup executives to raise their hands if they lost sleep over their role in the crisis. The bewildered (former) executives didn't react fast enough and received a verbal scourging (Nasiripour & McCarthy, 2010). Even though this formal series of depositions culminated in The Financial Crisis Inquiry Report (United States Financial Crisis Inquiry Commission, 2011), inquiries and discussions continue to go forward over the proper handling of the financial meltdown and what the professional responsibilities are of those who played a role.

Following this group of professionals came a media onslaught covering the material. Michael Lewis wrote *The Big Short*, which looked at the lead-up to the financial crisis through the action in the subprime mortgage markets (Lewis, 2011). *Too Big to Fail* offered a more complete view of the catastrophe, with private stories from individuals already known to be involved and painting them, if not in a sympathetic light, at least a human one (Sorkin, 2010). *House of Cards*, on the other hand, was a fierce attack on most every person involved in the crisis (Cohan, 2010). *Diary of a Very Bad Year* was a somewhat uncouth relating of the financial crisis narrated through an ongoing conversation between the author (a journalist) and an anonymous snarky hedge fund manager (Gessen, 2010).

These were accompanied by books which didn't specifically target the financial crisis, but rather the methods used by economists. *Models. Behaving. Badly.* cast light on the often tenuous assumptions which are needed to achieve certain complex financial models (Derman, 2011). Scott Patterson sounded the same alarm with *The Quants*, focusing instead on the personalities of the mathematical revolution rather than its properties (2010). There were also book releases from several well-established behavioral economists such as George Akerlof, Robert Shiller, and Dan Ariely, each encouraging us to step beyond the traditionally-held bounds of rationality (Akerlof & Shiller, 2009; Ariely, 2009).

Most of us in the financial and policy industries, however, will remember that such tales are not unique. The financial markets had been through the wringer before: Michael Lewis got his start with *Liar's Poker* (Lewis, 1989). There was also the debacle surrounding the junk bonds, well told in Bruck's *Predator's Ball* (Bruck, 1989). Even prior to that was the savings and loan crisis, brought about by a combination of swift deregulation and opportunists (Lowy, 1991). So, on some level, we in the industry expected this to pass. There may be new regulations or a new agency, but there was little mention of ethics outside of the press. There was no widespread mention of changes from inside the industry, and the American Economic Association (AEA) spent more time insisting that they were not a regulatory body than actually dedicating space to the discussion of a formal code of ethics. This is best illustrated in the words of Alfred Coats, who had stated over a decade prior that "[t]he AEA needed no special code of ethics because the canons of correct professional practice were too obvious to require specification" (Coats, 1985). Logically, if you would drop a stapler, the mathematical formulas which would govern its descent to the floor would apply, regardless of who pays your salary. How was economics any different?

Then came *The Inside Job* (2010). The constant trickle of calls for discussions on ethics that had been occurring for years from pioneers such as Deirdre McCloskey and, more recently, George DeMartino quickly became a chorus from inside the industry. In the opening days of 2011, over 300 economists and other social scientists signed an open letter to the President of the AEA calling for the creation of a code of ethics (Chan, 2011). In response, the AEA assembled the Ad Hoc Committee on Ethical Standards for Economists at their 2011 meeting (Berrett, 2011). Finally, the industry had begun to take notice.

1.2 Ethics and Social Science

Empirical social scientists generally come to ethics in one of two ways: a thought that has been simmering for a while in the back of the mind, or a pot that has just boiled over and requires immediate comprehension and clean-up.

I have no doubt that there will be many philosophers that disagree with the interpretation of a person or methodology in this text; we similarly believe that many statisticians will consider the use of statistical terms in what is often a verbally anecdotal way to be sophomoric, even scandalous. Bayesian theorists may very well weep knowing that copies of this book are available in the open marketplace. To us, however, the purpose of this book is very similar to trying to find the commode in a restaurant in a foreign country: everyone in the situation has an understanding of the process and necessity, but we can't seem to find enough common vocabulary to get the point across. If anything, we find ourselves in the more difficult scenario, there being few ways to easily pantomime to our bewildered audience any message regarding fiduciary duty or Pareto optimization. The language of hypotheses and statistics provides a translation of the often arcane people and formal processes of ethical theory and procedures into something tangible for policy scientists.

There are many books which have been written over the past few decades that make an elegant and powerful case for the involvement of ethics and moral concerns in economics and public policy. More recently, the first steps have been made into trying to codify such needs on a professional level; however, the lack of professional ethical training, whether in the classroom or the pit floor, in addition to the anemic standards put forth by many professional groups and exemplars highlight a continued need. A gap continues to persist between the acknowledgment that professional ethics is called for and the realization of such a tenet as a heuristic that any social science professional is comfortable using. This book attempts to operationalize that need.

1.3 Why Should I Read an Ethics Book?

Though we firmly believe that anyone is capable of making thoughtful and purposive ethical decisions, we also believe that this process does not always occur naturally. Numerous incentives and heuristics play into how we make decisions.

A great deal of the time, we are not even aware that we are calculating options or how we are doing so (for example, how long did it take you to decide which hand to use to turn the page just now? Were you aware you made a decision just then?)

Even when we are aware, we're not sure how we came to or how to express that process. Think of a child learning addition for the first time. They will understand conceptually, when holding an orange in each hand, that they have two oranges. The next step is counting each aloud, recognizing that there are separate pieces and words corresponding to each piece: ("one . . . two") two oranges. The step after that is the walking through the process of actual addition: holding one orange, then adding another one orange in the other hand. Finally, and perhaps not even on the same day, the child will learn to write the symbols that stand for the actions she just did.

Ethical decision-making is much the same way. We decide things every moment, with and without realizing we are doing so. We've been deciding things for so long (since birth, really) that it often doesn't require deliberate thought. But how well do you know how to make a decision? How do you tend to react when faced with ambiguous information? Do you have an innate tendency to dwell on conceptual and definitional issues? When you ask yourself what the "right" thing to do in a situation is, what percentage of the group normally ends up better off – a majority or a small section? As you can see, once you decompose the decision process, the elements become more complicated; things complicate further when you try to determine your own natural tendencies toward a method or moral approach (for example, you may already be familiar with utilitarianism, but maybe not other moral theories that have a different take on which actions and decisions are morally permissible and forbidden). This isn't to say you've been making decisions incorrectly – probably quite the opposite. But what this book does is help you slow the journey down so you can make the correct choices on your path and be able to navigate your way back, should you ever be called on the carpet to do so.

Just when you thought knowing thyself was enough, somewhere along the road, we became social and policy scientists. Even if we had years of philosophical or ethical training, the notion of professional ethics adds a different lens to the decision-making process. We are no longer asking ourselves what we believe is moral to occur in a given situation, but specifically asking what is ethical or ought to occur in a particular situation *due directly **to or through** the fact that we are public policy professionals.*

This is a point of departure between this text and many of the other quality works that exist in the field of normative elements in economics, including ethics. This text does not take a stand on acceptable usury, the existence or level of minimum wage in the United States, or on the supremacy of either utilitarian or rights-based reasoning in times when they conflict. There are many quality works that do, and we consider it your professional obligation to be familiar with their arguments. However, that is not why this book exists.

This text accepts that scientists of different religious, moral, cultural, and political ideologies all need to practice their professions with a guiding set of principles; we also understand that each of those scientists will be acting in a professional capacity with individuals who have different moral groundings and backgrounds. This book is built around the belief that simply approaching a decision from only one line of ethical reasoning is short-sighted. By using a portfolio of ethical tests representing the broadest spectrum of different moral theoretic traditions, even if you had been flawlessly separating facts from factual issues and filtering the information through your Benthamite calculus, you open yourself to new possibilities and improve your chances of finding the best course of action.

First, you may have overlooked a group of stakeholders or missed a potential externality. This occurs not necessarily because you neglected the process, but because there is an inherent heuristic conflict in what we do. For example, on an extremely simplified level, economists and policy professionals are utility aggregationists; yes, there are several ways of modelling the precise weights and sources of utility across the society, but on some level the whole is dependent on its parts. This means we often tend toward the utilitarian schools of thought when we rely on our basic tool set: we are trying to serve as many as possible with the limited resources we have available. Even those readers who are not economists are likely in the public sector and have an interest in serving as many of the public at large as possible. However, somewhat paradoxically, most of us in public policy are employed at least in partial answer to provide a public good or address a market inadequacy. We coordinate transfer payments, draft environmental policy, target inflation rates, forecast housing prices, fund schools, hunt fraud, and run nonprofit organizations. The largest aggregation of voters will help keep you employed, but one man with a computer can download top secret memos and bring down governments. You'd best know how to understand the needs of both these types of audiences.

Second, even if the initial analyses do not sway you from your original conclusion, you are now familiar with the objections that other points of view will have with your proposed course of action. Very few in our line of work have the ability (fortunately) to issue edicts without concern for who may object, so being aware not only of the dissenters' arguments, but of their underlying factual and conceptual assumptions and differences is a beneficial side-effect of having completed the analytical process. Very few times will you face an objection from a professional colleague that is being made simply out of thin air. Therefore, even if you remain completely convinced that your initial gut feeling was correct after subjecting it to more rigorous methods, you are better able to understand the objections of others and coherently defend your reasoning.

1.4 Why Should I Read This Ethics Book?

As previously mentioned, there is an existing literature on the role of morality in the markets, with additional branches that specifically address the need for professional ethics in our lines of work. So what is this text adding to the existing field?

This text is designed to be a standalone resource for a course on professional ethics. Ethics training of some type in professional programs is now often mandatory, but will come in a wide variety of forms. For example, at the home institution of one of the authors, a half day of in-person training and a short online module were required to acquaint the budding social scientist with research ethics. Exposure to professional ethics as a public policy professional was also required as a prerequisite to the program, but the actual course on ethics was never offered. At other academic institutions, requirements vary between full semester-long courses to one-credit seminar courses to administrative waiving (though the latter is diminishing as legal requirements for ethics training increases). Outside of academia, the state of ethical training varies widely between sectors and professions. The regulated professions which require credentialing, such as engineering and law, often require adherence to a code of professional ethics as a part of the licensure necessary to practice. Those that do not require credentialing but do have a dominant professional society, such as the fields of statistics and sociology, also have codes of professional ethics that are mandated for those who wish to join the ranks of the society. At the time of writing, economics is somewhat unique in that the dominant professional society has only recently considered itself in need of a code of ethics, and the code produced addresses only a few concerns that an economist encounters in professional experience.

Such a wide variety of preparation is best accommodated with a few things. First, few of us will assemble a list of reading materials to acquaint ourselves with the field of ethics: if we haven't read Aristotle or Hume already, we've likely resigned ourselves to the fact that we can live comfortably without doing so, especially given our busy lives. This is, however, unfortunate. There are several scholars who have made important contributions to the way we think, but have written in texts that are too long or too abstract for most of us to get through. If there was a kind of greatest hits collection of classical works that related to professional ethics in economics, it wouldn't necessarily be ideal, but would fill a gap that is often either left empty or filled with photocopied original readings that students skim right before lecture or professionals might get to "later."

Second, the process of actually making a decision of any kind needs to be walked through in detail so we can understand how we currently develop and process our choices and where we may be short-sighted in our approach and analytical depth. Part of this process is simply making the decision process much more deliberate. Different pieces need to be identified, such as facts, concepts, and values, with each of these being evaluated as to level of ambiguity and potential role in the situation. Stakeholder groups should be determined and causal linkages mapped. Gaps in information (factual and otherwise) need to be identified and either remedied or stabilized with an admitted assumption. This iterative process of making a map of the decision landscape is essential to both proceeding with an ethical decision and in explaining the reasoning post hoc.

Third, there needs to be a way to bridge the gap between the theoretical knowledge we have of ethics and the very real decisions that we find ourselves making. Many professionals consider concepts such as utilitarianism and rights-based reasoning (i.e., the deontological approach) to be abstract theories that have little practical value when an individual actually finds himself confronted with an ethical quandary (Guillemin & Gillem, 2004; Rallis & Rossman 2012). Part of this challenge comes from the breadth of ways that any course of action can be deemed ethical: based on a utilitarian calculus, using a deontological approach, or using virtue theory to determine the virtuous course of action. We touched on this previously in our discussion of the need to learn and use a portfolio of ethical approaches. However, we also need to adopt the language and procedure of ethics to a methodology that we find useful for our needs. Philosophers may enjoy series of thought experiments or leisurely sessions thinking about thinking, but we need to apply those ideas in a way that we can carry in our policy toolbox. This text has chosen the language of statistical hypothesis testing, which is a natural fit for the likely reader, as it maps our ethical algorithm to the methods we already use in practice. Further, it is a methodology that many, if not most in the policy sciences are familiar with and can provide a common tongue across sub-disciplines.

Finally, many of us do, in fact, think about ethics on a regular basis. Additionally, the fact that you're reading this book means that some element of selection bias is at play. However, we're not always sure what other people are thinking. Do our co-workers think about ethics? What about our mentors? In order to answer these questions, this book includes casual and personal stories about professional ethics from ten leading minds in their respective policy fields. We know that the opportunity to talk to someone else about ethics isn't always available, though we encourage you to do so and provide resources to make that easier. But since our ten notable authors are unable to sit down over a cup of coffee and offer their perspectives on professional ethics with each of us personally, they instead wrote what they would say in a form we could all share.

1.5 Contents of the Text

This book does not discuss, per se, potential moral transgressions in economics, nor does it seek to justify whether a code of ethics for economists should exist. Other texts have done very admirable jobs in doing this. Rather, this text is a handbook for those in the public policy profession who want to know why and how to incorporate professional ethics into the daily practice of their craft. We hope that this volume addresses that need, and it does so in three sections.

In Sect. 1.1, we discuss the role of ethics in the life of a professional: why it is present and, more importantly, why you should care. Chapter 1, which is underway, provides a general introduction to the book, its motivation, and its purpose. Chapter 2 contains biographies of a series of notable philosophers and economists whose works contribute largely to the body of modern ethical thought. The aim of this sizable chapter is to make available the names and concepts which may have passing familiarity and make their contribution accessible to the policy professional and to encourage you into deeper readings into the works of these notable figures. There will inevitably be disputes regarding the people included on any list of "necessary" philosophy reading; many will cringe to see Marx, while others will be angered to see Rand. However, the 16 people here are only meant as the bare minimum you need to know in order to responsibly conduct yourself in a conversation regarding the intersection of applied ethics and applied economics. This includes both the classic figures and those more divisive contributors from the last century, but without whom it would be difficult to understand the modern context in economics and public policy. I would highly recommend all readers to expand this list, not only to other traditional favorites such as Ricardo but also to heterodox scholars, institutionalists, social psychologists, and views of economic systems which originate outside of Western thought.[1] The number of viewpoints available in economics is diverse and rich, though they may not be on the front page of the newspapers or textbooks you may already have been exposed to. Of equal importance to reading about the original works and biographical details of the authors is understanding their ideas in their words by knowing the type of world that produced them.

In Sect. 1.2, we present an ethical problem-solving methodology tailored with the methods and vernacular of data analysis that is the constant companion of economists and policy professionals alike. Inspired by a model and teaching method in use for engineering ethics for almost 20 years (Harris, Pritchard, & Rabins, 2000; McLaren, 2006; Searing, 1998), decision components are broken down, analyzed, reassembled, and systematically tested in order to find the best solution to the problem at hand. Each step of the process directly mirrors and is explicitly linked with procedures already known to the reader and ties back to the theoretical materials touched on in Sect. 1.1. In Chap. 3, data collection and categorization is discussed; each piece can be classified according to known and unknown status, in addition to its nature as a fact, concept, value, or assumption. Following verification and explicit addressing of potential sources of bias, Chap. 4 discusses the formation and testing of ethical hypotheses. Said testing is actually a series of independent analyses each representing a different school of moral thought (utilitarianism versus the ethics of deontology) or process of moral reasoning (situational versus universal). Chapter 5 introduces moral reasoning techniques that are used to analyze the results of the hypothesis testing and generate ethical conclusions. Chapter 6 contains a pair of detailed case studies that are used as illustrations of the ethical decision procedure in real-life scenarios.

Section 1.3 marks the shift from internal justification and methods of ethical practice to their empirical relevance and use. It contains a series of short, casual

[1] An excellent and more exhaustive resource for the curious is *Handbook for Economics and Ethics* by Jan Peil and Irene van Staveren (2009).

essays from leading figures in a variety of subfields. Experts in topics such as nonprofit management and experimental economics were asked to share their own personal experiences and advice for practitioners who were beginning in their fields; here is a wealth of actual experience that can serve not only as an exemplar for your own specialty, but also as a window into the function of other specialties with which you may not be as familiar. As editors, we were constantly struck not only by the candid warmth of our contributors, but also of how much they had to offer each other when read together. The text concludes with an Ethical Analysis Workbook and links to various professional codes of ethics contained in the appendices.

Discussion Questions

1. Do you believe there should be a code of ethical conduct for economists? Why or why not?
2. If there should be a code of ethics for economists and public policy professionals, whom should be responsible for developing the cod
3. Should there be enforcement of ethical standards amongst policy professionals, and who should conduct the enforcement? Do you believe that a formal enforcement mechanism is important to the success of ethical practice?

References

Akerlof, G. A., & Shiller, R. J. (2009). *Animal spirits: How human psychology drives the economy, and why it matters for global capitalism*. Princeton, UK: Princeton Univ Pr.

Andrews, E. L. (2008, October 23). Greenspan concedes error on regulation. *New York Times*, New York.

Ariely, D. (2009). *Predictably irrational, revised and expanded edition: The hidden forces that shape our decisions*. New York: HarperCollins.

Berrett, D. (2011, April 19). The "Inside Job" effect. *Inside Higher Ed.*, Washington, DC.

Bruck, C. (1989). *Predator's ball*. London: Penguin.

Chan, S. (2011, January 4). Letter calls on economists to adopt code of ethics. *New York Times*, New York.

Coats, A. (1985). The American Economic Association and the economics profession. *Journal of Economic Literature, 23*(4), 1697–1727.

Cohan, W. (2010). *House of cards: A tale of Hubris and wretched excess on Wall Street*. New York: Doubleday.

Derman, E. (2011). *Models. Behaving. Badly.: Why confusing illusion with reality can lead to disaster, on Wall Street and in life*. New York: Simon and Schuster.

Ferguson, C. (Writer) (2010). *Inside job*. USA.

Gessen, K. (2010). *Diary of a very bad year: Interviews with an anonymous hedge fund manager*. New York: HarperCollins.

Guillemin, M., & Gillam, L. (2004). Ethics, reflexivity, and "ethically important moments" in research. *Qualitative Inquiry, 10*(2), 261–280.

Harris, C. E., Pritchard, M. S., & Rabins, M. J. (2000). *Engineering ethics: Concepts and cases* (2nd ed.). Belmont, CA: Wadsworth Publishing Company.

Lewis, M. (2011). *The big short: Inside the doomsday machine*. New York: WW Norton & Company.

Lewis, M. M. (1989). *Liar's poker: Rising through the wreckage on Wall Street*. New York: WW Norton & Company.

Lowy, M. E. (1991). *High rollers: Inside the savings and loan debacle*. New York: Greenwood Publishing Group.

McLaren, B. M. (2006). Computational models of ethical reasoning: Challenges, initial steps, and future directions. *Intelligent Systems IEEE, 21*(4), 29–37.

Nasiripour, S., & McCarthy, R. (2010, June 7). Greenspan testifies to financial crisis commission, blames Fannie, Freddie for subprime crisis. *Huffington Post*, New York.

Patterson, S. (2010). *The quants: How a new breed of math whizzes conquered Wall Street and nearly destroyed it*. New York: Random House.

Peil, J., & van Staveren, I. (2009). *Handbook of economics and ethics*. Cheltenham, UK: Edward Elgar Publishing.

Rallis, S. F., & Rossman, G. B. (2012). *Research journey: Introduction to inquiry*. New York: Guilford Press.

Rousseau, J.-J. (1899). *Émile, or treatise on education* (Vol. 20). Appleton.

Searing, D. R. (1998). HARPS ethical analysis methodology, method description, Version 2.0. 0. Taknosys Software Corporation.

Sorkin, A. R. (2010). *Too big to fail: The inside story of how Wall Street and Washington fought to save the financial system – and themselves*. London: Penguin.

United States Financial Crisis Inquiry Commission. (2011). *Financial crisis inquiry report: Final report of the national commission on the causes of the financial and economic crisis in the United States*. Washington, DC: Government Printing Office.

Chapter 2
A Basic Primer: People to Know

Elizabeth A.M. Searing and Donald R. Searing

Abstract This chapter contains brief synopses of 16 philosophers or economists that contributed greatly to the current understanding of ethics in the fields of economics and public policy. Very few fields outside of philosophy have the inclination to pick up the works of such authors, despite the incredible contributions that such scholars have on the day to day lives of each of us. In order to take the first step toward surmounting that hurdle, we have assembled a collection that contains enough information to give the reader a taste of 16 different points of view. Each scholar has a brief note on their biographical details and the world they lived in, followed by a discussion of their most notable achievements. Finally, the policy implications which have had the biggest impact on current understanding and practice are mentioned in order to gain perspective on why we bother studying these men.

Keywords Ethics • Economics and philosophy • Public policy and philosophy

2.1 Introduction

The authors highly encourage the reader to explore the works of these luminaries in detail once your appetite is whetted with these summaries. The references sections for each figure will point you to their most influential works and that of their critics and compatriots.

E.A.M. Searing, PhD (✉)
Assistant Professor, Department of Public Administration and Policy, Rockefeller College of Public Affairs and Policy, University at Albany – State University of New York, 305 Milne Hall, 135 Western Avenue, Albany, New York, USA
e-mail: esearing@albany.edu

D.R. Searing, PhD
CEO and Principal Scientist, Syncere Systems, Altamont, NY, USA
e-mail: dsearing@synceresystems.com

E.A.M. Searing, D.R. Searing (eds.), *Practicing Professional Ethics in Economics and Public Policy*, DOI 10.1007/978-94-017-7306-5_2

2.2 Aristotle

> Virtue is a state of character concerned with choice, being determined by rational principle as determined by the moderate man of practical wisdom. (Aristotle, *Nichomacean Ethics*, II.6)

Biography Aristotle (384–322 BC) was a Greek philosopher whose work now influences subjects from geometry to political science. He was the student of Plato, who was in turn the student of Socrates – the ideas of these three men provide the foundation for most of Western philosophical thought (Marino, 2010). Once he turned 18, Aristotle lived in Athens and taught at Plato's Academy for an additional 18 years before leaving to travel, indulge his love of natural sciences and zoology, and marry. Soon afterwards, he was asked to be the tutor of 12-year-old Alexander the Great; this position brought him additional repute and, when Alexander conquered Athens, he founded his own school in Athens at the Lyceum (Blits, 1999). Public opinion of Aristotle and the Lyceum were initially quite high, with crowds following Aristotle around as he lectured while walking (this is why the Aristotelian school of thought is often called the Peripatetic school, with *peripatos* meaning "walking" in Greek); Alexander also sent plant and animal specimens back to his mentor from all of the places he would reach during his war campaigns (Hughes, 2003). Over time, however, Aristotle's popularity faded and he was indicted for "impiety" by the Athenians after Alexander had died. Aristotle fled rather than face a trial, saying he did not want the Athenians to sin twice against philosophy – referring to the forced suicide of Socrates years earlier (McKeon, 2009).

Contributions As someone who researched and practiced in a multitude of topics, Aristotle created several strands of influential thinking; it is a shame that we are only able to cover the most relevant here. The most important for our needs is the writing of *Nicomachean Ethics*, where he outlines the pieces of his particular approach to ethical conduct. Unlike others who believed that traits such as divinity could be somehow bestowed on individuals, Aristotle believed that even the most intelligent person could be unethical if they did not have a record of experience to look back on and refer to. This type of thinking evolved into the canonical law of medieval Christianity, where clergy who were taking confessions created large books of every type of situation imaginable in order to precisely ascribe the atonement that needed to be made. Case-based reasoning also became the foundation for English Common Law and, thus, the law used in the United States today.

More important is his elevation of this type of experience to the level of a necessity for ethical thought. Aristotle believed the ideal moral citizen had two particular traits: *sophia* (wisdom) and *phronesis* (prudence). Someone could possess incredible amounts of knowledge on ethics and good intent, but not still not be able to act ethically in a situation because she does not have the experience to recognize what actions are occurring or being called for (Sisko, 2001). Aristotle laments (like many colleagues of mine) that youth nowadays are full of technical skill (*techne*), but without a sense of humility or ethics that would come with professional experience; he also did not imply merely chronological age, but also anyone who would treat resources as if they had no experience in working with them.

Also in *Ethics* is a brief discussion that would make any modern Institutionalist proud: the key to a city's strength is its faith in justice. Without the ability to reciprocate and exchange, Aristotle argues, then citizens will have no reason to trade or relate; likewise, without a sense of community, individuals would not come together to trade (Finley, 1970). People with diverse occupations, such as his example of a shoe-maker and a house-builder, use cities to find a way to exchange goods – there is some number of shoes that is worth some number of houses. Though he does not linger long on how such prices are formed (only that they must be), he has inserted another important modern market insight into an ancient text.

Not to be overlooked, however, is Aristotle's *Politics*, which was written shortly after *Ethics*. As Birkland notes in his text on the policy process, the great Greek thinkers were very interested in discovering how and why people could live together in a state and not constantly resort to violence (p. 5). Most of Aristotle's *Politics* is dedicated to descriptions of various types of governments, for which he forms a typology; however, within the first two books are more important contributions to economics and political thought. Like many contemporaries, he discusses both slavery and citizenship; unlike Plato, however, Aristotle considered most every citizen in a city to be capable of being a part of its political affairs.

Finally, the process of logical deduction was detailed and codified through several writings, most of which are contained in the collection of books called the *Organon*. For those of us who conjure up hazy memories of Boolean statements when we hear "logic," you may be surprised to learn that deductive logic has also contributed a great deal of behind-the-scenes structure to the social sciences. When the social sciences first started branching off as a formal field from the "natural" sciences of chemistry and physics in the middle of the twentieth century, this generated a great deal of debate regarding what the proper method of conducting research in this new field should be. At this time, logical positivism and its variants dominated the research landscape – stemming from Aristotle's tight descriptions of logical methods, all science was expected to not only be internally consistent (it didn't contradict itself) and falsifiable (there was a potential way for it to be wrong), but also able to be proven empirically (Toulmin, 1977). Though most social scientists no longer adhere to such a strong doctrine regarding falsifiability, the emphasis on causal reasoning that plays a role in modern science and statistics stems from the constructs in the *Organon*.

Policy Application Since Aristotle's intellectual contributions are so varied, some of his most important policy applications are synergistic. For example, on the more political side, Aristotle believed firmly in the empirical nature of things: science, wisdom, and most everything he considered important came through experience. It wasn't the young and the bold who made the good leaders – only those who had been around long enough to gather *phronesis* had any business trying to run a government.

Second, Aristotle is a precursor of the anti-bourguois pages of Thorsten Veblen, who wrote of the wasteful upper classes and their "conspicuous consumption" in the early twentieth century. Aristotle strongly instructs readers not to accumulate money for money's sake, or to buy things as a display of wealth. This type of behavior would symbolize bad resource management, which to the Greeks meant poor political leadership.

Virtue ethics is a modern movement which considers the "negative" language of most ethical codes to be antithetical to ethical purpose – individuals should not be concentrating on what not to do, but what they should do. Virtue ethics holds that people should have in their minds exemplars of virtue that can be emulated as one builds their own phronesis. A good example of this are the "WWJD" bracelets often worn by young Christians in the 1990s; meaning "What Would Jesus Do?', the bracelets encourage an adolescent who may be faced with a choice to try to emulate Jesus in their decision-making (Marino, 2010).

Finally, like Xenophon and other Greeks that wrote about *oikonomia*, Aristotle knew that the science of getting along stemmed directly from how resources were divided. Though *oikonomia* literally only refers to the management of the household, Aristotle considered the ruling of a man over his household, over his family and wealth, and over a city-state to be the same process with different matters of scale (Baloglou, 2012). Though we would consider such views as repressive in today's culture, the insights that management of all types revolves around the distribution of resources amongst the parties involved continues to hold. Whether we are discussing the proletariat repression of Marx or the bank bailout of the Great Recession, harmony often depends on the perception of fairness in the distribution of wealth.

2.3 Arrow

> If we want to rely on the virtues of the market but also to achieve a more just distribution, the theory suggests the strategy of changing the initial distribution rather than interfering with the allocation process at some later stage. (Kenneth Arrow, *Nobel Prize Lecture*, 1972)

Biography Kenneth Joseph Arrow was born in New York City in August of 1921. His undergraduate and master's degrees were both in mathematics, the former from City College of New York and the latter from Columbia University (Arrow, 1992b). His family lost a great deal in the Great Depression, and he credits the free tuition and high quality of students at City College to be one of the pieces of his success (Arrow, 2009). Following military service as a weather officer in World War II, Arrow returned to Columbia to earn his doctorate in economics; simultaneously, he also served as a research associate at The Cowles Commission for Research in Economics, which counts 25 Nobel laureates among the scholars it has employed or directly influenced (Cowles Foundation for Research in Economics, 2011).

Arrow's first teaching position following his doctorate was at Stanford University, which he returned to following an appointment at Harvard from 1968 to 1979; he retired from Stanford in 1991 and has remained there as Professor Emeritus (Arrow, 1992b; 2005). Throughout his career, Arrow has received numerous prestigious awards, such as the John Bates Clark medal in 1957, the Nobel Prize in Economic Sciences in 1972, and the von Neumann Prize in 1986, in addition to many honorary degrees and leadership positions in professional societies (Arrow). Though retired from academic life, Arrow continues to remain very active in public policy debates regarding economic and policy.

As an aside, Arrow's family is actually teeming with economists: his sister (Anita Summers), his brothers-in-law (Robert Summers and Nobel Prize winner Paul Samuelson), and his nephew (Larry Summers, who served in both the Clinton and Obama presidential administrations) (O'Shea, 2008). Ironically, there has been no modeling of the transmission mechanisms of being an economist.

Contributions Arrow's true academic loves were mathematical economics and statistics, which was largely self-taught, though encouraged by the faculty and mentors he had (Arrow, 2009). From these, he provided the base analysis for many ideas involving information, innovation, learning by doing, racial discrimination, and voting behavior. His seminal contributions, however, are his work on general equilibrium theory (for which he won the Nobel Prize) and further development of social choice theory.

Using the mathematical techniques that were coming into vogue in the middle of the twentieth century, Arrow used these sophisticated tools to update the analysis regarding general equilibrium theory (Nobelprize.org, 1972). General equilibrium theory had first been formalized in 1870s by Leon Walras (Arrow, 1992a); however, the analysis represented the first few steps of the "marginal revolution" and, arguably, relied heavily elementary calculus and analogies to physics (Ackerman, 2002, Mirowski, 1991). This was further developed in the 1930s by John Hicks, who fused the formal theory of Walras with more empirical concepts such as markets, the marginal rate of substitution, and the separate effects of income and substitution in determining consumption changes (Hicks, 1946). Arrow used these contributions to clarify and expand on the notions of both general equilibria and Pareto optimality using set theory. He found that, given certain assumptions about the set of potential allocations of goods being convex, all competitive equilibria are Pareto efficient, and conversely that it is necessary for a Pareto efficient outcome to be achievable as an equilibrium in the market (Arrow, 1951).

Arrow is also generally considered to be the founder of modern social choice theory, which combines elements of social welfare theory and collective decision-making (Dimitrov, 1983); Arrow describes himself as "almost completely the creator of the questions as well as some answers" in the field (Arrow, 2009). Arrow's interest in social choice stemmed directly from his experience with general equilibria and Pareto efficiency. As is commonly known, the market can create a Pareto efficient outcome given an initial allocation of resources, but the actual outcome is dependent on the initial distribution of goods and the ownership of the capital. Concepts such as justice or fairness are not answered, which Arrow recognized as a gap in the theory's application and usefulness to modern problems (Arrow, 1992a). Accordingly, Arrow began to search for ways to address this and accommodate the "great many other situations in which the replacement of market by collective decision-making is necessary or at least desirable" (Arrow).

Policy Application The most popular contribution in modern policy is Arrow's Impossibility Theorem, which broke the boundaries of economics and can now be seen as a staple in advanced courses in political science, sociology, and public policy. Simply stated, given certain assumptions, majority voting will not always produce a ranked list of alternatives and can produce anomalies such as voting cycles and other violations of transitivity. Initially described in his article "A Difficulty in the Concept of Social Welfare," Arrow develops and mathematizes a problem with simple majority voting that was initially discovered by Condorcet in 1785 (Arrow, 1950).

There are four assumptions required for the theorem. Most importantly, unlike Bentham and other utilitarian philosophers that encountered difficulties in developing ways to compare utility between individuals, Arrow only requires ordinal rankings of options: which option is first and second in order of preference to you, rather than how much more you prefer option one to option two. This means that an aggregation of those individual preferences into a social welfare function is possible and would accurately depict their preferences (Arrow, 1950). Second, the process of social choice will produce a Pareto efficient outcome (Arrow, 1992a). Third, the choice being made is independent of irrelevant alternatives, such as the inclusion on a ballot of every citizen of the United States, despite the fact that only a few are viable candidates interested and vetted for the office (Arrow). Finally, the social welfare function is not imposed by another source, which is often called the "Non-Dictatorship" condition (Arrow).

Given these assumptions, let's imagine that we have six friends: Adam, Alicia, Bella, Bishop, Candace, and Caleb. They are trying to decide what type of take-out food they will have for dinner between three options, and they have all agreed to abide by the will of the majority. Adam and Alicia rank their options as pizza, noodles, and curry. Bella and Bishop would prefer noodles to curry, and curry to pizza. Candace and Caleb want curry, with pizza as a second option and noodles as their least preferred. At the end of it all, they still haven't decided where to eat, and we have proven that, given the original reasonable assumptions, majority rule doesn't always give an ordered outcome of preferences. Under certain circumstances, this can even lead to voting cycles, where repeated rankings are called for, but no one option ever wins. Though many scholars have found ways to address the paradox through either weakening assumptions or providing ones of their own, Arrow's paradox provided a theoretical challenge based on a potentially real scenario in an era where the aggregation of preferences and collective rationality were taken for granted.

Arrow's work in social choice, however, has also evolved into several active lines of analysis in current policy debates, namely health care reform and global warming policy; not only are the ideas and research areas which Arrow helped found still active, but Arrow personally involves himself in these issues and continues to produce analysis. In medical and health care policy, Arrow's interest began in 1963 and continues to the present day (Arrow, 1963, Arrow, Akerlof, & Maskin, 2011). He chaired the Committee on the Economics of Malarial Drugs of the Institute of Medicine, which determined that financing from outside sources is necessary if the simultaneous treatment of malaria and race against treatment-resistant varieties were to continue (Arrow, Panosian, & Gelband, 2004). In the current debates over universal coverage, Arrow contends that individuals are unable to overcome the uncertainty that they may use the healthcare system or how much that usage may cost; this means most attempts to capture or discount this uncertainty is unreliable (Arrow et al., 2011); further, there are known cost externalities to the rest of society which should also receive weight, especially if the user had opted out of coverage. However, such a system should also include means for rewarding innovation and developing a system for measuring impacts and efficiency (Arrow et al., 2009).

Arrow's involvement in climate change policy stems not only from social choice, but in his work with information uncertainty. In 2007, Arrow came to the defense of fellow economist Nicholas Stern, who issued a report on climate change on behalf of the United Kingdom which encouraged engagement of policy alternatives to combat global warming (Arrow, 2007). Stern's report had drawn criticism for failing to address the possibility that future difficulties may be considered less important than current economic growth if subjected to proper time discounting (Stern, 2006); Arrow addresses this concern and calls for serious policy considerations, which he echoes in other works (Arrow, 1999, Arrow et al., 1996, 2009).

2.4 Bentham

> Nature has placed mankind under the governance of two sovereign masters, pain and pleasure . . . [t]he principle of utility recognises this subjection, and assumes it for the foundation of that system, the object of which is to rear the fabric of felicity by the hands of reason and of law. (~Bentham, *An Introduction to the Principles of Morals and Legislation*, Chapter I, 1979)

Biography Jeremy Bentham was born in a wealthy area of London on February 15 of 1748; though the oldest of seven children, only one other survived past their early years, and his mother died when he was 11 (Rosen, 2007). He was a very intelligent boy and attended college at Oxford when he was only 12 (UCL Bentham Project, 2013); however, he felt very socially awkward because of his age and small size, a sense that never seemed to leave him (Rosen). Bentham graduated with both a bachelors and a master's degree by the age of 19 with the intent of following his father's wishes and becoming a lawyer. In studying law, however, he found far more that he disagreed with than could support, and began a lifetime of critical discussion on legal and philosophical matters (Rosen). Bentham continued to be an active writer and commentator on policy, often writing 20 pages a day until near to his death (UCL Bentham Project). Afterwards, Bentham had several students which carried on the refinement of utilitarianism, the most famous of which was John Stuart Mill, the son of his collaborator, James Mill.

Almost as memorable as his life was Bentham's wishes for his body after death. From the age of 21, Bentham had wished for his body to be dissected and preserved after his death in order to further science. Known as the auto-icon, Bentham's actual skeleton has been fitted with a wax head, padding to fill out the clothes, and his favorite walking stick, and is displayed in a special cabinet in the South Cloisters of

University College in London (Richardson & Hurwitz, 1987, Rosen, 2007). His body was taken to the 100th and 150th year anniversary meetings of the College Committee, where he is listed as "Jeremiah Bentham, present but not voting" (UCL Chemistry, 2010).

Contributions Known for several contributions to political philosophy, Bentham is most well-known for his work on the principle of utilitarianism: "the greatest happiness for the greatest number," though this particular wording probably came from scholars that were active ahead of Bentham (Goldworth, 1969). Underlying his description of utility was a process which Bentham dubbed the "felicific calculus," which provided a way for individuals to calculate the quantity of happiness given by an action and use it for interpersonal comparison (Mitchell, 1918). Bentham suggested that human emotion was comprised of smaller elements: 14 simple pleasures and 12 simple pains (Bentham, 1879); even though the combinations of these elements could be exhaustive to track and quantify, the fact that utility could be aggregated on the individual level, then on the societal level, was key to his concept of an ideal society. In describing this calculus, Bentham postulates that each additional sum of money that a person gains will actually bring less and less quantities of happiness, introducing (though not formally stating) the Law of Diminishing Marginal Utility (Goldworth). The focus on individual happiness invited critiques from those who labeled his work as pure quantitative hedonism, including his protégé John Stuart Mill (Kreider, 2010). Further, the usage of a particular process with the focus on ends pre-empts any discussion of justice that is not based entirely on results (Diamond, 1967); this particular criticism of utilitarianism (called "consequentialism") is later addressed by philosopher Immanual Kant.

The difficulty with utilitarianism (and, for that matter, pure democracy), is that it permits a tyranny of the majority; the moral concept of fairness or justice is absent from Bentham's teachings since the morality of an act is determined by the aggregate hedonsim in the felicific calculus. This critique of Bentham, though one he could not overcome, left the gap in philosophical thought that would come to be occupied by John Rawls, who now provides the opposite side of the coin in terms of distributive fairness (Sen, 1974).

Bentham's reliance on the ability for people to see right and wrong as determinable via calculation is a major component behind his theories on criminal justice, which tend to be highly authoritarian by modern standards (Harrison, 1995). His most well-known element of work in this area was the development of the Panopticon, which was a concept for a prison inspired by his brother's tales of Russia and commissioned by the English government. The Panopticon consisted of a circular enclosed space with a tower containing an overseer in the middle of it: from this perch, the prisoners could be observed to both prevent trouble and to make sure that whatever task they were supposed to be accomplishing was done efficiently. Bentham not only designed the structure, but he also planned to be the central administrator of the system and make it profitable, thus solving a social ill through the effects of deterrence and gaining a stream of personal income. Unfortunately for Bentham, the government thought better of the plan and eventually compensated him for his several decades of devotion to the project (Harrison).

Policy Application Bentham's dream was to be instrumental in the passage of legislation that would bring about what he considered an ideal government (Harrison, 1995). By far, Bentham's most significant policy application is the continued use of utilitarianism in a variety of forms. It provides a relatively straightforward philosophical endorsement of democracy, where the moral outcome is defined as the one which satisfies the greatest number. This is ironic since Bentham never declared any particular fondness for democracy per se, only a growing sense of disenchantment with what he perceived was the ruling elite (Copleston, 1946); further, enough of his ideas contained such a powerful administrative element (such as the Panopticon) that some authors have accused him of endorsing despotism (Crimmins, 1996).

Far stronger is the link between Benthamite utilitarianism and social welfare economics; even the concept of a social welfare function, which presupposes the existence of some function which can provide a maximum level of satisfaction given the aggregation of individual utilities, is at its core utilitarian (Gowdy, 2004). Additive social welfare functions such as the kind used by Bentham, though no longer considered sophisticated, are common place in analysis (Harsanyi, 1955, Sadka, 1976). As emphasized by Harsanyi, there is an attractiveness to permitting each individual person to have their own unique utility function of an unlimited number of mathematical forms, but the society-wide results can be approximated through allowing individual forms to take a much more restricted set of options (1955). Aside from pure welfare economics, such analysis is heavily debated in both taxation (Feldstein, 1976, Sadka) and public goods literatures (Howarth & Norgaard, 1990).

Bentham's other lasting policy impacts stem from his involvement and writings on the extension of legal rights to those underserved by his contemporaries, such as women (Bentham, 1879, Williford, 1975). In his initial political works, he likens the treatment of women to slaves over whom tyranny is not questioned (Bentham). Bentham even attributes his dedication to combatting and improving English law to the plight of a woman, Teresa Constantia Philips, a courtesan whose unfortunate story was publicized during his youth (Bentham, 1843a). Later, Bentham makes several articulate arguments regarding the philosophical and case for women's suffrage, from the dramatic success of English queens to the rejection of the division of mankind into superior and inferior segments (Bentham, 1843b, 1843c, Williford, 1975). However, when asked whether he supported women's suffrage outright, he concluded that, though he philosophically supported it, there was too much opposition for it to be successful (Bentham). Bentham also wrote the first known appeal to decriminalize sodomy in England, which he considered a matter of personal expression (Bentham & Crompton, 1978). Ironically, despite Bentham's strong opinions on the extension of legal and civil rights, he had very little faith in "natural rights" such as those being invoked to justify the revolutions in France and the United States (Harrison, 1995).

Finally, Bentham's work underlies several current movements in the social sciences. First, cost-benefit analysis, which has its basis in additive utilitarianism, is still considered the standard evaluative tool in program development and evaluation; even though most talk is currently on outcomes, it is the weighing of the cost of such outcomes versus their monetary benefits that takes place inside the corporate, nonprofit, or public office. Further, now that the behavioral economics movement is taking hold and questions regarding the role of GDP per capita are surfacing, people are dusting off their copies of Bentham in trying to answer the question of how to effectively measure well-being and what really makes people happy (Gowdy, 2005).

2.5 Hayek

> The curious task of economics is to demonstrate to men how little they really know about what they imagine they can design. (~Friedrich A. von Hayek, *The Fatal Conceit*, 1988)

Biography Friedrich August von Hayek was born on May 8, 1899, in Vienna, Austria; his father was a renowned botanist and his family respected, though not as wealthy as the family of his cousin, famous philosopher Ludwig Wittgenstein (Von Hayek, Kresge, & Wenar, 1994). Before he could finish school, Hayek served on the Italian front in World War I, during which time he began to think and write on the importance of subjectivism and methodological individualism in the social sciences (Garrison & Kirzner, 1987). His service in World War I had a profound influence on his sociopolitical thought, however, and he began to think about the social and political realities of the world as opposed to the scientific or purely philosophical ones (Von Hayek et al., 1994). Following the war and the attainment of doctoral degrees on jurisprudence and political science, Hayek began an academic career which crossed several nations. He would eventually earn the Nobel Prize in Economic Sciences, sharing it with Gunnar Myrdal, for contributions to the understanding of business cycle fluctuations. During the banquet, he noted the irony of receiving an award for teachings which warned of the dangers of concentrating power in one person: "Yet I must confess that if I had been consulted whether to establish a Nobel Prize in economics, I should have decidedly advised against it. One reason was that I feared that such a prize, as I believe is true of the activities of some of the great scientific foundations, would tend to accentuate the swings of scientific fashion. This apprehension the selection committee has brilliantly refuted by awarding the prize to one whose views are as unfashionable as mine are" (Von Hayek, 1974).

Contributions Hayek's most well-known work, *Road to Serfdom*, describes how the behaviors of the collective tend to encroach on the freedoms of the individual (Hayek, 1973). Hayek's primary argument was through what was known as the economic calculation problem: if a socialist country was to develop a centralized way to distribute resources, then this huge task has to be entrusted to a person (think Social Planner from macroeconomic theory) who could not possibly have all of the information necessary to make adequate decisions. The concentration of such power in one point, therefore, makes the collectivist government transition to a totalitarian government (Hayek, 2001). The only reliable way of communicating such information in a functioning market was through prices. At the time is was published in

1944, the book was deeply unpopular since it equated the political system of an enemy (Nazi Germany) with that of a nation that was an ally at the time (the Soviet Union) (Boettke, 2005).

Unlike the classical belief that the market gradually groped its way toward equilibrium, the influence on Hayek from Wittgenstein and other philosophers of science led him to look for deeper reasoning. He discovered two things. First, there seemed to be a cyclical behavior of booms and busts in the savings and spending behaviors of the greater economy. Second, these trends in the macroeconomic records correlated with decisions that had been made by experts in charge of the central bank. If the central bank targeted interest rates and pushed them downwards, then there would be a reduced incentive to save for the private individual consumer, taking away a price signal that the market used to regulate its saving behaviors and prodding the individual to spend more. When the individual consumer finally reaches the end of his means, a slump or recession occurs in their spending habits as they endure the hangover that comes with spending binges. He considered the phenomenon of business cycles to be directly traceable to the meddling of the central bank (Hayek, 1931).

It was this idea which also brought him into a very direct and very public confrontation with another famous economist of the time, John Maynard Keynes. Keynes (see separate entry) was a strong proponent of government spending in times of recession, which is the exact opposite prescription than what Hayek would offer. Government stimulus, in Hayek's reasoning, was what caused the initial over-investment in the first place, so adding additional spending on top of this was simply deepening the problem. For a good (if unorthodox) summary of the dispute, I would suggest the same resource that I do to m undergraduate economics classes: find the song or music video "Fear the Boom and Bust" by Emergent Order (Papola, 2010). It's cheesy, but the facts are correct, and you'll remember it far better than anything I could write.

Policy Application Hayek was one of the primary movers behind the development of neoliberalism as an economic policy: the emphasis on freedom of expression began by Smith and Mill expanded from individuals out to corporate actors, as well. Hayek admitted that his approach to *laissez-faire* economics was more radical than those which were supported by classical economists such as Smith. Further, unlike classical economists such as Mill, Hayek believed that most social programs were distortions of the market signals and was dismissive of the need for social policy, seeing it as the first step toward socialism (Hayek, 1949). However, students of this branch of economics, called the Austrian School since many of its proponent were Austrian, continue to flourish in academia and specialized journals to this day. Though Hayek credits Carl Menger with the ideas and inspiration beyond the Austrian School, it is Hayek that developed the ideas enough to where they are active over a century later (Hayek, 1934).

Most scholars credit Hayek as being one of the founders of the modern Libertarian movement, though there is discussion over whether he would consider himself one (Boettke, 2005). Of primary importance is the strong opposition to the existence of the Federal Reserve Bank and its operations in the market. As described in *Road to Serfdom*, entrusting one small fallible group or person with the caretaking of a society is both an invitation to trouble and akin to a dictatorship (Hayek, 2001). Hayek saw very little use for the Fed (if any), and believed that inflation would be best controlled if the government did not have a monopoly on the printing of money; the market which appropriately allocated goods with multiple buyers and sellers would eventually settle on an optimum quantity of money (Hayek, 2009). This also meant that he objected strongly to the centralization or coordination of monetary policy, whether this was the ill-fated portion of the Bretton Woods agreement that fixed exchange rates or the unified European currency (Issing, White, & Vaubel, 2000). Notably, however, Hayek was not an isolationist – his desire to build an international network of scholars signaled that his dislike of international cooperation stopped at the economic policy level (Coase, 1993).

2.6 Hobbes

> In such condition, there is no place for industry; because the fruit thereof is uncertain: and consequently no culture of the earth; no navigation, nor use of the commodities that may be imported by sea; no commodious building; no instruments of moving, and removing, such things as require much force; no knowledge of the face of the earth; no account of time; no arts; no letters; no society; and which is worst of all, continual fear, and danger of violent death; and the life of man, solitary, poor, nasty, brutish, and short. (~Thomas Hobbes, *Leviathan*, 1651)

Biography Thomas Hobbes was born in Wiltshire, England, on April 5, 1588, there was such fear concerning the potential invasion of the Spanish armada that Hobbes' mother actually delivered Hobbes ahead of schedule (Martinich, 1999). Very little is known of Hobbes' early life, though his father left the family when Hobbes was young; he received a bachelor's degree from Magdalen Hall with good enough grades to enter a career of being a private tutor to the children of nobility (Bull, 1981). Through this, Hobbes travelled and made the personal connections necessary to survive as a political writer during a tumultuous time, fleeing England to Paris in 1640 following the circulation of a controversial political pamphlet, then fleeing back when the Royalists who fled the Civil War in England took issue to the permissibility of switching sovereign allegiance in *Leviathan* (Martinich). The political nature of his continued writings kept him controversial, and he was eventually banned from publishing inside of England (Lansford, 2007).

Contributions Hobbes' best known work, *Leviathan*, contains both of the elements of political philosophy for which he is most famous: the savage liberty of the individual and the necessity of the strong state. When man was in his natural state, Hobbes argued, he was interested in himself. This was a naturalistic approach to ethics and morality: that which was moral was what furthered the self (Donaldson, 1994). However, a group of purely self-interested people would always be at war with each other over resources; therefore, in his natural state, the life of man was "nasty, brutish, and short," with the potential for very little productive activity (Hobbes, 1887).

In response to these conditions, mankind would begin to band together for mutual protection. In forming groups, a person would willingly subject themselves to restrictions of personal freedoms in order to belong to the collective. Hobbes insisted that true security would only take place with a strong and absolute central authority, since the power to curb such an individual would cause jealousy and instability among the members (Lloyd & Sreedhar, 2008). Later social contract theorists would dispute the necessity of the ruler being a despot, but the underlying mechanics of a restriction on personal freedom in exchange for security in person and property remained.

Policy Application Hobbes was the first of the major social contract theorists, with others including individuals such as John Locke and Jean-Jacques Rousseau. The implication that a rational person would give up his or her natural rights willingly to a government, especially a despot, had not been made explicitly clear until *Leviathan*. Aside from the powerful effect this had on political discourse, this type of exchange would later become fundamental in the study of game theory; if one views the prisoner's dilemma game as one with despots and democracies, a perceived greater potential for civil war in democracy could lead to despotism being a Nash equilibrium (Binmore, 1998).

2.7 Hume

> We speak not strictly and philosophically when we talk of the combat of passion and of reason. Reason is, and ought only to be the slave of the passions, and can never pretend to any other office than to serve and obey them. (~David Hume, *A Treatise of Human Nature*, 1739, 3.3.3)

Biography David Hume was born in April of 1711 in Edinburgh to an upper-middle class family. His father died when he was still a baby, leaving his mother to raise him and two siblings (Hume, 1907). He did well in school and his family expected him to become a lawyer; however, Hume only had love for philosophy and literature. He left the practice of law to concentrate fully on writing A Treatise on Human Nature in England and France, then returned to live with his brother when he had spent his savings (Mossner, 1950). He served as a tutor, librarian, and as numerous small appointments, but spent most of his days writing (Hume). During his lifetime, his most famous work was the 6-volume *The History of England*, but most of his political and philosophical writing was dismissed due to his atheism (Jordan, 2002). In his autobiography, Hume admitted that his first aim in writing was always fame instead of truth, which further distanced him from other minds of his time (Hume).

Contributions Though not considered so at the time, Hume's *A Treatise on Human Nature* is one of the classics of Western philosophy (Rosenberg, 1993). It is made up of three sections, which build on each other: on cognition, on emotions, and on morality. In cognition, Hume discusses the nature of knowledge and introduces the role of logic and probability. In the second section, he describes the various passions that humans fell, and in the third describes theories of morality. In short, "[a]ll morality depends on sentiments; and when any action, or quality of the mind, pleases us after a certain manner, we say it is virtuous; and when the neglect, or nonperformance of it, displeases us after a like manner, we say that we lie under an obligation to perform it" (Hume, 2003).

Hume also made large contributions to method in the social sciences, including laying the foundations for positivism and introducing some of the problems with inductive logic. On the former, Hume considered only scientific observation of the empirical world to be an acceptable basis for any science (Rosenberg, 1993). This alone speaks more to Hume being an empiricist than a positivist, but he also devotes a portion of his discussion to problems with the process of induction. For example, suppose the only type of chocolate I knew of was milk chocolate; when I'm told that I will receive a chocolate bar as a present the next day, I instantly assume I'll be getting a milk chocolate bar. However, in no way is this a necessity – just because I have only had milk chocolate bars up until this point does not mean that is all I will ever receive is milk chocolate.

Policy Application Hume was not only able to formulate a hypothetical government that protected property and enacted justice, but that was built by people whom he felt we needed to assume were inherently self-interested (Bowles & Gintis, 2002). He was not a believer in social contracts per se, so instead used reason to walk his way through the potential courses of action available to people in social contact. In this, he anticipates modern game theory. For example, Hume tells a story about two neighbors who are growing corn, with one field ripening the day after the other one. Both farmers know that they would be better off helping each other, but because they don't trust each other, there is no coordination and both fields rot (Putnam, 1993). Binmore credits Hume as being the first to invent the concept of reciprocal altruism, showing that social functioning rests on such exchanges (1998).

Hume also draws attention to the difference between positive and prescriptive statements in the course of an argument. Specifically, he takes a close look at the point in an argument or line of reasoning where something "is" to when something "ought" to do something (Treatise); this phenomenon is known as "Hume's Guillotine" (Donaldson, 1994). Between the two verbs is the introduction of a normative or emotional element, and this brings any kind of deductive logical conclusions into question; similar to the role of emotions discussed elsewhere in Treatise, its introduction into the process changes the logical validity of the conclusions. As MacIntyre states, "factual statements cannot entail logical premises" (MacIntyre, 1959). This division is also a well-known one in economics, where scholars as diverse as Keynes and Friedman both concur that economics is a positive science which happens to often have normative implications (Friedman, 1953). However, with the development of specialized fields of applied economic policy such as health policy, the re-evaluation of concepts such as well-being in international development, and the advent of behavioral economics, the line between the fields continues to erode in importance or, at the very least, equalize the importance of both sides.

2.8 Kant

> All our knowledge begins with the senses, proceeds then to the understanding, and ends with reason. There is nothing higher than reason. (~Immanual Kant, *A Critique of Pure Reason*, 1781)

Biography Immanuel Kant was born on April 22, 1724, into a family of tradesman that, while not poor, occasionally had to rely on extended family for assistance (Rohlf, 2010). His family lived in Königsberg, which at the time was the capital of Prussia and enough of a metropolis at the time that Kant travelled more than 10 miles outside it during his life (Lewis, 2009). His family were very devout Pietists, and his schooling emphasized both Biblical study and emotional introspection; his distaste for this approach may have inspired his fascination with its potential antithesis, pure reason, in his own later work (Rohlf).

Following college at the University of Königsburg, Kant was a private tutor for several years before becoming an unsalaried lecturer at his alma mater for 15 years; this means that he was paid directly by his students for an income. Though this often meant very large teaching loads, he would also have bursts of publishing activity that steadily increased his reputation and roster sizes until he was offered a salaried position in 1770. He was then able to expand his lectures to include not only logic and philosophy, but also one of the first courses on anthropology (Kant & Louden, 2006). Kant, as an intellectual and an academic, was very popular and successful (Rohlf, 2010).

Kant was not, however, someone who was particularly well liked as a person. Much different than many of the minds of that time in Königsburg, Kant was determinedly unmarried, a potential atheist, and espoused many ideas on liberty that made his local government figures nervous (Kuehn, 2001). He was considered a local celebrity and did not seem to lack for guests at his dinner parties, which he held often. However, by the time of his death, most of the academic discussion regarding his work had already swung against it following its initial wave of enthusiasm.

Kant finally passed away on February 12 of 1804 following years of increasing seclusion and probable senility (Rohlf, 2010). Unfortunately, much of the biographical information stems from stories from his local town, so his context in relation to that place and time needs to be taken into account when you ascribe reliability to such sources (Kuehn, 2001).

Contributions Though he made several contributions to philosophy and ethics, *The Critique of Pure Reason* (1781) is considered the most important philosophical work. The text was written after an 11-year sequestration from research and general public life, often called his "silent decade" (Washburn, 1975). This was brought on by an increasing dissatisfaction with his work that was brought to a head when he read some of David Hume's papers. Hume argued that knowledge could only be based on sensory experience; Kant, however, was unsatisfied with the exclusion of human reason. After identifying what he considered the problem – uniting subjective sensory perception and objective human reason – Kant dedicated himself to reconciling the issue (Adler, 1997; Vasilyev, 2001).

For ethics specifically, *The Metaphysics of Morals* (1797) was the groundbreaking text. Kant attempted, in his own words, to conduct the "investigation and establishment of the supreme principle of morality" (Kant & Gregor, 1996), and in many ways did. As a way to escape what he considered the relativism of empiricist philosophers such as Hume, Kant insisted that a basis of morality must be one which is absolute and binding, regardless of society or situation that a person was raised in. This was called a "categorical imperative" – an individual must behave a certain way because they are a rational being, which they cannot opt out of and which exists regardless of end consequence (Kant & Gregor). There were four characteristics of the imperative: it must be universally applicable, not treat people as a means to achieve something, rely on full individual autonomy, and be applied in the "Kingdom of Ends" (Kant & Gregor). This final tenet, serving as a sort of summary of the first three, states that any imperative should be formulated in a way that could be followed in a society of rational people – one should act as a legislator in the Kingdom of Ends (Korsgaard, 1996).

Policy Application Kant's contributions were primarily philosophical or political theory, so a degree of latitude is needed to apply them directly to public policy choices (Gillroy & Wade, 1992). Kant often directly alluded to the construction of a society; for example, he noted that "the greatest problem for the human race, to the solution of which Nature drives man, is the achievement of a universal civic society which administers law among men" (Kant, 1963). Indeed, Kant was considered highly cosmopolitan for his time, believing that the world had become so tightly knit and interconnected that relations between states had to exist for any semblance of just relations between citizens to exist (Brown & Held, 2011). However, he did not spend time on specific mechanics (with the exception of how to properly educate children, on which he was extremely explicit (Kant, 2003)).

The best example of this application is one of his own, in the usage of the Kingdom of Ends. Kant's theory of ethics and governance stemmed from individual autonomy: not in its unbridled exercise, but in the exercise of it while constrained by its obligation to reason. This is very similar to the reasoning of the social contract theorists, though Kant was generally more concerned with the construct of thought than with the construct of society. The foundations are the same, however, which is why the final element of the categorical imperative is the construction of a society, if only in thought experiment form.

2.9 Keynes

> But, chiefly, do not let us overestimate the importance of the economic problem, or sacrifice to its supposed necessities other matters of greater and more permanent significance. It should be a matter for specialists-like dentistry. If economists could manage to get themselves thought of as humble, competent people, on a level with dentists, that would be splendid! (~John Maynard Keynes, *Economic Possibilities for our Grandchildren*, 1930)

Biography John Maynard Keynes was born on June 5, 1883, to parents active in the scholarly community at Cambridge, England. The academic environment of his family gave Keynes a level of comfort and optimism with culture and public policy that would serve him well. Despite being sick often as a young child, he excelled in school once he arrived at Eton, where he won numerous prizes scholastic prizes, but also gained the reputation of being slightly egocentric (Moggridge, 2002). Upon moving to London, he also belonged to the famous Bloomsbury group, which was a circle of friends that contained numerous literary notables such as Virginia Woolf and E.M. Forster (Leach, 2008). His early and numerous romantic relationships were primarily men, and he meticulously catalogued and coded such encounters (Zimroth, 2008); at 42, however, he married the Russian ballerina Lydia Lopokova. Described as "his greatest and most successful gamble," she was initially resisted by Keynes' friends in Bloombury, but was eventually accepted into the group (Levy, 1979).

Contributions Modern macro as a field owes its creation to the work of Keynes; he argues that there are such inherent differences in the dynamics and actors at the macro level that there are fundamental distinctions in the way the science should be approached. His principle work, *The General Theory on Money, Banking, and Employment*, is often a wholesale rebuttal to the classical view of economics on the aggregate level, especially in the realm of public policy. He rejects the core tenet of Say's Law, which states that the prices of aggregate supply will determine the prices of those goods as they are demanded. Instead, he introduces the concept of aggregate demand, which is comprised of consumption, investment, and government spending (Keynes, 2006). Further, by setting aggregate demand free of being determined by supply, he introduces the possibility that the two forces need not always automatically find each other in an equilibrium which is acceptable (Patinkin, 1984). This invites the use of macroeconomic policy to control the level of demand using different fiscal and monetary policies in order to steer the economy.

This approach, however, was not universally accepted – important dissenters included Joseph Schumpeter and Friedrich A. Hayek, with whom he had a vociferous debate through the media regarding appropriate policy; for a lighter (but accurate) take on their debate, watch the music video for "Fear the Boom and Bust" by Emergent Order (Papola, 2010). Modern critics often link his policies to soaring government deficits. Though often true, this is not so much definitive as it is a selective application of his policy recommendations: his advice that Britain should finance the war through taxation rather than debt does not find its way into the articles which target his profligacy (Keynes, 1940).

Keynes also provided an explanation for why unemployment existed, which was always troublesome for classical economists who firmly believed that the markets would clear, an equilibrium would be found, and all those who wanted employment would have it. On an individual level, Keynes argued that workers were not motivated to work by the real wage (which is the wage level divided by the price level), but by the nominal wage. This means that, even in a recession where the price level and wages could decrease proportionally and still retain the same purchasing power, the fact that the nominal wage would decrease would make the move intolerable to the worker. This is called the "stickiness" of wages – a person in a recession will not accept a wage cut because they succumb to the "money illusion" that their purchasing power is decreasing (Ekelund Jr & Hébert, 2007). This prevents the labor market from automatically adjusting to full employment as the classical economists would predict, and Keynes maintains that government intervention would be necessary.

Policy Application We have seen a lot of Keynes over the last decade as various pieces of the world economy began to stumble. The idea of government stimulus as a means to climb out of an economic recession was formally theorized and described by Keynes in General Theory. As policy, the reception of his ideas regarding stimulus spending have waxed and waned depending on the economic conditions at the time. Following World War II, Keynes' ideas grew in acceptance and became mathematized through the Neo-Keynesian school of thought, who included economists John Hicks and Paul Samuelson (though there continues to be discussion among Keynesians over how Keynesian the neoclassical synthesis was). The popularity of Keynesian ideas continued until the 1970s, when a combination of stagflation and the new Monetarist school of economic thought began to increase their critiques (Lucas & Sargent, 1979). With the global recession in 2008, however, Keynesian ideas and policy options have again come into favor (Akerlof & Shiller, 2009).

In addition to his contribution to economic policy per se, Keynes also understood the role which macroeconomic conditions could play in the relations between nations; he possessed remarkable foresight into the conditions that would cause the Second World War. Keynes had been a financial representative for the English Treasury at the Versailles peace conference, and had advocated for reasonable financial punishment for Germany on the grounds that the country needed to have the ability to recover (Keynes, 2004). Unfortunately, he was overruled, and the resulting treaty angered and repulsed Keynes so much that he resigned from his post and wrote *The Economic Consequences of Peace*. Here, he warns that, "[i]f we aim deliberately at the impoverishment of Central Europe, vengeance, I dare predict, will not limp. Nothing can then delay for very long that final war between the forces of Reaction and the despairing convulsions of Revolution, before which the horrors of the late German war will fade into nothing" (Keynes). This prediction of the economic crises in Germany, the ensuing Second World War, and his role in the establishment of the World Bank and International Monetary Fund gained him international fame as an economist, and remains a cogent reminder of the political and economic consequences of the dynamics of a country's debt, whether this is due to war reparations or World Bank loans.

2.10 Locke

> New opinions are always suspected, and usually opposed, without any other reason but because they are not already common. (~John Locke, *An Essay Concerning Human Understanding*, 1689)

Biography John Locke was born on August 28, 1632 in the country town of Pensford, in England (Chappell, 1994). His parents, both Puritans, bestowed on Locke a keen sense of religion and morality, which would permeate his later writings on political philosophy (Dunn, 1982). Locke attended Westminster School and then Christ Church at Oxford, where he chose to pursue research in medicine. This enabled him to become the personal physician of Lord Ashley (who would become the Earl of Shaftesbury and a leader in the overthrow of King James II), and it drew him into the world of English politics (Uzgalis, 2007). When he was associated with a rebel plot to assassinate the king, Locke fled to Holland for 5 years and worked tirelessly on his writings in political philosophy. He returned when the rebels were victorious and promptly published *An Essay Concerning Human Understanding* and *The Two Treatises of Government*, though the latter was published anonymously (Uzgalis, 2012). The last few years of his professional life were spent reorganizing the Board of Trade, which was the primary force in governing the colonies in addition to domestic trade and social policy (Uzgalis).

Contributions Many scholars actually consider the four-volume *An Essay Concerning Human Understanding* (1805) to be Locke's greatest work; here, he dismisses the concept that people are born with innate ideas, opening the philosophical debate to questions of free will and conceptual understanding that had previously been considered the material of theology. He proposes the simultaneous use of reason and religion, offering God as one of the few pieces of knowledge that could be relied upon while other elements of life need either deductive logic or the use of probability (Uzgalis, 2007).

Where Locke differed substantially from his predecessor Hobbes was in the permissibility and desirability of a dictatorial regime. Woodhouse argues that Locke considered the authority of parents to be a simple trusteeship of power on behalf of God (1997); a similar argument is made for the holder of political authority in the first Treatise of Government, with the analogy clarified in the second. Strongly influenced by the political tumult of his time, Locke believed that there were situations where citizens should resist their king or ruler, and both Treatises may have been written in order to build up to this particular conclusion (Ashcraft, 1994). Kings are not ordained to rule, but instead to enforce the natural divine law; if the king instead elects to use force to enrich himself or enact his will, then he becomes a tyrant who should be deposed. The obvious parallels between the acts of the tyrant and those of the English kings made Locke both an eloquent political philosopher and a revolutionary.

Policy Application Most people that have taken a high school civics course will remember that the famous phrase from the Declaration of Independence regarding the inalienable rights of life, liberty, and the pursuit of happiness had its roots in Locke (though there is not unanimous agreement on this, see Banning (1995)). In the *Second Treatise*, Locke describes the sovereign law of nature as something that is universal and derived from heavenly rule; in direct opposition to the nasty and brutish state of man in Hobbes's work, Locke notes that even though nature "is a state of liberty, it isn't a state of license," meaning that there are rules which govern behavior even absent formal society (Locke, 1980). Within these natural rights are contained life, health, liberty, and possessions, and every person both possesses these and had the right to punish anyone who infringes on the rights of another (Locke).

Concepts such as natural rights continue to exist and inform civil society, especially in matters of statehood or social welfare. Locke believed that man is entitled to that which he produces (Bankman & Griffith, 1987); however, this entitlement is tempered by a natural right to subsistence for all people (Locke, 1980). As described in the Second Treatise, a person has a right to the excess production of someone else because natural law "gives every man a title to so much out of another's plenty, as will keep him from extreme want, where he has not means to subsist otherwise" (Locke, 1988). This was the insight behind his calls for reform of the Poor Laws: since both government and fellow man were responsible for maintaining the order and sanctity of God's laws, then the death of any person due to the lack of a basic human need was criminal (Ashcraft, 1994).

Locke also was one of the pioneers of a revolution in the approach to education policy. Until this point, children were often viewed as property or as a subpar version of an adult; with his emphasis on free will and the open mind, Locke argued that children be treated as individuals with specific learning needs, who needed interaction from their parents. Since each child began life *tabula rasa*, then it was the function of their education to make them informed citizens that were capable of directing a good society (Uzgalis, 2007). He also considered both teachers and parents to be responsible for this upbringing, and his text on education was designed to serve as a reference text, offering hints topic by topic, for both audiences (Locke & Milton, 1830).

2.11 Mandeville

So Vice is beneficial found, When it's by Justice lopt and bound; (~Mandeville, *The Fable of the Bees*, 1705)

Biography Remarkably little is known about the life of Mandeville (Primer, 1975). He was born in Holland in approximately 1670, and pursued a medical career. He moved to London, where it is unknown whether he practiced medicine, but his penchant for alcohol was noted (Rousseau, 1975). In addition to *The Fable of the Bees*,

Mandeville also wrote other works with similar wit: a novella disguised as pornography, called *The Virgin Unmask'd*, is actually a harangue about women's rights aimed at the unsuspecting male reader (Vichert, 1975).

Contributions Mandeville is known for his political satire, *The Fable of the Bees or, Private Vices, Publick Benefits* (1957). The opening poem, the *Grumbling Hive; or Knaves turn'd Honest*, is presented as 200 rhymed couplets, concerns a hive of bees that convinces themselves that their success has made them lacking in morals; in response, they pass laws that outlaw some of the unsavory competitive behaviors. In doing so, however, they outlaw many of the behaviors which had caused their hive to thrive, such as (De Mandeville & Kaye, 1957). Finally, the hive is in a point of semi-starvation, but they reassure themselves that they are now all quite moral. The story was a direct commentary on society at the time when Mandeville was writing; this can be seen by the description of the monarchy and various legal initiatives even without the extensive commentary which Mandeville attaches to the poem.

Policy Application The contention that modern society is lacking in some kind of morality is a staple of modern politics; Americans have a "fascination with utilizing the force of law to repel people from sin" (Devins & Kauffman, 2012). Whether this missing element is referred to as family values or a concern for social welfare depends on which side of the political spectrum is talking. However, it continues to highlight a salient policy issue: when addressing a public need, the behavioral incentives and potential externalities of the decision need to be taken into account. Whether this is the proliferation of crime under Prohibition or the "boomerang effect" of posted warnings and product labeling causing an increase in use due to defiance (Ringold, 2002), unintended consequences of policy can leave the situation worse off than it was prior to the policy intervention.

2.12 Marx

> And how does the bourgeoisie get over these crises? On the one hand, by enforced destruction of a mass of productive forces; on the other, by the conquest of new markets, and by the more thorough exploitation of the old ones. That is to say, by paving the way for more extensive and more destructive crises, and by diminishing the means whereby crises are prevented. (~Karl Marx, *Manifesto of the Communist Party*, 1848)

Biography Karl Marx was born in Trier, Prussia, to a middle class and loving family. He attended the University of Bonn, but was transferred to the University of Berlin by his father after he became distracted by college life (Ekelund Jr & Hébert, 2007). After graduating from Berlin and then Jena with his doctorate, Marx returned to Bonn in hopes of teaching, but began a string of editorial jobs at philosophical and political journals. Unfortunately, his journal publications resulted in his expulsion from both Prussia and France, causing him to flee to first Brussels (where he published *The Communist Manifesto*) and then London; his best friend and collaborator, Friedrich Engels, was similarly banished, but was able to retain employment in Manchester (Marx & Nicolaus, 1993). In London, life was extremely difficult for Marx and his family, with constant illness and lack of income while Marx continued his research. Marx felt ashamed on behalf of his family, especially for his children, for having to endure this lifestyle (Blumenberg, 1998). Following Marx's death, Engels finished the manuscripts for the second and third volumes of Das Kapital, then left a significant portion of his estate to the two surviving daughters of Marx, both of whom were continuing in the footsteps of their father's activism (Montefiore, 2011).

Contributions Though support for Marxism has waned over the last few decades, Marx remains as one of the authors with the most cogent discussion of the potential problems with unbridled capitalism. The way he described the downfall of the capitalist system was through the "Laws of Capitalist Motion," which were five predictions on how the capitalist system would fall. First, the rate of profit will fall as technology improves the productiveness of capital, as opposed to labor. Second, the falling rate of profit will cause greater consolidation of companies within industries. Third, there will be increasing rates of unemployment as a result of capital substitution and overproduction. Fourth, the working class will become more miserable as the capital owners seek to squeeze more profit out of factor inputs such as wage. Finally, cyclical crises will grow in severity until the capitalist system collapses (Ekelund Jr & Hébert, 2007). Though political views will probably determine to what degree Marx appears to have been accurate, the fact that there are legitimate and consistent flaws to which capitalist societies are prone has become more obvious through the Great Recession.

Marx's second major contribution is the labor theory of value, which had been utilized before, but without such central placement in the theory. Though many people would hesitate to identify themselves as Marxist sympathizers, any time you have heard someone ask, "But what is it *really* worth?", they are probably ascribing to a labor theory of value which states that the final value of the good should have direct relation to the amount of hours that go into it. Unlike previous value theorists that did not necessarily seek empirical validation, Marx incorporated the surplus value often produced by laborers and exploited by capital owners into the mainstream of his sweeping historical political philosophy (Ekelund Jr & Hébert, 2007).

Policy Application One of the most memorable contributions of Marx to public policy stands at odds with those of other political philosophers: rather than describing only the assembly of a social contract, Marx dedicates more of his pages to describing the destruction of the state through revolution. Aside from the specific description of the failure of capitalism through the laws of motion, Marx emphasizes the need for revolution on a grander scale. He was a proponent of dialectical methods, which was a version of thought based on Hegel's ideas of progress: a thesis is formed, then an antithesis, and then both are annihilated to form a synthesis (Ekelund Jr & Hébert, 2007). In Marx's mind, the French revolution in 1848 was a failure because they only repeated the process of the larger French Revolution; successful revolutions could not be backward-looking, but must be forward-looking and prepared to be annihilated alongside their target in order to provide the needed social change (Puchner, 2006). The guidebook for this experience is *The Communist Manifesto*, which also created a literary genre for similar declarations of unorthodox belief.

Social policy and humanism are other lasting impacts from the bold strides taken by Marx and Engels. In addition to the more extreme characteristics of the new mode of production hinted at in the *Communist Manifesto*, the document also contained ideas which for now are taken for granted. For example, Marx called for the ending of child labor laws and the provision of free public schools, neither of which are very hysterical for modern times. Additionally, the conditions in many other areas of the world as trade has liberalized have drawn in humanist challengers, with some causes advancing far faster (such as the loss of rainforest) and some much slower (the poverty of sub-Saharan Africa). However you feel about Marxism, Marx had a profound impact not only on friends to his cause, but also on those who disagreed with some of his assumptions and results. Because of this impact, Karl Marx has been called one of the three founders of social science, alongside Emile Durkheim and Max Weber (Morrison, 2006).

2.13 Mill

> Many, indeed, fail with greater efforts than those with which others succeed, not from difference of merits, but difference of opportunities; but if all were done which it would be in the power of a good government to do, by instruction and by legislation, to diminish this inequality of opportunities, the differences of fortune arising from people's own earnings could not justly give umbrage. (~John Stuart Mill, *Principles of Political Economy*, 1900)

Biography John Stuart Mill was born on May 20th, 1806, in London, the eldest of what would be eight brothers and sisters. His father, James Mill, was the collaborator of Jeremy Bentham, and wanted to mold his son into a genius that could further the utilitarian cause (Mill, 2007). During an intense home education, John Stuart Mill threw himself into the Bethamite utilitarian cause until the strain of his doubts caused a mental collapse when he was 20; he overcame the severe depression though poetry and a kind of intellectual emancipation from his father and mentor (Mill, 1981). Though continuing on in utilitarianism, he broke with his predecessors on several counts and became fascinated with the concept of social justice.

Mill married at the age of 45 to a woman with whom he had been close friends for over 20 years, but who had married to another man and then widowed. Though the relationship was platonic during that friendship, one of the reasons that prompted the writing and publication of Mill's autobiography was the description and justification of the relationship to a scandalized and often cruel Victorian social class (Levi, 1951). Though able to enjoy marriage for only 7 years before his wife's death, his daughter-in-law continued to serve as his secretary and published may of his works following his death.

Contributions Mill's most prominent contribution to modern thought is his eloquent and impassioned defense of liberty. Best outlined in *On Liberty*, he considers every man to have sole control over his own mind and body, with a government only stepping in to protect him from others (or others from him). Many scholars contend that Mill had two versions of liberty: one regarding freedom of expression (which was wide and permissive) and one regarding economics and trade (where he considered taxation and wealth redistribution perfectly appropriate) (Stimson & Milgate, 2001). The authors of this text consider both to be complementary: given that liberty is fastened to the ability to exercise such, than the opportunity to do so must exist. As evidenced in the opening quote to this section, Mill's strong belief in social policies rested on access to opportunity. If one considers the right of liberty to be contingent on the exercise of liberty, then the redistribution of access to opportunity through wealth redistribution meshes with the more expansive discussions of political liberty found in Mill's works. On a societal level, he breaks new ground on the role of liberty and governance, describing not only the dangers of dictators, but also those of democracy; the latter condition, which he calls the "tyranny of the majority" (Mill, 1909), is commonly used in modern political discussion.

Though Mill continued the refinement of utilitarian thought following Bentham, he emphatically rejected the kind of quantitative element which Bentham had struggled to develop (Kreider, 2010); instead, he attempted to improve both the moral authority and the validity of the system by accounting for the qualities of feelings (Sigot, 2002). This stemmed from Mill's views on liberty: individuals cannot be reduced to aggregate numbers, and, further, these could not be simply augmented into a societal standard. For example, Mill states that it is of higher importance to be an unhappy human than to be a happy pig; the utility of the pig, when added to the disutility of the human, should not have the same weight in social policy (Mill, 2007). Additionally, one of his more famous quotes regards the pursuit of happiness: "Those only are happy (I thought) who have their minds fixed on some object other than their own happiness; on the happiness of others, on the improvement of mankind, even on some art or pursuit, followed not as a means, but as itself an ideal end. Aiming thus at something else, they find happiness by the way" (Mill, 1981). Though he continued to focus on the maximization of happiness and avoidance of pain as the primary motivators and foundations of a system of human behavior and morals, the appearance of other-concerning preferences set him apart from his predecessors.

Mill also wrote extensively on political economy as a field, and *Principles of Political Economy* was considered the standard text on the subject for over 60 years (Ekelund Jr & Hébert, 2007). This was partially due to the rationale he used to justify such study: he had read Comte and other members of the French enlightenment, gaining some degree of skepticism toward classical economics, but mostly a larger appreciation for empirical reality as opposed to theory. This faith in positivism led him to believe (and persuade others to believe) that, since economics' premises are rooted in the real world and you can use deductive logic to travel from its premises to its conclusions, then the science can generally be trusted as sound (Mill, 1994). His education had given him a firm foundation in Ricardo's classical theories of economic rent and limitations on growth due to land; he took this training and developed one of the first British formulations of static equilibrium. Though the last of the great classical economists, he split his greatest work into two pieces: the first three books on theory and the final two on applications to social policy reform (Ekelund Jr & Hébert).

Policy Application The largest contribution of Mill was the use of economic thought in approaching social policy. He advocated for a proportional income tax which had an exemption below a particular level to protect the poor; he also supported luxury and estate taxes on the grounds that they were the best candidates for redistribution of wealth (Mill, 1900). He supported the reformed Poor Laws and believed that large workhouses were the best way to provide the poor with both gainful labor and a disincentive to free-ride (Ekelund Jr & Hébert, 2007). Though the workhouses would become social policy problems of their own, Mill's attempt to fuse proper economic incentives and removal of legal barriers with government support for the very poor very closely resembles the political approaches currently used to address poverty in the United States. Further, the concept that liberty is the foundation for all other utility continues to inspire policy-makers looking for alternative ways to measure well-being, such as Amartya Sen.

Also, similar to his mentor Bentham, Mill took an extremely progressive stance on women's rights, comparing their contemporary treatment with that of slavery (Mill & Alexander, 2001). "On the Subjection of Women" was considered an especially strong statement, as it made logical arguments for not only suffrage, but also the education and employment of women; unlike his mentor, Mill never backed away from a strong policy recommendation on the matter, despite its unpopularity (Annas, 1977). Modern feminists, however, tend to downplay Mill's work since it only addressed legal rights and did not address the equality of domestic duties, assuming that most women would happily choose marriage as a career (Shanley, 1981). However, his firm belief in extending suffrage to women and minorities at a time where such views had serious social repercussions should not be dismissed.

2.14 Rand

> Achievement of your happiness is the only moral purpose of your life, and that happiness, not pain or mindless self-indulgence, is the proof of your moral integrity, since it is the proof and the result of your loyalty to the achievement of your values. (~Ayn Rand, *Atlas Shrugged*, 1957, p. 1059)

Biography Ayn Rand, whose birth name was Alissa Zinovievna Rosenbaum, was born in St. Petersburg in February of 1905 (Sciabarra, 1995). When she was twelve, the Bolshevik Revolution caused her family to flee from their home and helped nurture and enduring hatred of Russian government that would serve her writings (Heller, 2009). After returning to Petrograd (St. Petersburg's new name) and crushing poverty, Rand obtained a visa to visit relatives in the United States and emigrated.

Once in the United States, Rand worked as a writer in the film industry, though times became tough when movies began to include the spoken word; she began to find success when her philosophical leanings toward the Nietzschean superman allowed her to write aggressive characterizations that grabbed the attention of audiences (Burns, 2009). She also met her husband, Frank O'Connor, while he was an aspiring actor and they remained married for 50 years. Over time, the veneer of fiction over the philosophy became thinner, and Rand began to attract a following regarding her own version of the capitalist superman, eventually publishing both fiction and nonfiction on the theme. Following the publication of her magnum opus novel, *Atlas Shrugged*, Rand devoted herself full time to nonfiction and the teaching of her philosophy. Her teachings drew several devoted students, including famous individuals such as future Federal Reserve chairman Alan Greenspan and economist Milton Friedman, though the latter was an avowed statist (Friedman, 1991). However, her own personal popularity waned as she became older and more strident; her philosophy, however, continued to gain supporters. In 1991, Atlas Shrugged was listed as the second most influential book in the lives of Americans in a poll conducted by the Library of Congress, following only the Bible (Moore, 2009).

Contributions Objectivism is the title given to Rand's philosophy, called such due to its insistence on the existence of an objective reality and the rejection of subjective or collectivist interpretations that could be corrupted by government, society, or other people. Objectivism is not considered a formal school of thought by many philosophers, however the popular appeal of a system of value grounded in individual achievement and free trade has grown over the last several decades (Rachels & Rachels, 1986).

Objectivism's approach to ethics was described explicitly in *The Virtue of Selfishness*, which is a collection of essays written by both Rand and Nathaniel Brandon (Rand & Brandon, 1964). Rand describes mankind as holding to three values: reason, purpose, and self-esteem; these values are operationalized and achieved through three virtues which correspond to the values: rationality, productiveness, and pride (Rand, 1961). She considered reason to be the root of all values, and holds that a person should "never place any consideration whatsoever above one's perception of reality" (Rand). With the firm belief in an objective reality, there is an incentive to clear any obstruction that could be interfering with this accurate perception (such as external demands imposed by an authoritarian government or social mores).

Policy Application Modern political libertarianism derives a great deal of its philosophical development from Rand's works, though she considered much of the libertarian ideal of the time akin to subjective anarchy. Despite popular criticism to the contrary, Rand was always careful to separate hedonism from objectivism: the pursuit of irrational whims, whether selfish or selfless, was not tolerable (Rand, 1961). However, this was due to the belief that, so long as the individuals involved were rational, that conflicts between interests did not occur. This led to the conclusion that trade was the only true mechanism that should guide interactions between people, since such behavior would continue until all involved were better off. As you may notice from a previous chapter, this strongly resembles the concept of Pareto efficiency; Rand, however, extends the concept from one which dictates that such an action is *beneficial* to one that is *ethical*. Further, she outright rejects any merit which comes from altruistic behavior, believing that such activity breeds dependence and robs an individual of their ability to pursue their own values of productiveness and pride (Rachels & Rachels, 1986). This makes the discussion or even acknowledgement of several problems involving public goods and market failures an extremely difficult task. Though such opinions exist in the nonprofit sector with respect to trampling the solution through goodwill, few scholars will go so far to say that such involvement should not exist as a moral argument (though there are exceptions, such as Escobar (1995)).

Objectivism impacts the realm of public policy directly in its rejection of centralized authority in various contexts. Most famously, Alan Greenspan receives criticism from non-Objectivists for being a man of Rand's inner circle of friends and claiming her as a major inspiration (Martin, 2001, Weiss, 2012). However, he likewise incites strong dislike from Objectivists for his abandonment of ideas he held as a young man, such as a return to the gold standard, when he was confronted with the task of actually guiding the economy as Chairman of the Federal Reserve Bank (Greenspan, 1966, Taylor, 2002).

Rand's teachings also strongly influence the education policy field with the introduction of market mechanisms such as school choice and institutional closures under No Child Left Behind, among other policy measures. Rand personally believed that a centralized educational system run by the government was an unjust imposition of authority and generally advocated for the centralized system to be abolished (Reid, 2013); this view has continued in more and less virulent forms since that time (Attick & Boyles, 2010, Kirkpatrick, 2008).

2.15 Rawls

> The natural distribution is neither just nor unjust; nor is it unjust that persons are born into society at some particular position. These are simply natural facts. What is just and unjust is the way that institutions deal with these facts. (~John Rawls, *A Theory of Justice*, 1971, p.87)

Biography John Rawls was born in Baltimore, Maryland, on February 21 of 1921 (Freeman, 2007). His family was well-to-do, with his father being a successful lawyer and his mother active in women's rights causes, both of which can easily be considered a strong influence on his later political philosophy. Equally as strong, however, were the deaths of two of his brothers when he was a child, both from diseases they had contracted from Rawls; many scholars attribute both his shy personality and the emphasis on arbitrariness and chance in his writings to the loss of his brothers (Freeman, Pogge, 2007).

Rawls spent some of his preparatory school years immersed in Protestant theology, which can also be seen in his later writings (Weithman, 2009). He earned a degree in philosophy from Princeton and considered entering the seminary; however, he first served in the Pacific in World War II, which was an experience that both changed his religious views and propelled him further into philosophy and the concept of justice (Pogge, 2007). He returned to Princeton to complete his doctorate, then followed a Fulbright with faculty positions at Cornell and MIT before moving to Harvard, where he taught for 40 years. He was not an especially prolific writer, but he produced three major works, many articles, and several expansions and clarifications of the ideas he had put forward in *A Theory of Justice*. Rawls passed away in November of 2002, having continued to publish up until his death.

Contributions Rawls is most well-known for his initial book, *A Theory of Justice*, where he outlines a framework for a political philosophy which holds fairness to be the ultimate goal. Rawls was dissatisfied with what he considered to be shortcomings in the utilitarian approach to ethics: the ability for a tyranny of the majority to occur was too great to be considered a moral system (Kymlicka, 1988). In response, he makes two main arguments in *Theory*: the first regarding how to decide what is fair, and the second on how to achieve this fairness (Rawls, 1999).

First, Rawls recognized the human tendency toward self-advancement, whether on an individual level or in the tendency to form groups which will try to dominate the agenda. Accordingly, the problem became the identification of someone with such groups. Rawls reasoned that, if an individual didn't know what their group affiliations were (such as race, gender, or socioeconomic class), they would be unable to create preferential treatments for their group. This is very much a "what would like be like if you walked in someone else's shoes," only you're conducting a thought experiment and not sure whose shoes you're walking in. This is called the "veil of ignorance" (Rawls, 1999), where an individual pretends there is a veil between their eyes and the state of the world. This ensures that people will craft policy based on fairness, not knowing which groups they belong to.

Second, Rawls puts forth a more controversial theory on how to achieve this fairness, which relies on a concept of distributive justice. All individuals should have the same basic liberties, opportunities, and endowments; if some people are found to be lacking, then those who have been blessed by fortune to have large quantities of this endowment are morally obligated to share. This applies not only to certain levels of material goods or wealth, but also, more controversially, to fruits of labors that were gained by the lucky inheritance of traits such as talent or liking hard work (Rawls, 1999). This "difference principle" insists that the good of society is maximized when the long-term utility of the least well off group is considered the most important (Altham, 1973); unsurprisingly, it is also his most contentious idea.

Policy Application Rawls' primary contribution to economic policy is the formulation of "the maximin criterion," which was created as a method to achieve fairness since endowments will have already been made (and the veil of self-knowledge already pierced) (Rawls, 1974). It is the formalization and policy application of the "difference principle" – the maximum long term benefit for any society is for the allocation of resources to favor and compensate for the group which was the minimum amount of resource.

He did not originally intend it as an economic application and waives off many of the more formal critiques as being beyond his ability to answer (Rawls, 1974); however, this did not keep more vocal critics such as Harsanyi from pointing out empirical situations which would clearly favor a Bayesian approach (Harsanyi, 1975). In Rawls's defense, scholars such as Hammond consider the maximin to be an entirely acceptable form of generalized social welfare function (Hammond, 1976). Indeed, such reasoning continues in the modern economics curriculum in the form of Leontief curves: the level of utility is determined by the least-well-off partner, which results in players who are willing to pay for fairness (Jakiela, 2008).

2.16 Rousseau

> As soon as any man says of the affairs of the State "What does it matter to me?" the State may be given up for lost. (~Jean-Jacques Rousseau, *The Social Contract*, 1762)

Biography Jean-Jacque Rousseau was born on June 28, 1712, in Geneva, which was a city-state at the time (France, 1987). Having lost his aristocratic mother just a few days after he was born, Rousseau and his father moved to the highly politicized area of Geneva where the other artisans and watchmakers lived (Rosenblatt, 2007). Following the departure of his father when he was ten, Rousseau began a lifetime of living in different places, the transition to the next often beginning with an argument or publication of something incendiary. Rousseau was often described as egoistic and occasionally without tact (Levi, 1951); Hume, who sheltered Rousseau in some of the later years of his life, remarked that not veiling such strong political opinion in his works was unwise (Gay, 1996). According to his *Confessions*, Rousseau ended his years as a lonely and betrayed person who never grasped why he had been pilloried by the two countries he had always called home (France).

Contributions Known for several elements of philosophy and music, Rousseau's largest contribution was in his version of the social contract, which differs from those envisioned by Hobbes or Locke. Rousseau saw the state of nature as a place where man could survive and care for others, but who would constantly be comparing himself to those people or groups which had more possessions and worrying about protecting his own; by surrendering his natural way of living to the state, however, he gains strength and recognition for those rights, such as property (Wraight, 2008). This "surrendering" is essential since Rousseau sees the danger to peace not being inherent in a monarch, but in inequality between members of the contract, this envy and friction being what drove man into the contract originally (Wraight).

Rousseau is also known for pioneering the modern form of autobiography. Some scholars, such as Hazlitt (1930), consider it the greatest of all of Rousseau's work; at the time, however, it was considered scandalous (Mitchell, 1990). In four volumes, it abandoned the previous style of chronological ordering and layered in modern musings, romantic encounters, and asides to the reader (Beaudry, 1991).

Though nowhere near the level of precision that Keynes included in his diaries, Rousseau provides a very intimate look at his personality and beliefs in addition to the traditional retelling of his own story. Though he probably began writing the autobiography as an attempt to clear his name, it only added to the attacks made on his character (Levi, 1951).

Policy Application Like Locke, Rousseau had a profound impact on the founding of the United States and an even stronger one in France. In France, Rousseau became a cult figure that was radicalized by the revolutionaries and therefore despised by traditionalists (Swenson, 1998). His religious tolerance was reinterpreted as deism, and his abhorrence of historical study encouraged the winds of change that were sweeping the French nation (Kelly, 1968). In the United States, Rousseau had a much less vivid impact: the notion of surrendering oneself to the state, even in return for greater rights and for total equality, did not catch on in the States as well as it had in France.

What has lingered, however, is his deep reverence for civil society and participation in the democratic process. His ideal form of government was the direct elections that occur in a city-state, having ill memories of the representative assembly in his childhood Geneva (Wraight, 2008). This fervor for participation is echoed in modern civil society scholars such as Theda Skocpol, who decries the rise of organizations that subsist on member checks rather than ongoing and participatory member relationships (Skocpol, 1999). As Rousseau mentions in the *Social Contract*, yielding your voice and freedom to a subset of the population is the same as yielding it to a monarch and therefore wholly unacceptable (Wraight).

Rousseau, like fellow Enlightenment political philosopher Locke, helped to change the perception and practice of education. Children did not have the reasoning capabilities of adults, thus filling them with knowledge without wisdom would be counterproductive; the purpose of an education was to develop analytical and moral reasoning (Rousseau, 1899). To do this, Rousseau proposed a very child-centered approach which was very opposite the current fashion: in order to teach that something is wrong, such as tardiness, the key is not to lecture on it, but to convince the student through experience (Rousseau). Unfortunately, during the time when Rousseau published *Emile*, such practical lessons were overshadowed by the content of the book which addressed the loosening of restrictions on daughters of the time period (Rousseau). Like much of his work, however, the offensiveness faded over time, leaving the political philosophy to inspire for centuries.

2.17 Smith

> How selfish soever man may be supposed, there are evidently some principles in his nature, which interest him in the fortune of others, and render their happiness necessary to him, though he derives nothing from it, except the pleasure of seeing it. (~Adam Smith, *The Theory of Moral Sentiments*, 1817)

Biography Adam Smith was born in Kirkcaldy, Scotland, in June of 1723. His father died about the time he was born, and as a result Smith and his mother became very close (Rae, 2006). Smith was an excellent student, attending Glasgow College at 14 and then winning a fellowship to study at Oxford; his time at Oxford, though, was extremely unhappy. Since becoming a professor required ordination, Smith chose to return to Scotland, where he lived with his mother for 2 years until an opportunity to teach arrived. After 13 years of lecturing, Smith became a tutor to Charles Townshend's stepson and travelled Europe, meeting other members of the philosophical Enlightenment (Marroquin, 2002). When the tour ended, Smith returned to his mother's in Kirkcaldy and began to work on *Wealth of Nations*. Following its publication, Smith held a series of government positions, offered counsel on trade, and continued to write until his final night, where he reportedly mentioned to his gathered friends after dinner that, "I believe we must adjourn this meeting to some other place" before passing away later that night (Rae).

Smith was a lifelong bachelor and described his own physical characteristics as proving himself a "beau in nothing but [his] books" (Rae, 2006). He also had several quirky habits that one would expect to find in a stereotypical professor: absent-minded, prone to distraction, and often frail of health. Once, he was so distracted in talking about an idea that he fell into a tanning pit (Ekelund Jr & Hébert, 2007)! My advice: don't google the mechanics of tanning pits if you're eating something right now.

Contributions Smith's two primary works neatly summarize his two lasting contributions: that of moral philosophy and of classical economics. The *Theory of Moral Sentiments* forms the foundation for his later work on political economy, where he explores the caveat to the invisible hand: that "while self-love is a necessary condition for the unleashing of humankind's productive energy and creativity, it is not sufficient" (Evensky, 2005). In the opening words of the book, Smith comments on the presence of both self-centered and other-centered tendencies in each person (Smith, 1997); the key to being a virtuous person in a liberal society is balance between the three sentiments: anti-social (such as justice and punishment), social (such as beneficence), and selfish (such as grief and joy) (Evensky). Smith's views on capitalist society and economics presuppose workings of these three sentiments rather than simply selfishness in isolation, which is often left out of casual modern interpretations.

The *Wealth of Nations* held even greater insight, fleshed out with examples that are easy to recall, even for modern readers. The concept of a market was nothing new, nor was the apparent self-interest of mankind being used for public benefit – Mandeville's *Fable of the Bees* having been written almost 75 years before. The concept that the public welfare, embodied in the market, would naturally find its way to its optimum location on its own accord was novel, with the allegory of the invisible hand physically leading the individual "to promote an end which was no part of his intention" (Smith, 2006).

The other famous example from *Wealth*, that of the pin factory, is a very simple way of explaining both an empirical observation he noted and a powerful theory.

Here, Smith contrasted the working arrangements and output of two hypothetical pin factories: one had each worker create pins from beginning to end, while the other had individuals specialize in certain tasks, such as measuring the wire or sharpening the end. In the factory which allowed the workers to specialize, productivity would be astronomically higher (4800 pins per worker) than in the one where each worker did every task (an estimated 20 pins) (Smith, 2006). He then goes on to apply this division of labor to larger markets, such as across industries and countries, in order to explain comparative gains from trade. Smith's explanation that each country could have a comparative advantage in something without having an absolute advantage, resulting in a mutual gain between trade partners, was instrumental in the rejection of Mercantilist thought (Wilson, 1957).

Policy Implications The moral and mechanical justification of *laissez-faire* economics is rooted in the work of Smith. Though he did not use the term, the French phrase broadly meaning "let it be" is evident in the work: the markets will function best if left free of government intervention. The philosophy of *laissez-faire* has been the foundation of many policies, whether that is the spread of international trade or the decentralization of state industries in the developing world. As popular as the term is, however, there are very few who believe in totally government-free markets because of the existence of information asymmetries (where one party knows more than another) or public good problems (where something that is needed cannot be produced effectively in the private market due to an inability to exclude). Additionally, the concept of *laissez-faire* was declared dead by Keynes in 1926 and several times since, most notably after the Great Recession (Keynes, 1926). However, regardless of how strongly it lives, *laissez-faire* reasoning continues to guide capitalist markets.

Of the many mechanical achievements Smith made with policy implications, one which would provide the foundation for centuries of policy guidance involves his notes regarding wages. Though Ricardo used marginal analysis in looking at wages and rents, Smith was able to discern numerous relationships regarding wages and the traits of the job. For example, a public executioner commands a wage premium due to the unsavory nature of the job, whereas a bricklayer has a similar premium because his work is skilled, but sporadic. Additionally, jobs which require a lot of training (such as medicine) or trust (such as a jeweler) will also command higher wages (Smith, 2006).

Discussion Questions

1. What are the similarities and distinctions between Rousseau's concept of the collective will and Smith's concept of an invisible hand?
2. Marx and Smith are often considered polar opposites in worldview and empirical approach. How is this accurate, looking to both theory and practical reality? Do they have elements in common?
3. Which person included in this chapter has a view of society that you believe has the most in common with yours? Why do you feel their view is most accurate?

4. Compare and contrast different conceptualizations of the word "utility." What implications do the differences have for policy analysis?
5. If we expanded this section to include 17 individuals, whom should be the next person we include and why?

References

Ackerman, F. (2002). Still dead after all these years: Interpreting the failure of general equilibrium theory. *Journal of Economic Methodology, 9*(2), 119–139.

Adler, M. J. (1997). *Ten philosophical mistakes*. New York: Simon and Schuster.

Akerlof, G. A., & Shiller, R. J. (2009). *Animal spirits: How human psychology drives the economy, and why it matters for global capitalism*. Princeton, NJ: Princeton Univ Pr.

Altham, J. (1973). Rawls's difference principle. *Philosophy, 48*(183), 75–78.

Annas, J. (1977). Mill and the subjection of women. *Philosophy, 52*(200), 179–194.

Arrow, K. (1950). A difficulty in the concept of social welfare. *The Journal of Political Economy, 58*(4), 328–346.

Arrow, K. (1951). *An extension of the basic theorems of classical welfare economics*. Paper presented at the Proceedings of the Second Berkeley Symposium on Mathematical Statistics and Probability, Berkeley, CA.

Arrow, K. (1963). Uncertainty and the welfare economics of medical care. *The American Economic Review, 53*(5), 941–973.

Arrow, K. (1992a). General economic equilibrium: Purpose, analytic techniques, collective choice. In A. Lindbeck (Ed.), *Nobel lectures, economics 1969–1980*. Singapore, Singapore: World Scientific Publishing Co.

Arrow, K. (1992b). Kenneth Arrow – autobiography. In A. Lindbeck (Ed.), *Nobel lectures, economics 1969–1980*. Singapore: World Scientific Publishing Co.

Arrow, K. (1999). Discounting, morality, and gaming. In P. R. Portney & J. P. Weyant (Eds.), *Discounting and intergenerational equity* (Chapter 2, pp. 13–21). Washington, DC: Resources for the Future.

Arrow, K. (2005). *Kenneth J. Arrow – autobiography – addendum*, April 2005. Retrieved 20 Mar 2013, from http://www.nobelprize.org/nobel_prizes/economics/laureates/1972/arrow-autobio.html#

Arrow, K. J. (2007). Global climate change: A challenge to policy. *The Economists' Voice, 4*(3), 1–5.

Arrow, K. (2009). Kenneth J. Arrow. In W. Breit & B. T. Hirsch (Eds.), *Lives of the laureates: Twenty-three Nobel economists* (5th ed.). Cambridge, MA: The MIT Press.

Arrow, K., Akerlof, G., Maskin, E. (2011). Virginia v. Sebelius-Economics Professors amicus brief.

Arrow, K., et al. (2009). Toward a 21st-century health care system: Recommendations for health care reform. *Annals of Internal Medicine, 150*(7), 493–495.

Arrow, K., et al. (1996). *Intertemporal equity, discounting, and economic efficiency*. Cambridge, UK: Cambridge University Press.

Arrow, K., Panosian, C., & Gelband, H. (2004). *Saving lives, buying time: Economics of malaria drugs in an age of resistance*. Washington, DC: National Academies Press.

Ashcraft, R. (1994). 9 Locke's political philosophy. In P. R. Portney & V. Chappell (Eds.), *The Cambridge companion to Locke* (Chapter 9, pp. 226–251). Cambridge, UK: Cambridge UP.

Attick, D., & Boyles, D. (2010). Book review of Jerry Kirkpatrick's Montessori, Dewey, and Capitalism. *Education and Culture 26*(1), pp. 100–103.

Baloglou, C. P. (2012). The tradition of economic thought in the mediterranean world from the ancient classical times through the Hellenistic times until the Byzantine times and Arab-Islamic world. In J. G. Backhaus (Ed.), *Handbook of the history of economic thought* (Chapter 2, pp. 7–91). Dordrecht, the Netherlands: Springer.

Bankman, J., & Griffith, T. (1987). Social welfare and the rate structure: A new look at progressive taxation. *California Law Review, 75*(6), 1905–1967.

Banning, L. (1995). *Jefferson & Madison: Three conversations from the founding*. Madison, WI: Madison House Pub.

Beaudry, C. A. (1991). *The role of the reader in Rousseau's confessions*. New York: Peter Lang.

Bentham, J. (1843a). In J. Bowring (Ed.), *The works of Jeremy Bentham* (Vol. X). Edinburgh, UK: William Tait.

Bentham, J. (1843b). In J. Bowring (Ed.), *The works of Jeremy Bentham* (Vol. IX). Edinburgh: UK.

Bentham, J. (1843c). In J. Bowring (Ed.), *The works of Jeremy Bentham* (Vol. III). Edinburgh, UK: William Tait.

Bentham, J. (1879). *An introduction to the principles of morals and legislation*. Oxford, UK: The Clarendon Press.

Bentham, J., & Crompton, L. (1978). Offences against one's self: Paederesty (part 1). *Journal of Homosexuality, 3*(4), 389–406.

Binmore, K. G. (1998). *Game theory and the social contract: Just playing* (Vol. 2). Cambridge, MA: The MIT Press.

Blits, K. C. (1999). Aristotle: Form, function, and comparative anatomy. *The Anatomical Record, 257*(2), 58–63.

Blumenberg, W. (1998). *Karl Marx: An illustrated biography*. New York: Verso Books.

Boettke, P. J. (2005). On reading Hayek: Choice, consequences and the road to serfdom. *European Journal of Political Economy, 21*(4), 1042–1053.

Bowles, S., & Gintis, H. (2002). Social capital and community governance*. *The Economic Journal, 112*(483), F419–F436.

Brown, G. W., & Held, D. (2011). *The cosmopolitanism reader*. Cambridge, MA: Polity.

Bull, H. (1981). Hobbes and the international anarchy. *Social Research, 48*(4), 717–738.

Burns, J. (2009). *Goddess of the market: Ayn Rand and the American right*. Oxford: Oxford University Press.

Chappell, V. (1994). *The Cambridge companion to Locke*. Cambridge, MA: Cambridge University Press.

Coase, R. H. (1993). Law and economics at Chicago. *Journal of Law and Economics, 36*(1), 239–254.

Copleston, F. C. (1946). *History of philosophy: Bentham to Russell* (Vol. 8). Mahwah, NJ: Paulist Press.

Cowles Foundation for Research in Economics. (2011). Cowles Commission/Foundation for Research in Economics: Nobel Laureates. Retrieved 20 Mar 2013, from http://cowles.econ.yale.edu/archive/people/nobel.htm

Crimmins, J. E. (1996). Contending interpretations of Bentham's utilitarianism. *Canadian Journal of Political Science/Revue canadienne de science politique, 29*(4), 751–777.

De Mandeville, B., & Kaye, F. B. (1957). *The fable of the bees or, private vices, publick benefits*. Oxford, UK: Oxford University Press.

Devins, C., & Kauffman, S. (2012). Laws of unintended consequence: A warning to policymakers. In *Cosmos & cultre: Commentary on science and society* (vol. 2013). National Pubic Radio.

Diamond, P. A. (1967). Cardinal welfare, individualistic ethics, and interpersonal comparison of utility: Comment. *The Journal of Political Economy, 75*(5), 765.

Dimitrov, V. (1983). Group choice under fuzzy information. *Fuzzy Sets and Systems, 9*(1), 25–39.

Donaldson, T. (1994). When integration fails: The logic of prescription and description in business ethics. *Business Ethics Quarterly, 4*(2), 157–169.

Dunn, J. (1982). *The political thought of John Locke: An historical account of the argument of the 'Two Treatises of Government'*. London: Cambridge UP.

Ekelund, R. B., Jr., & Hébert, R. F. (2007). *A history of economic theory and method* (5th ed.). Long Grove, IL: Waveland Press.

Escobar, A. (1995). *Encountering development: The making and unmaking of the third world.* Princeton, NJ: Princeton Univ Pr.

Evensky, J. (2005). Adam Smith's "Theory of Moral Sentiments": On morals and why they matter to a liberal society of free people and free markets. *The Journal of Economic Perspectives, 19*(3), 109–130.

Feldstein, M. (1976). On the theory of tax reform. *Journal of Public Economics, 6*(1–2), 77–104.

Finley, M. I. (1970). Aristotle and economic analysis. *Past & Present, 47*, 3–25.

France, P. (1987). *Rousseau: Confessions.* Cambridgeshire, UK: Cambridge University Press.

Freeman, S. (2007). *Rawls.* New York: Routledge.

Friedman, M. (1953). The methodology of positive economics. In *Essays in positive economics* (pp. 3–43). Chicago, IL: Chicago UP.

Friedman, M. (1991). Say 'No' to intolerance. *Liberty, 18*, 17–20.

Garrison, R. W., & Kirzner, I. M. (1987). Friedrich August von Hayek. In J. Eatwell, M. Milgate, & P. Newman (Eds.), *The New Palgrave: A dictionary of economics* (pp. 609–614). London: Macmillan Press Ltd.

Gay, P. (1996). *The enlightenment: An interpretation: The science of freedom* (Vol. 2). New York: WW Norton & Company.

Gillroy, J. M., & Wade, M. L. (1992). *The moral dimensions of public policy choice: Beyond the market paradigm.* Pittsburgh, PA: University of Pittsburgh Pre.

Goldworth, A. (1969). The meaning of Bentham's greatest happiness principle. *Journal of the History of Philosophy, 7*(3), 315–321.

Gowdy, J. M. (2004). The revolution in welfare economics and its implications for environmental valuation and policy. *Land Economics, 80*(2), 239–257.

Gowdy, J. (2005). Toward a new welfare economics for sustainability. *Ecological Economics, 53*(2), 211–222.

Greenspan, A. (1966). Gold and economic freedom. In A. Rand (Ed.), *Capitalism: The unknown ideal* (p. 69). New York: Signet.

Hammond, P. J. (1976). Equity, Arrow's conditions, and Rawls' difference principle. *Econometrica: Journal of the Econometric Society, 44*(4), 793–804.

Harrison, R. (1995). Jeremy Bentham. In T. Honderish (Ed.), *The Oxford companion to philosophy* (pp. 85–88). Oxford: Oxford University Press.

Harsanyi, J. C. (1955). Cardinal welfare, individualistic ethics, and interpersonal comparisons of utility. *Journal of Political Economy, 63*(4), 309–321.

Harsanyi, J. C. (1975). Can the maximin principle serve as a basis for morality? A critique of John Rawls's theory: JSTOR. *The American Political Science Review, 69*(2), 594–606.

Hayek, F. A. (1931). *Prices and production.* London: George Routledge & Sons, Ltd.

Hayek, F. A. (1934). Carl Menger. *Economica, 1*(4), 393–420.

Hayek, F. A. (1949). The intellectuals and socialism. *The University of Chicago Law Review, 16*(3), 417–433.

Hayek, F. A. (1973). *Economic freedom and representative government.* London: Wincott Foundation.

Hayek, F. A. (2001). *The road to serfdom.* East Sussex, UK: Psychology Press.

Hayek, F. A. (2009). *Denationalisation of money: The argument refined.* Auburn, AL: Ludwig von Mises Institute.

Hazlitt, W. (1930). On the character of Rousseau. In P. P. Howe (Ed.), *The selected writings of William Hazlitt* (pp. 90–94). London: Dent.

Heller, A. C. (2009). *Ayn Rand and the world she made.* New York: Anchor.

Hicks, J. R. (1946). *Value and capital* (Vol. 2). Oxford, UK: Clarendon.

Hobbes, T. (1887). *Leviathan: Or, the matter, form, and power of a commonwealth ecclesiastical and civil* (Vol. 21). London: George Routledge & Sons.

Howarth, R. B., & Norgaard, R. B. (1990). Intergenerational resource rights, efficiency, and social optimality. *Land Economics, 66*(1), 1–11.

Hughes, J. D. (2003). Europe as consumer of exotic biodiversity: Greek and Roman times. *Landscape Research, 28*(1), 21–31.

Hume, D. (1907). *An enquiry concerning human understanding and selections from a treatise of human nature: With Hume's autobiography and a letter from Adam Smith*. Open Court.

Hume, D. (2003). *A treatise of human nature* (10th edition). Project Gutenberg Literacy Archive Foundation.

Issing, O., White, L. H., & Vaubel, R. (2000). *Hayek, currency competition and European monetary union*. London: Institute of Economic Affairs.

Jakiela, P. (2008). *Essays in experimental development economics*. Ann Arbor, MI: ProQuest.

Jordan, W. R. (2002). Religion in the public square: A reconsideration of David Hume and religious establishment. *The Review of Politics, 64*(4), 687–713.

Kant, I. (1963). *On history: An idea for a universal history from a cosmopolitan point of view*. Indianapolis, IN: Bobbs Merril Co.

Kant, I. (2003). *On education*. (trans. Churton, A.) Mineola, NY: Dover Publications.

Kant, I., & Gregor, M. J. (1996). *Kant: The metaphysics of morals*. Cambridge, MA: Cambridge University Press.

Kant, I., & Louden, R. B. (2006). *Kant: Anthropology from a pragmatic point of view*. Cambridge, MA: Cambridge University Press.

Kelly, G. A. (1968). Rousseau, Kant, and history. *Journal of the History of Ideas, 29*(3), 347–364.

Keynes, J. M. (1926). *The end of laissez-faire* (Vol. 16). London: Hogarth Press.

Keynes, J. M. (1940). *How to pay for the war: A radical plan for the chancellor of the exchequer*. London: Harcourt, Brace.

Keynes, J. M. (2004). *The economic consequences of the peace*. New York: Courier Dover Publications.

Keynes, J. M. (2006). *The general theory of employment, interest and money*. New Delhi, India: Atlantic Publishers & Distributors.

Kirkpatrick, J. (2008). *Montessori, Dewey, and capitalism: Educational theory for a free market in education*. Claremont, CA: TLJ Books.

Korsgaard, C. M. (1996). *Creating the kingdom of ends*. Cambridge, MA: Cambridge University Press.

Kreider, S. E. (2010). Mill on happiness. *Philosophical Papers, 39*(1), 53–68.

Kuehn, M. (2001). *Kant: A biography*. Cambridge, MA: Cambridge University Press.

Kymlicka, W. (1988). Rawls on teleology and deontology. *Philosophy & Public Affairs, 17*(3), 173–190.

Lansford, T. (2007). Hobbes, Thomas. In J. Patrick (Ed.), *Renaissance and reformation* (Vol. 1, pp. 542–547). Tarrytown, NY: Marshall Cavendish.

Leach, B. (2008 Oct 18). The great economist John Maynard Keynes: A biography. *The Telegraph*.

Levi, A. W. (1951). The writing of Mill's autobiography. *Ethics, 61*(4), 284–296.

Levy, P. (1979). The Bloomsbury group. In M. Keynes (Ed.), *Essays on John Maynard Keynes*. Cambridge, MA: Cambridge University Press.

Lewis, R. (2009). Kant 200 years on. *Philosophy Now, 49*, 4–4.

Lloyd, S. A., & Sreedhar, S. (2008). Hobbes's moral and political philosophy. In E. N. Zalta (Ed.), *The Stanford encyclopedia of philosophy* (Fall 2008 Edition). http://plato.stanford.edu/archives/fall2008/entries/hobbes-moral/

Locke, J. (1980). *Second treatise of government*. Indianapolis, IN: Hackett Publishing Company.

Locke, J. (1988). *Locke: Two treatises of government student edition*. Cambridge, MA: Cambridge University Press.

Locke, J., & Milton, J. (1830). *Some thoughts concerning education* (Vol. 1). Boston: Gray & Bowen.

Lucas, R. E., & Sargent, T. J. (1979). After Keynesian macroeconomics. *After the Phillips Curve: Persistence of High Inflation and High Unemployment, 19*, 49–72.

MacIntyre, A. C. (1959). Hume on " is" and "ought". *The Philosophical Review, 68*(4), 451–468.

Marino, G. (Ed.). (2010). *Ethics: The essential writings*. New York: Modern Library.
Marroquin, A. (2002). *Invisible hand: The wealth of Adam Smith*. Albuquerque, NM: The Minerva Group.
Martin, J. (2001). *Greenspan: The man behind money*. New York: Da Capo Press.
Martinich, A. P. (1999). *Hobbes: A biography*. Cambridge, UK: Cambridge University Press.
Marx, K., & Nicolaus, M. (1993). *Grundrisse*. London: ePenguin.
McCloskey, D. N., & Ziliak, S. (2008). *The cult of statistical significance: How the standard error costs us jobs, justice, and lives*. Ann Arbor, MI: University of Michigan Press.
McKeon, R. (2009). Biographical note. In R. McKeon (Ed.), *The basic works of Aristotle*. New York: Random House.
Mill, J. S. (1909). On liberty. In P. F. Collier and Son. *Autobiography and Essay on Liberty* (pp. 203–331). New York. Accessed at https://play.google.com/store/books/details?id=ENtXAAAAYAAJ&rdid=book-ENtXAAAAYAAJ&rdot=1.
Mill, J. S. (1900). *Principles of political economy: With some of their applications to social philosophy*. London: Longmans, Green, and Company.
Mill, J. S. (1909). On liberty. In *Autobiography and essay on liberty* (pp. 203–331). New York: P. F. Collier and Son. Accessed at https://play.google.com/store/books/details?id=ENtXAAAAYAAJ&rdid=book-ENtXAAAAYAAJ&rdot=1
Mill, J. S. (1981). *Autobiography and literary essays*. Toronto, Canada: University of Toronto Press.
Mill, J. S. (1994). On the definition and method of political economy. In D. L. Hausman (Ed.), *The philosophy of economics: An anthology* (Vol. 2, pp. 52–68). Cambridge, UK: Cambridge UP.
Mill, J. S. (2007). *Utilitarianism, liberty & representative government*. Rockville, MD: Wildside Press LLC.
Mill, J. S., & Alexander, E. (2001). *The subjection of women*. New Brunswick, NJ: Transaction Publishers.
Mirowski, P. (1991). *More heat than light: Economics as social physics, physics as nature's economics*. Cambridge, MA: Cambridge University Press.
Mitchell, W. C. (1918). Bentham's felicific calculus. *Political Science Quarterly, 33*(2), 161–183.
Mitchell, W. J. T. (1990). Influence, autobiography, and literary history: Rousseau's confessions and Wordsworth's the prelude. *ELH, 57*(3), 643–664.
Moggridge, D. (2002). *Maynard Keynes: An economist's biography*. New York: Routledge.
Montefiore, S. S. (2011, September 23). At home with Karl Marx. *The New York Times*.
Moore, S. (2009). 'Atlas Shrugged': From fiction to fact in 52 years. *Wall Street Journal*.
Morrison, K. (2006). *Marx, Durkheim, Weber: Formations of modern social thought*. London: SAGE Publications Limited.
Mossner, E. C. (1950). Philosophy and biography: The case of David Hume. *The Philosophical Review, 59*(2), 184–201.
Nobelprize.org. (1972). *The prize in economics 1972 – press release*. Retrieved 20 Mar 2013, from http://www.nobelprize.org/nobel_prizes/economics/laureates/1972/press.html
O'Shea, J. L. (2008, 24 Nov). 10 things you didn't know about Lawrence 'Larry' Summers. *U.S. News & World Report*.
Papola, J. (Writer) (2010). Fear the boom and bust. In J. Bradley (Producer). USA: EconStories.
Patinkin, D. (1984). *Anticipations of the general theory?: And other essays on Keynes*. Chicago, IL: University of Chicago Press.
Pogge, T. W. M. (2007). *John Rawls: His life and theory of justice* (trans: Kosch, M.). Oxford: Oxford UP.
Primer, I. (1975). *Mandeville studies: New explorations in the art and thought of Dr. Bernard andeville (1670–1733)* (Vol. 81). The Hague, Netherlands: Springer.
Puchner, M. (2006). *Poetry of the revolution: Marx, Manifestos, & the Avant-Gard*. Princeton, NJ: Princeton University Press.
Putnam, R. D. (1993). The prosperous community. *The American Prospect, 4*(13), 35–42.
Rachels, J., & Rachels, S. (1986). *The elements of moral philosophy*. New York: McGraw-Hill.

Rae, J. (2006). *Life of Adam Smith*. New York: Cosimo.

Rand, A. (1961). The objectivist ethics. In A. Rand (Ed.), *The virture of selfishness* (pp. 13–39). New York: Signet.

Rand, A., & Brandon, N. (1964). *The virtue of selfishness: A new concept of egoism*. New York: Signet.

Rawls, J. (1974). Some reasons for the maximin criterion. *The American Economic Review, 64*(2), 141–146.

Rawls, J. (1999). *A theory of justice* (6th ed.). Cambridge, MA: Harvard UP.

Reid, J. (2013). "The Ayn Rand School for Tots": John Dewey, Maria Montessori, and objectivist educational philosophy during the postwar years. *Historical Studies in Education/Revue d'histoire de l'éducation, 25*(1), 73–94.

Richardson, R., & Hurwitz, B. (1987). Jeremy Bentham's self image: An exemplary bequest for dissection. *British Medical Journal (Clinical Research Ed.), 295*(6591), 195.

Ringold, D. J. (2002). Boomerang effects in response to public health interventions: Some unintended consequences in the alcoholic beverage market. *Journal of Consumer Policy, 25*(1), 27–63.

Rohlf, M. (2010). Immanuel Kant. In E. N. Zalta (Ed.), *The Stanford encyclopedia of philosophy* (Summer 2010 Edition). http://plato.stanford.edu/archives/sum2010/entries/kant/

Rosen, F. (2007). Bentham, Jeremy (1748–1832). In H. C. G. Matthew, B. Harrison, & R. J. Long (Eds.), *Oxford dictionary of national biography* (Onlineth ed.). Oxford, UK: Oxford University Press.

Rosenberg, A. (1993). Hume and the philosophy of science. In F. N. Norton (Ed.), *The Cambridge companion to Hume*. Cambridge: Cambridge University Press.

Rosenblatt, H. (2007). *Rousseau and Geneva: From the first discourse to the social contract, 1749–1762* (Vol. 46). Cambridge, MA: Cambridge University Press.

Rousseau, J.-J. (1899). *Émile, or treatise on education* (Vol. 20). New York: Appleton.

Rousseau, G. S. (1975). Mandeville and Europe: Medicine and philosophy. In I. Primer (Ed.), *Mandeville studies: New explorations in the art and thought of Dr. Bernard Mandeville (1670–1733)* (Vol. 81). The Hague, Netherlands: Springer.

Sadka, E. (1976). On income distribution, incentive effects and optimal income taxation. *The Review of Economic Studies, 43*(2), 261–267.

Sciabarra, C. M. (1995). *Ayn Rand: The Russian radical*. University Park, PA: Penn State Press.

Sen, A. (1974). Rawls versus Bentham: An axiomatic examination of the pure distribution problem. *Theory and Decision, 4*(3–4), 301–309.

Shanley, M. L. (1981). Marital slavery and friendship: John Stuart Mill's the subjection of women. *Political Theory, 9*(2), 229–247.

Sigot, N. (2002). Jevons's debt to Bentham: Mathematical economy, morals and psychology. *The Manchester School, 70*(2), 262–278.

Sisko, J. E. (2001). Phronesis. In L. Becker & C. Becker (Eds.), *Encyclopedia of ethics: P-W* (2nd ed., pp. 1314–1316). New York: Routledge.

Skocpol, T. (1999). Associations without members. *American Prospect, 45*, 66–73.

Smith, A. (1997). *The theory of moral sentiments*. Washington, DC: Regenery.

Smith, A. (2006). *An inquiry into the nature and causes of the wealth of nations*. Cirencester, UK: Echo Library.

Stern, N. (2006). Review on the economics of climate change. *London HM Treasury*.

Stimson, S. C., & Milgate, M. (2001). Mill, liberty and the facts of life. *Political Studies, 49*(2), 231–248.

Swenson, J. (1998). Revolutionary sentences. *Yale French Studies, 93*, 11–29.

Taylor, J. (2002). The fish rots from the head down (vol. 21). www.MiningStocks.com

Toulmin, S. (1977). From form to function: Philosophy and history of science in the 1950s and now. *Daedalus, 106*(3), 143–162.

UCL Bentham Project. (2013 Feb 26). Who was Jeremy Bentham? Retrieved 21 Mar 2013.

UCL Chemistry. (2010 Sept 20). *History – chemical history of UCL: The Autoicon*. Retrieved 21 Mar 2013, from http://www.chem.ucl.ac.uk/resources/history/chemhistucl/hist03.html
Uzgalis, W. (2007). John Locke (Stanford encyclopedia of philosophy). In *Stanford encyclopedia of philosophy* (vol. 5).
Uzgalis, W. (2012). The influence of John Locke's works (Stanford encyclopedia of philosophy). In *Stanford encyclopedia of philosophy* (Fall 2012).
Vasilyev, V. V. (2001). The origin of Kant's deduction of the categories.
Vichert, G. (1975). Mandeville's the virgin unmask'd. In I. Primer (Ed.), *Mandeville studies: New explorations in the art and thought of Dr. Bernard Mandeville (1670–1733)* (Vol. 81). The Hague, Netherlands: Springer.
Von Hayek, F. A. (1974). Friedrich August von Hayek's speech at the Nobel Banquet. Retrieved 25 May 2013.
Von Hayek, F. A., Kresge, S., & Wenar, L. (1994). *Hayek on Hayek: An autobiographical dialogue* (Vol. 20). East Sussex, UK: Psychology Press.
Washburn, M. (1975). Dogmatism, scepticism, criticism: The dialectic of Kant's "Silent Decade". *Journal of the History of Philosophy, 13*(2), 167–176.
Weiss, G. (2012). *Ayn Rand nation: The hidden struggle for America's soul*. New York: Macmillan.
Weithman, P. (2009). John Rawls and the task of political philosophy. *The Review of Politics, 71*(01), 113–125.
Williford, M. (1975). Bentham on the rights of women. *Journal of the History of Ideas, 36*(1), 167–176.
Wilson, C. (1957). 'Mercantilism': Some vicissitudes of an idea. *The Economic History Review, 10*(2), 181–188.
Wraight, C. D. (2008). *Rousseaus's the social contract: A reader's guide*. London: Continuum.
Zimroth, E. (2008, January 28). The sex diaries of John Maynard Keynes. *Intelligent Life*.

Part II
Ethical Decision-Making

"The human faculties of perception, judgment, discriminative feeling, mental activity, and even moral preference, are exercised only in making a choice. He who does anything because it is the custom, makes no choice. He gains no practice either in discerning or in desiring what is best. The mental and moral, like the muscular powers, are improved only by being used. The faculties are called into no exercise by doing a thing merely because others do it, no more than by believing a thing only because others believe it. If the grounds of an opinion are not conclusive to the person's own reason, his reason cannot be strengthened, but is likely to be weakened, by his adopting it . . .

He who lets the world, or his own portion of it, choose his plan of life for him, has no need of any other faculty than the ape-like one of imitation. He who chooses his plan for himself, employs all his faculties. He must use observation to see, reasoning and judgment to foresee, activity to gather materials for decision, discrimination to decide, and when he has decided, firmness and self-control to hold to his deliberate decision."

-John Stuart Mill, *On Liberty,* 1859

Chapter 3
Framing the Problem

Elizabeth A.M. Searing and Donald R. Searing

> *"If while traveling in a mountain range you notice that the apparent relative height of mountain peaks varies with your vantage point, you will conclude that some impressions of relative height must be erroneous, even when you have no access to the correct answer. Similarly, one may discover that the relative attractiveness of options varies when the same decision problem is framed in different ways. . . The susceptibility to perspective effects is of special concern in the domain of decision-making because of the absence of objective standards such as the true height of mountains."*
>
> -Daniel Kahneman and Amos Tversky (1981)

Abstract This chapter contains a description of the framing process in the ethical decision-making methodology. Before attempting to handle questions of ethics, a scenario must be deconstructed into component pieces. Facts, concepts, and morals are defined and discerned from like objects that contain some degree of ambiguity (known as factual issues, conceptual issues, and moral issues). Gaps in these components are filled with assumptions, an important but often insidious part of the decision process. Finally, process can continue iteratively until stopped by the decision-maker.

Keywords Decision • Framing • Factual issue • Concepts • Conceptual issue • Morals • Moral issue • Recognition of priors • Iterative looping

E.A.M. Searing, PhD (✉)
Assistant Professor, Department of Public Administration and Policy, Rockefeller College of Public Affairs and Policy, University at Albany – State University of New York, 305 Milne Hall, 135 Western Avenue, Albany, New York, USA
e-mail: esearing@albany.edu

D.R. Searing, PhD
CEO and Principal Scientist, Syncere Systems, Altamont, NY, USA
e-mail: dsearing@synceresystems.com

E.A.M. Searing, D.R. Searing (eds.), *Practicing Professional Ethics in Economics and Public Policy*, DOI 10.1007/978-94-017-7306-5_3

When the unlikely team of an economist (Amos Tversky) and a psychologist (Daniel Kahneman) began working together in the early 1970s, no one anticipated the radical shift that mainstream economic thought was about to make. Though not the first to notice the importance of subjectivity to the theory of value (which has been a concern from the very beginning), Kahneman and Tversky were the first to formalize the impact of the description and surrounding of a problem on the actual choice made. This environment would vary from person to person, even decision to decision, depending on how the problem was viewed and the nature of the person making the decision. This understanding paved the way for the development of prospect theory (we hate losses more than we like wins) and other forms of subjective expected utility; more importantly, it explained instances of reference-dependent scenarios, which explained preference reversals, one of the fundamental underlying assumptions of Neoclassical economic theory.

So what is framing? Think of it as a picture frame: it surrounds the problem and influences how you view what's inside. Even given the same picture, an ornate gold frame will influence your estimate of the picture's value compared to a faded wood frame full of chips and dents. Thus, the price that you would bid an auction would be influenced not only by the quality of the painting, but also its environment and the priors that you have about what such a frame implies. Framing, according to Kahneman and Tversky, is "controlled by the manner in which the choice problem is presented as well as by norms, habits, and expectancies of the decision maker" (Tversky & Kahneman, 1986). For our purposes, framing is the descriptive environment of a decision, including both the perception of the problem by the decision agent and the nature of the agent herself.

The exploration of framing effects already occurs in several subfields of economics. In experimental economics, documenting humanity's biases and inclinations often yields brilliant (and very publishable) results. For example, Kahneman and Tversky describe a situation where individuals will value a mug at a lower value when observing it than if they own it; owners estimate its value much more highly and are much less likely to give it up than those simply viewing the mug ("loss aversion") (Kahneman, Knetsch, & Thaler, 1990; Tversky & Kahneman, 1991); Thaler describes the reluctance of someone who had bought wine at a bargain to sell back the same wines for a profit later ("endowment effect") (Kahneman et al., 1990; Thaler, 1980) The importance of framing also appears in the tax and public finance literature. People are much more willing to overpay tax and receive a bonus than underpay and pay more fees (McCaffery & Baron, 2004; Schelling, 1981); further, payers have different feelings toward the fairness of progressive taxation depending on whether the same amount is reported in dollars or percentages (Heath, Chatterjee, & France, 1995; McCaffery & Baron, 2004). Finally, an entire school of economic thought called behavioral economics has developed over recent years specifically dedicated to the impacts of human behavior on and in economic science.

All of these contributions highlight an especially salient point: the strong desire for economics to be a positive science does not, in reality, excuse it from normative or subjective considerations. As modern philosopher Lorraine Code said, "[o]bjectivity requires taking subjectivity into account." (Code, 1991, p. 31). We can prove intransitivity mathematically or derive a precise estimate of industrial sector growth using parameters and calibration, however each of these positive figures is influenced by our determination of salient information, our design of the models, our interpretation of the results, and the underlying assumptions and eccentricities of all data and previous models involved. This axiom exists even before we explicitly begin considering the traditional "ought" questions of norms and ethics that are the primary concern of this text. It is only natural, therefore, that we consider such framing in "ought" questions, as well.

How do we accommodate framing in the ethical decision process? We methodologically collect and assemble our data on the agents involved (including ourselves), the facts as we know them, the concepts in play as we understand them, and the values involved in the case. Each piece of information is classified and vetted from numerous angles, and missing gaps are filled with explicitly acknowledged ex post facto assumptions. Understanding the environment of the decision is just as crucial as the mechanics of resolution.

3.1 Assemble the Data

As in all sciences, including and especially the social sciences, the key to understanding is the data. Without observations on the way things are, we step away from the empirical nature of our disciplines and toward a more sterile world of theory and philosophy. Both theory and philosophy have their place (including very shortly in this handbook); however, our foundations lay in the world and situation that we find ourselves in.

As policy professionals, we are generally familiar with the importance of and efforts required to get good data. Whether we are working on growth forecasts using 30 years of aggregate numbers or the results of a single round of an ultimatum game, the reliability of our analysis rests on the quality of the information used to draw those conclusions. Additionally, unlike many of those aggregate datasets that are compiled, tidied, and released by others according to strict standards and established instruments, when describing your own decision scenario, you have no one to rely on to vet your data and only a handful of instruments to guide you (including, hopefully, this book). The rest of this chapter will be spent exploring how to describe the decision scenario in unambiguous detail, as displayed in Fig. 3.1.

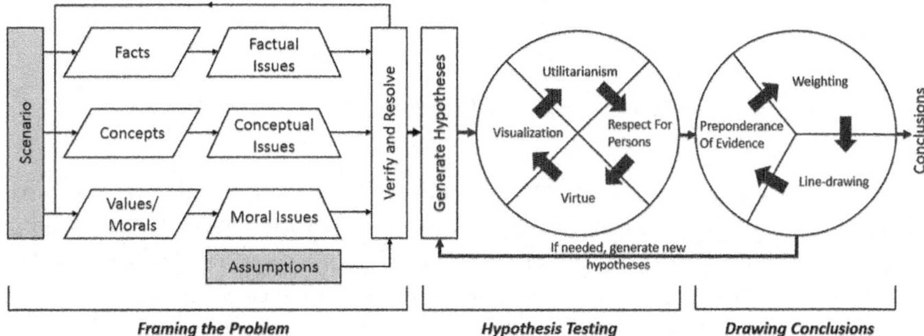

Fig. 3.1 Framing the problem

3.1.1 What Is Data in an Ethical Decision Scenario?

Decision data is any piece of information, disputed or commonly accepted, that may be relevant to the decision at hand or its consequences. Examples are facts, beliefs, opinions, projections – anything that will help explain the numerous facets of the situation you are being asked to analyze. Some of these are obvious, such as needing to know the time to incorporate for a small business if trying to design an incentive system to encourage the formation of home-based businesses. This can be gathered from a large statistical powerhouse or by hand. However, you also need to know with whom any interactions have to be made: will an individual need to travel a great distance to meet with a local magistrate? Will this official expect a bribe? What is the community attitude toward bribery? Toward the government in general? And vice versa? This is a very small part of the process of business formation, but each of these can be a deal-breaker.

So how do you tell what is salient? In an ethical situation, it is best to be risk-averse – better to err on the side of being ethical than otherwise (we will talk more extensively about this in hypothesis testing later in the book). Deciding what is salient is a crucial part of the framing process whose importance should not be overlooked. During the initial data-gathering process, all possible information should be considered; however, due to cognitive constraints, the massive set of information compiled about the situation will need to be pared down to only the most relevant data. Ask yourself for each piece: do I believe this could be helpful in understanding this event? If so, store it in the active part of the decision space (e.g., write it down); if you currently do not feel it is helpful, then store it in the inactive portion. This step is important for two reasons. First, you are evaluating the merits of information, which will help you simplify your decision space and classify it further. Second, should it become salient at a later point (and many questions are resolved with information stored "outside of the box"), you have a brief recognition of where this information can be accessed again. You do not have to store it in the active decision space to recognize where it is. Like a forgotten recipe from your Great Aunt Betty, you know roughly where to find it on your shelf when you discover she'll be stopping by for dinner the next day. You didn't think it was important previously, but it has become so, and knowing its approximate whereabouts will help you hunt it down when needed.

3.1.2 How Is Decision Data Gathered?

Physically, data is gathered in ways very similar to those you use in any other sort of analysis: by research, interview, introspection, and extrapolation. Research, in a broad sense, is any gathering of information. Here, we refer to it as the familiar hunting and mining of information through inanimate sources, such as books, journals, the internet, etc. The definition of "full disclosure" according to the Code of

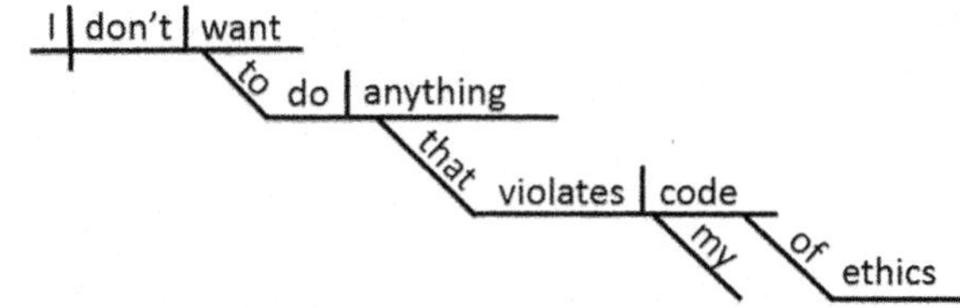

Fig. 3.2 Syntax method example

Ethics for the Central Bureau of Statistics, the median age of the worker in a textile factory, or the most effective way to measure subjective utility are all examples of data of different types. They vary in description, ease of acquisition, level of ambiguity, and traditional use, but they are all necessary pieces of information salient to the dilemma.

So where would you start? Even the task of physically describing the room you are currently in is daunting if you are trying to be thorough, to say nothing of the beliefs and expectations of those around you. How would you begin, and how would you proceed?

A simple approach is called the syntax method. The syntax method provides an approach to your surroundings based on the elements of grammatical syntax (those rules about how to build sentences that you thought you had forgotten since middle school). Remember what we said about storing things in the inactive space until you suddenly found a situation where they were salient? Here's your chance to practice (Fig. 3.2).

The place to start in gathering information is with the subject (like in diagramming a sentence): you, the decision agent. Who are you, and what roles do you play in the situation? Do you hold supervisory power over other agents, over this subject matter area, or are you an observer of peers? What are your political or religious views? Have you historically dealt with similar situations, and how did they resolve themselves? How did those situations differ from the one at hand? What history do you have with the other agents involved?

Don't forget to include in your discussion of the subject the perceptions that others may have of you. Are you known as a risk-taker around the office? Even if you consider yourself someone who slowly and deliberately thinks things out, make note of the fact that others may have noticed something, and this observation may have a hand in the scenario (regardless of which party is correct). Remember, just as many ethical situations arise from perceptions as they do from facts, and the recognition and understanding of each is prudent when attempting a thorough analysis.

Next move to the verb(s). What action is either taking place or being evaluated in the scenario? This can include a suspected transgression (accepting a bribe), evaluation of a current act (is accepting a consulting fee really a bribe?), and potential avenues of resolution (should you report your boss for a suspected breach of professional ethics?) For example, Janet has a growing suspicion that her co-author, who is responsible for conducting the experiments that were jointly designed by the both of them, may not be reporting the results accurately. All of the results are very clean, very direct, and very supportive of their hypothesis. Janet suspects that her co-author may have cleaned some unfriendly data from their dataset. Concerned, she collects data concentrating on verb syntax- the action. For example, she asks herself how would this have happened: omission, deletion, misinterpretation, or fabrication. What methods would have been used? Why and how did she begin to come about her suspicion? And, finally, what are her potential courses of action? Is she considering confronting her coauthor? Conduct polite inquiries with former colleagues of his? Get advice from a senior department member? Each of these is both potential actions and possible resolutions that will need evaluation.

Next are the objects that receive an action, what your Language Arts teacher called "direct objects." These will often be more agents and can be investigated in the same ways that you described yourself. Janet can list what she knows about her co-author: attitudes toward conduct such as this, in addition to other salient facts concerning past incidents of this nature, current salary, status of his tenure clock, any developments in his personal life, etc. This can also be, depending on the situation, other colleagues, a sample population, a journal, the scientific community, or the citizenry of a town or nation. The traits and elements of this recipient of action are integral to understanding how the action being evaluated or contemplated will actually occur; it is necessary not only to determine the ethical implications of all agents involved, but also to grasp the empirical realities of any course of action taken. Ethics is about the application of theory to the reality, and the traits of all agents involved must be included.

The syntax allegory can be continued *ad nauseum*: indirect objects (the recipient of the direct object, such as I throw the ball to you), adjectives and adverbs, conjunctions, etc. Further structured research is available to suit your needs. However, we feel that the three discussed (subject, verb, direct object) are of primary importance, forming the base of any coherent sentence or ethical thought. Further elaboration in both cases (writing and decision-making) is very useful and increases the value of the final product.

3.1.3 How Is Decision Data Recorded?

This is another area where personal preference holds great importance. The old favorite of simply writing things down has many benefits, regardless of whether such information is written by hand, typed into a laptop, or dictated into a recorder. Such records allow physical organization of information into various classifications and progressions; facts can be gathered according to syntactical source, then rearranged into different groupings when analysis begins. Further, such recording removes the cognitive limitations of memory from the subject syntax area – how much information you can store in accessible memory will no longer hold such an influence on your judgment (my own recollection is, for example, quite poor, which is why I am an intractable list-maker).

Depending on the situation, however, you may be unable to record information in such a fashion due to circumstance, available time, or under outside counsel. In such cases, two steps must be taken. First, keep the information in cognitive groupings. Whether these classifications are initially syntactical or whether they proceed directly to the mental baskets labeled according to type, the human brain is a relational beast that recalls best when there are close associations between concepts. Second, you should include the various ramifications specifically relating to the information storage, such as memory, time available, or ongoing emotional states, in your subject information.

3.1.4 How Is Decision Data Classified?

Once the data has been gathered, you now possess a wealth of inter-related facts associated by their subject of origination. This can be quite helpful; however, the "locational" groupings which helped you gather data is not necessarily the groupings where associations for evaluation will be the most beneficial. You wash your dirty laundry according to color, but that's normally not the way things hang in your closet. Pants are with pants, shirts with shirts, etc. The same applies to pieces of a decision. In addition to making things easier to sort and compare, this helps you distinguish which elements have ambiguity attached to them, which is an important factor in the analysis.

3.1.4.1 Facts and Factual Issues

As economists and policy professionals, we are particularly fond of facts, those delightful nuggets of information that are uncolored by normative taint and form the framework for our art, or rather, science. Facts are descriptions or statements about the nature of an object or situation which can be disproved through observation. The percentage of time spent at a university office, the amount of money spent on your 2 week consulting trip to Ghana, the GDP per capita of Bolivia in 1998: all of these are factual figures. These are all obvious examples of facts.

Not all facts are easily proven or disproven. Conflicts can stem from just a disagreement over the facts, for example, consider the question of which tax system will raise more revenue? Each side's policy advocates will have their own data. Some effort can be dedicated to discovering which may be resting on faulty data, however, assuming that each party is professionally competent, both projections may be technically valid. At this point, such revenue outcomes should rather be considered a factual issue because of the ambiguity involved in determining which state exists or may come to pass. We refer to it as an issue since we want to be sure to call out the disagreement over the data that will need to be resolved in order to come to a conclusion.

This tax situation is not an ethical issue as presented. Many factual disagreements do not need to be resolved through moral reasoning, though this does not mean that a preponderance of facts in a situation excludes it from being an ethical issue. For example, as suggested above, if Alexander spends a lower amount of time at his university office than a certain threshold in favor of an outside consultancy in Ghana, this may imply negligence of his professional ethics. This situation can be easily resolved through the accurate comparison of his time allotment against any stated requirement in his employment contract or university code of ethics. Should his colleague, Taneisha, mention the transgression to the department head? This is a more complicated issue that could have factual components (i.e., is reporting such behavior obligated by her employment contract or code of ethics), but also other factual issues (how accurate are her assessments? Does Alexander work from home?), conceptual issues (will the university see any benefit, even prestige, from this venture?), and moral issues (Alex helped her land this job – doesn't she owe him the benefit of the doubt?).

What if facts exist, but there is ambiguity? Taneisha doesn't know what the true percentage of time that Alexander spends working on his university duties. How should this be classified? This is an example of a factual issue – the nature of the data is factual, however the ambiguity of the fact is itself a salient part of the analysis. *Theambiguityitself is important to working through the situation* (Table 3.1).

Also, in the same line of thinking that you needed to include information on the subject (you) in gathering data, do not forget to include ambiguity which may be seen from other points of view. If it's your tax projections versus someone else's, it is tempting to consider there to be no factual issue at all – after all, you wouldn't be championing something that was wrong! However, the reality that the facts are in dispute is central to the situation. Even though you don't consider them disputable, the decision environment that you are in does, and any courses of action will need to reflect this status. For example, Taneisha and Alexander may differ on the amount of time that Alexander spends in the office; each considers her- or himself in custody of irrefutable fact. However, this is clearly a factual issue since any course of action will need to reflect a period where additional resources are used to help document and prove more conclusively whose assessment is correct before deciding on punitive action. The entire situation may stem from a factual error: perhaps Alexander truly does not realize that his hours are as lopsided as they are. The ambiguity in the fact played a crucial role in both the analysis and the resolution of the situation, which is why this ambiguity if flagged outright during classification as a factual issue.

Table 3.1 Facts and factual issues

Facts	Factual issues
The town does not have a highway running through it	What will be the volume of traffic on the proposed highway?
The plan for the highway has it running through the town	What will be the economic impact of new highway on the town in terms of traffic?
Six houses will have to be demolished in order to construct the road	Can eminent domain be used to seize the necessary property in the town?
The budget for constructing the new highway	Before the project is complete, the actual final cost for constructing the highway

What about someone's state of mind? If you felt that something suspicious might be going on with the local tax authority because of the way that the representative dodged questions at your meeting and appeared "uneasy," is this a factual issue? The answer is yes: whether the person is or is not acting a certain way can be verified. But where does the ambiguity in this observation stem from? It is not the factual state of being, but rather what you would define as uneasy. The prefecture's representative being uneasy is a fact or factual issue, but it relies on a concept or conceptual issue.

3.1.4.2 Concepts and Conceptual Issues

Sometimes conflicts can stem not from whether a fact exists, but what that fact existing means. A concept is the definition of an idea or issue which uses words as description to separate it from other concepts. For example, a good definition of a horse would be a four-legged mammal which eats grass, travels in herds, and has hooves, a mane, and a tail. This definition is perfectly functional unless you've never seen a horse before and are trying to identify one in a herd of zebra. The difficulty doesn't arise from whether the horse exists, but rather what one would consider a horse.

Concepts and conceptual issues are no stranger to economic thought. Even the Greek economists were concerned with the efficient allocation of resources, which inherently requires a definition of efficient. Following the Greeks, the Medieval and Classical scholars were concerned with the theory of value; Adam Smith's water-diamond paradox is at heart a discussion of concept. What does "valuable" mean? Water is plentiful, but we die without it; diamonds are trivial, but rare. Hence, price derives from the quantity supplied and demanded, reflecting a larger price for the scarce good and settling on a (relatively) uniform definition of value. Once "valuable" is defined, there is no paradox.

More recently (and closer to the core of this handbook) is the debate over how to accurately measure well-being. The economics profession has long used GDP per capita as the de facto measure of well-being for a society, especially when tackling issues such as poverty and economic growth. However, scholars such as Andrew Oswald began calling for a re-examination of that metric, arguing that very well-to-do societies have miserable people, and that there are other measures of quality-of-life such as cultural ties and health care which should be given more emphasis when charting the "development" of an economy. This culminated in a report commissioned by the French President Nikolas Sarkozy concerning alternatives to measuring well-being; the Commission on the Measurement of Economic Performance and Social Progress was headed by Nobel Laureates Joseph Stiglitz and Amartya Sen, along with pre-eminent economist Jean-Paul Fitoussi and a host of other leading figures. The Commission finds a host of other indicators that should be used to expand the definition of "well-being" in order to more accurately measure the success and failures of programs designed to boost general welfare (Stiglitz, Sen, & Fitoussi, 2010). This debate is only beginning to heat up and will be one of the central discussions for economics over the coming decades.

Table 3.2 Concepts and conceptual issues

Concepts	Conceptual issues
Welfare is defined as "the health, happiness, and prosperity of a group of people"	What is definition of 'impact'?
A Need is defined as "something required or essential"	What is the definition of "murder"? (e.g., is war-time killing technically murder?)
	What is the definition of "exploitation"?

The presence of ambiguity differentiates between concepts and conceptual issues in much the same way as for facts and factual issues. Does everyone involved agree on the definition of key concepts? What does "negligent" mean? Or "inappropriate"? Or, for that matter, "economist"? Also, be sure that you own level of commitment to a particular definition does not preclude the rest of the group having a differing opinion; just because you are convinced that an acceptable level of fees have been paid for a company to "own" their share of carbon emissions may not imply that the definition of "own" is the primary point of contention in ongoing discussions (Table 3.2).

At the heart of many debates over "morals" are actually debates over concepts. Much of the heated debate over abortion concerns the definition of "life": when does it begin and what does it constitute in the terms of rights. However, even if the definition of "life" were agreed upon, there would still be conflict over whether someone *ought* to be able to have an abortion. The introduction of the *ought* implies moral weight, which is beyond the question of fact (whether it is) and concept (what it is) and into normative values (what should it be).

3.1.4.3 Morals and Moral Issues

Values and morals are, in your principles of microeconomics textbooks, that which are referred to as normative concerns and dismissed as being outside the realm of mainstream economics. Ironically, however, they never have been. Adam Smith's first (and, in his opinion, the best – see Rae, 2006) publication was *The Theory of Moral Sentiments*, having recognized that any science dedicated to the study of relations between people would have a moral component. Unlike philosopher David Hume, who was Smith's friend and contemporary, Smith didn't even use the concept of utility in his initial descriptions of human interactions, but rather that of sympathy (Smith, 1997). The inherent social component of economics, of the exchange in markets, was never lost to Smith and to many economists who have come after. However, it is one of the purposes of this handbook to emphasize to those who have forgotten that, in any science involving allocation or interaction, several ethical considerations in both content and application exist.

This is not to say, however, that economics currently exists purged of normative considerations. A great body of literature has been dedicated to moral consideration in economics, especially with respect to social welfare and just distribution of resources. However, these are viewed as subfields and are often antagonistic toward

Table 3.3 Morals and moral issues

Moral	Moral issues
Hold paramount the health, safety, and welfare of the public (from the NSPE code of ethics)	Is it more important to tell the truth or to be a good
Do not lie	Is it ok to lie if it prevents physical harm to another?

mainstream economics. What this handbook hopes to do is make such petitions unnecessary by systematizing the treatment of factual, conceptual, and moral concerns as a matter of professional concern; ethics exists not only in *what* we do, but in *how* we do it.

As an aside, this handbook will often use the words moral and value interchangeably, though to ethics professionals there can be a great difference. Since the methodology incorporates elements of both the traditional schools of value clarification (for a good summary, see Kirschenbaum, 1992) and moral development (see Kohlberg & Hersh, 1977), we are comfortable doing so. Additionally, the term "value" has many pre-existing meanings in the field of economics, so we choose to avoid the semantic confusion and stick primarily with "moral."

So how will you know morals and moral issues? A good rule of thumb is the "normative" rule you learned in principles: if "ought" or "should" is involved, the statement probably involves values. Second, almost any time a moral consideration is involved, it will be a moral issue. This is because morals are often beliefs strongly and internally held, which means they have been able to develop a sense of sanctity that aren't attached to facts and concepts (Table 3.3).

You may be asking whether there are moral issues; after all, as discussed above, aren't many dilemmas that are perceived as moral actually conceptual? There are three responses to this. First, always verify that facts and concepts have been gathered and classified before delving into the moral issues. It may very well be that your moral issue is actually conceptual. Second, even if definitions agree, there may still be *intra*-value conflict. Two colleagues could both consider "advocacy" to include, with respect to one's duties as a graduate program advisor, the ability to "effectively understand and represent student interests." However, Jacob could consider bar-hopping with the graduate students on Friday nights as necessary to achieving this goal, whereas Jon could consider this a gross breach of professional etiquette. Each faculty member agrees on what professionalism and effective advocate means, but could vary widely on professionally ethical forms of application based on their own personalities and values. Third, there could be *inter*-value conflict. With a finite supply of resources, whether you're working with the budget of an elementary school or a nation, there will be needs unmet. Do you spend the money you have on tutoring (or fiscal stimulation) for those with the most need, or for those on the margin whom you can help more of? In the public sector, policy makers and analysts are more familiar with these concerns: efficiency or equity? End-results or process? Rawls or Bentham (or Nozick or Marx)? Morals and moral issues, though rarer than the other pieces of information you assemble, are powerful and often fundamental to the decision scenario.

3.2 Verify the Data

Once you have your data assembled, as in any other data you work with, you need to test and verify it to ensure its validity. As mentioned previously, a written or other physical record helps keep things organized and is simpler to review; however, the process of re-examining, filling gaps, resolving conflicts, and other means of cleaning the data can occur regardless of the storage medium.

3.2.1 *Recognition of Priors*

You, the agent, are very important. We began with listing and recording information about ourselves first: our definitions, roles, forecasts, values, etc. These are called priors, and their recognition is an important step in our assessment of this situation. However, we need to anticipate the existence of bias in our own analysis. Just as if we were approaching bias in an econometric analysis, there are steps we can take to minimize the impact of bias in our analysis to produce a sound conclusion.

First, look for trend. Have you experienced situations like this before? How similar were those situations, and what elements set it apart from the one you are currently facing? Your record of previous successful resolutions may indicate a series of successful analyses; however, what we are compensating for is the automatic tendency or heuristic to lean in that direction instinctively in the current situation. If you, as department head, have often heard calls of biased grading from a particular student as he progresses through the departments' class offerings, however you must acknowledge your instinctive desire to dismiss this student based on historical behavior. Peter may have cried wolf several times before, which is salient in considering whether a wolf is actually present; however, you should acknowledge your prior that Peter is a trickster before heading into a situation where you instinctively lean one direction. Having a prior is normal, acceptable, and useful, but only if you acknowledge that it exists and can handle it as its own factual issue. De-trend your analysis or you will have biased and unreliable results.

3.2.2 *Resolution of Conflict*

Ayn Rand, a much-ballyhooed philosopher quite popular among economists, once observed of factual dispute that "[c]ontradictions do not exist. Whenever you think that you are facing a contradiction, check your premises. You will find that one of them is wrong" (Rand, 1992, p. 199). Though it is an entertaining thought experiment to devise ways that she is mistaken, as a rule of thumb this stands true. When reviewing your data, should a contradiction occur between facts, they become (categorically) factual issues that require further investigation.

3.2.3 Iterative Looping

Reality is not static. The information involved in your ethical decision scenario will change for at least one of the following reasons. First, your process of finding gaps and resolving contradictions leads to the discovery of new relevant information and new questions. Second, the same processes lead to the correction, repair, or abandonment of pre-existing information. Third, even given perfectly (and unrealistically) accurate information, the situation evolves with time, requiring constant iterative looping to occur. Iterative looping is the constant revisiting and adding of information at various steps of the decision process, causing you to go back to the beginning and re-process the whole unit of information to search for new gaps, conflicts, etc.

This may soundonerous, perhaps even impossible. But, the good news is that, in practice, you will develop heuristics that will help you process the information more efficiently as you delve into the analysis. As new information comes in, your developing sense of wisdom (What did Aristotle call this? *Phronesis!*) will offer advice on the salience of the new pieces and your gathering, classification, and verification skills will become more automatic (though, of course, still diligent). However, it is the premise of this text that such actions and ways of thinking are, in fact, not the norm in our profession. So, as in learning to ride a bicycle or perform a double integral, the process will begin slowly and carefully only to become something that can be done as a matter of day-to-day life.

3.2.4 Assumption Formation

When all of your data is gathered, classified, and verified, there will continue to be gaps. You have diligently attempted to fill in those gaps and resolve those outstanding factual, conceptual, and moral issues, but some will always remain. This could be due to an inability to locate the information needed, an inability to reach consensus on a definition, or the immediate lack of a metric to establish the hierarchy of personal friendship and professional conduct. However, there are two additional steps that can be made to accommodate these features.

First, any fact, concept, or moral with salient ambiguity should remain a respective "issue." The hint of unknown or risk, just as it does not erase itself from consideration in economics, does not remove the piece of information from analysis here. Keeping it classified as an issue continues to alert us to the presence of significant ambiguity so that we can identify what conflicts underlie the ethical situation. Further, when hypothesis testing and moral reasoning are underway, we can locate what could be a keystone in resolving the dilemma.

Second, if there are gaps in the information that require some form of bridge to proceed, we can form assumptions. Many students of economics are accustomed to seeing assumptions appear at the beginning of a problem; in doctoral courses in microeconomics, one of the first steps is to prove the axioms of consumer choice and move on from there. Those underpinnings are taken as given for much of the ensuing analysis. Here, however, we do not assume that anyone has tread this exact path prior to us, and we explicitly create our assumptions prior to the analysis. Consider them the bottom rung on the hierarchy of ambiguity: there are facts/concepts/morals, issues for the above categories which contain a salient measure of ambiguity, and assumptions, which contain copious amounts of ambiguity and risk. Assumptions should be the first place you look when a contradiction appears; they are simply placeholders for information that has not yet been obtained. Treating them as such keeps us from relying on them as fundamental, since this is often the difference between theoretical and empirical work. Using an assumption is not a passive act. You choose an information placeholder on which to act. Our tendency to call such things "given" at the outset of analysis does not absolve us of the implications of their use. You assume when you do not know; they are not "given" at the outset.

3.3 Conclusion

Framing, as demonstrated, is a crucial part of the ethical decision process. The gathering of information according to the syntax method helps ensure both that the scenario if thoroughly covered and that emphasis is given to the often-overlooked perspectives and biases of the agent. After gathering, the data can be classified according to type (factual, conceptual, or moral) and the level of ambiguity. Following classification, the data needs to be verified, contradictions resolved, and assumptions made to fill any remaining gaps. The process can be restarted or re-engaged at any time due to the iterative looping which is required of the constant flow of new information. As in economic analysis, the quality of the analysis and conclusions relies on the strength and validity of the data; when performing ethical analysis, the same criteria holds.

Discussion Questions

1. Name a situation (either hypothetical or in the news) that involves disputes on factual, conceptual, and moral issues. Which do you feel dominates the argument?
2. Why is stating the assumptions important?
3. What is the difference between an assumption and the recognition of a prior? How can they function in the same way, and how are they different?
4. Find a news story or journal article which addresses a policy issue that you believe the authors have mislabeled (i.e., the article describes the conflict as a factual one whereas you believe it is a conceptual issue, etc.). What about the situation leads you to believe that you are correct? How would the situation need to be different if the author was correct?

References

Code, L. (1991). *What can she know: Feminist theory and the construction of knowledge*. Ithaca, NY: Cornell University Press.

Heath, T. B., Chatterjee, S., & France, K. R. (1995). Mental accounting and changes in price: The frame dependence of reference dependence. *Journal of Consumer Research, 22*, 90–97.

Kahneman, D., Knetsch, J. L., & Thaler, R. H. (1990). Experimental tests of the endowment effect and the Coase theorem. *Journal of Political Economy, 98*, 1325–1348.

Kahneman, D., & Tversky, A. (1981). The framing of decisions and the psychology of choice. *Science, 211*, 453–458.

Kirschenbaum, H. (1992). A comprehensive model for values education and moral education. *The Phi Delta Kappan, 73*(10), 771–776.

Kohlberg, L., & Hersh, R. H. (1977). Moral development: A review of the theory. *Theory Into Practice, 16*(2), 53–59.

McCaffery, E. J., & Baron, J. (2004). Framing and taxation: Evaluation of tax policies involving household composition. *Journal of Economic Psychology, 25*(6), 679–705.

Rae, J. (2006). Life of Adam Smith. New York: Cosimo.

Rand, A. (1992). *Atlas shrugged* (35th Anniversary Edition). New York: Dutton.

Schelling, T. C. (1981). Economic reasoning and the ethics of policy. *The Public Interest, 63*, 37–61.

Smith, A. (1997). *The theory of moral sentiments*. Washington, DC: Regenery.

Stiglitz, J. E., Sen, A., & Fitoussi, J. P. (2010). *Mismeasuring our lives: Why GDP doesn't add up*. New York: New Press.

Thaler, R. (1980). Toward a positive theory of consumer choice. *Journal of Economic Behavior & Organization, 1*(1), 39–60.

Tversky, A., & Kahneman, D. (1986). Rational choice and the framing of decisions. *Journal of Business, 59*, S251–S278.

Tversky, A., & Kahneman, D. (1991). Loss aversion in riskless choice: A reference-dependent model. *The Quarterly Journal of Economics, 106*(4), 1039–1061.

Chapter 4
Hypothesis Testing

Donald R. Searing and Elizabeth A.M. Searing

> *"I cannot give any scientist of any age better advice than this: the intensity of a conviction that a hypothesis is true has no bearing over whether it is true or not."*
>
> ~Peter Medawar (1990)

> *The method of science is "the method of proposing bold hypotheses, and exposing them to the severest criticism, in order to detect where we have erred."*
>
> ~-Karl Popper (1974)

Abstract This chapter covers the construction of ethical hypotheses and four different types of ethical hypothesis testing. Visualization tests are thought experiments used to test hypotheses in simple hypothetical environments. Virtue analysis uses exemplars in order to inspire ethical behavior. Utilitarianism-based analyses utilize different rules in order to maximize aggregate levels of utility. Respect for Persons tests hold the tiers of rights of any person to be paramount, often in conflict with utilitarian analyses.

Keywords Hypothesis testing • Null hypothesis • The golden rule • Anticipatory self-appraisal • Virtue ethics • Utilitarianism • Act utilitarianism • Rule utilitarianism • Cost-benefit analysis • Black swans • Respect for persons • Pareto efficiency

D.R. Searing, PhD
CEO and Principal Scientist, Syncere Systems, Altamont, NY, USA
e-mail: dsearing@synceresystems.com

E.A.M. Searing, PhD (✉)
Assistant Professor, Department of Public Administration and Policy, Rockefeller College of Public Affairs and Policy, University at Albany – State University of New York, 305 Milne Hall, 135 Western Avenue, Albany, New York, USA
e-mail: esearing@albany.edu

E.A.M. Searing, D.R. Searing (eds.), *Practicing Professional Ethics in Economics and Public Policy*, DOI 10.1007/978-94-017-7306-5_4

4.1 Hypothesis Testing in Ethics

By offering a description of something, whether you're describing your ideal car to a friend or offering an opinion on a particular bond issue, you are declaring several things. First, you announce your perception of something, which is primarily a passive behavior. The receipt of input from your sensory organs, either happening concurrently or being assembled from a past incident for a contemporary "thought experiment," is a step before the translation into what the situation is or implies. Second, you utilize this passive information to make a statement about that perception.

For example, I would like to know more about what you would consider the ideal car and inquire. By vividly describing a hot red Porsche, the performance handling and the way the interior reflects the car's elegance and sportiness, you are making an active statement about both positive description and normative judgment. I'm receiving the information, and with these pieces of information I construct in my head what I consider your ideal car to look like. You feed me the information, which I then process and assemble. How closely this resembles experiencing an actual Porsche is another matter: you can take steps to improve accuracy such as loading up details or including more than one sensory avenue (for example, what does it smell like, or what does the gear shifter buttons on the steering column make you think of). I know very little of cars, so it may or may not resemble a true depiction of a Porsche. The more information you feed me and the more pieces I accurately receive, the more accurate my inner picture will be.[1] It also matters what my own frames are. I would personally prefer a maroon Ford F150 pickup truck to your Porsche; it's less expensive, easier to service, and will carry a much larger quantity of garden mulch. Upon hearing that this car only has two seats, I may inadvertently picture something far more Lilliputian than it actually is given my preference for garden supply capacity. This preference (or bias) may be reflected in my mental reconstruction of your received information, but it did not impede my receipt of the information itself.

You can also think of this in a less frivolous sense. Let's say you are a financial advisor. You've formed an opinion on what level of risk and returns you'd like to see over the last 5 years before you recommend that stock or mutual fund to a client on the brink of retirement. You have gathered information in the course of your work, and the weight of that information has given you a particular level of comfort: if the relative return is below a certain threshold, the option is not considered. It is up to the company's performance or some other windfall of new information to move you past that default position. It is a cognitive and professional heuristic called the status quo, an automatic reflex that keeps us from repeating the same search-process-stop rule each time we need to exercise agency and make a decision.

[1] Delicious epistemological questions about whether the true ideal car is an objective "truth" or the truth as constructed in your own head (i.e., what if you are wrong in your perception of Porsches) is not going to receive the treatment it deserves here. I applaud you for your philosophical prowess, but you'll need to read another book to get into that.

For those of you with statistical training (which I hope is all of you), this should strike you as extraordinarily familiar. The null hypothesis, the status quo, is the state of the world as it has been perceived.[2] It is also how we expect the world to remain unless some additional information or new force acts on it. Though it may seem odd to think of your daily life as a series of surviving or falling null hypotheses, this is to a large extent what happens.

This implies two interesting things. The first is that the null I formed on the basis of previously acquired information about risk. It is chosen because the ramifications of what would happen if it were wrong while we assumed it was correct have been minimized (a type I error).

The second is that we have built a conclusion – that the null hypothesis will still stand – into the remaining bits of our worldview. Our beliefs do not stand in a vacuum, but rather play a role in both the vertical and horizontal chains of actions. When one element shifts, the other assumptions and hypotheses that were formed when the original hypothesis was considered true may fall or be strengthened.

So what does this have to do with ethics? You are familiar with hypotheses: the Porsche 911 is the most desirable car or the independent variable has no impact on the dependent variable. Both are statements of perception, belief, and expectation, but both are also subject to the arrival of potentially damaging or confirming additional information. Both are also direct comparisons to the process of ethical decision-making.

The process with which we will learn to gauge the degree of moral correctness of our actions is one which follows the same scientific steps as chemistry and statistics: assume a null whose testing minimizes the most harmful error. Then, using a series of tests, we will subject that assumption to different established ethical methods to establish the probability level of moral correctness of the assumption. You don't need to perform an exhaustive battery of tests for every notion, just as you don't routinely conduct every known test of fitness on every regression or attach weights to the potential consequences each morning of failing to brush your teeth (unless you're in preschool). Once the tests have been conducted, you can gauge whether they have passed an acceptable threshold for your extended environment. If your assumptions prove wrong, you have a formal process that you can revisit. Here, we can learn a great deal from qualitative research approaches: when there are questions of procedural legitimacy, transparency and documentation are paramount for validity (for an excellent explanation of such matters, see Yin (2009)).

This method is, at its core, very uncomplicated – it mimics both a science with which we are familiar and the epistemological process by which we go through everyday life. This is the central contention of this text: practicing professional ethics is not beyond the hope or scope of economics and public policy. Rather, it is a process we already know and use, but may not have been organized or self-aware enough to recognize it, especially when faced with a situation with ethical concerns or normative values in play. The next steps of the analysis are modelled in Fig. 4.1, which is the second portion of the figure shared in Chap. 3.

[2] There is also another popular viewpoint that the null hypothesis is simply that property or assumption that is being tested, regardless of whether this statement does or does not reflect the current state of reality. Grounded in context as we are, however, we will use the status quo interpretation.

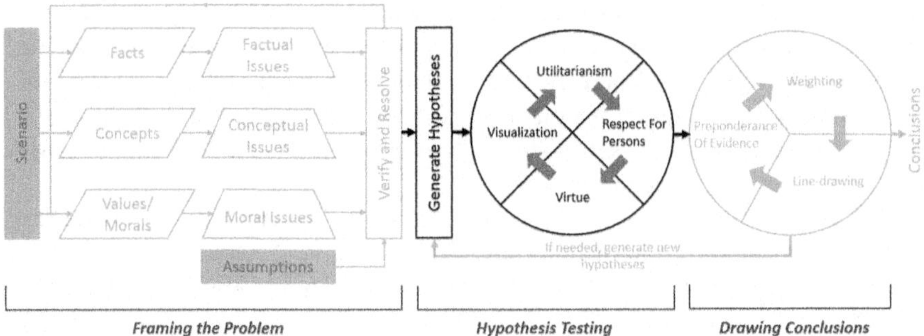

Fig. 4.1 Hypothesis testing

4.2 The Hypotheses

4.2.1 Forming the Null Hypothesis

When addressing the process of ethical decision-making, the most daunting step is deciding where to start. Even as someone who has likely developed their own assumptions, models, and projections for our occupation, we often have years of formal data and formal methodology to guide our thinking. Putting together a forecast for the retail sector? You'll need current and historical information regarding sales, sentiments, and costing information for the last few years to form your view of the world and make a prediction. Trying the gauge the impact of a 1-cent SPLOST on a region's budget for transportation? Dig out reactions to other SPLOSTS, some elasticity measures, and transportation and housing information for the last 10 years and projections for growth for the next 20. What is the starting point for a professionally ethical act?

Let's revisit what we know about null hypotheses. First, they are the description of the world as we feel it is most likely to be and remain as. If we rely on the perception of our profession in the popular press, we don't gain a lot of useful insight. In fact, it may make us reactive: if the world believes that we are a bunch of unethical louts, just wait for next earnings season! We may also, however, earnestly feel that we should be given the benefit of the doubt, much like English common law: we are ethical until proven otherwise. The fact that you picked up this book implies that, somewhere in your head, you believe firmly that you are or should be an ethical professional. Approaching null hypotheses from this angle is accurate from an ethnographic standpoint, but quickly can run aground in our own feelings of self-worth or indignation. Though there may be several of you out there with fists pumping – *YES*! *I am an unethical lout*! – there is a slightly less personal and more procedurally legitimate way to form the null.

Rather than starting with yourself and your personal traits as the object of consideration, shift your focus to the role of any given null. Shift that frame away from your personal feelings about your own ethical nature and into a more benign environment. Remember a project or client or situation where you went in with very little else to go on in the way of status quo. You had to spend more of your time gathering information, trying to fit the received information into a worldview, then a hypothesis, all the while keeping in mind the appropriateness of fit and error minimization. This process can be used to walk through the building of our ethical null.

First, let's revisit the popular medical example you probably encountered in your introductory statistics course. When discussing types of errors in your analysis regarding hepatitis B testing, you were asked which structure would be most appropriate: a test with a higher false positive (type II) or a higher false negative (type I)? A false negative in this situation is clearly the more grave: people who are infected, but received a false negative, will continue to spread the disease and infect other people.

The same line of reasoning supports the contention that our null regarding our own professional ethics behavior is the assumption that our assumed path is unethical. In doing so, we hold that the chance of a Type I error, the chance that the null hypothesis is not rejected when it should be, as the most grievous. Judging that an unethical act is ethical is far more damaging to the client and the general welfare than deciding not to embark on an ethical path that was wrongly deemed improper. The latter situation is a loss, no doubt, and I bet at least some of our readers are now sketching the math for such an instance in the margins. However, our profession has endured a great deal of damage over the last decade, much of it rightfully so. The emergence of further unethical behavior, especially if assumed otherwise, would be disastrous not only to the professional and situation at hand, but also to our larger profession.

Even if we were to assume a benign professional environment, Tversky and Kahneman (1991), in their studies of loss aversion, found that people in experimental studies felt and dreaded losses more that they enjoyed gains of equivalent worth. We can apply the same principle here: a decision which is shown to be unethical will do more harm than an unlauded ethical deed.

What might this look like? Perhaps you are considering the ethical implications of the decision regarding placement of a congestion-easing rail line through a particular neighborhood. You could form the null hypothesis to reflect a status quo of ethical – unless convincing evidence is shown otherwise, you assume than the plan and procedure used to reach it will be ethical. However, this approach will produce more false "ethical" during testing than assuming the plan is unethical. This is bad! We would rather be cautious and have an ethical action unlauded than do something which is truly unethical. (We will see how to arrive at this judgment later on in the book).

4.2.2 The Alternative Hypothesis

For some of you, the formulation of the alternative hypothesis is an afterthought now that the null has been decided. This, however, overlooks its purpose. The alternative hypothesis is the second state of being that is accepted should the first be proven false (or, to be precise, when we reject the null hypothesis that our action is unethical). So, in the very plainest terms, if our H_0 is:

H_0: The maintenance of Facebook friendship between an elected official and a paid lobbyist who lobbies the official is unethical.

Then the broadest possible H_a would be:

H_a: The maintenance of Facebook friendship between an elected official and a paid lobbyist who lobbies the official is not unethical.

This need not be so. Even though we don't need to worry about one- versus two-sided testing necessarily, we are free to tailor our hypothesis to a scope which we feel is useful as an alternative. We may very well be preparing to test a proposed course of action where we know the cost-benefit relationship and utilitarian concerns are in its favor – what you're concerned about is the rights-based and reciprocity tests. Take, for example, the potential question of whether to allow Big Box Grocery (a national chain) to open a location on the main street of your town. Assume further that the downtown has been recently revitalized, with several small family businesses now located there; several of these shops are specialty grocers. Your primary concern even before your analysis is not whether the townspeople would be better off with cheaper goods, but what the potential impact of the chain store would be on these small businesses. A potential null for this situation would be:

H_0: Granting permission to Big Box Grocery to open in the revitalized downtown district would be unethical.

Accordingly, the alternative hypothesis is likewise tailored to the null:

H_a: Granting permission to Big Box Grocery to open in the revitalized downtown district would not be unethical.

4.2.3 The Role of the Environment

Ethics and ethical decision-making do not exist in a vacuum – the tenet that each ethical hypothesis is independent is even more unlikely than when such an assumption is used in traditional statistical modeling.[3] Similar to McCloskey and Ziliak's (2008) emphasis on the importance of real-world results, the ignorance of context (especially since we make allegorical use of statistical language) is a grievous one. So despite the purpose of this text being entirely applied, let's look at the theoretical implications of our hypothesis construction.

[3] For reasons on why you should always ask yourself about the real-world implications of your assumptions, we suggest beginning with Berk and Freedman's (2003) excellent chapter "Statistical Assumptions as Empirical Commitments." When you're ready for a stronger dose, we recommend the McCloskey and Ziliak (2008).

First, we would like to emphasize that, even if an ethical state is considered the null, the decision procedure and validity would not change. The meanings and probabilities of errors would alter, but the methodology is still procedurally valid. Think of the above example of hepatitis B: both are testing the same condition using the same process. One is more accurate, which means there is a preferable approach. But don't let the fear that you are going to worsen the situation by picking the incorrect null keep you from the attempt.

Second, the dynamic aspect of the decision cannot be ignored, whether this involves the interdependency of one person's decisions, the interconnectedness of that person's decisions with the decisions of others, or the constant iterative loop of information, processing, and adaptation that is any cognitive process. You'll notice in Fig. 4.1 at the steps leading up to the formation of the hypotheses al easily loop back into each other as the process of learning and verifying constantly adds new issues and information. However, you don't see the same loop in the hypothesis section. This is not to say that you're tied to the mast of your initial hypothesis until you've reached a conclusion. It does mean, however, that one of two options occurs.

Option A is that the addition of enough information to alter your confidence level in your hypothesis has probably come about through the discovery of additional information or insight. This means that you leave the singular path that you're currently on and re-enter Framing. For example, imagine that you are working for a small consulting firm that specializes in education policy; your firm has just shifted views on a controversial piece of legislation involving vouchers for parochial schools. You grab a bite to eat later that day and consider the situation from several angles. Now that your personal views on the subject do not align with your work, do you feel that it will impact your advocacy? As you mull this through, one of the partners from your firm walks in and sits down with someone you recognize as the headmaster for a school that would stand to benefit from your firm's change in stance. This doesn't strike you as distressing until they spend more time with their hands on each other than on their silverware. As they leave together, you realize that enough additional information has surfaced that your position on whether you can effectively advocate this position needs to be fully re-evaluated – leave the hypothesis phase and re-enter framing.

Option B is that, rather than immediately packing up and going back to Framing, you finish the path that you were headed down as a thought experiment and then begin again. This provides a comparative context: without the introduction of the conclusion-changer, what would your results have shown? Then repeat the process, taking full account of your recent insight. You can also use this to perform a kind of "ethical differencing" to gauge the impact of your recent knowledge, which is very useful in its own right. In the previous scenario, you could finish your ethical evaluation in the assumed absence of the knowledge of the potential conflict of interest for your firm from the partner's behavior. Then, consider the situation again with the new information: this will give you the approximate ethical impact you attach to the conflict of interest on its own. Though I wouldn't advocate this as an approach to every ethical scenario due to resource requirements, the differencing process can nonetheless be quite valuable.

There are epistemological concerns here, however: for a truly accurate differencing, you have to assume that the impact of knowing the new information will not influence your processing of the original analysis. Does knowing you're going to change the assumptions and inputs alter the conclusion that you intend to use for comparison? If this degree of precision is necessary in the result, make note of the issue in your analysis and include the "new" original analysis as a potential proxy for the "true" original analysis, which can then be compared to the analysis that utilizes the conflict of interest information. Few of us will find it necessary to be that precise; however, the methods and tools are present for you to do so (remember to document!)

4.3 Ethical Analysis

You have now gathered facts, recognized assumptions, and developed hypotheses based on your materials. All of this has been in preparation, getting you carefully ready to analyze the information and test your hypotheses' ethical fitness. At this point, let's think about applied statistics. Your information is, to the best of your ability, accurate, clean, and organized. You have formed hypotheses. Now, however, you need to conduct testing: using established schools of ethical thought and models, how does your hypothesis hold up?

In theory, in order to achieve "perfect" moral correctness, you would need to conduct analysis using all codes of ethical thought (in addition to the more familiar, often ludicrous assumptions of perfect information, etc.). One of the central tenets of this book is that perfect moral correctness should be treated like perfect equilibrium or perfect democracy: ideals of great significance and little practical relevance. We are trying to maximize our ethical accuracy, which occurs to greater degrees the more and better we can explore our data. However, we also don't expect an exhaustive test of all ethical theories due to resource constraints. Eventually, to borrow a phrase from bounded rationalist Gerd Gigerenzer, we would like you to have several ethical heuristics in your cognitive adaptive toolbox, which could be accessed practically subconsciously when needed (Gigerenzer & Selten, 2002).

In this text, we have gathered the most popular and most representative analyses that represent the varied schools of ethical thought and grouped them together according to theme. Ideally, you should consider performing all of the analyses: at a minimum, try and include one from each group, since they are grouped according to school of thought. Even prior to picking up this book, most of us considered at least two out of habit. That is the natural part of the methodology – it is a process you were already conducting, simply formalized, clarified, and expanded. Don't worry about reconciling or interpreting the findings just yet – just conduct the testing and record the results.

As these analyses are processed, you will definitely find yourself revisiting your frame. It will initially have all of the information you deemed necessary before you began your analysis. But as you progress through the analysis, you will need to adjust your decision's frame (it's best to view this as an iterative process) to add additional facts, concepts and moral conclusions as well as introduce new factual, conceptual, and moral issues that need to be resolved as part of the analysis process. This revisiting is a natural process, and is indicative not of an incomplete initial analysis, but of a maturing understanding of the problem as you proceed through the analyses. This growth in the understanding of the problem and the subsequent gains in reasoning will be as valuable to you as the calculated final results and is the hallmark of mature ethical thinking.

As the consideration of the hypotheses is really a consideration of a future state of the system, there will always be some guesswork and estimation inherent in the resolution of these types of issues that arise during the analyses. Our recommendation is that you use actual data when available, data from similar events when actual data is not available, or your best guess when neither form of data is available. In scenarios where you have adequate lead time in your decision-making process, the list of factual issues with uncertain answers becomes the primary driver for the topics of additional research. Use this and other data from your framing to back up your conclusions regardless of where they are generated from; you are building an argument for your selected course of action and the more grounded that analysis is in the context of the problem, the better the final argument.

Regarding the testing and evaluation, we would urge the reader to be as honest and objective as they can be when processing these tests. The analyses being performed are dependent on YOUR assessments of the values and skewed or biased assessments will definitely affect the outcome of the analyses. The tests outlined below are designed to help you apply your judgment to the situation in a reasoned and thorough way- not to provide you with those judgments. People make bad decisions every day. It is our contention that it is easier to make bad judgments when the problems are approached superficially and quickly, and that the power of the methodology being outlined is that it slows this process down and ensures greater care is taken in considering the details of the situation as well as encourages you to explore alternate points of view that you might have glossed over in a snap judgment of a situation. That being said, a detailed approach does not guarantee a fair, unbiased solution. Tools such as these can be used to rationalize bad decision-making after the fact as well. We urge all readers to keep an open mind when using these tools and use them as they were intended- as tools that can help a reasonable user thoroughly evaluate a problem, avoid their own biases, and find the best solution.

A note about keeping records: We have included a sample form at the end of this book for you to keep track of your tests, in addition to space at the end of the chapters for notes. Unlike most authors who include such things, we fully expect you to use them if you wish now, but we hope that you will use them as inspiration for your own, personalized system. Being ethical doesn't require every decision to be documented in one of our forms. Hopefully, a few years from now, you'll be jotting down in the margins of the report you're reviewing which of the tests gave results that were of concern to you during your mental assessment. However, in the beginning, it's convenient to have a place to practice, so we encourage you to utilize the provided tools.

4.3.1 Visualization Analyses

The least complicated forms of ethical analysis, at least procedurally, are the visualization analyses. In these analyses, the consequences of the null hypothesis are visualized using a number of devices to help you see the actual consequences of the hypothesized action being put into effect. The results of these types of tests tend to be binary- morally acceptable or not morally acceptable. They can be a good first filter for determining whether the null should be rejected. These tests are not as comprehensive as Utilitarian or Deontological/Respect for Persons analyses (discussed in the next sections), which can also help rank hypotheses in the circumstance of having several potential alternates.

4.3.1.1 Expected Reciprocity Analysis (The Golden Rule)

This analysis is usually the first that springs to mind for most when they consider moral reasoning. The basic concept of this analysis is to consider what it would be like to be the recipient of the action you are considering instead of its instigator. This consideration is most commonly known as the Golden Rule and colloquially known by the formulation, "Do unto others, as you would have done unto you." It is as close to a universal ethical rule as can be found across cultures and religions (Pfaff & Wilson, 2007). The goal of this analysis is for you to visualize what the action you are considering looks like to those affected. You have already likely visualized what it looks like from your point of view while you were formulating the hypotheses in the earlier steps of this process. But this test demands that you look at the results of the hypothesis from the role of those people affected by it. If your hypothesized solution affects multiple people or groups of people, you will need to visualize the results from each of their perspectives.

Some things to consider in this analysis:

- Take your time to really examine who the affected people are for this hypothesis.
  - If the action affects a given person, how does it affect their neighbors, families, coworkers?
  - Are there any side effects that could affect someone you have not considered?
  - Are there cultural differences between yourself and those affected? Do you really understand the differences?
- Check your premises and your personality.
  - Are you more or less tolerant of behavior or change than the average person?
  - If you are unsure, role-play as someone who is less tolerant of change than you think you are.

- Be objective about the risk (magnitude of effect and likelihood of it occurring) that your solution poses to those affected.

Example

Your lawnmower unexpectedly stops working halfway through mowing your lawn. It's late on Sunday afternoon, and you know that no repair shops will be open anywhere at this hour. You would like to finish mowing your lawn today since you have an important work deadline on Tuesday and you know you will not be able to get back to finish the lawn at least until next weekend. You happen to glance into your neighbor's yard and see that their garden shed is unlocked. You had seen the leave for vacation this morning, so you know no one is home. You realize you could borrow their lawnmower from their shed and finish your yard and no one would be the wiser. Should you borrow the lawnmower in this situation?

The Golden Rule test would require you ask of yourself how you would feel if it were the neighbor in your situation who was going into your shed to borrow your lawnmower without asking. How do you think you would feel in this situation? Would you feel violated or ill-used? Would it matter that you likely wouldn't know that the neighbor had borrowed it? Do your answers provide sufficient reasoning to reject the null hypothesis that such behavior is unethical?

4.3.1.2 New York Times Analysis

This analysis is another quick test for determining the fitness of a given hypothesis. The test requires that you formulate a headline for a national paper that states that you advocated and executed the action currently deemed unethical in your null. For example, if you are advocating for the location of a landfill in a region with a lower socio-economic status than the region you live in, imagine the following headline in the paper: "Reader Advocates Dump among Working Families of Nearby City." Is that something for which you would proudly bear responsibility? Is that something with which you would want your name associated?

In keeping with our stated risk aversion, we recommend emphasizing the negative effects of the hypothesis, as would be done in a none-too-flattering headline, and imagine your friends, family, and coworkers reading the headline. If the headline makes you queasy or unsure, it is likely what you are advocating is not something that is at its root morally acceptable to you.

Some things to consider when applying this analysis:

- This test is effective because it makes you visualize publicly taking responsibility for your decisions. More than likely, if you are uncomfortable with the headline, then it is something you would only do if you could quietly get away with it, which tends to be a hallmark of questionable behavior.

- Read the headline and imagine you are questioned by your mother/father/children as to why you made this decision; can you explain or justify your decision?
- If the headline seems too negative, add in some of the benefits or qualifications used in your reasoning to justify the statement. "Reader Advocates Dump in the Slums of the Nearby City, Tens of Jobs Created," "Reader Advocates Dump in the Slums of the Nearby City, Tourists Don't Go There, So They Won't Notice The Smell," "Reader Advocates Dump in the Slums of the Nearby City, It's Already Polluted, So No One Will Notice the Run-Off." Do the qualifications make it more palatable for you to take responsibility?
- We acknowledge that journalists are talented at making almost any act appear unpalatable. If you prefer, visualize your rebuttal or explanation of your act, whether it is in the paper or to a relative. Are you still uneasy?

Example

Using the example from the previous section regarding the secret borrowing of a neighbor's lawnmower, you can construct a headline of the following sort, "Reader Secretly Borrows Neighbor's Property While They Are Away on Vacation". Is this a headline you would be able to defend? Is it one you would be proud of?

If we add some justifications to the headline, "Reader Secretly Borrows Neighbor's Property While They Are Away on Vacation, But Reader's Lawn Looks Nice", does it make it sound any better to you? What about "Reader Secretly Borrows Neighbor's Property While They Are Away on Vacation, Then Leaves Twenty Dollars"?

4.3.1.3 Anticipatory Self-Appraisal Analysis

In this analysis, the effects of the solution being put into effect are considered for the implementer. In effect, you will imagine what it will be like for you after the null hypothesis is rejected. This is similar to the technique many athletes use to visualize their successful completion of their endeavor and use those feelings of pride and success to motivate them through the hours of repetitive practice required for their success. You need to imagine your hypothesized solution in place and imagine what you will experience at that time in terms of your feelings of accomplishment or what the solution may mean for your career or personal development. This technique is similar to the *New York Times* Analysis in that it drives you evaluate the effects of the hypothesized solution, but differs from that test by focusing on the effects on you and your opinions of yourself as opposed to the effects on others and their opinions of you. The motivation to dig deeply into the set of effects is motivated by your own self-interest and the understanding of the benefits or harms the solution will bring that will reflect poorly on yourself.

Some things to keep in mind while performing this analysis:

- Think through the effects of the rejected null in as detailed a manner as possible. This analysis is only as good as the detail of the effects that can be imagined.
- Focus on the changes in your professional standing as a result of the effects of the alternative hypothesis.
- Are there any negative consequences to rejecting the null that would be a black mark on your life story or career development?

Example
In the continuing saga of the secret borrowing of the lawnmower, you would need to imagine how you would feel after you borrowed the neighbor's lawnmower and completed your yard. You would feel good that you had accomplished your Sunday afternoon chore and could focus on the work needed for your looming deadline. When the neighbor returned, would you resolve to tell them of your borrowing? If not, why not? Would you feel awkward around them if you did not tell them? Would you be worried that they would notice that the lawnmower had been borrowed? What would you tell them if it broke while you were finishing up your lawn? If another neighbor saw you borrowing the lawnmower or even if they just saw you using a mower that was not yours, what might they think of you? These are all good questions that arise from the type of visualization of the future that are dictated by this analysis.

4.3.1.4 Aggregate Application Analysis (Kantian Categorical Imperative)

Immanuel Kant and his work were discussed earlier in this book (in Chap. 2), and this analysis is a direct offshoot of his primary approach to moral reasoning: the categorical imperative. Kant's first formulation of this imperative is stated thusly, "Act in accordance with a maxim that can at the same time make itself a universal law." (Kant, 1785). The categorical imperative is Kant's attempt to ground moral theory in reason, removing one's own calculation of well-being for oneself and others from the equation, such as you would find in the other analyses discussed above. Restating the imperative in a slightly different way gets us close to the formulation of the test we need for this analysis; moral acts are ones that if when generalized into a law, would lead to a non-contradictory state.

The standard example used to illustrate this point is that of the person who borrows money from a friend and lies to that friend about their intention to pay the money back. If this scenario is universalized such that the law is that all borrowers of money will lie about their intention to pay back the money to those who lent it, then with a little imagination and logic it is possible to envision a world where this law holds sway. In this world, everyone lies about their intentions to pay the money back, and thus if we assume the world to still be populated with rational, reasoning people, then no one would actually lend anyone else money, since never in the history of this world would anyone ever have been paid back. Thus, the action, when universalized and made into a law creates a contradiction- all borrowers lie and do not pay money back, and the conclusion that no one would lend money to anyone will lead you to the final contradiction that one could not be a borrower in a world where there was no one willing to lend money in the first place.

Some things to keep in mind while performing this analysis:

- It is not as easy as it may appear to state your action in a generalized way such that a meaningful law can be generated. You will need to generalize the specific situation into its basic behavioral elements, not just in terms of the generalization of the actors.

Example
In the lawnmower borrowing case discussed in a number of examples above, it would not necessarily be helpful to generate a law that stated, "All neighbors who need to finish cutting their lawn should borrow their neighbor's lawnmowers that are found to be easily available without asking permission." While this is truly a universal formulation of the specific problem at hand in those examples, it can be more enlightening to generalize the problem, not just the scope of the actors (you to all neighbors). If we generalize the behavioral elements of this problem (the taking of property from an acquaintance and the lack of permission), the universal law to consider in this analysis becomes much broader and it is much easier to come to a conclusion based on its formulation. In a world where the general rule was that anyone could take someone else's property without asking as long as it was easily available, is one in which people would own nothing, since they would use someone else's property for their needs and have no property of their own for someone else to take. This leads to a contradiction, in that in a world where property rights are not respected, no property would exist.

4.3.2 *Virtue Analysis*

Virtue ethics is one of the oldest schools of thought when it comes to ethical thinking, as it is rooted in the ethical contemplation of thinkers in ancient Greece like Plato and Aristotle and similar thought in ancient China predating even the Greeks (Hursthouse, 2013). While the schools of thought we are going to consider in the next two sections of analyses are focused on the outcomes (or consequences, if you like) of the actions performed (utilitarianism) or the duties owed to others in society (respect for persons[4]), virtue ethics is focused on the internal state of the actor, or more specifically their intentions and aspirations. These intentions and aspirations are referred to as

[4] The formal name for what we are referring to as "Respect for Persons" is deontology and it refers to ethics that are duty-based (i.e., your duties to others, like respecting others' rights for example).

moral character and the development of an understanding of the aspects of this character required to make one moral forms the basis of this analysis.

The quest for understanding of the defining characteristics of what is a moral (or good, if you will) life must start by understanding what you are aspiring to be when you are desiring to be moral. Much of what people think about when asked what it means to be moral revolves around what we will call proscriptive directives such as the ten commandments of Judeo-Christian belief system (e.g., thou shall not kill, thou shall not lie). Ethics according to this formulation is a list of things one should **not** do; You should not kill someone and steal their livestock, You should not lie, etc. These kinds of formulations of ethical rules get you quite far down the path of building an ethical system but they are not at the root of some of our better behaviors. Those behaviors are not driven by what we should not do, but by what someone who wishes to be "good" should do. These are not the things to avoid, they are the things to aspire to, and hence the school of thought built upon these foundations is often called aspirational ethics.[5]

So in the operational form of this analysis, there are two main steps. First, identify the virtues/traits you are aspiring to in order to be a good person in the scenario being examined. It may be difficult to express precisely what characteristics you are trying to follow, so here are a few helpful hints. One, think of the kind of adjectives you would use to describe someone you admire, such as responsible, respectful, caring, fair, just, loving, honest, selfless, friendly, neighborly, wise, giving, focused, intelligent, competent, professional, loyal, brave, steadfast, etc. These are the types of characteristics that begin define someone with moral character someone you can admire and aspire to emulate yourself.

Two, if the words don't leap to mind immediately, think instead about someone you admire for their moral character: someone you know of in your field, someone you have read about, or someone you know personally. We have included luminaries from several fields as a part of this text in order to provide a portfolio of potential ethical exemplars. Use that person as your example for your behavior, your exemplar.

Exemplar is the word that philosophers use to describe such people, and a quick search on the Internet for "moral exemplars in" and fill in your field will usually return a number of references that can provide you with lists of people in your field who didn't just behave ethically to stay out of trouble, but who exemplify moral characteristics that you could aspire to emulate in your behavior. If you are religious in nature, there are likely exemplars in your tradition that you can use as an exemplar as well.

In the analysis you will be performing, some of the virtues you are aspiring will be applicable to the situation under consideration. You should list and describe the

[5] You can see the switch from proscriptive to aspirational in approach for example in the Christian teachings between the Old and New Testament approaches to ethics. As stated before, lists of rules like the Ten Commandments are proscriptive, relating what you shouldn't do, whereas the teachings of Jesus in the New Testament are more aspirational; for example, love thy neighbor as you love yourself (Mark 12:31). The approach has evolved from telling you what evils not to do to what character traits (love) you should be aspiring to express in your character.

virtue you are trying to achieve in the situation. Once you have a list of those that you believe will be applicable, then you should consider each of your hypotheses (the null, and any alternatives each in turn) and ask yourself the following questions:

- Would a person I describe as having the virtue in question behave as the hypothesized action states I should behave?
    - If not, what would a person who was purely following that virtue do?
- Could you see your exemplar rejecting the null hypothesis that the action was unethical and proceeding to bring it about?
    - If not, what do you think they would do instead?[6]

Once you have determined how each course of action would be looked upon from each of your virtues or exemplars, you should be able to identify the hypothesized action that would be best aligned with your aspirations, and that should be the course of action that you should follow according to this analysis.

The powerful aspect of this approach is that by appealing to virtue ethics, you get away from the relatively pessimistic approach of determining whether or not your action is impermissible according to the minimal standards of your ethical school of thought, and start to evaluate and guide your actions by what you want to be, not by what you do not want to be. It may sound like a subtle difference, but it is not as we can look at in the example below.

Imagine that during the winter months your hometown receives a snow storm that drops a few inches of snow on the ground in your neighborhood. The driveways and sidewalks are covered in snow. You dress in warm clothes, a hat, and gloves and head out to clear the snow off of your driveway and sidewalks. It takes you an hour to clear away the snow that has fallen on your property and you see a number of your neighbors clearing their walks as well. Your next-door neighbors are an older couple that recently had experienced a number of medical events which has left both of them relatively unsteady on their feet and easily tired. You notice that their driveway and walks are not cleared and their car parked there is also covered in snow. Nothing in a proscriptive ethics make your morally culpable for hustling inside to warm yourself up now that your job is done. But you spend the last few minutes of your snow clearing thinking about what it means to be a good neighbor and how you wish your community was friendlier and watched out for each other. Perhaps you think back to the summer when your wife had a horrible reaction to an insect sting and had to be rushed to the hospital by a neighbor who you admired after that for their selflessness and caring nature. You aspire to be that kind of person, and even though you have no moral obligation to clear the snow from their walks, driveway, and car, you go ahead and do it anyway. Another hour later and every walkway on your neighbor's property is snow-free so you head inside feeling good because you behaved not as you had to but as you ought to if you were the person you aspire to be.

---

[6] Some of you may remember the WWJD (What would Jesus Do?) meme that swept through the American Christian community in the 1990s that is essentially this exact same kind of approach.

This example should illustrate to you the power of considering the aspirational aspect of ethics in one small and rather pedestrian instance, but that same approach can guide you in the bigger and thornier ethical decisions you may face. And that guidance, paired with the insight from the next two schools of thought and their analyses, should get you closer to making the right decision.

4.3.3 Utilitarianism-Based Analyses

The term 'utilitarianism' identifies one of the most influential schools of thought in the history of moral philosophy. Colloquially, most understand its tenets from the simple formulation, "the greatest good for the greatest number." John Stuart Mill and Jeremy Bentham (see Chap. 2) detailed this consequentialist approach in their works, primarily as a way to operationalize moral theory into a calculative tool for assessing policies and laws (Driver, 2009). When given a choice between alternate policies, the morally right activity or policy would be the one that provided the greatest good as summed across all of those affected by the problem being solved (i.e., focusing on the outcomes or consequences of the action- hence, consequentialist). This approach should seem familiar as it is commonly experienced by economists and policy makers as a cost-benefit analysis (which will be discussed below) and also as a maximization problem. Utilitarianism is praised for being rational and fair, with the calculation clearly ignoring the social hierarchy of those affected or the influence of the individual doing the calculation.

While the utilitarian formulation does in fact provide a compelling tool, it must be used with extreme care as there are a number of issues that can make its use more difficult than you might imagine at first glance. There are scenarios where the calculation can in fact recommend outcomes that most people would consider ethically suspect.

In terms of the issues that deserve careful consideration when applying utilitarianism, the first is the consideration of what is meant by 'good.' Since we are treating it mathematically, we must understand how we can measure this 'good' so it can be related in the equations that will need to be processed. Mills defined this term in terms of the subjects' feelings of happiness or pleasure (which is why utilitarianism is sometimes labeled hedonistic) while Bentham focused on the concept of pleasure as it related to the expression of personal or social virtue not just of the subjects' base feelings (Driver, 2009). Of course, defining 'good' as pleasure, happiness, or well-being doesn't immediately get us to a quantitative value that can be used in the calculations, but it gets us a step closer. Concepts like happiness or pleasure can be expressed in ways that can be captured in the types of instruments that are common in policy research and analysis (e.g., Do you feel that you and your family are better off?) or can be proxied for by a more tangible measure like a monetary currency, which in truth is done more often than not. In our culture, well-being and money often are tied fairly tightly together, and money can be used as a fair approximation for well-being in many cases, but we would caution the reader that a broader view of the types of currency that are available to an individual usually provides a better proxy for any given individual's well-being than just monetary currency alone.[7]

In terms of the definition of the concepts of happiness or well-being, you must also be wary in that these definitions can also vary on a person by person basis (i.e., there is a conceptual issue here). This problem is not a problem of measurement as was discussed previously, but a problem of definition. A sociopath or masochist has a different conception of pleasure than the non-sociopath or non-masochist, to the degree that their valuations of happiness with certain situations may be the complete opposite of one another (e.g., pain as pleasure for the masochist). While the examples provided to make this point so far may be viewed as extreme, this problem can more subtly affect our reasoning, especially when the subjects of the calculation constitute members of a culture, country, religion, or socioeconomic situation different than those of us doing the calculation. For most reading this book, the concept of working at a job in sweatshop conditions would be considered definitely not pleasurable, but for someone living in a constant state of starvation and privation, an uncomfortable job experience that provides the resources needed for survival is definitely a benefit.

Utilitarianism and its primary focus on the aggregate effects of a policy can also lead one applying its calculations to come to conclusions that are morally suspect as well. The focus on the group or society can blind the user to the effects that these policies may have on one person. We can use an extreme case to illustrate this point. If you can imagine that there are five people who are on the organ donation waiting list with each person requiring an organ that would be necessary to continue their lives, then purely mathematically, you could rationalize causing the death of one donor and harvesting their organs for implantation into the five people waiting. In the sums at the end, five people gained a life's worth of well-being at the cost of only one person's well-being- a gain of 400 % on the well-being ledger. This result should sound suspect to you, and rightfully so.

These issues should not dissuade us from using utilitarian analysis as a valuable tool in the moral toolbox, though. In fact, the monetary-currency version of the utilitarian analysis, the cost-benefit analysis, is widely used when analyzing decisions and policies. But, like all powerful tools, it is best that you understand their limitations before you start swinging them around.

For our analytic purposes in this book, we will operationalize utilitarianism as the application of three different analyses: act, rule, and cost-benefit analysis.[8] Each analysis takes a slightly different approach to calculating the overall utility with the benefit of the avoidance of some of the pitfalls and issues outlined above. The approach you

[7] The concept of non-monetary currencies is a relatively modern one which expands upon the argument that money is not an adequate proxy for utility for many people. Social status, responsibility, honor, and social justice are examples of other 'currencies' that people trade in, often at the expense of their available monetary currency (Searing, 2009).

[8] Though some philosophers reading this text may shudder at the inclusion of cost-benefit as a utilitarian philosophical approach, in truth it is. As defined here, it is a utilitarian analysis utilizing only a monetary currency to measure well-being or utility. Additionally, the cost-benefit analysis is a tool that is readily accepted and used by economic and policy professionals.

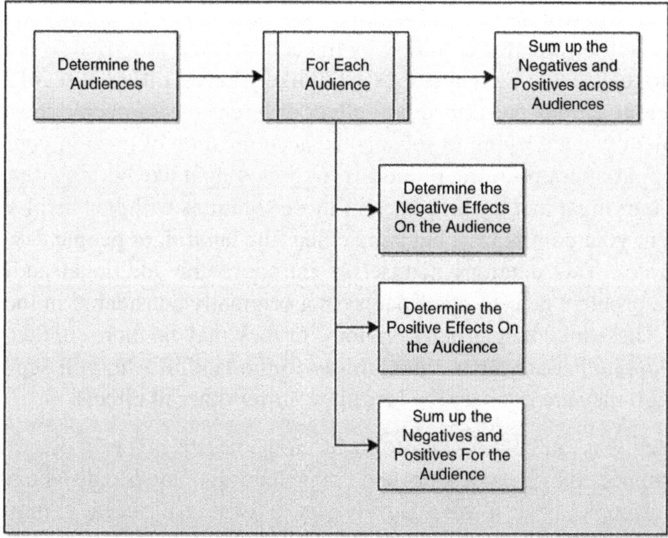

Fig. 4.2 Act utilitarian analysis flowchart

should take in using these tools is to do all three analyses and carry each of their recommendations separately into the final stages of the ethical decision-making process.

4.3.3.1 Act Utilitarian Analysis

In this analysis, the results will be determined based on the utility difference as caused by one specific act. This act can be considered a single decision or application of a policy[9] (i.e., the action called for in one of your hypothesized solutions). By defining the analysis as being confined to a single act, this helps us identify the necessary boundaries in time, space, and society to allow us to calculate the caused increases and decreases in utility. Having these boundaries is also a necessary condition for us to do a consistent and relevant comparison of your different hypotheses to provide you with usable results.

The process for performing an Act Utilitarian Analysis is outlined in the figure below (Fig. 4.2).

You will perform this analysis for each of your hypotheses separately. For each hypothesis, you will first determine who the audiences are that are affected by the actions outlined in the hypothesis, determine how each of the audiences are affected by the actions called for in the hypothesis, and then sum up the total change in well-being for each hypothesis (null and the proposed action). The hypotheses can then be ranked by the amount of well-being they provide in the analysis and the one with the greater net benefit would be the appropriate action to select morally per this analysis.

[9] This single decision is often referred to as a situation and thus this type of focused analysis on the outcomes of this single action are referred to as situationalist. So more formally, the Act utilitarian analysis is a consequentialist and situationalist analysis.

Determining the Audiences At its most basic, an audience is a person or set of people who will be affected similarly by the action being proposed. It is important first of all to realize that each hypothesis will likely have a different set of audiences as the different actions prescribed will affect different sets of people. For example, if the problem you are trying to solve is the accumulation of trash in your community, you might offer up several proposals for removing it like burning it in an incinerator or a burying it in a landfill. Each of those solutions will then involve not only the people in your community, but people near the landfill, or people downwind of the incinerator. The solutions themselves introduce the additional audiences by moving the problem near to other people not originally considered in the problem statement. These may be glaringly obvious, or they may be more subtle (e.g., consider the people that are along the highway to the landfill who will see increased traffic though they are not near the landfill to suffer other ill effects.

Additionally, it can be very easy to focus on the negatives (i.e., those who will be negatively impacted by the decision) and not include all of the people who might benefit. In our example above, it was relatively easy to focus on the negative impacts of the landfill, but not on those positively affected such as the new employees of the landfill.

Besides taking care to make sure you include all of the audiences who might be affected, you might have non-human audiences to consider such as the flora and fauna of the local ecosystem. These types of audiences can be problematic, as determining their well-being will fall outside of the realm of what can be measured directly through survey instruments, as well as the fact that there may be a moral bias that favors human well-being over non-human well-being. This kind of concern may bring to light a moral issue that you may have not considered in the original framing of your problem. This will commonly happen, as your hypothesized solutions will bring in areas of concern outside of your established frame and the remedy to it is to revisit your frame and record the new pieces of information and resolve any of the new issues that arise. This is not a setback in the analysis, but the evidence of a maturing understanding of the problem and its potential solutions.

Regarding the non-human populations, there are a number of ways to resolve this that can range from including them as full-fledged audiences with indirect scientific measurement of their well-being (e.g., population counts or other health-assessment methods) to the use of human proxies for these concerns (e.g., asking affected human audiences how a given impact to the surrounding natural environment will affect them).

Some things to keep in mind when defining audiences:

- Decide early on whether you will include non-human audiences or whether you will use human audiences to proxy the effects on the non-humans.
  - If you include non-human audiences, ensure you have a moral rationale for doing so and can express the determined equivalence ratios between entity types (e.g., is one wolf life worth a human life? Half a life?)
- Include all people/entities that are in the base problem space as well as those who will be introduced through the application of each of the solutions.

  - If you move a problem somewhere else, don't forget those audiences along the route.

- Focus first on the direct recipients of the effects of the actions (both positive and negative), then examine the relationships of those audiences to determine the indirect consequences and so on and so on until you reach a point that the effects felt by the audience would be something that they would face regardless of the action under consideration being performed. For example, if we were considering terminating an underperforming employee from a company, we would most definitely include as audiences the employee, his or her coworkers, and managers in the company as the first level of audiences due to the direct effect on them. From there, we can expand our audiences to those related to the directly affected audiences, such as the employee's spouse and children, our customers/clients whose service may be disrupted, and even look at the families of the other coworkers who may be affected due to the stress or anger felt by the coworker. We can look at other relationships as well, such as the fact that with one less worker in our company, the small business owner who owns the restaurant in the building will have one less customer and thus our decision will reduce their income. But this is a good place to draw the line, since the employee had to make a choice to eat in that restaurant on any given day, so the income of the restaurant owner was not a given and that the loss of one customer would be a normal occurrence on any given day and should not be attributable to the action of terminating the employee in the same way the effects on the employee's family should be included.

Determining the Effects Once we have our audiences, the next step is determining how each of our hypotheses will affect those audiences. We must determine how much the hypothesized action will affect the audience's well-being either positively or negatively. This can be a qualitative or quantitative assessment, but in the case of both, we encourage you to consider (a) both positive and negative effects on each audience member, and (b) consider well-being across the currencies (i.e., not just monetary- if you want to purely focus on the monetary, then the cost-benefit analysis will be more what you are looking for). Estimate the values if you have to (or drive research topics off of the gaps in information) but be objective about the valuation you provide and provide a detailed explanation of the reasoning behind your score.

The primary quantity you will be considering is the change in well-being as a result of the hypothesized action. While the size of the change normally is a good indicator of the fitness of the hypothesis, there are scenarios where it is also important to consider where the audience you are considering was in the absolute scale of well-being before the hypothesized actions were applied. If the people living next to the proposed landfill are already living next to a larger landfill, the negative consequences of the additional landfill will be much reduced as compared to the scenario where they live next to a national park to begin with. To restate, the change in well-being is most important not as an absolute value, but as a comparative value with respect to the audience's existing measure of well-being.

Some things to consider when calculating the effects on an audience:

- Consider positive effects as well as negative effects. It can be easy to focus on one or the other depending on your natural biases or through how the issues have been framed. People living next to a landfill experience negative consequences like smell, increased traffic, runoff concerns, BUT they also reap the benefits of local employment and the benefits of all of the possible uses for the land after the landfill has reached completion.
- Not all effects can be defined with a monetary value. Think about self-worth, satisfaction, responsibility, honor, justice and the like. People will often trade their monetary resources to gain value in these areas.
- Be consistent in your well-being measures across hypotheses and across audiences. You will be aggregating the results at the end of this process, so you need to be able to compare the numbers.
- Keep in mind that the well-being we are explicitly considering in these analyses is aggregate, so the number of people in each audience multiplies the well-being change they are experiencing.
- Be aware that the hypothesized action may result in lethal consequences for an audience and that the valuation of the harm caused may bring up some uncomfortable concepts for you to consider (e.g., the monetary/non-monetary value of a human life).
  - Sticking with the risk-averse stance taken in this book, it would be our advice to bias your measurements such that the negative score of a number of harms outweighs the positive score of an equivalent number of benefits.

Summing the Well-Being Once you have analyzed both (or all, in the case of multiple alternatives) of the hypotheses across all of the audiences, you can generate the sum the utility/well-being for each hypothesis. If you were consistent in the measures of utility for each of the audiences and hypotheses, then you will end up with each hypothesis having a number or rank associated with it. The hypotheses that have the higher aggregate benefits to well-being will be ranked as more attractive than those that have lower benefits or costs.

The results of this analysis will be a relative ranking of the hypotheses under consideration. The ranking will not just be an ordinal ranking, but will be a score which can be used in further comparisons, so it is important to retain the scores not just the rank order of the hypotheses.

4.3.3.2 Rule Utilitarian Analysis

In this analysis, the same basic steps of the calculation are followed as were outlined in the Act Utilitarian Analysis, but the way in which the hypothesized action is evaluated is different. This analysis is designed to better analyze scenarios like that of the organ donor from above that would pass an Act Utilitarian Analysis. The basic flow of the analysis is outlined in Fig. 4.3.

The difference in the analysis is that we are no longer analyzing the net benefits and costs (positives and negatives) from a single act. In the Rule Utilitarian Analysis, the

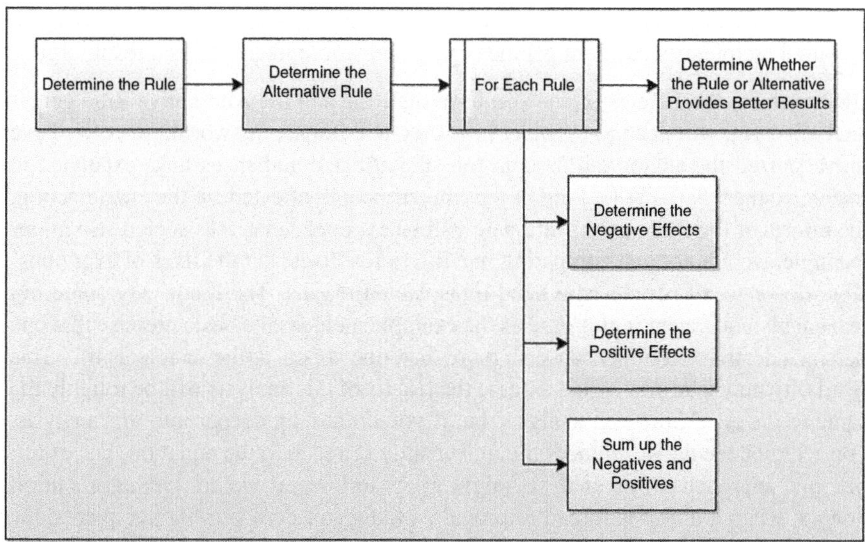

Fig. 4.3 Rule utilitarian analysis flowchart

consequences being measured are based on the universalization of the action (i.e., the making of the proposed action into the rule). So, the first step of this analysis is to generate the rule from the hypothesized action. The second step is to generate the alternative rule which is the opposite of the rule generated from the proposed hypothesis. The rest of the analysis continues on similarly to the Act Utilitarian Analysis. The negatives and positives from the rule and its alternative are generated and summed to determine which leads to the greater benefit. If the rule has the greater net then that indicates that the hypothesized action should be performed. If the alternate rule provides the greatest net benefit, then it would indicate that the hypothesized action should not be performed.

Determining the Rule Generating the Rule from your proposed hypothesis can be done by formulating a statement such as "Everyone will do the proposed action when faced with a situation like this one." Of course, in the formulation of your rule you will include the specifics of your situation and hypothesized action. In our organ donation example above, we can formulate a rule such as "Every time that the death of one person can provide organs to multiple critically ill recipients, that death should be caused and the organs harvested and donated." The Rule captures the details of the situation and universalizes the proposed action. We will come back to this Rule in the analysis step.

Determining the Alternate Rule The Alternate Rule is developed in order to provide an additional option for analyzing the hypothesis. The additional option in this case is an expression of the universalization of the exact opposite of the action proposed in the hypothesis. To develop this alternate, you would take the Rule generated in the previous step and negate it. For example, the Alternate Rule to the organ donation example's Rule would be "Every time that the death of one person can provide organs to multiple critically ill recipients, that death should not be caused and the potential recipients would not get the organs and would likely die as a result of it."

Determining the Effects Once you have the Rule and the Alternative Rule generated, then you will need to consider how they will impact the world. Since we have universalized the action and its converse, the affected audiences have expanded to match. Rather than just looking at the limited people affected by the single action, the effects of the Rule and its alternate will be experienced across society. So in our example, we are not just comparing one life to five lives, but the lives of every possible donor to all people who need transplanted organs. The math may come out reasonably equivalent in this case as the example includes the basic premise that one person's death (the donor) can save more than one person's (the recipient) life. This similarity may lead you to just assume the results of this analysis will be roughly the same as the Act Utilitarian analysis, but if you do not dig deeper into this analysis, you will not see the differences the universality brings into the equation. For example, one approach to the analysis might go as follows; if we are talking about all donors, when a donor is forced to provide a kidney or cornea to the recipients, the donor then becomes a candidate recipient as they are now in need of their missing organ. Conversely, the recipient now becomes a donor candidate following the same logic. This role reversal then alternates as the organs are cycled from one person to the other and back again. As you can see, the benefits that were mathematically obvious from the Act Utilitarian Analysis disappear very quickly as we start to talk about more than just an isolated incident involving one donor and the potential recipients.

Next, you should analyze the Alternative Rule in a similar manner; looking at the plusses and negatives of the case where the exact opposite of your hypothesized is universally performed. In the example scenario, we posited that no person should be harmed in order to provide donor organs to needy recipients. Looking at this from a strictly utilitarian point of view, the end result is likely a lot of dead potential recipients who never had the chance to receive the organ they needed. So in this example, the Alternative Rule also leads to a generally negative outcome.

Summing the Well-Being Once you have analyzed both the Rule and the Alternate Rule, you now need to determine which course of action leads to the best overall outcome. This can be somewhat difficult as the universalization of the rule itself can cause negative consequences regardless of the action being universalized. In general, it is rarely the case that everyone doing some one thing or the thing's opposite all at the same time will lead to a beneficial outcome. For example, if everyone stopped eating meat tomorrow due to ethical concerns for the animals providing the meat, there would be a lot of chickens, pigs, and cows stuck in feedlots either waiting to be set free into the countryside or starving to death because the people raising them wouldn't have the means to continue feeding them without the sales of their end product. There would be some extremely negative consequences for the animals involved if the action was taken in concert across society. Of course, the opposite rule, that everyone should eat meat tomorrow would be exacerbating the original problem regarding the ethical treatment of the animals.

It is just these sorts of society- or market-wide effects and interactions we are trying to understand in the Rule Utilitarian analysis. If in the final accounting though, if the Rule seems like it will benefit society more, then it would indicate your hypothesis is the proper course of action. If the Alternate clearly provides more benefit, then the hypothesized action should not be pursued. Of course, if like in the above examples, the Rule and the Alternate both lead to negative consequences, then you may want to consider revising the rules to be a bit less restrictive and downplay the immediacy inherent in the rule in order to eliminate the self-defeating nature of the universalization itself and focus on the outcome. The example in the box gives an example of this process from an economic point of view for comparison.

Example

Imagine a situation in a small town where a person was trying to decide whether or not to buy an ice cream cone this evening as they were walking by the ice cream shop. We could generate a rule that said "Every time that anyone in the town walks past the ice cream shop they will buy an ice cream cone." If we consider this effect immediately we can imagine long lines outside of the store or the store running out of ice cream. On the opposite side of the coin, we could focus on bigger picture items that would affect the society of the town should everyone get ice cream, like increased tooth decay and obesity that would result from the increase in ice cream consumption in addition to the gustatory pleasure brought to the townsfolk.

Though they can appear similar, rule utilitarianism and the aggregate application (Kantian categorical imperative) are quite distinct. In aggregate application, Kant addresses the conceptual problems that come from universal application: if everyone borrows without asking, then there are no property rights, so what would "borrowing" mean? In contrast, rule utilitarianism is not a question of definition, but what is best for society in terms of consequences (Tännsjö, 2013, p. 61). If everyone in town went for ice cream at the exact same time, there would be massive lines of unhappy people. However, the meaning of buying ice cream is still intact. It is simply a question of welfare.

Some things to keep in mind when performing this analysis:

- Focus on the overall effects on society beyond the immediate possible self-defeating nature of universal rules.
- Adjust your rules to be more general and less specific as related to your hypothesized action, this can help you avoid the self-defeating trap discussed above.
- Look for effects that come about due to the effects of scale on your action as well as network and cyclical effects (like the donors becoming recipient candidates and then donors again in the example above) that can amplify the positive and negative outcomes.

4.3.3.3 Cost-Benefit Analysis

Cost-Benefit Analysis is a specialized form of the Act Utilitarian Analysis and follows much the same process. The specialized portion is that instead of looking at overall qualitative positives and negatives for the audiences, the analysis requires that these values be quantified into a currency (usually dollars or euros, but there are other forms of currency to consider using) so that precise mathematical judgments can be made in order to determine whether the hypothesized action is the right one to perform. The general flow of the analysis is outlined in the Fig. 4.4).

This analysis should be familiar to most of the readers of this book as it is a common decision-making tool used in policy analysis and economics. The costs associated with the hypothesized course of action are summed and simply compared to the sum of its benefits. If the benefits are greater than the action's costs, then the action should be performed. If the costs outweigh the benefits, then the action should not be performed.

The structure and method of this analysis appeal especially to our (referring to ourselves and our readers) scientific proclivities and the soundness of the numbers and its mathematics often bolster the confidence in its conclusions. This confidence can be quite misplaced though, as the numerical accuracy often masks the underlying uncertainty and subjective judgments that were used to derive the "sound" numerical values found in the cells of the analysis. Below, we look at some common roadblocks to performing a good cost benefit analysis that should be avoided by its users.

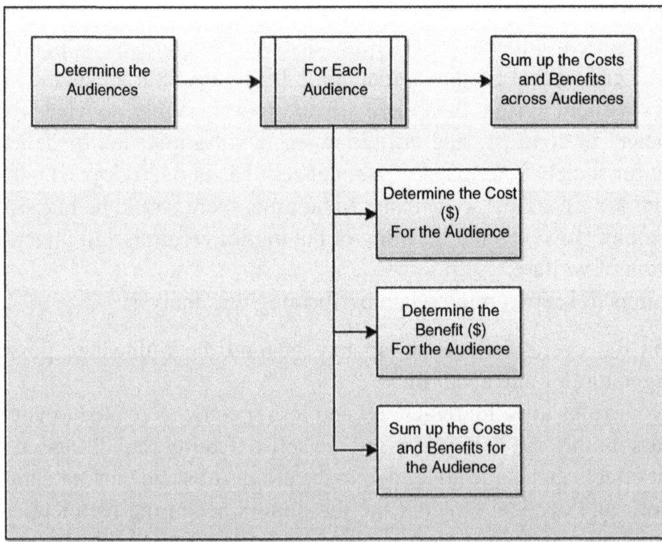

Fig. 4.4 Cost-benefit analysis flowchart

Avoiding the Uncomfortable One of the most common difficulties encountered when performing a cost benefit analysis on situations involving moral judgment is that the costs incurred end up either being difficult or uncomfortable to quantify. In situations where life and death are possible outcomes (e.g., treatment decision-making by doctors or design decision-making by engineers), you will inevitably require a value for a human life, a value for the reduction in length of a life, or a value for a human arm or leg. These values are quantifiable using several different methods, many of which can be found when surveying the recent awards in wrongful death lawsuits. Often, the risk premium paid in workers' wages for performing high-risk jobs is modeled, as was done by W.K. Viscusi (2003), the U.S. Federal Aviation Administration (FAA), and the Environmental Protection Agency (EPA), in order to calculate the value of a life. Models of lost potential earnings for each death and the provision of equivalent compensation is the basis of the model used by Kenneth Feinberg, the Special Master of the U.S. Government's September 11th Victim Compensation Fund (Marsh 2007). The risk-based numbers essentially treat each life as equivalent at least in the value assigned to the life, while the lawsuit summary and earnings models methods generate different numbers for different people. The latter summations can be difficult to use before an action has occurred unless the target of the action being contemplated is a specific individual whose identity is already known.

One of the best examples of a cost-benefit analysis gone awry is that of the case of the Ford Pinto. The Pinto was designed to be an entry-level car that Ford could sell for under $2000 in the early 1970s.[10] The design process was hurried as Ford needed to get their sub-compact to market to compete with the new foreign imports entering the market at that time. In order to keep the weight and costs down, the engineers had to utilize as much of the available space within the already small body as possible. This lack of space forced the gas tank to be placed between the rear axle and the rear bumper. This placement puts the gas tank in the direct path of the damage that would be caused in a rear-end collision. During subsequent collision testing, the fuel tank ruptured on several test vehicles spilling fuel into the passenger compartment at least once.

Based on these statistics, Ford knew that a fix should be put in place to reduce the risks of fire. An $11 per vehicle fix was developed by the engineers and the estimate for retrofitting all production vehicles was calculated to be $137 million (12.5 million vehicles at $11 a piece = $137 million). These were the obvious costs to the solution, not to mention the damage to Ford's reputation with a recall of this magnitude. The safety office at Ford decided to calculate the benefits that those costs would offset. Based on risk studies of collisions, they determined that fixing this problem would reduce deaths by 180, burn injuries by 180, and vehicles damaged

[10] This case summary is based on the case study, "#34 Pinto," from Harris et al. (2000). The authors would highly recommend this book or its subsequent editions as a great source of ethical case studies presented in a format amenable to classroom discussion. While the main focus of that book is engineering ethics, most of the cases are quite controversial and thus interesting not only from an engineering standpoint but from a societal and policy point of view.

by 2100. Based on National Highway Traffic Safety studies at the time, saved lives were valued at $200,000, saved burn injuries at $67,000, and reduced vehicle damage of $700. These counts and values worked out to a benefit of around $49 million. So, based on the calculation, it was decided that it would be far more affordable to leave the problem in place in the Pinto and deal with the deaths and injuries that occurred when the collisions did happen. After a number of fires and burn deaths had occurred in Pintos on the road, they gained a reputation as a death trap and became a public relations nightmare for Ford. When the cost-benefit analysis that had been performed was exposed in the subsequent court proceedings, Ford's nightmare only got worse.

One might argue that in the example, Ford used far too low a value for the lives that were lost, and by modern standards it was quite low; however, it would be easy to construct a hypothetical case in which a similar outcome could be created even with higher values placed on the lives lost. If this whole notion of putting a value on human lives (or lives in general) is a bit off-putting to you, then you will find your solace in the Respect for Persons analyses in the next section. Delicate sensibilities, however, are no excuse for a subpar ethical analysis.

Egocentricism Egocentrism, or the focus on the benefits and costs for the decision-maker, played a supporting role in the Pinto case discussed above in that Ford focused on how much the litigation for the lives lost would cost *them* and how much the fix would cost *them*. By being entirely focused on the costs and benefits as they perceived them to be for them, you might argue that they undervalued the lives that would be lost (especially with regards to the natures of the deaths). Keep this in mind when assessing costs, which should be the costs encountered by those who are the affected by the hypothesized action, **not** the costs that those losses will cause you, the decision-maker, to incur (e.g., legal defense costs, etc.). Ford's focus on the direct monetary costs also failed to predict the huge loss in prestige and brand value that the entire Pinto escapade cost them.

Mistaken Odds and Black Swans The last pitfall to avoid in your cost-benefit analyses is that of avoiding overestimating the probability of the benefits and underestimating the probability of the costs. This is an important concept since most of the costs and benefits used in our calculations are not givens based on the hypothesized action being executed; the action simply adjusts the probabilities of the costs and benefits being realized. Thus, our estimation of the probabilities of a certain effect being realized plays a major role in our calculated values for our costs and benefits.

It is natural for most of us to overemphasize the positive (e.g., I might win the lottery this time!) and play down the chance of the negative outcomes from occurring (e.g., most people's propensity to exceed the speed limit in their cars despite the increased likelihood of an accident). You must be aware of your biases regarding the respective odds of the costs and benefits so as to avoid unintentionally introducing error into your calculations.

Besides our general predisposition to err when assessing probabilities of benefits and costs occurring, there are problems that can occur just from the fact that the enterprise is probabilistic in nature. Most statistical models are based on the normal distribution, as this is a fairly accurate estimate of the distribution of probabilities for natural systems. But as recent events have shown, even Nobel Prizes don't guarantee your risk assignment formulas will work in all conditions. In *The Black Swan: The Impact of the Highly Improbable*, the author examines the effects that can happen when the normal distribution is not followed and the extremely improbable event, the "Black Swan" occurs (Taleb, 2010). These types of events, he argues, are not well understood and are the ticking time bomb inside many risk calculations that are relied upon to shape our decisions and thus our world.

While worrisome, these pitfalls and roadblocks should not preclude the use of the cost-benefit analysis, as it can be a very valuable tool in our toolbox; however, they should remind us to stop and reflect on where the numbers in the analysis actually come from. Those same numbers which give this analysis its feeling of objectivity and certainty can be hiding dark secrets and masking true uncertainty when dealing with matters of ethical concern the ramifications of getting something wrong can be dire.

Some things to keep in mind when performing this analysis:

- Spend time considering where the numbers used for costs and benefits are from.
  - What assumptions are present in that innocent-looking value you are assigning?
- Focus on determining the costs and benefits from the point of view of the audience, not from the point of view of the decision-maker.
- Be extra careful when assessing values on lives and injuries caused to audience members. Use conservative numbers for values of lives. If you find yourself looking for a lower value of life to make your calculation work out, then you are already treading on thin ice morally-speaking.

4.3.4 Respect for Persons Analyses

If, while studying the previous section describing the utilitarian analyses, those analyses seemed to be missing something or felt like they were actually condoning something that was morally questionable or wrong, then you may intuitively base your judgments off of your understanding of the ethics of respect for persons or more formally, deontology. This school of thought bases morality not on the maximization of utility (i.e., consequences measured in happiness or well-being) across the audiences affected, but on the minimization of harm to those audiences regardless of the benefits that might accrue. This theory is based on the idea that each of the members of the affected audiences has a shield of rights that protect them from the negative effects of the decision-maker's hypothesized action. An action that would be uncontroversially correct according to this moral theory would be the one that did not violate any audience's rights at all. An action that would be completely condemned would be the one that violated the most fundamental of the audience's rights; the right to life. Rarely are such black and white situations encountered though. In most analyses, you will find yourself having to decide between violating one audience's rights instead of another, so this straightforward theory requires some additional structure to its analyses. The two respect for persons analyses deal specifically with how best to trade off the rights violations of one audience versus another. We will outline the Rights-Based Analysis first, followed by the Pareto-Efficiency Analysis (which should be familiar ground for our readers.)

4.3.4.1 Rights-Based Analysis

The Rights-Based Analysis examines the effects of the hypothesized action in terms of the violations of the audiences' rights incurred by the performance of the action. Not all rights violations are equally heinous nor are they guaranteed to occur if the action is performed. A fairly efficient way of processing these rights can be created by grouping the rights into three tiers (Harris et al., 2000) and then classifying the violations based on the certainty of the violation of the rights should the action be performed (i.e., does the action necessarily cause the violation, or does it just increase the likelihood of said violation).

The most important rights in our hierarchy are the Tier 1 rights, also known as the "basic rights." These rights include the right to life (i.e., the right to not be deprived of life), the right to mental and bodily integrity, and the right to be safe from torture. The next tier of rights is known as the Tier 2 or "maintenance rights." These rights include the right to maintain your current status or situation (e.g., right to private property, right not to be lied to). While important, these rights are not as important as the tier 1 rights, as can be witnessed by the fact that most people would trade away their property in order to save their life. The lowest tier of rights in this hierarchy is the "advancement rights" or "purpose-fulfillment rights," which are rights that protect your ability to grow and advance (e.g., the right not to be discriminated against). Violations of these Tier 3 rights don't deprive you of your life or even of your current property, but they do restrict your chances to advance socially or economically.

In addition to the severity of the harm, the effect on the probability of the harm must also be taken into account, just as you would account for both magnitude and probability of the harm in a standard risk calculation. Some violations of rights are not actual immediate violations of rights, they may in fact be only increases in the likelihood that the rights violation would happen. For example, if I dropped you off against your will in the middle of crime-ridden area, I have increased the likelihood that you will be mugged, but it is not the same as if I had personally pulled out a gun and mugged you. Both lead to violations of your Tier 2 and possibly your Tier 1 rights, but one I am directly responsible for and the other I played a slightly lesser role. Thus, while both are ethically wrong, there is still a difference in exactly how the rights were violated. Much of our moral judgment here follows our legal judgment (or is it the other way around), in that we tend to hold someone in greater contempt for acts in which they directly cause as compared to acts in which they were

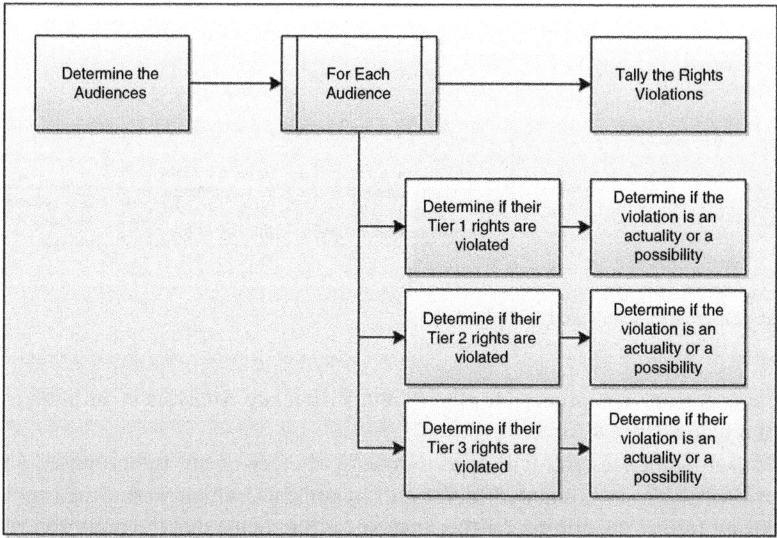

Fig. 4.5 Rights-based analysis flowchart

less directly involved. So, when assessing rights violations it is equally important to assess the actuality versus the possibility of the harm as well as its magnitude.

The process involved in this analysis is outlined in Fig. 4.5. Again, each audience is considered in turn with the hypothesized action and the null and for each we consider which of their rights, if any, are violated by it. We need, at this point, to understand the nature of the harm and rank the violation according to the tier or tiers of rights that are being violated or threatened to be violated. Then, we need to assess whether or not the violation is an actual violation or whether it is a possible violation (i.e., whether or not it is a direct violation of just increases the likelihood of a violation of the right).

Once you have assessed the violations or lack of violations for each of the audiences for each of the actions, then you can determine that the one with the least rights violations is the better action, with the ideal being a complete lack of violations due to the action.

4.3.4.2 Pareto Efficiency Analysis

The concept of Pareto efficiency should be familiar to the readers of this book. Pareto efficiency is when it is impossible to make anyone involved any better off without making at least one person worse off. This is normally not a concept directly linked to ethical analysis, but its fundamental principle aligns with the ethics of Respect for Persons due to its focus on the prevention of harm to a single individual. This function then matches the principle of protecting an individual regardless of the benefits that their harm might provide. This analysis then looks very much like the Rights-Based analysis in terms of its process with a far stricter

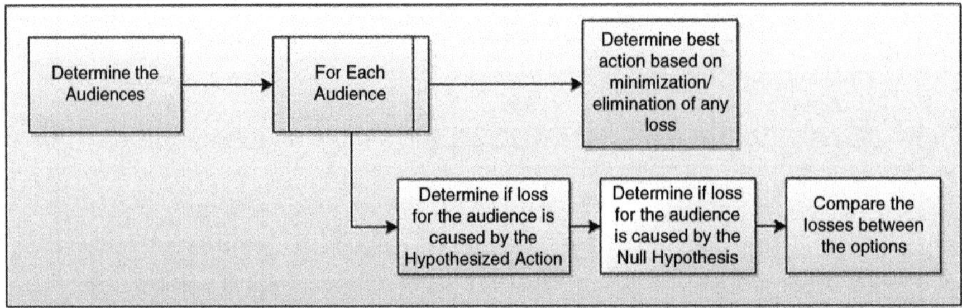

Fig. 4.6 Pareto efficiency analysis flowchart

success criterion. The process for the Pareto Efficiency Analysis is outlined in the diagram below (Fig. 4.6).

For each audience, you will need to assess whether or not the proposed action causes them harm as compared to the null hypothesis, which would then indicate that we are failing the criteria for this analysis will indicate that the proposed action will be considered unethical.

4.4 Presenting Results

Congratulations! You have hopefully amassed a lengthy list of ethical tests and results. In doing so, you have considered the ethical implications of the decision you are facing with respect to several separate philosophical approaches. Just as many of these ethical approaches are rooted in different and often opposing moral theories, you may also have amassed a large quantity of detailed and conflicting information. You're more enlightened, but you feel no more close to a conclusion that you did prior to testing. What do you do?

Remember – this is just like any other research methodology, such as applied statistics. Right now we have *results*, but we do not yet have *conclusions*. There are several steps that we can undertake to draw that moment closer.

First, if you did not use the provided worksheet or something similar of your own devising, you need to organize your findings. Even the most rigorous and harmonious of results will appear haphazard if they are not properly organized. Our suggestion is to group the tests according to philosophical approach so that you can more clearly see any conflicts (see the worksheet in the Appendix A for an example). Inter-group conflict is more common than intra-group conflict, but is by no means exclusive. In addition to clarifying the results of the testing for your own purposes, his also benefits any future parties interested in your thought processes. You've chosen a career that handles politically and emotionally sensitive materials, so when someone demands to know what in the world you were thinking (and they will), you can provide it to them in tabular format.

Second, we must undertake the third phase in ethical decision-making: moral reasoning. Just as in ethical testing, there are several approaches to reconciling the conflicts between results, and each can be employed alone or in turn, depending on your resource constraints. In doing so, we can order and resolve the testing results and either reject or fail to reject our hypotheses that our course of action is unethical.

Discussion Questions

1. Which of the philosophers that you learned about earlier in the text would be the best champion for each of the ethical approaches? Which would be that approach's strongest opponent?
2. Propose a modified version of the Cost-Benefit Analysis that uses an alternate currency instead of dollars or euros? Where might this type of analysis be better than the standard analysis?
3. The concept of utility has always been a good candidate for being a not easily resolvable conceptual issue. Propose at least three ways that you could use to measure utility in a manner useful in the Act Utilitarian test described in the chapter?
4. Develop another scenario in which the results of an Act Utilitarian Analysis on the proposed action would be contradicted by a Rule Utilitarian Analysis of the same proposed action.
5. Discuss some of the difficulties you might encounter in practically using the Aggregate Application Analysis or Expected Reciprocity Analysis.

References

Berk, R. A., & Freedman, D. A. (2003). Statistical assumptions as empirical commitments. In *Law, punishment, and social control: Essays in honor of Sheldon Messinger* (2nd ed.). Hawthorne, NY: Aldine de Gruyter.

Driver, J. (2009). The history of utilitarianism. In E. N. Zalta (Ed.), *The Stanford encyclopedia of philosophy* (Summer 2009 edition). http://plato.stanford.edu/archives/sum2009/entries/utilitarianism-history/

Gigerenzer, G., & Selten, R. (2002). *Bounded rationality: The adaptive toolbox*. Cambridge, MA: MIT Press.

Harris, C. E., Pritchard, M. S., & Rabins, M. J. (2000). *Engineering ethics: Concepts and cases* (2nd ed.). Belmont, CA: Wadsworth Publishing Company.

Hursthouse, R. Virtue ethics. In E. N. Zalta (Ed), *The Stanford encyclopedia of philosophy* (Fall 2013 ed.). http://plato.stanford.edu/archives/fall2013/entries/ethics-virtue/

McCloskey, D. N., & Ziliak, S. (2008). *The cult of statistical significance: How the standard error costs us jobs, justice, and lives*. Ann Arbor, MI: University of Michigan Press.

Pfaff, D. W., & Wilson, E. O. (2007). *The neuroscience of fair play: Why we (usually) follow the golden rule*. Chicago: Dana Press.

Popper, K. (1974). *Unended quest: An intellectual autobiography, Karl Popper*. London: Routledge.

Searing, E. A. (2009). Casuistry: The tape measure in the cognitive toolbox. Unpublished manuscript, Atlanta.

Taleb, N. N. (2010). *The black swan: The impact of the highly improbable fragility*. New York: Random House Digital.

Tännsjö, T. (2013). *Understanding ethics*. Edinburgh, UK: Edinburgh University Press.

Tversky, A., & Kahneman, D. (1991). Loss aversion in riskless choice: A reference-dependent model. *The Quarterly Journal of Economics, 106*(4), 1039–1061.

Viscusi, W., & Aldy, J. (2003, February). *The value of a statistical life: A critical review of market estimates throughout the world* (NBER Working Paper No. w9487). Cambridge, MA: National Bureau of Economic Research.

Yin, R. K. (2009). *Case study research: Design and methods*. Los Angeles: Sage.

Chapter 5
Drawing Conclusions

Donald R. Searing and Elizabeth A.M. Searing

> *"Nothing is more difficult, and therefore more precious, than to be able to decide."*
>
> ~Napoleon Bonaparte (1769–1821)

Abstract This chapter discusses what to do after the different types of ethical tests have been conducted and the results assembled. There will almost always be a conflict between the recommendations of different ethical tests, so different methods for addressing this conflict are explored. A preponderance of evidence, different weightingtechniques, and the use of casuistry and line-drawing are all explored as ways to synthesize the results of the hypothesis tests into a final conclusion and recommendation.

Keywords Drawing conclusions • Null hypothesis • Casuistry • Line-drawing

5.1 Coming to a Conclusion

Each of the analyses performed in the last chapter represents a different moral theory (consequentialist or deontological) or method of moral reasoning (situationalist or universalist). These differing approaches and views are critical in helping you come to a final conclusion regarding your proposed hypothesis. They were meant to stretch your moral reasoning and force you to examine different points of view on the same problem. If you approached each analysis objectively and built your arguments up from the components of your frame, it is possible that you are now in

D.R. Searing, PhD
CEO and Principal Scientist, Syncere Systems, Altamont, NY, USA
e-mail: dsearing@synceresystems.com

E.A.M. Searing, PhD (✉)
Assistant Professor, Department of Public Administration and Policy, Rockefeller College of Public Affairs and Policy, University at Albany – State University of New York, 305 Milne Hall, 135 Western Avenue, Albany, New York, USA
e-mail: esearing@albany.edu

E.A.M. Searing, D.R. Searing (eds.), *Practicing Professional Ethics in Economics and Public Policy*, DOI 10.1007/978-94-017-7306-5_5

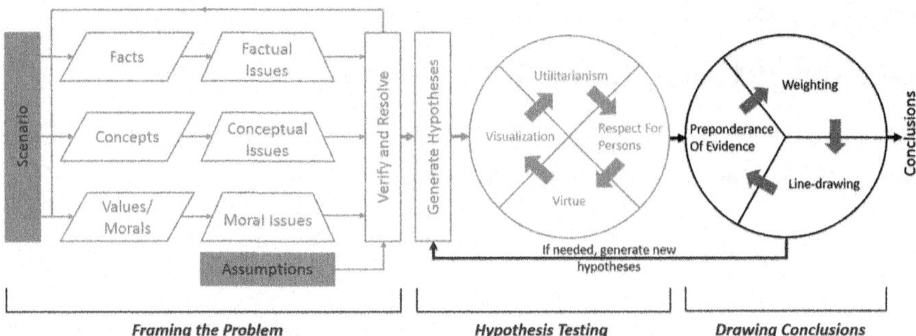

Fig. 5.1 Drawing conclusions

a state of mild confusion as it is very likely you have taken both sides and built up arguments both for and against your hypothesized action. You may be asking yourself, "Now what do I do?" In Fig. 5.1, the final piece of the process diagram begun in the prior two chapters offers some insight.

5.2 All Analyses Agree to Reject the Null Hypothesis

If your problem was particularly clear-cut, it is possible that you ended up with unanimous agreement among the conclusions of all of the performed analyses. If the analyses all agreed that your proposed action would provide a benefit, then this is the simplest case for determining the final conclusion. The analyses in this case are telling you that the hypothesis you put forward to solve your problem is an acceptable solution regardless of how you look at it. Before you pat yourself on the back though, keep in mind that the odds that you have managed to satisfy all of the analyses of all of the different moral theories are fairly low. With that being the case, we would recommend that in this scenario that you go back and re-examine your analyses, be sure that you did not fall into any of the traps we have outlined for those analyses (e.g., maybe your analyses were egocentric- and thus missed another audience that should have been included).

5.3 All Analyses Agree to Fail in Rejecting the Null Hypothesis

If your analyses all agreed that the hypothesis was harmful (i.e., caused more harm than benefit), then you have a simple case in terms of the results of the analysis, but not a simple resolution to your problem- which in the end is the ultimate goal of the entire process. So unanimity in this case does not get you to a clear path to a resolution, it just closes the door on this path. All is not in vain, though: the additional information you gathered throughout the analysis will aid in reformulating your hypothesis for the next attempt at finding an acceptable solution.

5.4 When Analyses Disagree

The most likely outcome of your set of analyses will be that they do not agree on the acceptability of your hypothesis. There are several methods for proceeding to a conclusion given a disagreement in the conclusions of the analyses that will be outlined in this section of the chapter. The first of these methods is to judge the hypothesis based on a preponderance of evidence; like a direct democracy, each ethical test is worth one vote, and a majority of votes wins the outcome. This is a quick and useful rule, bordering almost on a heuristic, but there are drawbacks.

The second method is an adaptation of the simple aggregation found in the method outlined above that uses a preponderance of evidence. Rather than having an equal importance assigned to each test, a weighting schema can be used to incorporate elements which you feel are of greater salience to the situation or to the general state of things. It is important, however, that such considerations be made prior to the amassing of the final data, which will minimize the temptation of post hoc rationalization.

The third method is an adaptation of a decision-making approach used since Aristotelian times and made famous (and infamous) by medieval Jesuit priests: casuistry, also known as the method of line-drawing. Using the line-drawing technique utilized by Rabins, Pritchard, and Harris (2000) we can use a visual balance to help assign the relative values to each ethical test.

These methods may seem odd from the standpoint of someone familiar with the standard methodology used in applied statistics in judging hypotheses. In that domain, you do not normally conduct tests of data characteristics or hypotheses that outright conflict, but such conflicts do occur.[1] However, these situations are normally the exception in statistical data analysis and the rule in ethical data analysis. This is primarily due to the varied schools of thought (e.g., utilitarianism and the respect for persons approach), that form the basis for the various analyses. These schools of thought approach the judgment of ethical acceptability from diametrically opposed viewpoints and this leads to the conflict inherent in this process.

5.4.1 *Preponderance of Evidence*

The simplest and most direct way of drawing a conclusion from your ethical findings is through the use of a preponderance of evidence or democratic standard. This kind of reasoning can be truly likened to a direct democracy, with each ethical test possessing one vote on the final outcome. Such a process was the preferred method of governance by the ancient Athenians, and is still in active use for political

[1] I am thinking specifically of the *brant* and *omodel* tests for violations of the parallel odds assumption in an ordered logistical regression model using Stata, but feel free to substitute your own practical experiences here.

purposes in countries such as Switzerland (Frey, 1994). Though a simple majority is not a mandatory threshold in such modern systems, it is suitable for our purposes here.

However, just as there are notable drawbacks to the philosophical ramifications and implementation of a direct democracy, similar problems are found here. In order for this resolution process to work correctly, a balanced set of analyses must be considered so as to not inadvertently weigh one school of thought (utilitarianism versus respect for persons) or conceptual approach (situational or universal) over another. The analyses provided in the previous chapter provide the required balance, assuming that you performed all of the analyses listed.

The employment of this analytical tool is relatively straightforward. Using the results of your ethical tests, assign each a value of +1 for those results which indicate that the course of action is ethical. For those tests which indicate your chosen course of action is not ethical, assign a value of −1. Then provide a simple sum of the values. If the summation of the ethical test results are greater than one, H_0 = *unethical* is rejected; if the summation is less than one, we fail to reject the null hypothesis that the course we are about to embark on is unethical.[2] If the summation balances out at zero, then you should try the weighted or line-drawing forms of analysis to address the ethical indifference and come to a more definitive conclusion.

Example

Abena, a consultant to the office of the state land commissioner, is contemplating her position on the construction of a bypass around a small rural town for the major highway running through it. Though the highway has a stoplight, there have been a number of fatalities at that intersection over the last 3 years. However, there is fear that bypassing the town will irreparably damage the local economy. Abena has carefully outlined and clarified the facts, concepts, and values in play using the necessary resources; this can look very much like a summative evaluation, comprising record reviews, interviews, and similar data collection in order to distill information. She remembers that her conclusions rest upon reliable and transparent methods, and that both determining someone's values and proving to her employer the justifications for her decision are contingent on valid data collection (Wholey, Hatry, & Newcomer, 2010). She has filled in assumptions where necessary, and conducted the ethical tests outlined in Chap. 5. Her final tabulation looks like this:

(continued)

[2] Some may feel that a positive value should represent affirmation of the null hypothesis; here, it is easier to visualize the process as a one-sided *t*-test where the higher values increase the likelihood of rejection.

H_0: It is unethical to build the bypass	
Visualization analyses:	
Expected reciprocity analysis:	+1
New York times analysis:	+1
Anticipatory self-approval analysis:	+1
Aggregate application analysis:	−1
Utilitarianism-based analyses	
Act utilitarian/cost-benefit analysis:	+1
Rule utilitarian analysis:	−1
Respect for persons analyses:	
Rights-based analysis:	+1
Pareto efficiency analyses:	−1

$$\sum t_n = (+5) + (-3) = +2:$$

Thus, it is ethical to proceed based on this analysis

Therefore, Abena decides that, though there are definite drawbacks to the plan, it would be ethical to proceed. She has also gained two advantages. First, she has identified which stakeholders may suffer adverse consequences, which can be compensated during the project design and implementation phases. Second, she is now more fully equipped to explain her thinking to anyone who may be interested in the ethical considerations of the matter, whether that's a client, reporter, or herself in a future time period.

While this approach seems relatively straightforward and fair, there are drawbacks to this approach; the same ones faced by the ancient Athenians. First, it ignores the salience which different ethical tests may have to different scenarios. For example, rights-based testing may matter more in legislation about the death penalty than in raising the budget ceiling (though rights-based analysis should by no means be excluded from the latter) due to the greater relevance of rights-based approaches on a situation that focuses primarily on one person and a great deal of harm focused on them. Further, expected reciprocity is practically meaningless when evaluating things such as potentially toxic effluent rates as it takes a rather binary view in its analysis which isn't necessarily amenable to determining a more nuanced type of threshold. Second, it allows the opinion of the majority to dominate the minority in a consistent fashion. Because of their similarity, most analysts naturally include all three utilitarian methods with some Pareto efficiency and perhaps a New York Times test. Here, the main fact that you have three probably similar answers are what will determine your ethical outcome, regardless of the scenario that you are evaluating and whether utilitarian concerns should be held paramount. This also means that selection bias can easily creep into your choice of ethical tests.

Alternately, a weighting schema allows you to take into account not only salience and appropriateness of the ethical tests, but also potential correlation between test results when evaluating your final outcome.

5.4.2 Weighting Schemas

If the preponderance of evidence is equivalent to state representation in the U.S. Senate (each state gets two senators and thus two votes), then the use of a weighting schema is equivalent to the U.S. House of Representatives (each state gets a number of representatives and votes in direct proportion to its population, so California, the most populated state, has proportionately more votes than Wyoming, the least populated state; 53 votes to 1 vote in 2013). Since the number of states in the United States is an accident of history and bears no relation to the actual demographic distribution of population, such a weighting mechanism is necessary in order for the government to be fairly representative of the population of citizens. While there might be other distributions that could be used, population percentages represent a simple, just way to distribute votes to achieve equal representation for each citizen in what would otherwise be a fairly arbitrary bucketing of people by state boundary.

Equivalently, the analyses provided above don't always balance each other out in a way where a simple preponderance of evidence scheme works any better than the state boundaries do in dividing up the population for governmental representation. As discussed earlier, the ethical analyses represent several competing schools of thought and several ways of judging the effects of a hypothesized action. In the previous section, we noted that the equal representation scheme only works if **all** of the analyses are completed since we provided a fairly balanced list to you. In practice, it will likely be the case that a given analysis does not provide a clear-cut evaluation of your hypothesis. Alternatively, you may not have the detail to be able to perform some of the more intensive tests satisfactorily (e.g., the Cost Benefit Analysis). So having a weighting schema is a necessary part of coming to a good conclusion on your hypothesis.

So, you may be convinced that using a weighting schema is a good idea in your analysis, but it still begs several questions. First, do we have to use all of the analyses in the conclusion? Second, what type of schema should be used to weight the analyses: what weights are acceptable in the final scheme (are they based on a rank, can they be utilized more than once, are they limited within a range, and can they be zeroed out)? Third, once we agree on the schema type, how do we assess the weight for each analysis? Fourth, are there ways to interpret the results of the analyses in a non-binary fashion? Let's address these questions in order.

Do we have to use all of the analyses? We are of the firm belief that you shouldn't throw out completed analyses that actually have answers that make sense. The power of the methodology outlined here is that you are encouraged to slow down your though processes and approach the problem from a myriad points of view. If those analyses resolve (i.e., provide a conclusion that you can evaluate), then you should definitely consider that answer in your final determinations. Now, that being said, there are scenarios that we discussed in each of the analyses where it becomes clear that the test is not going to provide you with any meaningful answer. For example, the more universal in nature that the analysis is, the more likely it will be that you had to remove the nuances of your hypothesized solution to generate the universal rule you ended up analyzing. With these generalized rules, it often is the case that the mode of the analysis really does not provide a good way to properly come to a definitive conclusion for what started as a very specific hypothesis. So, in these types of situations you might want to not consider those results. But, sticking with our theme from earlier, we would strongly discourage you from eliminating them completely from your analysis. Keep them in the final determination, just use their lack of conclusiveness as a reason to weight their contribution very lightly.

Next, what type of weighting schema do you use? There are numerous weighting schemas that you can utilize:

- A simple ranking-based weight scheme: rank the analyses from n to 1 and use the inverse of their rank as their weight,
- A simple "heuristic"-based[3] weight scheme: weight the analyses either a 0 or 1; 0 to ignore the analysis' result or 1 to include the result in the total,
- A more complex "heuristic"-based weight scheme: weight the analyses 0, 1, or 2; use the 2 to weight more relevant analyses,
- A weighting scheme of your choice.

Our preferred method is the complex heuristic method that allows for the inclusion/exclusion with the additional option of weighting some of the analyses more than the baseline analysis weighting. We find that it is more natural for decision-makers to follow a method that allows for the pruning of the analyses that do not provide useful results before the weighting based on importance is processed. The complex heuristic method gives you best of both worlds; pruning and weighting of the remaining items. Feel free to use one of the other schemas if you are more comfortable with its application, though with only nine analyses to operate over you should be careful not to apply too much weight to any one analysis' conclusions or risk reducing your conclusion process becoming based on one analysis alone.

With the weighting schema selected, then you can concern yourself with actually determining the weights for each of the analyses in preparation for the final calculation. The weights you provide are subject to your judgment, much like the rest of this process, and as in the rest of the process, you should strive to not make your analysis a post hoc rationalization. You should approach the weighting of the analyses with

[3] This scheme is referred to as heuristic because unlike other weighting schemes, its structure is meant to allow numerically for the removal of the weighted items from the final determination. This "pruning" of the items being weighted can best be thought of as the application of a set of heuristic rules to the items being considered to remove those not being considered. This process is an adaptation of the poliheuristic model of decision-making (Mintz, 2004). As an example, if you were considering the purchase of a vehicle, you would not create a table of all possible vehicles and compare their various weighted attributes. The more realistic process would be that you have already made up your mind that you want a four-door compact car and you would confine your attribute comparisons to the subset of vehicles that were four-door compact cars. So, in our weighting scheme, this would be equivalent to providing a weight of 0 to the comparable items we wish to eliminate from further consideration.

as little bias from their conclusions as possible. Focus instead on the applicability of the moral theories being espoused in each of the analyses to the situation at hand and the context of the decision. If the decision will adversely affect a small number of people in a very drastic and harmful way, then most professions and policy-making bodies would give more weight to the respect for persons analyses, as these tend to be protective of individuals' rights and heath.[4] If the situation at hand focuses primarily on a larger-scale policy decision, then the utilitarian analyses would likely be weighed more, assuming that there are not major rights violations of other audiences (e.g., loss of life). The context provided by your professional codes can be very helpful in weighting the solutions as well. In the codes of ethics for engineers, it is clearly stated that the health, safety, and welfare of the public (and the individuals that make it up) are of paramount importance (NSPE, 2007). This statement of paramountcy in their code helps engineers weight their analyses appropriately- any analysis that has costs that can be measured in those terms (health, safety, welfare) can be given more weight. In the professions of economics and finance, their societies are still deciding on which principles to define their codes. But, we have a great deal of confidence that these professions will settle on the same sort of approach to seek truth and promote the maximization of public welfare without doing harm to the public or individuals therein. So, using this "do no harm" logic when recommending policies is a good place to start when determining the weight values for your analyses. Let's look at an example of this weighting scheme in practice.

Example

Let's reconsider the situation that Abena, the consultant to the office of the state land commissioner, is contemplating on the construction of a bypass around a small rural town for the major highway running through it.

In the analysis above, her final tabulation looked like this:

H_0: The highway bypass should be built	
Visualization analyses:	
Expected reciprocity analysis:	+1
New York times analysis:	+1
Anticipatory self-approval analysis:	+1
Aggregate application analysis:	−1
Utilitarianism-based analyses	
Act utilitarian/cost-benefit analysis:	+1
Rule utilitarian analysis:	−1
Respect for persons analyses:	
Rights-based analysis:	+1
Pareto efficiency analyses:	−1

(continued)

[4] Much as the Bill of Rights (the first ten amendments) in the U.S. Constitution is included to protect the individual from the federal government policies and enforcement actions.

If instead of the preponderance of evidence model of assessment, we use a complex heuristicweighting scheme, we can outline the desired value of the weights on each analysis. As this is a public works project and none of the effects of the construction lead to particularly heinous rights violations (no one dies, for example), we will go ahead and provide extra weight to the utilitarian analyses. Additionally, let's imagine that the Anticipatory Self-Approval Test did not provide us with a definitive answer. With those concepts in mind, we can provide a new tabulation with the weights added in.

H_0: It is unethical to build the bypass	
Visualization analyses:	
Expected reciprocity analysis:	+1
	(weight = 1)
New York times analysis:	+1
	(weight = 1)
Anticipatory self-approval analysis:	+1
	(weight = 0)
Aggregate application analysis:	−1
	(weight = 1)
Utilitarianism-based analyses	
Act utilitarian/cost-benefit analysis:	+1
	(weight = 2)
Rule utilitarian analysis:	−1
	(weight = 2)
Respect for persons analyses:	
Rights-based analysis:	+1
	(weight = 1)
Pareto efficiency analyses:	−1
	(weight = 1)
$\sum t_n w_n = (+5) + (-4) = +1$:	
Thus, it is ethical to proceed based on this analysis	

Therefore, Abena decides that, though there are definite drawbacks to the plan, it would be ethical to proceed. So, the addition of weights in this scenario did not change the overall conclusion, though the weights did weaken the confidence in the overall solution.

The last part of the weighting process to discuss is whether or not these schemes will work if the values being summed are not binary. Up until this point, we have really focused on the analyses providing a definitive ethical or unethical determination, in the parlance of the conclusion process, a +1 (ethical) or a −1 (unethical). When we sum these conclusions up, with or without weights, we create a score between +9 and −9 with the sign of the value really being what we are using to consider the overall conclusion on the hypothesis to be ethical or unethical. When we are considering the null hypothesis, the signs are adequate, but if instead of a satisficing answer, we were seeking a more optimal answer, for example, if we were comparing more than one hypothesis pair to each other, the actual magnitude of the assessment could play a role in ranking which of the hypotheses was considered the best solution. And it is not just the weighting schemes that would affect that, the actual judgments from each of the analyses can also be expressed in non-binary format (for example, you could use scores between −1 and 1). A given hypothesis could receive a more descriptive conclusion, such as absolutely unethical, or mostly unethical, or fairly ethical, etc. Additionally, if the hypothesized action didn't directly cause the harm or the benefit, but instead only increased the likelihood that the given effect would happen to the audience, then the judgment output from the analysis could take into account the confidence that you have in the effect being realized or its numerical probability. These scores could be derived much as you might derive a risk assessment; through the multiplication of the magnitude of the outcome by the likelihood of that outcome occurring. These non-binary judgment values can be multiplied by the weights just as the binary values were and the conclusions can be generated. This concept of the judgments coming from the analyses not being completely defined by the ethical and unethical values alone leads us to another method that can be used to determine our final conclusion and even help us find alternative solutions when the hypothesis we are working on fails to meet our ethical standards. This alternate method for coming to a conclusion is covered in the next section.

5.4.3 Drawing a Line – The Method of Casuistry

There is another method that we recommend when you are faced with an especially tough set of contradicting analyses: the method of casuistry. Casuistry is a very old method for reasoning across multiple dimensions in a very visual and natural way.[5] It is a good way to visualize your way through a situation where there may not be

[5] Casuistry gained quite a bit of notoriety through Blaise Pascal's criticism of its use by the Jesuits in the 1600s as a tool for helping absolve the wealthy of their sins by using its ability to help rationalize flexibility in the moral absolutes. In fact, if you look in many dictionaries to this day, the definition of casuistry is not flattering. The revival in the use of casuistry came in the 1990s with the publishing of the book *The Abuse of Casuistry: A History of Moral Reasoning* (Jonsen et al., 1990) where they argued it wasn't the method per se but its usage in those situations. Its use has blossomed since them in both the moral reasoning and artificial intelligence realms.

clear black and white solution, much like the situation you probably find yourself in with your analyses. It is the method's efficacy in being able to help one find a line in the gray area between the ethical absolutes that has earned it one of its other designations: line drawing analysis (Harris et al., 2000). It is also known as the powerful algorithm used in many case-based reasoning systems, and we will look at how this method can help us come to a final conclusion in cases where your weighting schemes tried in the previous step weren't enough to complete the process.

The line-drawing method is relatively straightforward in its setup when used to help conclude after the analyses have been run. You will begin by setting up a chart as shown in the figure below.

Each analysis gets its own row, also known as a dimension in case-based reasoning (each row is one dimension of a multi-dimensional comparison[6]). Each row gets its own continuum that stretches from the left to the right of the chart. This continuum represents the area between the two extreme positions we are going to call the positive paradigm and the negative paradigm. The positive paradigm is a visualization of the value in the row in its most positive terms. In this instance, since the rows are representing the analyses we have completed, the most positive an analysis can be is that its result says the action is morally permissible. The negative paradigm represents the visualization of the most negative outcome for that row; moral impermissibility.

The next step of the analysis is to evaluate each row and determine where on the continuum your conclusion from the analysis in the row falls. This is where the explanation of each conclusion and our exhortation to not always describe the outcome in absolute terms of yes or no. You have to ask yourself if the conclusion you reached was uncontroversial for that analysis, or if there is something about the conclusion that leaves some doubt as to the perfectness of the conclusion. You might be saying to yourself, that according to the analysis, the hypothesized solution is morally permissible, but it isn't quite the perfect permissibility because you had to make some concessions in the analysis or the probability of the positive values occurring as a result of your solution are not 100 %. This little bit of doubt or uncertainty is exactly what can be expressed in the line-drawing analysis. If your hypothesized solution was analyzed as having absolute moral permissibility, then you would put an 'X' on the far left of the continuum directly under the "Positive Paradigm" label, as shown below (Figs. 5.2 and 5.3).

If the conclusion of the analysis is the absolutely most morally impermissible outcome, then you would put the 'X' at the other extreme as shown below (Fig. 5.4).

Most conclusions will not fall at these extremes, but will end up somewhere in the continuum between the extreme endpoints. If you had a conclusion that was

[6]For those of you with a geometrical bent, you can imagine the line-drawing analysis as a N-dimensional space where N is the number of rows (dimensions) in your analysis. Joining the positive and negative paradigms to each other will outline an N-dimensional hypercube. As such, the absolute best solution is located at the positive apex point and the worst solution is located at the negative apex. Your solution, when mapped, will be located somewhere in the space bounded by this cube nearer to one apex or the other.

Analyses	+ Positive Paradigm	Negative Paradigm -
Expected Reciprocity	. . . .	. . . .
New York Times	. . . .	. . . .
Anticipatory Self-Appraisal	. . . .	. . . .
Aggregate Application	. . . .	. . . .
Act Utilitarian Analysis	. . . .	. . . .
Rule Utilitarian Analysis		
Cost-Benefit Analysis	. . . .	. . . .
Rights-Based Analysis	. . . .	. . . .
Pareto Efficiency Analysis		

Fig. 5.2 Line-drawing template

Analyses	+ Positive Paradigm	Negative Paradigm -
Expected Reciprocity	X	. . . .
New York Times	. . . .	. . . .
Anticipatory Self-Appraisal	. . . .	. . . .
Aggregate Application	. . . .	. . . .
Act Utilitarian Analysis	. . . .	. . . .
Rule Utilitarian Analysis		
Cost-Benefit Analysis	. . . .	. . . .
Rights-Based Analysis	. . . .	. . . .
Pareto Efficiency Analysis		

Fig. 5.3 Line-drawing analysis: positive paradigm

Analyses	+ Positive Paradigm	Negative Paradigm -
Expected Reciprocity	. . . .	 X
New York Times	. . . .	. . . .
Anticipatory Self-Appraisal	. . . .	. . . .
Aggregate Application	. . . .	. . . .
Act Utilitarian Analysis	. . . .	. . . .
Rule Utilitarian Analysis		
Cost-Benefit Analysis	. . . .	. . . .
Rights-Based Analysis	. . . .	. . . .
Pareto Efficiency Analysis		

Fig. 5.4 Line-drawing analysis: negative paradigm

Analyses	+ Positive Paradigm	Negative Paradigm -
Expected Reciprocity	. . . . X	. . . .
New York Times	. . . .	. . . .
Anticipatory Self-Appraisal	. . . .	. . . .
Aggregate Application	. . . .	. . . .
Act Utilitarian Analysis	. . . .	. . . .
Rule Utilitarian Analysis		
Cost-Benefit Analysis	. . . .	. . . .
Rights-Based Analysis	. . . .	. . . .
Pareto Efficiency Analysis		

Fig. 5.5 Line-drawing analysis: generally positive

Analyses	+ Positive Paradigm	Negative Paradigm -
Expected Reciprocity	. . . .	X. . . . .
New York Times	. . . .	. . . .
Anticipatory Self-Appraisal	. . . .	. . . .
Aggregate Application	. . . .	. . . .
Act Utilitarian Analysis	. . . .	. . . .
Rule Utilitarian Analysis		
Cost-Benefit Analysis	. . . .	. . . .
Rights-Based Analysis	. . . .	. . . .
Pareto Efficiency Analysis		

Fig. 5.6 Line-drawing analysis: morally neutral

morally permissible, but there was some uncertainty, you would put your 'X' on the chart for that row in the positive (left) half of the continuum and you would use your judgment to determine how close to the positive paradigm to put it. An example of a generally positive conclusion being placed on the chart is shown below (Fig. 5.5).

There is one special case, and that is the position of morally neutral. Any analysis that produced a conclusion that was not helpful (i.e., provided no guidance one way or the other) would fall in this category. The location for moral neutrality on this chart should be fairly obvious; the center line as shown below (Fig. 5.6).

You would then go through each of the analyses (i.e., rows) and make a judgment about where its conclusion falls on the continuum. We have included an example of a completed chart below (Fig. 5.7).

So a number of analyses came out positive, a number came out negative, and two did not have a meaningful conclusion one way or the other. The final conclusion can then come from some visual analysis of the chart. One method we like to use as a first pass is to look at the chart and pretend it is balanced on a fulcrum centered right under morally neutral axis on the chart. You then imagine that the chart tips one way or the other based on the heavy 'X's (you could view this as a form of weighting).

Analyses	+ Positive Paradigm	Negative Paradigm -
Expected Reciprocity	. . . . X	. . . .
New York Times	. . . .	. . . . . X . . . . . .
Anticipatory Self-Appraisal	 X	. . . .
Aggregate Application	. . . X	. . . .
Act Utilitarian Analysis	. . . .	 X
Rule Utilitarian Analysis	. . . .	. . . X . . . .
Cost-Benefit Analysis	. . . .	. X . . . .
Rights-Based Analysis	 X	. . . .
Pareto Efficiency Analysis	 X	. . . .

Fig. 5.7 Line-drawing analysis: complete

The direction the chart tips based on this weight is the direction that the analysis "leans" in terms of an overall conclusion. Now, it may not be obvious from that first test which way it will lean, and if that is the case you can dive into the analyses themselves. We like to look for any conclusions that are nearly paradigmatic one way or the other. For example, in the chart above, you can see that the Act Utilitarian Analysis conclusion is essentially at the negative paradigm, while nothing on the positive side is even close to the paradigmatically positive conclusion. This would be a good sign that this analysis probably should come to the negative conclusion, as the negative conclusion seems much more definitive for at least one of the analyses. If nothing jumps out at you as tipping the decision one way or the other, then you will need to do dig deeper into the analyses:

- You might want to go back to the analyses and ensure your conclusion is as firm as you have portrayed it in the analysis.
- You might want to add some more dimensions to your analysis. Is there are issue with feasibility for you hypothesized solution? Do you think you really can execute it? Have you underestimated/overestimated the impediments you might face in implementing your solution? Is cost a factor in implementing your solution? Look at adding an extra dimension to help tip the conclusion one way or the other.
- You may need to do some soul searching and realize that there is no good solution to your problem and you will have to just make a decision based on your experience and instinct and live with the consequences.
- Or, you may just need to try a different solution (see the next section).

In the end, you will need to use your judgment to determine what the conclusion is for a given chart, but likely this one act of judgment is easier and less biased then just coming to the overall moral judgment in a snap, off-the-cuff way. But that description fits more than just the line-drawing analysis – it is the theme of the entire process we have outlined here. By slowing down, analyzing your frame, proposing a hypothesis, breaking the problem into more easily analyzable chunks, being objective, and then aggregating the partial judgments into one overall final conclusion for that hypothesis, you will end up at a much more defendable and reasoned argument for your actions. We cannot guarantee that you will always perfect decisions using this method, as biases can always creep in and the future always brings surprises. However, if you follow a process to make your decisions, you will be able to sleep comfortably in your knowledge that you did your best to think through all of the consequences and that you had a well-reasoned argument for your actions.

5.5 So Your Proposed Solution Is Unethical- Reformulating the Hypothesis

One last thing to consider in the overall process is that it is not a one-shot game. That is, if your first hypothesis doesn't end up with a positive overall assessment, that is not the end of the game. You should generate a new hypothesis and commence the process again for that hypothesis. To make it easier on the second time through, don't start with a brand-new hypothesis; instead, make it a variation of the one you just analyzed. The variation you introduce should be informed by the results of the analyses. If, like in our sample chart above, the results for the hypothesis were fairly balanced except for one analysis, then when you generate your new hypothesis, do so with an eye towards minimizing the aspects of it that caused the result to be so negative for that test. In this way, the line drawing chart can serve one final purpose, that of helping to shape the next hypothesis so that you get a better result in the next pass through the methodology and in the end have a better solution to the problem you face.

5.6 Conclusion

Now that the discussion of the methodology is complete, some of you may feel frustrated: wasn't this book supposed to tell you what was ethical? However, hopefully the use of the process (shown fully in Fig. 5.2) has demonstrated why the opposite – that shades of grey are dominant – is the norm. This book is not concerned with finding the only ethical decision, but in helping you determine the most ethical one based on a thorough understanding of the contents and biases of the situation and the application of different tests. Further, though the decision to reject or fail to reject the hypothesis that the behavior is unethical is a binary one, the degrees of certainty that this decision reflects are just as myriad here as they are in econometrics.

Perhaps most importantly, this text does not eclipse the reader's responsibility to thoroughly explore and test the situation. The ethical responsibility of an economist and public policy professional cannot be outsourced to someone other than the

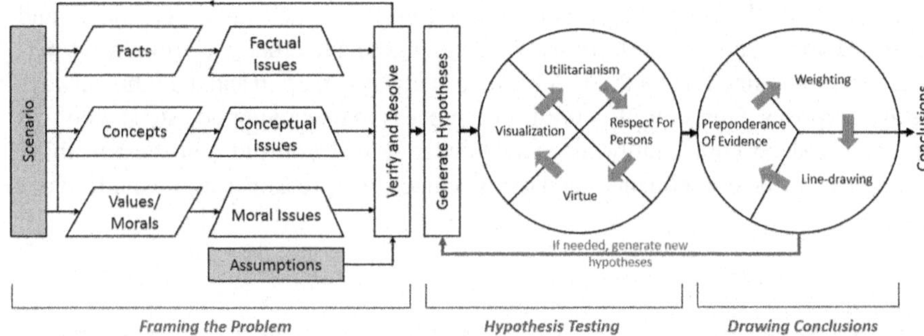

Fig. 5.8 Ethical decision-making methodology

maker. One of the reasons economists were mocked in The *Inside Job* was over the belief that the objectivity of the mathematics itself was transferrable to the design of the model and analysis of the findings. The existence of a code of ethics or decision-methodology does not absolve anyone of their responsibility, just the same as the notion of the invisible hand or the use of a DSGE model does not automatically validate our results. The description of the original conditions, choice of ethical tests, assessment of their results, resolution of any disputes, and interpretation of the conclusions all fall on the decision-maker. This book, like the theory or the model, is here to guide and improve the process while providing a road map for others to follow, should you need to provide it. The map is helpful, often crucial, but the decision to put one step after another down the path of improvement for our profession is yours (Fig. 5.8).

Discussion Questions

1. Which of the conflict resolution styles feels more "natural" to you? Why do you think that is, or what about the style makes you prefer it?
2. What are some difficulties that you can see in the utilization of the offered conflict resolution methods? How can these be overcome or, if this is not possible, at least accommodated?
3. It is highly unlikely that all ethical tests will come to the same conclusion. Why is this?

References

Frey, B. S. (1994). Direct democracy: Politico-economic lessons from Swiss experience. *The American Economic Review, 84*(2), 338–342.

Harris, C. E., Pritchard, M. S., & Rabins, M. J. (2000). *Engineering ethics: Concepts and cases* (2nd ed.). Belmont, CA: Wadsworth Publishing Company.

Jonsen, A., & Toulmin, S. (1990). *The abuse of casuistry: A history of moral reasoning*. Berkeley, CA: U. California Press.

Mintz, A. (2004). How do leaders make decisions?- A poliheuristic perspective. *Journal of Conflict Resolution, 48*(1), 3–13. Sage Publications.

National Society of Professional Engineers. (2007, July). *Code of ethics for engineers*. Alexandria, VA: NSPE.

Wholey, J. S., Hatry, H. P., & Newcomer, K. E. (2010). *Handbook of practical program evaluation* (Vol. 19). San Francisco, CA: Jossey-Bass.

Chapter 6
Case Studies

Donald R. Searing and Elizabeth A.M. Searing

"If you would convince a man that he does wrong, do right. But do not care to convince him. Men will believe what they see. Let them see."

~Henry David Thoreau (1817–1862)

Abstract This chapter includes two case studies which utilize the ethical decision-making methodology. The first case involves an academic setting with an ethical situation involving proper research behavior; it is relatively uncomplicated, so additional alternate hypotheses from potential later iterations of the methodology are included. The second case is more complex and deals directly with some of the larger issues currently in public and nonprofit policy, such as what a policy needs to accomplish before it is considered justified.

Keywords Case studies • Professional ethics • Academic ethics

6.1 Case Study 1: Frederick

6.1.1 Introduction

Four years ago, Frederick graduated from a reputable doctoral program in political science and landed his first job as an assistant professor at ReQua University. He's responsible for teaching one or two courses every semester, but one of the reasons he chose to work at ReQua was because of its reputation as a leading research university. There are six other members of the political science department: two

D.R. Searing, PhD
CEO and Principal Scientist, Syncere Systems, Altamont, NY, USA
e-mail: dsearing@synceresystems.com

E.A.M. Searing, PhD (✉)
Assistant Professor, Department of Public Administration and Policy, Rockefeller College of Public Affairs and Policy, University at Albany – State University of New York, 305 Milne Hall, 135 Western Avenue, Albany, New York, USA
e-mail: esearing@albany.edu

E.A.M. Searing, D.R. Searing (eds.), *Practicing Professional Ethics in Economics and Public Policy*, DOI 10.1007/978-94-017-7306-5_6

assistants, two associates, and two full professors. One of the full professors, Dr. Bekah Gregson, is the department head, while the other full professor had been the department head prior to Dr. Gregson. Everyone is friendly to each other – no one goes out together for beer after work, but it seems to Frederick that everyone appears to enjoy coming into the office.

Frederick has been generally on track with his publications and passed his third-year review a few months ago, but he was told by the department chair that he really needed to branch outside of his narrow subspecialty and into the larger field journals. He has a couple projects in the beginning-to-middle stages, so he talked to some colleagues and thought that he could re-target a couple of them for a more general journal. After getting one that he thought had good potential polished enough to potentially submit, he sends it to Dr. Gregson for her input on the paper quality and the chances of being placed in one of the major field journals.

When they meet to discuss the paper, her reply unsettles him. She has lukewarm, but constructive things to say about the paper: expand the literature review in a particular direction, tighten up the regressions, spend a little longer on policy implications. But what concerns him is that she says that, in her opinion, his paper will not make it past the editor's desk at any of the major journals. "Too fringe," she had said. And he was still too unknown. She said it would be a waste of time that he could put to use on better things.

At the end of the meeting, she suggests that perhaps, with her name on the article as well, it might give him the credibility the paper needs in order to pass that first hurdle and come under more serious consideration, where his paper would have the opportunity to shine. She said that this is often done with grad students and young faculty – in fact, her mentor had helped her land her first major journal publication in the same way. Frederick thanks her for the opportunity and says he'll get back to her after he thinks about the future of the paper.

That evening, Frederick takes a closer look at the publications of the faculty and graduate students in the political science department at ReQua. Sure enough, Dr. Gregson is listed as an author on the first publication or two of almost every new faculty member and student that graduated. He also talks to a couple of his friends who are already faculty in chemistry and virology, and both say they have long lists of co-authors, with the final person listed being the person who runs the lab. But Frederick also vaguely remembers what he learned in his state-mandated ethics training prior to graduation: practices such as "honorary" authorship – where someone is listed as an author despite not making a qualifying contribution – were discouraged in the social sciences. At least, he had been told this by the ethics instructor. Troubled, he wonders what to do next.

6.1.2 *Framing (See Chap. 4)*

6.1.2.1 Facts

The table of facts below is an accurate reflection of the objectively-known, incontrovertible facts surrounding the situation being analyzed.

#	Fact	Source
1	Frederick is an assistant political science professor	Case
2	Frederick has worked at ReQua University for almost 3 years	Case
3	Bekah Gregson is Frederick's department head	Case
4	Frederick has several papers he is trying to publish	Case
5	Publishing papers is necessary for Frederick to advance	Case
6	Bekah told Frederick that he needed to publish some of his papers in larger journals	Case
7	Bekah told Frederick his paper is "too fringe"	Case
8	Bekah told Frederick that having a more established researcher, like herself, listed as a coauthor on the paper might make it more palatable to the journal	Case
9	Frederick learns that Bekah is a coauthor on all of the first and second papers published by junior faculty while she has been department head	Case
10	Frederick took an ethics class that dealt with something like this issue	Case
11	Political Science is a social science	Common knowledge

6.1.2.2 Factual Issues

The table of factual issues below is a list of the known bits of information that are factual in nature but are controversial or unsubstantiated. A good example of this type of issue is an unknown future effect of a given action. Your goal should be to resolve these issues through additional research and turn them into facts, or through making an educated assumption of its resolution.

#	Factual issue	Assumed resolution
1	Frederick's papers are publishable in larger journals without a more well-known co-author	If Frederick knew whether or not this was the case, it would eliminate some of the concern about this situation. That being said, this is not likely to be known without submitting the paper
		This may point us in the direction of a possible solution, though

(continued)

#	Factual issue	Assumed resolution
2	Bekah did not contribute to the authoring of the papers in question	From the information in the case, we are assuming that she did not contribute to the papers in any material way
		Though this may also point us in the direction of a possible solution- with the idea of actually engaging Bekah in revising the paper and giving her the opportunity to "earn" the co-authorship
3	Having non-contributors listed as coauthor is not an acceptable practice in the social sciences	It would seem to us that Frederick isn't quite sure about this fact based on his discussions about other fields and his vague memory of an ethics course
		We would suggest that this is an area where some additional research by Frederick would help resolve this issue:
		Frederick should ask a colleague at another school if this common practice
		Frederick could find the notes he had from his ethics course and freshen up his understanding of "honorary authorship" and whether or not it is permissible in some form or the other (these resolutions are linked to conceptual and moral issues below)
		Frederick could inquire at one of the journals if this is an allowed practice
		Frederick should consult with his professional organization ombudsman or look at their code of ethics to see whether or not this is a topic that is already covered
4	What will happen to Frederick in terms of retribution from Bekah if he submits his paper without her as a co-author?	Frederick knew that she would not retaliate against him for not including him as a co-author, his decision would be much easier. His assumption from the narrative is clearly that he is fairly sure she would retaliate, thus creating the dilemma
5	If Frederick submits his paper to the smaller journals and is accepted, will this be acceptable with regards to his 3-year progress review?	Frederick might ask other faculty in his department, including the former department head, to see if this might be an acceptable approach
6	Is Frederick's work "fringe"?	Based on the definition of "fringe" below, we will assume that Frederick's work is out of the mainstream and thus less likely to be published in the mainstream journals in his field
7	If Frederick allows Bekah to be an honorary coauthor and it is discovered, will that impact his career or her career?	Again, if we knew this we would not have quite such a dilemma. If no punishment would be meted out for Frederick's behavior, and this was known, then Frederick's decision would be straightforward- allow the authorship, like they do in other fields
		That being said, as honesty is the cornerstone of academic research, we will assume that Frederick's allowing of Bekah to be a co-author without providing material or qualifying contributions would be akin to falsifying one's research and thus would lead to punitive measures for both he and Bekah

6.1.2.3 Concepts

The table of concepts below is a list of the concepts and their definitions that bear on the situation at hand. This section is used to clearly define these concepts so that someone reading your analysis understands the concepts and definitions being used in your later analyses.

#	Concept	Definition
1	Co-authorship	From the narrative it is clear there are different standards or definitions of what co-authorship means. In certain sciences, co-authorship is defined broadly to include those that materially contribute to the creation of the paper/work as well as those whose contribution is the creation and maintenance of the laboratory facility being utilized in the research
		That being said, it is clear the Frederick's interpretation of this concept includes only those who have had a material, "qualifying" contribution to the paper. What is defined as a qualifying contribution will be discussed as an issue below
2	Fringe	The definition of fringe in this scenario is any concept/work outside of the primary focus of the known journals in political science. Which journals are known as mainstream for their fields is a well-defined and known quantity in almost all academic fields
3	Honorary authorship	In the narrative this is defined as "where someone is listed as an author despite not making a qualifying contribution"

6.1.2.4 Conceptual Issues

The table of conceptual issues below is a list of the concepts that bear on the situation at hand that have ambiguous or controversial definitions. This section is used to state the definitions assumed in the rest of the analyses. They are stated here to clearly outline any controversial definitions separate from their use within the moral analyses.

#	**Conceptual issue**	**Assumed definition**
1	Qualifying contribution	A qualifying contribution will be defined for this analysis as having written at least one section of the paper/work OR having been involved in or responsible for the formulation of the hypotheses or analysis methods

6.1.2.5 Morals/Values

The table of morals below is a list of the values that will be brought to bear on the situation at hand in the subsequent analyses. This is a good location to clearly elucidate the pieces of a code of ethics (especially a professional code of ethics) that will be brought to bear in this analysis. For example, in most engineering codes, it clearly states that the public's health, safety, and welfare are the paramount virtues and this section of the document would be where you would outline the values that will be used in the analyses.

#	Moral/value	Source
1	Researchers should be honest (academic integrity)	General professional/academic codes of ethics (e.g., tenets of academic integrity). The scientific enterprise is built around the integrity of its participants that prevents fabrication of results, manipulation of processes, etc. It is also likely that Frederick has pledged to be honest in his research in the employment contract he has with his university
2	Taking credit for others work is wrong	General morality. Taking credit for other people's work is a form of theft and is therefore wrong (it wrongs the actual creator of the work)

6.1.2.6 Moral/Value Issues

The table of moral/value issues below is a list of the values that while being followed by the decision-maker in the situation are controversial in nature. These are moral conundrums whose interpretations and proposed answers can change the outcome of the analyses.

#	Moral/valueissue	Assumed rule/resolution
1	Is "honorary authorship" acceptable in Frederick's field?	While Frederick reveals that he believes it is not acceptable in his field to allow this practice, he is unsure, as it is acceptable to some degree in other fields
		If we were in Frederick's shoes, we would encourage him to

6.1.3 *Ethical Analysis (See Chap. 5)*

Now that you have framed your decision with the information you know from your initial analysis, you are ready to start the ethical analysis phase of your decision-making process. First, define your hypothesis with a null reflecting a status quo of unethical behavior for the proposed action; also, specify an alternative hypothesis of appropriate scope for the situation. Second, you will define your audiences (i.e., those affected by the action being proposed in the hypothesis). Third, you will process some set of the analyses, basing your evaluations and observations on the data resolved and stated in your framing. Fourth, you will interpret the results of the analyses and select the most ethical course of action. As a note, we have included in this simple case the additional hypotheses which would have come around in the exercise.

6.1.3.1 Generate the Hypotheses

There are two generally two hypotheses: the null hypothesis, which is the assumption of an unethical status quo or assumed course of action, and the alternative hypothesis. However, since this is a relatively simple case, we have included what would be the product of future iterations in this analysis. In other words, though we encourage you right now to test the null hypothesis of the action being unethical versus its counterfactual, you should become skilled enough with time to complete a few rounds of iterations in your head. Below, the first alternate hypothesis is the counterfactual to the null. The second is a more extreme potential course of action that we could evaluate if we determine (or sense) that the null will not be rejected. The third is an option that would have been arrived at during even later iterations and reflects the synthesis of several elements. However, even hypotheses that come about after a great deal of iterations should still undergo testing. This case study will present the tests from multiple iterations of the case study for the sake of space.

The null hypothesis
Adding Bekah as an honorary author on scholarly papers in order to get them published in mainstream journals and cultivate a professional relationship with Bekah is unethical

The alternative hypotheses
1. Adding Bekah as an honorary author on scholarly papers in order to get them published in mainstream journals and cultivate a professional relationship with Bekah is not unethical
2. Frederick can go to the Dean and report Bekah's behavior and try to have her removed as department head
3. Frederick asks Bekah to review his paper and help author/revise existing sections to make his papers more acceptable for the mainstream journals, thus getting Bekah to contribute in a meaningful, qualifying way and thus earning the co-authorship she desires

6.1.3.2 Determine the Audiences

The audiences of any given hypothesis set are all of the entities with moral standing that are affected by the proposed hypotheses. Depending on your moral philosophy these can either be limited to people only or to other living creatures or to large scale systems like the environment. Who you include is really a reflection of your answer to the moral issue surrounding who has moral agency (i.e., someone or something that is free to make their own moral decisions and be affected by them) and who has moral patiency (i.e., someone or something that is not at the level of autonomy to be considered a moral agent, but yet can still be affected by the decisions made around them).

Audience	Description
Frederick	Faculty member at ReQua University approaching his review date
Bekah	Frederick's department head at ReQua University
Other professors in the department who have added Bekah as author to their papers	The other professors in the department who have already accepted Bekah's offer
Future professors in the department	These are professors in the department who might be asked to provide the honorary authorship credit in the future

6.1.3.3 Visualization: Expected Reciprocity Analysis

Audience	Audience analysis
Bekah	If Frederick puts himself in Bekah's place, here is how he would interpret the various hypothesized actions:
	Null Hypothesis (refuse the unethical offer)- Frederick has to consider whether he would be accepting of a professor reporting to him that would not accede to his wishes if he made this request. Frederick would likely be upset that his direct report was not doing as they were told, but he might respect them for taking a stand for academic integrity
	First alternative (accept coauthorship) – Frederick would, based on the concerns he raised in the narrative, would likely not put a professor in his department in the same position. Although, this may be due to the fact that Frederick has an incomplete or unrealistic picture of the concerns and struggles related to this position (e.g., the department head may be being pressured by the dean or other school officials to publish despite the other responsibilities that are placed on them, leading to this honorary authorship being the only viable means to resolve that situation)
	The second alternative (go to the dean)- Frederick would likely be upset if one of his direct reports went around him in the "chain of command" and exposed his request for honorary authorship. He would likely feel betrayed and possibly ashamed that this request was brought to the attention of his boss
	The last alternative (offer the opportunity to provide a contribution to the paper)- Frederick would likely be somewhat upset that his direct report refused to provide honorary authorship, but likely would understand their argument for academic integrity and appreciate the opportunity to get the desired outcome (a publication credit) with a little extra work and both their honors intact
Other professors who have already provided honorary authorship	If Frederick puts himself in the shoes of the other professors in the department, then:
	The Null Hypothesis- Frederick, as the other professor, will likely respect the professor making the stand against Bekah, but will likely be upset that they did not and be worried that if this situation escalates, their prior actions will be brought into question
	First alternative- Frederick will not be affected if the new professor accedes to Bekah's request
	Second alternative- Frederick, as the other professor, will be very upset as a direct escalation of this situation to the dean will probably open up lines of inquiry into Bekah's behavior in the past and will likely expose his prior granting of honorary authorship to her- making him look bad
	Third alternative- Frederick, as the other professor, will likely be unaffected by this course of action as there will be no affect or inquiries necessarily into their previous behavior

(continued)

Audience	Audience analysis
Future professors	If Frederick puts himself in the shoes of the future professors in the department, he will have little to lose in any case where Frederick does not give in to Bekah's request, in that they will not be there for any fallout, but they will have much to gain in that they will not have to face this same situation with her in the future
	Frederick, as a future professor, would most likely find himself facing this same ethical situation if nothing was done by the professor facing the situation now. He would likely want this situation to be resolved before he had to face it, and thus he would prefer a solution that resolves it in such a fashion that Bekah will not make the same request in the future (likely alternative 1 and 2, and possibly 3)

Conclusion
This analysis provides anything but a crystal clear conclusion, as the effect of Frederick putting himself into Bekah's position or even that of the professors who had previously agreed to her demands is that he also would like to not be caught asking or caught acceding to the request. Frederick's feelings on academic integrity also gets in the way of this analysis as it is unlikely that he would have ever made this request of a new professor in the first place (which is in itself telling, and it is likely we will see this issue pop up in other areas of this analysis)

6.1.3.4 Visualization: New York Times Analysis

Proposed headline- for null hypothesis
Professor citing academic integrity concerns denied tenure after he refuses to grant department head authorship credit

Analysis for headline
This headline does capture the essence of what is being asked of Frederick, and it has pretty obvious negative estimates of what happens. There is a lack of integrity by the professor and the department head requesting the credit

Proposed headline- for alternative 1 and 2
Professor grants department head authorship credit despite the lack of a contribution!
Full investigation called for by Dean at ReQua University after academic integrity concerns are raised by professor

Analysis for headline
These headlines do have some positive connotations to them although there are the negative outcomes related in each regarding what happens to Frederick. While the actions outlined might seem extreme, this is the sort of extrapolation this analysis calls for (as this is a headline). It may not actually turn out that Frederick is fired, or a full-blown public investigation would necessarily happen, but it is not outside the realm of outcomes that could be reasonably expected in this situation given Frederick's hypothesized actions. It is this sort of extrapolation that helps hone in on the problems with these hypotheses; in both of these scenarios, there are consequences for Frederick. He is taking a moral stand for academic integrity, but it is not without cost to him, which is something that should be taken into account as an effect of these hypotheses

Proposed headline- for alternative 3
Professor and department head publish paper together

Analysis for headline
This headline is really not even news and I think all involved would be fine with the fact that this headline was published in the paper. That being said, this outcome is based on the assumption that Bekah goes along with Frederick's suggestion that she actually contribute to the paper. If she does not, then the situation will revert back to one in which the null hypothesis and the first two alternatives become the only available options

Conclusion
We feel this analysis is fairly clear. Academic Integrity is a large concern in academia and should be taken quite seriously, as the outcomes outlined above represent quite possible outcomes (investigations, etc.) of the null and the first two alternatives. In each of the options, someone or possibly everyone involved in the situation may end up with negative consequences and no one will look good
The analysis shows that the third alternative, which is not as confrontational as the other alternatives and has the distinction of trying to find a way to satisfy the concerns of all parties, has the opportunity to defuse this situation. That being said, it will also be the option that requires the most work by all parties involved

6.1.3.5 Visualization: Anticipatory Self-Appraisal Analysis

Analysis
If Frederick rejects the null hypothesis, then all of his apprehension and concern expressed before he made the decision will continue to be unresolved in him. He may attempt to rationalize it away as something he just had to do to get closer to the tenure he desires, but he will always wonder what would have happened had he stood up for his belief in academic integrity and held his department head to those standards
If Frederick is openly confrontational over this issue, he may find himself having made enemies of powerful people in his life, and may find himself unable to reach his goals while still at that institution (and possibly have difficulties finding a position elsewhere if he needs recommendations)
We think Frederick would have the best vision of himself in the future if he is able to hold onto his integrity and yet still find a way to work with his department head in a constructive manner like alternative 3 provides. Frederick would keep his integrity, help his boss find her integrity, and provide a way for everyone involved to get what they want (which will also make Frederick feel good about himself)

Conclusion
Little can come out of <u>just</u> being openly confrontational without providing alternative actions, while providing someone with a reasonable alternative while confronting them usually leads to a better outcome. This path, though, usually requires finesse in convincing the other person that it is in both of your best interests to find a compromise. The other benefit of this approach is that you do have the other confrontational options to fall back upon

(continued)

Conclusion
So, this analysis would point towards alternative 3 as the best approach for Frederick's future vision of himself. He would keep his integrity, likely get published, likely earn his boss' respect for a solution that gets her what she needs, and satisfaction that he successfully managed to create a win-win situation. And in the worst case, he also has the other confrontational options to fall back upon

6.1.3.6 Visualization: Aggregate Application Analysis (Categorical Imperative)

Use the tables below to develop your proposed universal rule and to capture its analysis. Remember, we are testing the underlying premise of the null hypothesis, so it can be framed in a positive fashion. Be sure to base your analysis on the data from your frame so you have a solid argument.

Proposed universal rule- for the null hypothesis
People who hold power over contributors to a work should always be given contributory credit on the works of the actual contributors

Analysis for rule
Referring back to the concept of contribution that was discussed earlier, this rule would contradict the whole essence of the definition. A contributor is someone who provides meaningful content for the work, and this rule would rank the bosses of those people who are contributing as also contributors. If you extend this rule to the next level, what about the boss' boss. If the author's boss is by this rule a contributor, then so is their boss and their boss, ad infinitum. Each level of boss would provide less and less of a contribution due to their distance from the work in question
So the rule itself leads to a contradiction in terms of the definition of a contribution

Conclusion
This analysis is used to show that the null hypothesis itself should stand. This analysis is good at getting to the essence of the conflict in this situation and that what Frederick is being asked to do is definitely not something he should consider doing. That essence can be defined as on one hand conceding to Bekah's proposition and giving her credit and on the other hand rejecting her proposition. The alternatives all fall on the side of opposing Bekah's proposition, they differ in the method by which Frederick would go about doing that, as some of them are openly confrontational, while others seek a way to bring Bekah around to the conclusion that the credit is not a good idea. Thus, the conflict being examined in this rule is whether or not the null hypothesis is an acceptable action or not. The rule and its analysis are pretty clear on that fact

6.1.3.7 Virtue Analysis

Use the tables below to describe your desired virtues or admired exemplars and your analyses related to each of the hypotheses as it relates to the virtue or exemplar.

Virtues/exemplars
Academic Integrity- This was brought up in terms of the Moral values we wanted to bring to bear on this case. It is central to the whole academic enterprise. Without integrity in our research and publications, knowledge cannot be built upon and no advances can be made in any sort of trusted fashion. Research is by its nature a relatively solitary process in its initial phases, and the darker sides of our personalities can influence our outcomes through plagiarism, cherry-picking or falsifying results for our experiments to match our pet theories, etc. It is only through open and honest communication that we can be assured that the results we are producing are correct and not subject to our own biases. All academics involved in the enterprise should strive for the highest levels of integrity and openness
Professionalism- All of us working with others in organizations large or small expect those who work around us to be professionals, that is be trustworthy, truthful, respectful, and responsible. Organizations only ever function well if the people who make them up exhibit these virtues, which we will lump collectively into the concept of professionalism. This concept as a whole is a virtue that can and should be strived for by all people working in organizations

Analysis
As has been shown above in other analyses, the idea of academic integrity is challenged by the first alternative hypothesis. Giving people credit for work they have not contributed too in a meaningful way directly contradicts the idea of open and honest communications between academics. So this is yet another analysis that sides with the null hypothesis and would point in the direction of the later alternatives being a better moral course to steer
With regards to professionalism, we will first point out that Bekah's request is in itself disrespectful of Frederick and untruthful, lending us to conclude that Bekah's actions themselves are not only controversial for their affront to academic integrity, but in that they are also unprofessional
But we include Professionalism here for additional effect, in that we do need to continue to be able to decide which of the alternatives is the best course of action for Frederick. Confronting Bekah and explaining why he cannot give her honorary authorship credit is the root of each of these alternatives since that is the core issue at odds with the null hypothesis. We now come to the method for confronting her. Bekah still is the department head and Frederick's boss, so she is due some respect and deference due to her position within the organization relative to Frederick's and sue to the influence she can have over Frederick's future. One of the tenets of professionalism described above is that of respect for your coworkers. That being said, the idea that Frederick should immediately go to the Dean (alternative 2) would be disrespectful to Bekah. Frederick should raise his concerns to her first. He should be open and honest with her as to his ethical concerns regarding academic integrity. He should give her the chance to see the error of her ways, or to provide the rationale for her request. If after this discussion with her, he feels that she is still asking him to do something he is uncomfortable with, then he should pursue other options (e.g., calling the ethics hotline, talking with an ombudsman, and talking to the dean) for raising this issue above Bekah. But, he should discuss it with her first, she is owed that respect. So while alternative 2 still remains on the morally right side of the argument here, we think it should in fact be a secondary option to be tried only after trying one of the other options

Conclusion
Based on the virtues we assume Frederick would espouse based on the narrative, we believe that Frederick should confront Bekah and proceed with one of the alternatives that includes direct confrontation with her (the null or #3) before escalating this to the dean or other administrator

6.1.3.8 Utilitarianism: Act Utilitarian Analysis

Use the matrix below to help detail out the effects of the hypothesized action on the audiences identified earlier. We find the use of '+' and '–' symbols a way to easily document the increase or reduction in utility for an audience, with '++' being a greater increase than '+' for example. Be sure to base your analysis on the data from your frame and the audiences identified earlier so you have a solid argument.

	Turn down Bekah	Discussion	Give Bekah credit	Discussion
Frederick	++,–	+: Frederick will have his integrity –: It is highly likely he will not get a good review due to his papers not being in the best journals and he will have made an enemy of his boss	–, +	–: Frederick will feel he traded his integrity for his position +: But, he will likely get a good review
Bekah	–	She will not get the credit for the paper	+	She will get the credit for authoring a paper
Other Profs	–	The other professors will be exposed in their acceptance of her offer, bringing their academic integrity into question	+	They will not be exposed in their actions
Future Profs	+	They will not have to be in this situation in the future	–	They will likely find themselves in the same position as Frederick in the future

	Go to the dean	Discussion	Offer opportunity to earn credit	Discussion
Frederick	++,–	++: Frederick has his integrity –: He went around his boss and has brought questions about her integrity to a wider audience, which will cause her a great deal more pain. Escalating this is going to be painful for him as well, career-wise	+	+: Frederick will have his integrity, though he will need to convince Bekah of the correctness of this action and she may not be open to it
Bekah	–	She will not get credit for the paper, plus she will likely be facing a review by the dean	+,–	+: She will get the credit for the paper she deserves –: She will actually have to work a bit to get there

(continued)

	Go to the dean	Discussion	Offer opportunity to earn credit	Discussion
Other profs	–	The other professors will be exposed in their acceptance of her offer, bringing their academic integrity into question	+	The other professors will not be exposed and may learn by example from Frederick how to navigate their way through these types f situations
Future profs	+	They will not have to be in this situation in the future	+	They will not have to be in this situation in the future- assuming Bekah sees the error of her ways and she adopts the idea that she can help these younger scholars by being involved in their research

Conclusion
The third alternative seems to have the best overall score when adding up the plusses and minuses (4 +, 1 –). This is to be expected as this alternative was originally envisioned as a creative way to confront Bekah without incurring some of the negatives associated with the more direct confrontation-only options
Notice too that the analysis doesn't really help distinguish between the null hypothesis and the confrontational options alone: The null hypothesis has equal numbers of +s and –s, as does the direct confrontation with Bekah, while the escalation to the dean's office option is the most negative of the set. If there was not a well thought-out third alternative, this analysis would have told us little. This is an example of what we discussed in Chap. 5 about coming up with additional alternate solutions that address the problems that you can foresee in the analyses. We have the benefit of hindsight and a lot of experience doing these analyses so while this option appeared evident to us from the start, it is likely the beginning moral analyst that you are might not reach this option until the latter phases of the analysis when you have done all of your analyses on the null hypothesis and its simple opposite and reached an unsatisfactory conclusion (i.e., indeterminate). It is at that point that in the analysis methodology that we encourage you to go back and look at your alternatives and tailor them to perform better in the areas where they did not perform as only a simple opposition to the null hypothesis. With more experience, you will be able to see these alternatives from the beginning of the process as you will be able to anticipate where each option might run into trouble in the analyses that are to come

6.1.3.9 Utilitarianism: Rule Utilitarian Analysis

Use the matrix below to help detail out the effects of the universalization of the hypothesized action. Be sure to base your analysis on the data from your frame and the audiences identified earlier so you have a solid argument.

The null hypothesis rule
Sometimes it is easier to phrase the rule as a question and then answer that question in the analysis. So here is our question:
If everyone were required to meaningfully contribute to a paper in order to get authorship credit, what would the world be like?

The null hypothesis rule analysis
This is similar to the analysis that was done for the other universalist test (i.e., the Categorical Imperative) in that we must imagine a world where all people behave according to the rule codified from our situation's null hypothesis. But, in this analysis we are not looking for a contradiction per se, but to understand the implications on the world as a whole from a well-being standpoint
If only meaningful contributions got authorship credit, papers could be used as good judges of a person's contribution to their field and academics would have great motivation to be involved in expanding their field's through the publication of original papers. This rule actually describes the idealized world of what those espousing the tenets of academic integrity would expect; fields of knowledge being continually expanded in an honest and open way for the betterment of society and the world

The alternative hypothesis rule
If everyone were to grant their boss credit on their works, what would the world be like?

The alternative hypothesis rule analysis
If all bosses were given undeserved credit on authored papers, then the actual worth of a paper to an author would be very little, as those looking at the papers would never know who actually contributed to the paper and who just got their named tacked on due to their privilege to be the actual author's boss (or their boss' boss, etc.). The usefulness of using papers to judge someone's contribution to the field would be completely negated. With no impetus to author a paper (i.e., no distinguishing of your individual effort, and no use of the output in advancing your career) the fundamental driving force in academia as we know it would be squelched and few, if any, papers would even be written thus slowing down our advances in knowledge to the detriment of society at large

Conclusion
Like the other universalist analysis, this analysis shows that the null hypothesis is desirable; the prospect of granting honorary authorship is not something we would want to follow in a general way, since the consequences would generally be quite negative as compared to the rule generalized from the null

6.1.3.10 Utilitarianism: Cost-Benefit Analysis

Conclusion
As the situation is not particularly amenable to dollars and cents type analysis, we will forgo this analysis and rely upon the more qualitative analysis of Act Utilitarian Analysis above, which captures the same ethical principles and approach in its function

6.1.3.11 Respect for Persons: Rights-Based Analysis

The rights-based analysis processes how the proposed actions affect each of the audiences in terms of the actual or possible violation of their rights expressed in tiers. The Tiers to use are:

- Tier 1- Basic Rights- Life, bodily and mental integrity, freedom from torture
- Tier 2- Maintenance Rights- Maintenance of position, livelihood, emotional state
- Tier 3- Advancement Rights- Ability to advance or grow, achieve goals.

We have found that the table below can be used effectively by putting a 1, 2 or 3 in the grid for each violation, and you can subscript it with a 'p' or 'a' for whether it represents a possible or actual violation respectively. Be sure to base your analysis on the data from your frame and the audiences identified earlier so you have a solid argument.

	Turn down Bekah	Discussion	Give Bekah credit	Discussion
Frederick	3	Bekah controls his ability to be reviewed well and advance in his quest for tenure. If he displeases her, his career will likely suffer	2	Frederick would suffer from a violation to his rights to feel honest and would be second guessing his integrity forever after
Bekah				
Other profs				
Future profs				

	Go to the dean	Discussion	Offer opportunity to earn credit	Discussion
Frederick	3	Frederick will have not only confronted his boss but escalated this to the point that Bekah's career will be harmed and thus, likely will his		
Bekah	3, possible 2	This will harm Bekah's reputation and her career		
Other profs	3	They risk being exposed in the ensuing investigations		
Future profs				

Conclusion
Alternative 3, if Frederick can convince Bekah of its value, is the only option that does not appear to violate the rights of someone involved. Alternative 2 is the worst in terms of its violation of more people's rights. One might argue that those whose rights are being violated, other than Frederick, are already people who ostensibly have committed unethical acts (Bekah's request, and the other Professors going along with her request), but as we mentioned before there may be extenuating circumstances that aren't known to Frederick. And just because someone has behaved unethically, that does not give the other actors carte blanche to violate theirs- two wrongs don't make a right

6.1.3.12 Respect for Persons: Pareto Efficiency Analysis

The Pareto efficiency analysis processes how the proposed actions affect each of the audiences in terms of the actual or possible benefit or harm the audience might face with the enactment of the proposed action. In this analysis, you will compare the change in benefits or harms with the enactment of the alternative hypothesis as compared to the null hypothesis. Ideally, your action will only provide benefits or no change for all audiences in order to satisfy the principle. Be sure to base your analysis on the data from your frame and the audiences identified earlier so you have a solid argument.

	Turn down Bekah	Discussion	Give Bekah credit	Discussion
Frederick	Benefit/harm	While he will have his academic integrity, his career advancement will most likely be harmed	Harm	He will have to live with his failure to uphold academic integrity
Bekah				
Other profs				
Future profs			Harm	They will be in the same situation in the future

	Go to the dean	Discussion	Offer opportunity to earn credit	Discussion
Frederick	Benefit harm	While he will have his academic integrity, his career advancement will most likely be harmed		
Bekah	Harm	She will likely be investigated at a minimum and punished		
Other profs	Harm	They will likely be implicated in the investigation due to their acquiescence to Bekah's request in the past		
Future profs				

Conclusion
This analysis tracks with the other respect for persons analysis in terms of alternative 3 being the best of the solutions and alternative 2 being the worst

6.1.4 Overall Conclusion (See Chap. 6)

The overall conclusion should take into account the conclusions drawn from the analyses performed. Ideally, you should have performed at least one test from each of the types of tests; Visualization, Utilitarianism, and Respect for Persons. It is also a good idea to ensure you have used at least one situational (i.e., act-based) and one universal analysis to give you a well-rounded, well-reasoned overall analysis.

6.1.4.1 Concluding Judgment

The table below can be used for you to look at the results of all of the analyses you have performed in one location to do your final comparison and judgment either by collecting the conclusions from the analyses and solving by summation, observation or through the use of a line-drawing (casuistic) analysis.

Analysis	Reject	Null	Fail to reject
Visualization analyses			
Expected reciprocity		X	
New York Times			X
Anticipatory self-appraisal			X
Aggregate application (categorical imperative)			X
Virtue analysis			X
Utilitarian analyses			
Act utilitarian analysis		X	
Rule utilitarian analysis			X
Cost-benefit analysis		N/A	
Respect for persons analyses			
Rights-based analysis	X		
Pareto-efficiency analysis	X		
	+	0	–

The table above can be used either as a summary table or as a line-drawing tool for helping you decide the final judgment. If you want to use the table for line-drawing, you would represent the conclusion from each of the tests as a point somewhere in the horizontal width of the grid cell according to the poles indicated at the bottom of the table (left-hand side represents absolutely morally permissible and the rejection of the null hypothesis, whereas the right-hand side represents the absolutely morally forbidden action and a failure to reject the null hypothesis that the action is unethical).

6.1.4.2 Final Conclusion

After all of your framing, analysis, and judgment, you should be able to determine whether you have sufficient evidence to reject the null that the proposed course of action is unethical. If you fail to reject the null, ask yourself where the crucial issues in the process for the proposed course of action are. These will guide you in a redesign of a potential ethical solution to the situation at hand.

Final conclusion
Frederick should not acquiesce to Bekah's demands for honorary credit. Academic Integrity is the bedrock of the enterprise they are involved in and Bekah's request is a direct affront to that. He will have to face the facts that there will likely be consequences from a career standpoint for not going along with her, but the analyses and the virtues espoused in Frederick's analysis really point that the cost would be too high for him to go along and let her have the undeserved credit. We fail to reject the null hypothesis that the action is unethical
But, Frederick should be intelligent in the way that he goes about confronting Bekah. As he wants to be a professional, he owes it to her to have a conversation with her first, and ideally, he should explain his reasoning to her. The reasoning performed in this analysis would drive that conversation, and the additional alternate that allows her to get what she wants and allows Frederick to get what he wants should be the first approach he takes. The hope is that (1) she will listen to his argument and agree, however grudgingly, that it is best that she not get undeserved credit, but that he should give her the opportunity to provide a meaningful contribution to the paper to make it more acceptable to the journals that will look better on his C.V. and reflect better on him and his department. In this ideal world, Bekah would see that there are better ways to get what she wants (publication credit) than to put people in these types of ethical situations. As a professional and a manager, she will need to recognize that she will not be able to attract and keep the talent she needs to make her organization a success if she continues to treat her new hires with the disrespect she showed Frederick
In the not so ideal world, where Bekah may not listen to Frederick and mend her ways, then Frederick may be forced at that point to refuse to have her involved in any of his papers and to go to the dean or ombudsman or ethics hotline in order to see her unethical behavior remedied

Discussion or formulation of new hypothesis
We had a creative solution dawn on us from the start of the analysis, and the analysis is fairly clear cut, so there is not a need to revisit this analysis at this time
Frederick may need to come back to this analysis at a later point depending on how Bekah relies to his overtures for a more meaningful contribution to his work in order for her to get credit. If this is the case, then one or more of the alternatives may have to be reformulated and the analyses completed again in light of the further action and additional knowledge that came from the first attempt at resolving this conflict

6.2 Case Study 2: Johanna

6.2.1 Introduction

Johanna has been working at a Bretton Woods institution for just over 10 years. She has worked on several projects ranging from tariff redesign to better documentation of seasonal workers in order to capture true market activity. Her specialty has become centered on Africa, and as a more senior analyst she now has supervisory obligations and real input into the direction of relationships between potential client states and her institution. Though she has yet to run a project on her own, she is often the second-most senior individual on a project and has a working familiarity (and often experience) with all of the economies, histories, and political regimes of the African continent.

Her current project is advising the country of Bechumazwe, which emerged from under an extremely repressive dictatorship 5 years ago and has been gradually introducing democratic reforms. The country has been wracked with difficulties: the previous regime fixed the exchange rates to absurd levels, which caused a thriving black market in currency exchange and further devalues their money. Additionally, the records which tracked the monies of the central government (including those monies from foreign governments and NGOs for aid purposes) were anemic, nonexistent, or fabricated. Infrastructure and even basic public services were crumbling or predominantly unavailable. Since the regime had changed, however, the wobbling government which had been put in its place made enough positive progress that they could be considered for financial advising and assistance from her organization in order to remedy what was becoming a dangerous situation for the fledgling democracy.

Bechumazwe has had one good stroke of luck recently, however. In 2010, two scientists working at the University of Manchester won the Nobel Prize in Physics for their creation and exploration of the material called grapheme. Scientists have discovered many new uses for a material: it's lightweight, strong, flexible, and, when used as a replacement for silicon-based computer hardware, can store much more data in a much smaller area with much faster processing time (Shah, 2011). Until recently, it had been prohibitively expensive to work with, but the manufacturing technology has improved enough that the demand for graphene has begun to rise.

Why is this good news for Bechumazwe? Because they are the leading provider of graphite in Africa, which is a major component of graphene. Though the mining operations are run by a state-owned company and are not up-to-date, it has been one of the most profitable of the national ventures. This is what has made its privatization one of the top priorities in the Poverty Reduction Strategy Papers drafted for Bechumazwe by Johanna and Daniel, the senior analyst from her organization who is leading this project.

Johanna knows that the efficiency and level of production of graphene would greatly increase under private ownership; however, she has concerns on the ability for the Bechumazwe government to replace its revenue source with tariffs and the remaining state-owned enterprises. The graphite extraction is the best candidate for privatization primarily because it is the most lucrative, but that's the same reason that such an industry should be left in the hands of what appears to be a stable and modernizing state. Other industries that have potential but less current profits, such as telecommunications, could be a more attractive candidate for privatization. Further, there has been growing resistance among the workers at the mine that their opinions do not count in the process.

Johanna knows that she will be expected to back up Daniel and the organization on the recommendations, but she has doubts on whether this approach is the most effective option based on its performance in the past and the potential impact on the citizens.

6.2.2 Framing the Situation (See Chap. 4)

6.2.2.1 Facts

The table of facts below is an accurate reflection of the objectively-known, incontrovertible facts surrounding the situation being analyzed.

#	Fact	Source
1	Johanna works for a Bretton Woods institution as a mid-level analyst	Case
2	Johanna's area of expertise is Africa	Case
3	She is currently assigned to a project advising the country of Bechumazwe	
4	Bechumazwe is a fledgling democracy in Africa that recently was ruled by a dictatorship	Case
5	The new government of Bechumazwe is making progress at improving the economy and infrastructure of the country but it still has significant challenges to overcome	Case
6	Bechumazwe has made enough progress to warrant the policy and financial advice of Johanna's organization	Case
7	Bechumazwe is a major source of graphite in Africa for use in graphene manufacturing	Case
8	The graphite mining operations are currently managed by the government of Bechumazwe	Case
9	The graphite mining operation is one of the most profitable ventures in the country	Case
10	One of the top priorities outlined in the current version of the policy advice being prepared by Johanna and Daniel is the privatization of the graphite mining industry	Case
11	The telecommunications industry is less profitable than the graphite mining, but is also a candidate for privatization	Case
12	There has been growing resistance among the workers at the mine that their opinions do not count in the decision process	Case
13	Johanna has doubts that the privatization of the graphite mining operations is actually the best route for Bechumazwe	Case

6.2.2.2 Factual Issues

The table of factual issues below is a list of the known bits of information that are factual in nature but are controversial or unsubstantiated. A good example of this type of issue is an unknown future effect of a given action. Your goal should be to resolve these issues through additional research and turn them into facts, or through making an educated assumption of its resolution.

#	Factual issue	Assumed resolution
1	Involvement of the Bretton Woods organization is *desired by Bechumazwe*	We are assuming that Bechumazwe is actively seeking the advice of Johanna's employer and will attempt to follow the advice
2	Selling the graphite mine will yield acceptable levels of cash for the government's needs	We are assuming, due to the language of the article, that selling the graphite mine will yield a non-trivial amount of money
3	The future values of the money streams from selling the graphite mine and other industries are calculable	We pick a reasonable level of projected cash flows, inflation, and time discounting
4	Bechumazwe will remain tolerably uncorrupt	Assumption based on 5-year trend
5	The graphite mine will be sold to a foreign-owned private company or conglomerate of private companies	Assumed that a wealthy domestic concern would have already acquired the company if it had been able to
6	The graphite mining operation will become more efficient	Assumption based on the goals of privatization and experience
7	The graphite mining operation will not worsen the working conditions of the current employees	Assumption based on an absence of evidence to suspect otherwise in Bechumazwe
8	The sale of the graphite mine will not be corrupt	Assumption contingent on the existence of a non-corrupt government

6.2.2.3 Concepts

The table of concepts below is a list of the concepts and their definitions that bear on the situation at hand. This section is used to clearly define these concepts so that someone reading your analysis understands the concepts and definitions being used in your later analyses.

#	Concept	Definition
1	Non-corrupt government	That tax or other government revenues will remain in government channels until officially disbursed in the interests of the citizenry
2	Improve efficiency	The mining company will maximize profits while minimizing the amount of externalities
3	Privatization	The acquisition of a publicly-owned firm by private interests; here, by factual assumption, we mean specifically a private company or collective of private companies
4	Working conditions	The wages, employment status, safety, and environmental quality of the employees of the mining concern
5	Citizenry	Those individuals living in Bechumazwe that do not hold positions of political power

6.2.2.4 Conceptual Issues

The table of conceptual issues below is a list of the concepts that bear on the situation at hand that have ambiguous or controversial definitions. This section is used to state the definitions assumed in the rest of the analyses. They are stated here to clearly outline any controversial definitions separate from their use within the moral analyses.

#	Concept	Assumed definition
1	Better off	An increase in standard of living (measured through wages and the resumption of utilities). Governmental stability is not necessarily a part of this measure
2	Government stability	The likelihood of an unplanned change in political leadership in a country

6.2.2.5 Morals/Values

The table of morals below is a list of the values that will be brought to bear on the situation at hand in the subsequent analyses. This is a good location to clearly elucidate the pieces of a code of ethics (especially a professional code of ethics) that will be brought to bear in this analysis. For example, in most engineering codes, it clearly states that the public's health, safety, and welfare are the paramount virtues and this section of the document would be where you would outline the values that will be used in the analyses.

#	Moral/value	Source
1	Maximize the public welfare of the Bechumazwe citizenry	Case
2	The advice of the Bretton Woods organization is *desirable*. Since Johanna is employed here, we should acknowledge the potential conflict of interest in that she would not work for a company whose mission she considered immoral	Case

6.2.2.6 Moral/Value Issues

The table of moral/value issues below is a list of the values that while being followed by the decision-maker in the situation are controversial in nature. These are moral conundrums whose interpretations and proposed answers can change the outcome of the analyses.

#	Moral/value issue	Assumed rule/resolution
1	Public involvement in policy-making is desirable	We assume that the citizenry will select what is in its own best interest
2	Foreign direct investment is socially and politically permissible	Historical, political, and social contexts do not prevent foreign direct investment

(continued)

#	Moral/value issue	Assumed rule/resolution
3	Foreign ownership of local resources or extracting interests is socially and politically permissible	Historical, political, and social contexts do not prevent foreign ownership of local resources or commercial interests
4	The government actions will reflect the will of the citizenry	We assume that not only is the government not corrupt, but that it is a legitimate proxy for the citizenry's opinions

6.2.3 Ethical Analysis (See Chap. 5)

Now that you have framed your decision with the information you know from your initial analysis, you are ready to start the ethical analysis phase of your decision-making process. First, define your hypothesis with a null reflecting a status quo of unethical behavior for the proposed action; also, specify an alternative hypothesis of appropriate scope for the situation. Second, you will define your audiences (i.e., those affected by the action being proposed in the hypothesis). Third, you will process some set of the analyses, basing your evaluations and observations on the data resolved and stated in your framing. Fourth, you will interpret the results of the analyses and select the most ethical course of action.

6.2.3.1 Generate the Hypotheses

There are two hypotheses: the null hypothesis, which is the assumption of an unethical status quo or assumed course of action, and the alternative hypothesis.

The null hypothesis
The recommendation that Bechumazwe privatize the graph mining operation is unethical

The alternative hypothesis
The recommendation that Bechumazwe privatize the graphite mining operation is not unethical

6.2.3.2 Determine the Audiences

The audiences of any given hypothesis set are all of the entities with moral standing that are affected by the proposed hypotheses. Depending on your moral philosophy these can either be limited to people only or to other living creatures or to large scale systems like the environment. Who you include is really a reflection of your answer to the moral issue surrounding who has moral agency (i.e., someone or something that is free to make their own moral decisions and be affected by them) and who has moral patiency (i.e., someone or something that is not at the level of autonomy to be considered a moral agent, but yet can still be affected by the decisions made around them).

Audience	Description
Johanna	The protagonist of the example who works for a Bretton Woods institution as a mid-level analyst with a specialty in Africa
Daniel	Johanna's immediate supervisor
Co-workers	Other employees of various levels in the Bretton Woods institution
Government of Bechumazwe	The current officials in the government of Bechumazwe
Bechumazwe citizenry	Those individuals living in Bechumazwe that do not hold positions of political power
Graphite mining company workers, current	The individuals currently working at the graphene mining company who do not have ownership rights.
Graphite mining company owners, future	The future private, foreign owners of the graphene mining company
Graphite mining company workers, future	The individuals who will work at the graphene mining company in the future who do not have ownership rights; these may or may not be the same people as the current employees
World community	The abstract body to which the Bretton Woods institution is also held accountable
Other potentially salable state industries	The individuals who currently work at the other state-owned companies

6.2.3.3 Visualization: Expected Reciprocity Analysis

Use the table below to organize the analysis results for each audience being considered. Be sure to base your analysis on the data from your frame so you have a solid argument.

Audience	Audience analysis
Daniel	If Johanna put herself in Daniel's shoes, then the facts as presented would lead us to believe that Daniel would disagree with the null hypothesis; not only that, but he could potentially consider it an insult to his own professional credibility that she would consider him potentially unethical. He may also doubt her commitment to her own work. However, he could also respect her for raising issues regarding the suitability of this solution that other professionals have raised, especially if the null stands and the act is considered unethical
Co-workers	Johanna's coworkers could share several of the same reactions that Daniel would, depending on their status is whether they would have any power regarding her employment situation. There is actually more of a potential positive from co-workers in general since a voice of dissent could empower others who have felt in similar ways to speak out and be more comfortable in the workforce

(continued)

Audience	Audience analysis
Government of Bechumazwe	If the null hypothesis holds, then Johanna should visualize what the options remaining to the government are. They will be unable to divest themselves of their most successful enterprise (which may not be optimal), but they should be able to privatize other industries. They will also continue to operate the graphite mine, which will continue to be a source of income. However, if the advice is packaged properly to them and alternatives provided (e.g., privatizing another industry), they will still have received the advice they were soliciting and would have a source of cash, albeit likely less cash than they may need currently
Bechumazwe citizenry	If the null hypothesis holds, then Johanna should visualize what the citizens of the country would experience if the graphite mine is not privatized. Per our assumptions, there is no ill will in the country for foreign investment in their industries, so they would likely not feel upset either way with regards to the mine being privatized or not. It is likely, though, that they are concerned as to the general poverty of the country and the weakness of the government. They will recognize that something needs to be done to increase investment in the country and thus in them. If the government does nothing regarding the economy, especially not embracing foreign investment, then they may begin to question its ability to grow the economy and deal with the general standard of living in the country. They would, however, probably be receptive to any serious grievances lodged by their countrymen, the current miners
Graphite mining company workers, current	The workers of the current mining company would likely agree with the null hypothesis. The mining industry is something they have built, and while they have no current direct ownership in the mine (though indirectly as citizens they hold "ownership"), the idea of selling the mine to foreign interests without considering local management, would likely be seen as a betrayal or as their government selling them out. So it is likely they would agree with null hypothesis
Graphite mining company owners, future	The future owners of the mine will likely already be a large international mining business or consortium of businesses. They would welcome the opening up of natural resource extraction opportunities in what previously was closed off to them. We assume that they would see this as an opportunity for themselves and the government and local citizens to reap the benefits of a more efficient operation as well as providing much needed capital to the government at a critical time. They would reject the null hypothesis
Graphite mining company workers, future	The future workers of the graphite mine would reject the null hypothesis due to the fact that they have no vested history in the industry being privatized. They will only have ever worked for the international organization that owns the more efficient mine
World community	Provided our assumptions hold, the world community would probably reject the null hypothesis since the international organizations such as Johanna's exist to help provide advice to struggling countries looking to stabilize their governments and currencies, as well as opening up more of the world to free trade. Countries like Bechumazwe that can raise its citizens out of poverty while embracing freedom and avoiding corruption are the exact sort of success stories the world community is looking for

(continued)

Audience	Audience analysis
Other potentially salable state industries	The sales of the graphite mining industry would at first have an impact on the sales of the other industries, as it would be the first industry to be privatized. In the long run, though, increased foreign investment in the country would not only provide the cash the government needs, but also will bring more economic activity to Bechumazwe which will likely increase the activity and thus value of these other industries. Plus, if the sales of the mining concern is successful, then it is more likely that other industries may be privatized; providing benefit for the government financially as well as increasing the efficiency of the industries. They would thus reject the null hypothesis

Conclusion
Based on the assumptions made in the framing of the problem and the analysis provided above, it would appear that the preponderance of audiences would reject the null hypothesis and would find the privatization of the graphite mining industry to be an ethical act
The sole outlier would be the existing workers in the graphite mining industry who likely will feel that their livelihoods and legacy are at risk with the sales of their industry to an international firm. Their concerns could potentially be addressed through some additional requirements, such as requiring the international firm to use local workers instead of imported workers or giving the mining workers or their communities a portion of the purchase price to improve their lives or their communities. If the local workers are content, then this will also help the larger citizenry maintain a positive attitude toward privatization

6.2.3.4 Visualization: New York Times Analysis

Imagine the proposed action will be announced in all its glory/infamy in the New York Times tomorrow. Generate the headline and analyze how you would feel if it was published in the paper for all of your friends and acquaintances to see. Be sure to base your analysis on the data from your frame so you have a solid argument.

Proposed headline- for null hypothesis
International Economic Development Organization blocks privatization over fears of local protest

Analysis for headline
This headline does not appear to be something that would cause an issue if published. Though a potentially beneficial act has not occurred in the form of the privatization, the mention of the reason might actually gain public sympathy rather than impede it. We do not find cause to reject the null hypothesis here

Proposed headline- for alternative hypothesis
International Economic Development Organization urges sale of graphite mine for cash-strapped Bechumazwe

Analysis for headline
This headline is a representation of the rejection of the null hypothesis and also seems to be a perfectly acceptable headline, given the assumptions. A development organization promoting foreign investment that is beneficial to a target country and its people as well as evolving a successful, efficient new industry from the existing structure would be touting this achievement as admirable. The only sour note that could mar this conclusion would be if the investment created more of a corruption problem for the government, but this is not currently a problem in Bechumazwe (according to our assumptions); additionally, this is something that can be monitored by the organization to mitigate the concern as time goes on

Conclusion
This test has ambivalent results since neither the null hypothesis nor the alternate hypothesis generate statements that would be objectionable if publicized

6.2.3.5 Visualization: Anticipatory Self-Appraisal Analysis

Use the table below to detail your vision of yourself after you have performed the hypothesized action. Be sure to base your analysis on the data from your frame so you have a solid argument.

Analysis
Johanna will feel a great deal of accomplishment should her organization's recommendations for Bechumazwe play out in a positive light. If, as we have stated in our assumptions, the sales of the graphite mining industry would be a positive financial move for the government, especially at this critical time in its evolution away from a more autocratic form. With the proper monitoring in place to mitigate the risks of corruption and a modification to the policy to placate the current mining workers, Johanna would have little to be concerned about for her future vision of herself
There is always a chance that this rosy future will not materialize for Bechumazwe by following the recommendations of Johanna's organization, though based on the facts in the case and the assumptions made, this risk can be minimized through the use of the other interventions mentioned above (corruption monitoring, etc.). That being said, though, it is likely that even if there are problems in the future Bechumazwe, there will be enough good done for the country and its citizenry to outweigh any of those possible downsides

Conclusion
Thus, as Johanna would actually view herself in a more positive light in the future if the recommendations are followed and were reasonably successful, this would constitute a rejection of the null hypothesis for her

6.2.3.6 Visualization: Aggregate Application Analysis (Categorical Imperative)

Use the tables below to develop your proposed universal rule and to capture its analysis. Remember, we are testing the underlying premise of the null hypothesis, so it can be framed in a positive fashion. Be sure to base your analysis on the data from your frame so you have a solid argument.

Proposed universal rule
All international development organizations should always encourage rising countries to privatize state-owned industries

Analysis for rule
Per the analysis' primary principle, the question that must be asked is whether or not the rule itself leads to a contradiction or more practically to a situation where the rule itself cannot be executed per its original formulation
The rule outlined above, if followed universally, would result in every state-owned industry being privatized until the point that no state industries were left. Though the absolute application of the rule would eventually make the rule inapplicable, unlike the lawnmower example, it does not interfere conceptually with the definition of privatization. This does rest, however, on the assumption that privatization is a positive act and will continue to be seen as so, as long as the rule was put into effect
(By way of comparison, think of how this test might have changed if we had used the word "enterprise" rather than "industry"? Would this have resulted in the privatization of postal service, defense, taxation, and other services of government and, if it did, what would be left for government to provide? This would be a potentially problematic case for the Aggregate Application Test.)

Conclusion
The universal application of the rule that represents the rejection of the premise of the null hypothesis would not conceptually interfere with the application of itself. Further, provided our assumptions hold, this could result in a perpetuating benefit to greater welfare

6.2.3.7 Virtue Analysis

Use the tables below to describe your desired virtues or admired exemplars and your analyses related to each of the hypotheses as it relates to the virtue or exemplar.

Virtues/exemplars
Amartya Sen- This Nobel prize-winning economist could exemplify what Johanna and her co-workers strive to emulate. His work in welfare economics and human development indices have provided a strong voice of reason advocating for the wise use of aid and its incumbent measurements. Sen has managed to maintain credibility inside the economics field while still being accessible to the popular press, and he has helped turn the focus of development toward the well-being of citizens

Analysis
Johanna's concern for both the workers in the potentially privatization-affected industry and the overall effect that the privatization might have on the long term prospects of the economy and the citizens of Bechumazwe come from her research into Sen's work and an admiration of his philosophy and approach to the problems. There have been many examples of misapplied or misused aid to developing countries, and Johanna wants to make sure that her guidance is provided to the government with the concern for the citizens and their growth/advancement as her primary focus

(continued)

Analysis
The recommendations in this case give her pause because the privatization of the most profitable state-owned industry, which could provide only a short term boost to the government to get it through a time of potential instability. Sen has cautioned against the universal application of privatization as a tool, but does believe it can be warranted. The description, analysis, and (most importantly) the assumptions which have been made in this scenario all indicate that this relatively stable and uncorrupt political environment could be an ideal situation where an industry that could reap great benefits from modernization exists in this case. Private capital and ownership incentives could improve the lives, including both wages and working conditions due to advancements in technology. Further, a more profitable operation could result in a steady supply of taxable income in addition to the initial cash from the sale. These additional insights (and additional assumptions about potential risks) would make Johanna more likely to believe that Sen would find that the null hypothesis could safely be rejected

6.2.3.8 Utilitarianism: Act Utilitarian Analysis

Use the matrix below to help detail out the effects of the hypothesized action on the audiences identified earlier. We find the use of '+' and '–' symbols a way to easily document the increase or reduction in utility for an audience, with '++' being a greater increase than '+' for example. Be sure to base your analysis on the data from your frame and the audiences identified earlier so you have a solid argument.

	Do not recommend	Discussion	Recommend privatization	Discussion
Johanna	–	Johanna is invested in the mission of her organization, so being unable to provide development guidance would be a negative to her	+	Johanna is invested in the mission of her organization and providing a recommendation for privatization would living up to that mission
Johanna's organization	–	The organization exists to provide guidance and investment for developing countries, so its mission would not be accomplished	+	Johanna's organization would benefit from promoting growth in rising countries and opening their markets

	Do not recommend	Discussion	Recommend privatization	Discussion
Bechumazwe government	–	The government is supportive of the development organization providing it guidance. They need the revenue as soon as possible and recognize the opportunity to achieve economic growth. Not recommending this course of action would be harmful to them	+	The privatization will provide the government with needed cash during this critical time. They are welcoming of the advice and opportunities Johanna's organization can provide
Bechumazwe citizenry	–	Without external investment and the revenue that would bring for the government, there is likely to be increased instability as well as a lack of growth	+	The investment will help stabilize their new government as well as open the doors to foreign investment and the growth that should entail
Current mining workers	0	There would be no change to their situation	–	They perceive that they will be disenfranchised after the purchase
Future mining workers	0	There would be no change to their situation	+	They will have an efficient industry to work in
Future mining owners	–	They will have missed out on an opportunity to be able to grow their business	+	They will have access to a previously closed resource extraction opportunity
World	–	The world will not see a likely successful investment in a developing country guided by the organizations it created and supports for that purpose	+	Development in a country, guided by an international development agency is achieving the goal of the development agencies, which is economic growth and poverty reduction around the world

(continued)

	Do not recommend	Discussion	Recommend privatization	Discussion
Other salable industries	–	Without the graphite mining industry, the most attractive industry in Bechumazwe, being privatized through foreign investment, the chance that these companies will see the same sort of investment is relatively low	–/+	They will have a negative in that they were not the ones purchased/privatized in the first round, but overall the growth of the economy due to the foreign investments being made will only benefit their growth and provide future sales opportunities

Conclusion
The act at the root of the scenario – the recommendation of privatization of the graphite mining industry – is judged by this analysis to be ethically allowable (8+ and 2–) and thus the null hypothesis is rejected. The alternative, which would be to withhold the recommendation, is judged to be unethical since the purpose for organizations like Johanna's is to provide expert guidance to emerging economies to increase openness, foreign investment, and growth so as to raise the general standard of living and reduce poverty in the target country. Again, this is highly dependent on assumptions of organizational efficacy

6.2.3.9 Utilitarianism: Rule Utilitarian Analysis

Use the matrix below to help detail out the effects of the universalization of the hypothesized action. Remember, we are testing the underlying premise of the null hypothesis, so it can be framed in a positive fashion. Be sure to base your analysis on the data from your frame and the audiences identified earlier so you have a solid argument.

The null hypothesis rule
All international development organizations should always encourage rising countries to privatize state-owned industries

The null hypothesis rule analysis
As was briefly stated in the other universalist analysis (Aggregate Application Analysis) the application of this rule in a universal sense would end up with a world where, in general, emerging countries and their citizens would be better off than they are today. Again, however, this does rest on the assumption that privatization is a positive act and will continue to be seen as so, as long as the rule is put into effect

Conclusion
The premise at the root of the null hypothesis would lead us to the fact that a universal application of it would cause a general increase in the well-being of the people in the emerging countries of the world. Thus, the null hypothesis is rejected, as its root premise is ethical and not unethical

6.2.3.10 Utilitarianism: Cost-Benefit Analysis

Use the matrix below to help detail out the effects of the hypothesized action on the audiences identified earlier. Be sure to use a consistent currency and remember to be consistent in the evaluation of the costs and benefits in terms of their likelihoods and expected values. Also, if you are time discounting or using any other parameter involving ambiguity or risk, be sure to note this. Base your analysis on the data from your frame and the audiences identified earlier so you have a solid argument.

Conclusion
This analysis is skipped here due to the fact that the numerical values in this case, while available to Johanna and her organization, are out the scope of this book
Based on the fact that the strategy papers as written are advocating the privatization of the mining industry, we can assume that the cost/benefit analysis performed as pointing at that course of action being the most advantageous for all involved. The Bretton Woods institution would have, at the very least, conducted tests that considered the prospect of their primary recommendation (the privatization of the graphite mine) to be numerically optimal. It is crucial, however, that such information as estimated sale price, potential tax revenue stream, potential market impacts, etc. all be recorded in the assumptions of the scenario
Assuming professional competence of the organization, the null hypothesis should be rejected

6.2.3.11 Respect for Persons: Rights-Based Analysis

The rights-based analysis processes how the proposed actions affect each of the audiences in terms of the actual or possible violation of their rights expressed in tiers. The Tiers to use are:

- Tier 1- Basic Rights- Life, bodily and mental integrity, freedom from torture
- Tier 2- Maintenance Rights- Maintenance of position, livelihood, emotional state
- Tier 3- Advancement Rights- Ability to advance or grow, achieve goals.

We have found that the table below can be used effectively by putting a 1, 2 or 3 in the grid for each violation, and you can subscript it with a ‘p’ or ‘a’ for whether it represents a possible or actual violation respectively. Be sure to base your analysis on the data from your frame and the audiences identified earlier so you have a solid argument.

	Do not recommend	Discussion	Recommend privatization	Discussion
Johanna	3	If she is unable to provide guidance, then her career will not advance		
Johanna's organization	3	The mission of the organization centers on providing guidance, so if they are blocked from providing it because it is unethical, then the organization cannot advance		
Bechumazwe government	3p	The third tier rights of the government and its ability to grow are threatened with violation if there is no investment in their country		They have asked for this guidance, so there is no violation of their sovereign rights
Bechumazwe citizenry				
Current mining workers			2p	There is a possible violation of their 2nd tier rights to continue their livelihood if we assume that during the privatization they will be losing their "ownership" of their industry as well as there might be reductions in the labor force due to increased efficiency or possible influx of foreign labor with the investment
Future mining workers				
Future mining owners				
World				

(continued)

	Do not recommend	Discussion	Recommend privatization	Discussion
Other salable industries	3p	Without the most profitable industry becoming privatized, there is a possible future violation of the other industry's rights to grow and possibly be bought out as well		

Conclusion
The null hypothesis potentially violates 3rd tier rights of multiple audience members, whereas the alternate hypothesis would only appear to possibly violate the 2nd tier rights of one audiences; the current mining industry workers. This would indicate that the null hypothesis' course of action is less ethical than the alternative, and thus the null hypothesis should be rejected

6.2.3.12 Respect for Persons: Pareto Efficiency Analysis

The Pareto efficiency analysis processes how the proposed actions affect each of the audiences in terms of the actual or possible benefit or harm the audience might face with the enactment of the proposed action. In this analysis, you will compare the change in benefits or harms with the enactment of the alternative hypothesis as compared to the null hypothesis. Ideally, your action will only provide benefits or no change for all audiences in order to satisfy the principle. Be sure to base your analysis on the data from your frame and the audiences identified earlier so you have a solid argument.

	Effects of not recommending privatization	Effects of the recommending privatization	Change
Johanna	Harm	Benefit	Positive
Johanna's organization	Harm	Benefit	Positive
Bechumazwe government	Harm	Benefit	Positive
Bechumazwe citizens	Harm	Benefit	Positive
Current mining workers	No change	Harm	Negative
Future mining workers	No change	No change	No change
Future mining owners	Harm	Benefit	Positive
World	Harm	Benefit	Positive
Other salable industries	Harm	Benefit (in the long run)	Positive

(continued)

Conclusion
The values in this chart are based on the discussion had in all of the previous analyses, so we won't rehash them here. The null hypothesis clearly is not a Pareto-efficient solution, as most of the changes in outcome are negative. In fact, the null hypothesis' action is almost all negative except for the harm that may befall the workers of the mining industry. However, the alternate hypothesis, though clearly superior, is also not Pareto-efficient based on this analysis. We can, however, reject the null hypothesis
Here, we also see another benefit of this type of analysis: we now know that an alternate hypothesis which makes the harm to the workers go away without adding harm to any of the other audiences would be a better solution. So the test not only gives you a determination on the null hypothesis, but it points you in the right direction for generating alternatives that would be better than the null and the current alternate. Some of these alternatives we have discussed in earlier parts of this example (e.g., using some of the privatization investment money to specifically aid the mining industry workers who may experience or perceive the experience of harm to themselves)

6.2.4 Overall Conclusion (See Chap. 6)

The overall conclusion should take into account the conclusions drawn from the analyses performed. Ideally, you should have performed at least one test from each of the types of tests; Visualization, Utilitarianism, and Respect for Persons. It is also a good idea to ensure you have used at least one situational (i.e., act-based) and one universal analysis to give you a well-rounded, well-reasoned overall analysis.

6.2.4.1 Concluding Judgment

The table below can be used for you to look at the results of all of the analyses you have performed in one location to do your final comparison and judgment either by collecting the conclusions from the analyses and solving by summation by observation or through the use of a line-drawing (casuistic) analysis.

Analysis	Conclusion reached
Visualization analyses	
Expected reciprocity	Null hypothesis rejected
New York times	Ambiguous
Anticipatory self-appraisal	Null hypothesis rejected
Aggregate application (Categorical Imperative)	Null hypothesis rejected
Virtue analysis	Null hypothesis rejected
Utilitarian analyses	
Act utilitarian analysis	Null hypothesis rejected
Rule utilitarian analysis	Null hypothesis rejected
Cost-benefit analysis	Null hypothesis rejected

Analysis	Conclusion reached
Respect for persons analyses	
Rights-based analysis	Null hypothesis rejected
Pareto-efficiency analysis	Null hypothesis rejected

The table above can be used either as a summary table or as a line-drawing tool for helping you decide the final judgment. If you want to use the table for line-drawing, you would represent the conclusion from each of the tests as a point somewhere in the horizontal width of the grid cell according to the poles indicated at the bottom of the table (left-hand side represents absolutely morally permissible action, whereas the right-hand side represents the absolutely morally forbidden action).

6.2.4.2 Final Conclusion

After all of your framing, analysis, and judgment, you should be able to determine whether you have sufficient evidence to reject the null that the proposed course of action is unethical. If you fail to reject the null, ask yourself where the crucial issues in the process for the proposed course of action are. These will guide you in a redesign of a potential ethical solution to the situation at hand.

Final conclusion
First, the results were fairly conclusive that the null hypothesis of considering the recommendation of privatization of the graphite mine to be unethical is rejected. Based on the analyses completed above, the recommendation to move forward with the action described in the premise of the null hypothesis is fairly straight-forward
But, as you may have noticed, much of this analysis is based on a number of assumptions that were made during the framing steps of the process (e.g., Bechumazwe is supportive of the development organization giving them advice; corruption is not an issue nor is it foreseen to be an issue in Bechumazwe in the future; etc.). You may think that we made best-case assumptions so that the analysis would be an obvious rejection of the null hypothesis. In a real-world situation, the values would not have to be assumed away and could potentially be researched or directly measured. The likelihood of governmental corruption is something that is measured by a number of different methodologies, and that could be what you base your "Bechumazwe doesn't have a corruption problem" assumption on. It still involves a level of risk and should probably still be considered an assumption, but it will be a better informed one with less risk. In the situation where you have a lack of information, make an assumption with the necessary documentation and full understanding of its limitations. These assumptions then become the basis for warning flags that can be used to help deliver the guidance or program
This framing method of using assumptions is there precisely for the purpose of coming to a conclusion in cases where there is a lack of necessary information at hand in order to make a decision. A well-thought-out assumption can stand in for the missing information, while still clearly standing out as an assumption. An assumption that should be challenged and changed as the underlying situation warrants it. The completed analysis should then be revisited, since one of its premises has been invalidated. Thus, the power of the assumption is that (1) it lets you move forward in the case of missing information and (2) stands out as an assumption and thus as a guidepost for the critical factors of the situation that warrant monitoring and as triggers for reanalysis

(continued)

Discussion or formulation of new hypothesis
As discussed above, the effect on the current mining employees was consistently the sticking point in a number of analyses. Thus, as a consistently thorny problem across the tests, it makes sense that we may want to adjust our proposed action to work around and remove that issue. One of the benefits of testing the null hypothesis is that we often get additional information about how to hone our solutions so that they can remove the negatives that the action will incur while not removing any of the benefits. The Pareto efficiency approach works well here – you want to find a solution that turns the harms of the null hypothesis' actions into benefits without causing additional harms to crop up. The tabular layout of the various analyses make this much easier to do as you have already broken all of the benefits and harms out in different ways according to different philosophical approaches. So the tables can be reused to help identify better alternatives, and these alternatives can be run back through the analyses as the null hypothesis until you find the optimal solution
Here, the optimal solution here looks to be that Johanna and her organization should move forward with the recommendation for the privatization of the graphite mining in Bechumazwe, but they should find a way to appease the mining employees so as to minimize the amount of opposition this policy might face

Part III
Perspectives on Professional Ethics

"The quality of a leader is reflected in the standards they set for themselves."

-Ray Croc

Chapter 7
Ethics and the Central Bank

Harold A. Vásquez-Ruíz

> *"Ethics is an objective necessity... for survival of mankind, not by supernatural grace,..., but by a mandate of reality and natural life."*
>
> ~Ayn Rand in *The Virtuous Egoist* (2007).

Abstract This essay discusses, from my personal experience, a number of professional ethical issues that might arise while working for a developing country's central bank. Having no an specific set of ethical guidelines on how a policy maker must perform his duties, we try to answer from personal experience how issues on economic research and policy making are handle in similar environments at developed economies.

Keywords Economics • Professional ethics • Central banking • Policy • Research ethics

After being immersed in a developed economy's culture—specifically, living, studying and working in the United States—it is possible to get a flavor about the ethical values upon which its citizens rely. These values are the core underlying interactions—either personal or professional—among individuals, which sometimes contrast significantly with values from other societies, such as those from less developed economies. During my experience in the U.S., I had the opportunity to relate at very different academic and professional environments. First, I worked as a teaching assistant at my alma mater, Georgia State University (GSU), and, later, as a research assistant at the Federal Reserve Bank of Atlanta. Finally, when I was writing my Ph.D. dissertation, I occupied a position as a Research Economist at the Economic Forecasting Center at GSU. Through this essay, I will discuss from my personal

H.A. Vásquez-Ruíz (✉)
Instituto Tecnológico de Santo Domingo Escuela de Negocios,
Av. Los Próceres, Los Jardines del Norte, Apartado Postal 342-9,
Santo Domingo, Dominican Republic
e-mail: email@haroldvasquez.com

E.A.M. Searing, D.R. Searing (eds.), *Practicing Professional Ethics in Economics and Public Policy*, DOI 10.1007/978-94-017-7306-5_7

experience a number of professional ethical issues that might arise while working for a developing country's central bank, always trying to use as a reference how these issues are handle in similar environments at developed economies.

After finishing my Ph.D. in economics, I returned to my native country and started to work as the Deputy Director of Research at the Central Bank of Dominican Republic, where I am responsible for conducting research and building models to analyze how changes in the international economy might affect the macroeconomic stability of the Dominican economy, a typical Latin American small developing country. Here, the objectives of professional economists at the Central Bank are not so different from a similar position in any other country: a group of professionals try to analyze the major economic challenges affecting the economy and recommend policy advice and lines of actions to policy makers. However, I believe that there are a number of ethical issues—which cannot be understated—related to different aspects in our duties (such as the process of data collection and analysis, research, and policy making) which professional economists need to consider, especially while working for a developing economy's institution.

Before addressing ethical issues in the policy maker's working environment, it is important to ask in first place: why would economists (or any other person) need a code of ethics? What is the role of ethics in guiding macroeconomic policy decisions? Why would individuals interacting both inside and outside an organization (such as a central bank) need to constrain their behavior within the parameters of a certain code? Why must individuals who behave outside of what is considered ethical norms are penalized? Is ethics really an "objective necessity"?

These questions concern the work of philosophers and researchers working in the field of ethics, and I will be very pretentious if I try to answer them in this essay. However, something for sure is that individuals have been concerned about ethics for centuries. For example, in the ninth century, Japan developed Bushido (which translated means "the way of the warrior") as a "code of moral principles which the knights (samurais) were required or instructed to observe" (Inazo, 1904, p. 6). These principles or moral codes have been part of the Japanese culture for generations and, even today, Japan is regarded as a developed market economy with a culture based on values of duty, loyalty, and goodwill (Morishima, 1982). For a developing country, such as Dominican Republic, I believe that it is very important to establish a moral code that guides individual interactions and addresses issues of responsibility within governmental institutions because it improves the quality of the job and the public perceptions about the institution.

Central banks are institutions committed to macroeconomic stability. To achieve this goal, a central bank must rely on the confidence and trust of the economic agents who are making decisions everyday within the markets. Thus, the credibility of central bank policies and announcements play an important role in the achievements of the central bank's targets. For this reason, I believe that it is important for a central bank to have a strong ethical framework that guides all decisions related to policy making, research, and economic analysis.

7.1 Ethics in Policy Making

There are many factors that might affect the performance of a public institution, including the political environment, the lack of accountability to the public, and the level of educational attainment or expertise of the decision makers, among others. These elements could divert an institution from achieving its major goals and harm its reputation.

Thus, a question of interest is how does a developing country's central bank manage to pursue its goals when it faces a political environment that might hamper policy making? To avoid the conflicts between policy and political decisions (which most of the time are not set to attain the same objectives), central banks, in most countries, have objectives and targets that are stated in law constitutional mandates, or treaties. Usually, these mandates are very simple and clearly stated. For example, the main objective of the Central Bank of Dominican Republic is to maintain "price stability," (Law 183-02, Art. 2-a). A similar mandate is established for the European Central Bank (Treaty on the Functioning of the European Union, Art. 127). Sometimes, these mandates are further clarified with the specification of quantitative targets—e.g., inflation must be within or below certain threshold.[1] In other countries (e.g., the United States before year 2012), central banks maintain multiple goals which, according to a number of authors, might increase the level of uncertainty related to the institutional objectives. In any case, these simple or multiple mandates contribute to the complexity of addressing any ethical problems that might arise from the political environment.

Although laws specify the central bank's major goals and, therefore, constrain policy actions, these institutions still have a lot of discretion in conducting their policies, including the selection of instruments and intermediate policy objectives and the elaboration of new financial markets' regulations. For instance, when deciding how to achieve an inflation target, central banks might choose among interest rate policies, exchange rate policies, money market interventions, or any combination among them. In each particular case, policy decisions need to consider the reaction of the different economic agents or sectors in the market, which might be benefited or harm with the decisions taken. For example, let's say the central bank needs to implement a policy to slow down the growth rate of inflation. Among its policy decisions, the central bank might choose whether to increase interest rates or to appreciate the exchange rate. In the former case, the central bank might find opposition from financial institutions because higher interest rate will reduce bank lending, therefore harming their business. In the latter case, a exchange rate appreciation increases the cost of goods sold at international markets, therefore the central bank might face complaints from a number of exporting sectors such as agricultural or manufacturing. Thus, ethics must place a role in central bank inter-

[1] In the case of Dominican Republic, the Central Bank's Monetary Program for 2012 establishes an inflation target of 5.5 % with a range of tolerance of ±1 %. For the European Union, the Governing Council of the European Central Bank established in 1998 that inflation must be below 2 %.

vention in the sense that, with multiple instruments that will all produce adverse effects on some audience, the central bank needs to be unbiased in exercising its judgment. Economic agents representing different sectors of the economy, being aware of the implications of central bank policies, use a number of mechanisms to show their concerns from policy decisions, including political influence, communications through the public media, etc. Here, the central banks act with *prudence* which, as the great philosopher Adam Smith defined in his 1970 *Theory for Moral Sentiments*, is the combination of three qualities: "reason and understanding" and "self-command," to communicate and to increase confidence about its policies, always keeping in sight the objective of price stability. When multiple pathways can be used to achieve the central bank's main target, although it is not clearly stated as a mandate, the central bank will chose the policy option that provide the best macroeconomic stability, or harm the lowest number of individuals at the bottom of the income distribution.

7.2 Ethics in the Research Environment

Besides policy making, the production of research is another area in which central banks must deal with ethical issues. The economic adviser must provide estimates to the best of his knowledge, which policy makers use as inputs to take decisions. However, it is challenging to produce high quality research in developing countries for a number of reasons, including difficulties obtaining high quality data, lack of research training or experience of the staff, and the inability to access good technical resources. This situation might open the case for a self-regulatory code of ethics that promotes the best research standards and improve the quality of information management and research analysis. Since there can be such a large difference in the needs and workings of a central bank across countries, this is an argument for customized ethics policies for each workplace.

The research in developing countries is focused on the analysis of how short-term events might affect the economy. For example, the major economic problems that affect small developing economies are related to the effects of short-term fluctuations in the exchange rate, the sustainability of debt and external economic disequilibrium (or balance of payments disequilibrium), or the effect of international commodity prices on the local economy. The analysis of these issues requires a very sophisticated level of technical information and rigorous knowledge of economic concepts that are not usually found in developing countries. These problems can be enhanced if analysts are under pressure to provide a given quantitative answer. This situation contrasts significantly with the working environment of research economist in the developed world, where they operate as if they were in an academic environment—with a great degree of freedom and independence—and their work is based on a long-term personal and institutional research agenda.

In developing countries, it is important to rely on a strong ethical code to guide the work of research and economic analysts so that they can provide the best answers to the people in charge of formulating policy prescriptions. The ethics code must promote research and economic analysis that follow international guidelines on the management of intellectual property, plagiarism, and manipulation of data.

7.3 Ethics in Data and Statistics

In developing countries, central banks are major producers of economic statistics. That is, central banks do not only produce and collect information on monetary aggregates, as it is commonly found in the developed world, but also they produce statistics on the balance of payments and external accounts, the financial sector, the government sector, the labor market, the consumer and producer prices, among others. Often, this happens even if governments have other public institutions that are supposed to fulfill this task.

The major reason that causes central banks engage in the responsibility of compiling statistics is the lack of human resources and technical capabilities of developing countries' National Institutes of Statistics. In general, central banks are decentralized public institutions with independent budgets that spent a lot of resources in human capital formation, international technical assistance, and modern equipment compared with the rest of the public sector, which makes them capable of conducting and managing national surveys and compiling all kinds of information for economic analysis. In addition, policy makers at the Central Bank have the incentive to invest in units that collect and manage statistical information because they need to rely on high quality statistical information for policy making.

A number of authors argue that central banks, especially those with a mandate of price and economic stability, should not be involve in collecting and elaborating certain types of statistics (such as statistics on price indexes, production, and national accounts) because this may create a conflict of interest and undermine the central bank's credibility (Tuladhar, 2005). Although, even in developing countries, central banks tend to separate information analysis and data collecting units; they might need to hire independent agencies to collect these information, or information on other relevant indicators, such as inflation expectations, to improve agents' assessment and credibility on monetary policy stance (Svensson, 2001). However, I believe that in developing countries, where political decisions might influence the behavior of some institutions, the level of transparency and reporting is more important in the agency compiling and using the information then in the one that is collecting the information. Therefore, central banks—as the institutions with the technical capability to best perform the job on data analysis and collection—should focus on making as clear as possible their methodologies and having a strong communication channel with the public to avoid these criticisms.

7.4 Ethics in the Exercise of Authority

In developing economies, central banks' authorities play an important role in regulating financial markets. For example, to pursue the price stability mandate, policy makers might delimit the operations and transactions of financial institutions, establish the role and activities of each type of financial agent, regulate exchange rate market operations, and so on. In exercising its power, policy makers must avoid the abuse of authority which might undermine the central bank's credibility and reputation.

Abuse of authority may arise since legislation defines a set of actions and orders that the Central Bank can legitimately demand of the regulated agents. However, some of these actions might, under specific circumstances, create a heavy burden for the financial institution, which is never compensated for the costs of compliance. This burden may also occur under a particular state of the world that was not considered a potential possibility when the legislation was passed, causing additional duress on both the institution and, potentially, the larger economy. Here, the Central Bank needs to possess a good reputation that will increase the likelihood of trust and compliance in this process; one of the ways to achieve this trust would before the institution to have and follow a publicly available code of ethics. That is, when a central bank exercises its powers, it is important that the financial system perceive its actions as "fair" and within the scope of the law to avoid a hostile financial environment between regulators and regulated agents. An environment of cooperation, in which all agents agreed on their rights and responsibilities, will enhance the stability of the financial system and the conduct of monetary policy. A code of ethics that regulates how central banks treat financial institutions in addition to the final constituency of citizens can achieve this goal.

7.5 Concluding Remarks

In general, a code of ethics can be seen as rules of conduct that are necessary for the functioning of markets and institutions. These rules are intended to improve the relationship between the agents that participate in the market and reduce the possibility of opportunistic behaviors that can destabilize the compliance with the economic institutions of the society.

The implementation of ethical codes across private firms and government institutions has been increasing over the years. These codes reflect the idea of transparency, honesty, responsibility, and the moral principles that individuals could rationally be agreed upon. As long as these codes provide incentives for compliance, they will be self-enforcing.

For a Central bank, a code of ethics could improve a number of aspects within the institution including the decision making process of policy makers, the work of research economist, and the task of collecting and managing statistical information.

Further, the relationship between regulators and regulated agents would improve as those who work in the central bank more fully understand the limits of their power and their responsibilities to the public and other institutions.

References

Faust, J., & Svensson, L. E. O. (2001). Transparency and credibility: Monetary policy with unobservable goals. *International Economic Review, 42*(2), 369–397.

Morishima, M. (1982). *Why has Japan succeeded? Western technology and the Japanese ethos*. Cambridge, NY: Cambridge University Press.

Nitobé, I. (1904). *Bushido: The soul of Japan. A public domain book* (13th edn.), Japan: Kodashan International Ltd.

Rand, A. (2007). *Normative ethics: The virtuous egoist* (1st ed.). New York: Cambridge University Press.

Tuladhar, A. (2005). *Governance structures and decision-making roles in inflation targeting central banks*. IMF Working paper no. 05/183.

Chapter 8
Ethics and Climate Change Policy

Julie A. Nelson

Abstract Climate change is changing not only our physical world, but also our intellectual, social, and moral worlds. We are realizing that our situation is profoundly *unsafe*, *interdependent*, and *uncertain*. What, then, does climate change demand of economists, as human beings and as professionals? A discipline of economics based on Enlightenment notions of mechanism and disembodied rationality is not suited to present problems. This essay suggests three major requirements: first, that we take action; second, that we work together; and third, that we focus on avoiding the worst, rather than obtaining the optimal. The essay concludes with suggestions of specific steps that economists should take as researchers, teachers, and in our other roles.

Keywords Climate change • Ethics • Catastrophe • Uncertainty • Interdependence • Responsibility • Embodied reason

Climate change is changing our world. Not only is it changing our physical world, but also our intellectual, social, and moral worlds, in ways that we could not have imagined a generation or two ago. The science of climate change, and the political impasses associated with dealing with climate change, demonstrate that we are in a profoundly *unsafe, interdependent,* and *uncertain* world. We are already experiencing levels of greenhouse gasses, the likes of which have not been seen on earth for at least 800,000 years (Weitzman, 2011, p. 3). We are facing a need for globally coordinated action that humans, having evolved in smaller groups of kin and nation, have never before attempted. We are—contrary to our usual processes of learning or transformation—facing a problem of having to act largely in advance, instead of after, actually experiencing the consequence of our actions (Stern, 2011, p. 2). We are, if we are honest about it, facing the possibility that all the skills and knowledge we've gained through our physical and social evolution and scientific investigations

Reprinted with Permission

Originally published as: Nelson, J.A. 2013. Ethics and the economist: What climate change demands of us, *Ecological Economics*, *85(0)*, 145–154.

J.A. Nelson (✉)
Department of Economics, University of Massachusetts Boston, Boston, MA, USA
e-mail: julie.nelson@umb.edu

E.A.M. Searing, D.R. Searing (eds.), *Practicing Professional Ethics in Economics and Public Policy*, DOI 10.1007/978-94-017-7306-5_8

to date may not be adequate, or of the right kind, to save the human race (and the rest of the life on the planet) from catastrophic, dislocating changes.

While having these facts right in front of us does not necessarily mean that we all see them—denial being one habitual human response to difficulties—this essay leaves the task of describing and defending climate science to others. Likewise, many cogent critiques of the application of standard economic benefit–cost approaches to climate change, and many convincing arguments about the impossibility of ignoring the ethical dimensions of climate change economics, have already been written.[1] Rather than repeat these arguments, this essay is forward-looking and practical. What does climate change demand of economists? That is, what should professional economists (such as myself and some readers of this journal) be doing—and what should non-economist scholars, activists, policymakers, officers of funding organizations, and members of the general public (such as other readers of this journal) legitimately be insisting that economists do? Given that economists need to grapple with ethical issues, how can we best do so? Given that economists do research and/or teach, how should what we now know—and, perhaps even more importantly, what we should now know that we do *not* know—affect our practices in these areas?

8.1 Enlightenment: Beyond the Beta Version

Nicholas Stern has said that we need a "new industrial revolution" to address climate change (Stern, 2011, p. 6). He also suggests that economists must consult other fields—including "science, technology, philosophy, economic history, [and] international relations"—as we develop our economic analysis (Stern, p. 19). An even *more* basic revolution is, however, needed as well: An overhaul of the ideas of the Enlightenment, Beta Version,[2] of the eighteenth century. This first version, based on a mechanical metaphor for nature along with notions of ideal Reason and individualism, got off the drawing-boards of philosophers and was put to use in scientific, economic, and political practices worldwide. But it seems that a great many of the assumptions underlying Enlightenment Beta and early scientific thought were wrong, or at best very incomplete. The continued advance of science has, in fact, revealed serious flaws in the earlier version—and in the economics based on it.

It has long been a central tenet of economic analysis, for example, that the best decision-making comes from having as much information as possible about the options at hand, and then—setting emotions aside—coolly performing a thoroughly

[1] See, for example, DeCanio (2003), Howarth and Norgaard (1992), Howarth (2003), Dietz and Stern (2008), and Ackerman (2009).

[2] In computer-speak, a potentially buggy version of a software package released for testing by prospective users is called a "beta version." Later releases considered error-free and stable enough for general use (though they will usually be further revised) are often referred to by version numbers.

rational (in the sense of following rules of logic) comparison and ranking of various outcomes. More recent work on decision-making, in contrast, demonstrates that less information and deliberation can sometimes lead to *more* satisfactory outcomes. Faced with too many choices, too much information, and/or too much emphasis on weighing and comparing, psychologists have found, people may make worse choices on decisions ranging from purchases of jams to comparisons of houses (Dijksterhuis, Bos, et al., 2006; Iyengar & Lepper, 2000). Use of intuition, rules of thumb, and unconscious processes may lead, in some cases, to better outcomes with less regret (Gigerenzer, 2007). Emotions have been found to be essential to rational (in the broad sense of reasonable and goal-serving) decision-making (Damasio, 1994). A newer view of reason that is rapidly gaining ground (outside of economics) emphasizes the embodied nature of our consciousness. As put by George Lakoff and Mark Johnson,

> ...[R]eason is not...a transcendent feature of the universe of or disembodied mind. Instead, it is shaped crucially by the peculiarities of our human bodies, by the remarkable details of the neural structure of our brains, and by the specifics of our everyday functioning in the world...Reason is evolutionary...Reason is not completely conscious, but mostly unconscious. Reason is not purely literal, but largely metaphorical and imaginative. Reason is not dispassionate, but emotionally engaged. (Lakoff & Johnson, 1999, p. 4)

Nor is reason something that is possessed by a lone agent in isolation: "The full understanding of mental phenomena should be sought in the context of an organism that is interacting with an environment" (Damasio, 1997, p. 170).

To give an example relevant to the case at hand, suppose you are taking a walk in a forest at dusk. You suddenly see something long, thin, and curving before you on the path and instinctively jump back. On second glance, it turns out that this object is just a piece of discarded rope. Was it rational for you to have recoiled? Defining rationality in the narrow sense of referring to only logic and deliberation, it was not rational. Because a piece of discarded rope is not dangerous, your recoil was neither reflective nor rationally justified by "the facts." Considering rationality in a broader and evolutionary sense, however, jumping backwards was a perfectly reasonable and, on average over such cases, likely survival-enhancing response. Instinctual recoil comes from a part of the brain that acts before the analytical processes have a chance to kick in. Had the rope been a snake, you could have been bitten while standing still waiting for your slower neural processes to inspect the object, weigh the evidence, and come to a decision. Holding out for the thoroughly informed and justified response is a sort of rationality that may be serviceable in simple, safe, and slow environments, but quite unserviceable outside of them.

It has also long been believed that individuals' preferences are stable, and immediately accessible for use in our rational deliberations. Our social and physical environments, however, have been shown to affect how we act in ways that are quite inaccessible to our conscious mind. Psychological studies of framing effects show repeatedly that exposure to movies that are funny or sad, drinks that are cold or hot, or smells that are good or bad, as well as minor changes to the wording of questions, can change our expressed opinions, stated reasons, and decisions.[3] The conscious

[3] See, as one examples of this now vast literature, Williams and Bargh (2008). Some of these phenomena have been incorporated into behavioral economics (Kahneman, 2003).

preferences thought to be sacrosanct in the rational choice view may in fact often not exist until they are unconsciously, externally, and perhaps somewhat capriciously created.

Likewise, while individual freedom has long been taken as the *summum bonum* to be aimed for, especially in regards to economic systems, new science is pointing to our deep ties to one another, though processes such as mirror neurons which make us feel and repeat in our own bodies the motions we see others enacting (Iacoboni, 2008). The point is not that individual freedom is unimportant, but that a monomaniacal focus on this "good" above all others leads to a serious neglect of—and even a blindness to—the interdependencies of family and community.

And, perhaps even more importantly, it has been assumed that the world we live in is such that it is amendable to cool, detached investigation and deliberation, and analytical models based on the mathematics of physics and engineering. In Enlightenment Beta the central metaphor used to think of natural processes is that of clockwork: Nature, by analogy to complex machinery, is imagined to be intricate but also thoroughly knowable and controllable. If the world was made by (Divine) Reason, and our species was uniquely (it was assumed) endowed with reason in order to know it and control it, then our technology and our philosophy makes us into demigods. But, as mentioned above, new generation science demonstrates that our human abilities of perception and cogitation are, in fact, evolved and embodied rather than being ethereally transmitted from a transcendent source. Even if we are convinced that there is a fundamental mathematical structure to the universe, new science suggests that a comparison of the complexity of this structure, vis a vis the limitations of our human wet-ware (brains), should be humbling. Epistemologically speaking, our knowledge is unavoidably limited and incomplete.

In Enlightenment Beta, the Divine Clockmaker set the world into ticking for our benefit. Such a helpful world, under our dominion, would provide for us and be safe. It would wait while we make our investigations and thoughtfully consider our next, progress-making interventions, quite free from worry about our own survival or subsistence. Yet as early as the 1890s, and exactly in the center of the newly forming Neoclassical school of economics, such an image was already being questioned. Writing in 1898 Alfred Marshall, the original great systematizer of Neoclassical economics, warned us about taking this image too seriously. Marshall recognized that Neoclassical economic models were based—not on revealed truth—but on metaphor: "There is a fairly close analogy between the *earlier stages* of economic reasoning and the devices of physical statics," he wrote, whereby by treating certain phenomena in isolation from each other can give some "exact and firm handling of a narrow issue" (Marshall, 1898, p. 40, emphasis added). In particular, he noted, Western Europe was, at the time in which he was writing, in a unique window of time and space uniquely free of the "black shadow" (1898, p. 41) of ecological limits. Consistent with what had been historically experienced up to his time, he conceived of these limits in terms of constraints imposed by agricultural fertility on population growth. Even with no knowledge of climate change, however, Marshall perceived that within some generations this unique window would close and ecological limits would again become important. To address this development, he said, economics would need to go beyond the "early stage" of physics analogies and notions of stable equilibria, and develop "later stage" organic notions of permeating "mutual influence" (43) based on biological analogies of "life and decay" (43). Marshall also recognized, as just discussed above, our epistemological constraints: "Man's [sic] powers are limited: almost every one of nature's riddles is complex" (40). Unfortunately, however, Marshall's warnings that holding onto the physics metaphor beyond its usefulness would tend to "confuse and warp the judgment" (39), and that freedom from limits was only temporary, seem to have been thoroughly forgotten by most economists in the orthodox mainstream where Neoclassical theories remain the touchstone.

The natural sciences have long since extended beyond the Newtonian mechanics on which Neoclassical economics modeled itself. The new science of climate change points out the (rather obvious, if we learn from the transition from our past to our present) fact that the future is unpredictable and that our well-being or even survival are not guaranteed. Climate change tells us that the world is not passive, submissive, willing to wait, and in existence simply for our benefit. Far from being a clockwork under our dominion, the climate system is, as one climate scientist has put it, "an angry beast and we are poking it with sticks."[4]

In Enlightenment Beta, the world was seen as supportive of the rational individual, predictable, and safe. The fields of physical science, philosophy, and economics that grew out of this mode of thought reflected these bedrock assumptions, employing a process in which bits of the world were analytically separated and explored. The goal was to find the universal rules and principles governing the world mechanism. Great strides were made, particularly in areas in which this world view and the actual world have some resemblance. But new science—science based not on Enlightenment Beta, but on a new world view that what we might call Enlightenment 2.0—points out that the world is also alive—and profoundly *unsafe, interdependent*, and *uncertain*. In the context of climate change, what does this demand of us? This essay suggests three central demands: first, that we *take action*; second, that we *work together*, and third, that we *avoid the worst cases*. But first, a few words are needed about some current views on ethics and economics that might seem to negate the need for any changes at all.

8.2 Ethics and Economics: Beyond the Split

To many who deal with economic issues, of course, discussion of ethics seems to be beside the point. Economic analysis is sometimes perceived of as value-free and objective, in contrast to ethical judgments that are normative and subjective. Such a view has been debunked at length by climate economists (e.g., Dietz & Stern, 2008; Howarth, 2003; Howarth & Norgaard, 1992), as well as philosophers (e.g., Kitcher, 2011; Putnam, 2003), and a full analysis will not be attempted here. Suffice it to

[4] Weitzman (2010), quoting climate scientist Wallace Broecker.

note that contemporary Neoclassical orthodoxy contains myriad value-judgments that only appear as objective from within a culture of disciplinary group-think in which alternatives are simply not entertained. The unquestioned priority given to individual freedom of choice, for example, is clearly a value judgment, in that it ranks freedom above other possible values—for example, ones that are more pro-social or pro-environment. The methodological valuing of the elegance, precision, and "artificial crispness" (Weitzman, 2009, p. 18) of mathematical models of optimization involves a normative and subjective judgment that these qualities are of more worth than other possible methodological goals, such as richness or realism. And, of course, economists should recognize the issue of opportunity cost: Research is not done in a vacuum, and the determination of our salaries and research budgets is based on decisions that value some lines of research above others. If economists are absorbed in rearranging deck chairs on the Titanic when we could have helped chart another course, we will bear some moral responsibility for the ship going down.

Alternatively, economists (and others interested in economic issues) may realize the relevance of ethical concerns, but consider ethics to be in the domain of the Philosophy Department. Paying more attention to ethics might seem to mean that we must become versed in deontology, consequentialism, virtue ethics, Kant, Rawls, Aristotle, and the like—or at least read those economists who try to translate such material into more familiar terms. Believing that such an investment is necessary before one can take an ethical stand, however, could be compared to believing that one must invest in economics graduate training before one can be allowed to make a purchase at the grocery store. Ethics is not something owned by the philosophy department, but rather something we, inescapably, *do*—just as we also, by virtue of being human, participate in economic life.

In fact, by deflecting our attention from the world we actually live in to the artificial rarified worlds lived in by the "liberal man" of traditional analytical philosophy and the "economic man" of orthodox Neoclassical economics, some discussions of moral philosophy and economics can be actively harmful. For example, Oxford economist and moral philosopher Jonathan Broome has penned, among other works, a background piece for the *Stern Review on Climate Change* (2006) and a high-profile article on climate ethics for *Scientific American* (2008). His background piece is thoroughly based on economistic expected utility theory and the reductionist ethics of aggregating quantities and qualities of life dependent only on utilities from the consumption of goods (2008, p. 15). In his 2008 article, Broome's assertion that future generations will "be richer than we are" seems to be borrowed from economists who project GDP growing forever. Such an assertion, of course, is based on nothing more than unscientific extrapolation about the entire future based on the very recent (in human history) past, supplemented by extreme assumptions about the substitutability between natural and other forms of capital. Broome's "elementary moral principle" that "you should not do something for your own benefit if it harms another person" or at least "compensate" them for it if you do (2008, p. 97)—reflects the generally status-quo-preserving criterion of Pareto Efficiency enshrined in orthodox economics. While Broome uses his principle to argue that "the better-off among the current generation" should take the first steps towards climate change mitigation, this "elementary moral principle" could also be used to argue that if protection of the residents of Bangladesh from climate change harms living standards in industrialized countries, then Bangladeshis should pay compensation to residents of those countries.

Also reflecting his economics training, Broome insists that the ethical question be formulated in terms of a search for the "correct discount rate" and that philosophers concerned with the extinction of humanity must express the badness of this loss "in quantitative terms" (2008, pp. 102, 100). While taken as a whole Broome's work comes down on the side of doing *something* about climate change, he suggests that detailed and quantitatively sophisticated work by ethicists and economists must precede democratic rational deliberation, which in turn much precede action on a societal scale. As in other studies of this ilk, the immediate prescription is not for action, but for further research. That might be a proper and reasonable view—were the world safe, rational, and certain. But what about the world that we live in?

8.3 We Must Take Action

What climate change demands of us has extremely little to do with becoming well-versed in academic moral philosophy and everything to do with how we understand our situation as human beings facing a crisis of potentially immense magnitude.[5] Recent studies of actual human moral action, in fact, suggest that the traditional focus of moral philosophy on principles and deliberation may be nearly beside the point. Principles may be based on reason, but action is based on motivation. The important roles that emotion, imagination, narrative, socialization, and bodily activity play in shaping moral action are now being more strongly recognized.

Consider first the case of moral emotions. Most economists and analytical philosophers consider these to be unnecessary, or even distracting and detrimental, to moral judgment. Yet psychological studies using brain imaging, observation of people with specific brain damage, and other techniques are demonstrating that moral judgment is—initially at least, and often entirely—more a matter of affective moral response than of moral reasoning. Moral reasoning, rather than being part of the process of coming to a judgment, is more often—as a practical and empirical matter—involved in possible *post hoc* justifications of a judgment already arrived at intuitively.[6] That is, we often sense the "rightness" or "wrongness" of something,

[5] Or, as put by a broader-thinking ethical philosopher: "Ethics is not about what detached, impersonal, objective, rational agents engaged in grand theorizing deduce. Rather, ethics is and should be about what imperfect human beings living in particular historical, socioeconomic contexts can and should do, given those contexts" (Warren, 2000, p. 114).

[6] Or, perhaps, we arrive at the judgments opportunistically. Mary C. Gentile recounts this tale of an MBA graduate being asked about what he had learned in a traditional course on business ethics graduate explained that he had "learned all about the models of ethical analysis…and that when-

and then may work to come up with reasons for what we feel (Greene & Haidt, 2002; Greene, Sommerville, et al., 2001; Haidt, 2001). This is not to say that introspective moral reasoning plays *no* role—people may in some circumstances consciously reflect on their intuitive judgments, and then change their mind. While the willingness of an individual to rationally pore over and consider revising his or her moral views is admirable, in practice this seems to occur relatively rarely.

The word "*mot*ivation" has the same root as "e*mot*ion." For questions of positive moral action—as opposed to moral judgment—emotional responses such as empathy, sadness, and shame seem to be particularly important, while the role of moral reasoning is particularly weak. One can be an expert on the many ways of formulating principles of justice, but—as a number of commentators are now pointed out (Haidt, 2001; Jonas, 1984, p. 85; Warren, 2000, p. 112)—if one does not have some emotional motivation—if one does not *care* about acting justly, for example—all the principles in the world will have no effect on behavior.

A motivating emotion of particular importance to the case of climate change, may be, as suggested by noted environmental ethicist Hans Jonas in his 1984 book *The Imperative of Responsibility*, that of fear. While much of Jonas' argument is phrased in the traditional styles of philosophical argument, he also points out that our development of technological powers with potentially profound and irreversible effects on the environment has created a world in which past and present experiences (Jonas, 1984, p. 27) and the traditional ethics of rights and duties (Jonas, p. 38) no longer serve as adequate guides. Linked to the point (to be argued at more length below) that what we need now is more attention to the avoidance of catastrophes than the achievement of best outcomes, he argues that fear is a useful emotion for promoting action.

Notions of *moral imagination* and *narrative* are also central to the questions of ethical motivation. As Jonas put it, our "first duty" is to "visualize" the effects of our harmful environmental practices (27): "[T]he creatively imagined *malum*," he wrote, "has to take over the role of the experienced *malum*, and this imagination does not arise on its own but must be intentionally induced" (27). The by now *pro forma* introduction of articles on climate change with extensive reviews of specific, concrete dangers (e.g., sea level rise, methane clathrate releases, disruption of the thermohaline circulation, floods, droughts, storms, and so on—often expressed with vivid geographic specificity) can thus be seen as an essential and vitally important part of a responsible ethical practice. So, also, are narratives which (while they may seem wildly overoptimistic given current political conditions) encourage people to have some hopefulness and a "can-do" attitude about addressing climate change. As long as there is life, there is hope.

Our actions are often also based on simple heuristics (Gigerenzer, 2007) and good narratives (Lakoff, 2004, Chap. 6; Taleb, 2010), more than the logical weighing of alternatives. This suggests that, for inspiring action on climate change, detailed, rational, technocratic arguments—e.g., debates on the parameterization of climate and cost-benefit models—may be less useful than economists generally prefer to think. While there is an important, *defensive* role to be played by economists

ever he encountered a conflict, he could decide what he wanted to do and then select the model of ethical reasoning that would best support his choice" (Gentile, 2010, p. xi).

who critique existing models that prescribe inaction (e.g., Ackerman & Finlayson, 2006; Ackerman & Munitz, 2011; Stanton, 2011), it would be a profound mistake to think that the creation of models *prescribing* action would do much, by itself, to avert catastrophe. Models—unlike emotions, moral imagination, and the stories that generate them—simply do not motivate. What gives "go slow" economic models their current power in directing (in)action is not the elegance of their equations—though this does create a barrier-to-entry effect, putting them seemingly beyond the critique of non-economists and non-mathematicians. Rather, they are but one small part of a general narrative of "regulatory burden," "costs," "price increases," and "job losses"—said to arise if mitigation efforts interfere with the "engine" (note the mechanical metaphor) of GDP growth. This narrative is being widely hyped throughout our societies by powerful coal, oil, and other interests with something to lose.

Can the powers of fear and story-telling be abused? Absolutely. We have seen this to the *n*th degree in the United States, in fear-inspiring narratives of "weapons of mass destruction" and color-coded terrorism alerts. Do we need to continue to think rationally about outcomes and weigh risks, in cases where this can be productively accomplished? Absolutely. Nothing in the above should be taken as supporting an abandonment of reason in favor of "anything goes" emotionalism and con-artist story-spinning. But is there any good alternative to using emotional energy and effective storytelling to get societies moving on climate change? Letting things proceed with "business-as-usual" is profoundly unsafe. Attempting to create motivation through strictly cool, rational processes is profoundly ineffective. There is no rational, clockwork, safe world to which we can retreat from this dilemma, brushing messy decisions off our hands. The question is not whether to tap emotions and narratives or not, but how to come up with good and useful ones that foster the sorts of changes that are needed. We should, given the contemporary state of the world, be required to attach a large red health-warning label. Perhaps, it might be argued, that while all this is necessary, it is not the role of economists to work on narratives. Such a view, however, ignores the fact that contemporary mainstream economics is a narrative (McCloskey, 1985), and an extremely culturally powerfully one at that. While we are accustomed to hiding the story under layers of physics-emulating math, the story we tell is about a fictional world of mechanism and control, where a focus on small (marginal) changes is appropriate. When we use such a story in our research or teaching we should, given the contemporary state of the world, be required to attach a large red health-warning label. And in particular, we should flag the part of the story that glamorizes individual self-interested choice.

8.4 We Must Work Together

Reflecting on Republican narratives on health care, climate change, and nearly every other issue that has recently come before the United States Congress, the parody on-line magazine *The Onion* recently suggested a scenario: A massive asteroid is hurtling towards earth, threatening massive conflagrations and extinctions.

The "article" quotes fictional Republican congresspersons arguing that government spending on trying to change the asteroid's course would involve "big government" and "lost jobs." "We believe" they state, "that the decisions of how to deal with the massive asteroid are best left to the individual" (*The Onion*, 2011).

While the fundamental unit of both Neoclassical economics and analytical philosophy is the human individual, and a fundamental ethical value is that of individual freedom, mitigation of climate change requires action on a vastly broader scale. Not only must people cooperate within communities and nations, but across national boundaries. We need to work together. Our abilities to think about how we might do this, however, are hampered by Enlightenment Beta habits of narrowly focusing on the single value of individual freedom, to the exclusion of other values.

In particular, the long-running central narrative of economics has contributed greatly to the current U.S. sentiments in favor of permissive indulgence of economic self-interest and the radical weakening of regulation or any form of centralized government power. Although Adam Smith would no doubt be greatly alarmed to see the exaggeration and distortion that this particular idea of his has suffered over the centuries, the story about the "invisible hand" of decentralized markets making individual self-interest serve the social good has become not only an economic but also a political and cultural mantra. Markets, it is now believed, vacate the necessity for ethics or shame.

Much as we, as economists, may try to nuance this story of radical self-interested individualism by pointing to insights about externalities and public goods, those are usually part of Lesson 2 (or, more likely, Chap. 14), and only picked up on by our better students. Lesson 1, from the way we currently teach economics—and blared incessantly from right-wing blogs and institutes—is that social cooperation is not necessary, and even becomes detrimental (i.e., freedom-reducing) in a competitive-market-based, GDP-growth aspiring economy. For keeping this as Lesson 1, the economics discipline carries a good deal of responsibility for the cultural shift towards radical individualism that underlies the current failure of climate policy.[7] We have actively helped to create a climate of, as Amartya Sen and Jean Drèze expressed it (in the context of global hunger), "complacent irresponsibility" (1989, p. 276).

A second legacy of Enlightenment Beta is a preference for thinking in terms of easily separable, analytically-well-defined concepts, and ignoring actual multi-level interdependencies and feedback loops. When pressed to go beyond the assumption that people are self interested, we may flip to an opposite assumption of altruism. When we find that pure free markets do not work quite right, we flip to an assumption of top-down public policy-making. In political philosophy, either we have a participatory democracy based on rational conversation, or we have oppression. Let us re-examine these Enlightenment Beta assumptions, first at the level of the propensities of individuals to cooperate or not, and then at the level of social and institutional organization.

[7] See Frank, Gilovich, et al. (1993) for evidence that economics teaching has this effect.

8.4.1 Not Just "Altruism"

Within economics, "self-interest" is thought of in terms of a utility function that includes only one's own consumption (including, perhaps, leisure and various intangibles), while "altruism" is represented by a utility function that includes the utility (or consumption) of others. This totally inadequate vocabulary severely distorts our thinking, directing attention away from our fundamental physical, social, and emotional interdependences—as well, as many others have pointed out, from issues of what really gives us satisfaction (Haidt, 2006).

The term "altruism," in fact, is given the impossible duty of covering everything from my taking minor notice of your interests as a way of furthering my own "enlightened" self-interest, to you sacrificially throwing yourself in front of a bus to save a child's life. More nuance is clearly required, and particularly in the context of the issue of climate change where the nature of our interdependence with future generations is rather different from that across contemporary people and nations.

The issue of how the current generation interacts with future generations is characterized by extreme non-reciprocity.[8] The fact that future generations cannot give us anything in return for actions we may take out of our concern with their well-being means that liberal theories of ethics based on enlightened self-interest and reciprocal relations among agents of equal status are hopelessly inadequate.

Fortunately, scholars who study moral action cross-culturally have identified individualistic principles as only one cluster among three that tend to inspire and inform cultural moral codes. Individualistic principles are concerned with individual goals, reciprocity, and nonharming. The second cluster revolves around community, loyalty, ingroups, hierarchy, and wise leadership. The third emphasizes divinity and purity (Gigerenzer, 2007, p. 187; Haidt, 2006, p. 188). What is striking about these later two clusters, to one coming from an Enlightenment Beta background, is their radically un-self-centered core. There is a sense in these that something is *demanded of* us, rather than merely subject to our choice or created in order to further our individual freedom. Unlike individual goals that can be traded off, issues related to community and purity are usually perceived of as in some way non-negotiable and absolute—or, as put by scholar of decision-making Gerd Gigerenzer, "not up for sale" (2007, p. 206). In the global scheme of things, our Western—and more specifically, U.S. and secular academic—predilection to emphasize only one of these clusters is a historical and geographical anomaly.[9]

Can the moral clusters that revolve around community and divinity serve oppressive ends? Certainly. Enlightenment Beta was initially in some sense a highly progressive force, given the feudal political and religious hierarchies of the time. The popularity of individualist approaches in recent history may be in part a reaction to

[8] In Nelson (2005) I call this "asymmetric mutuality."

[9] While U.S. culture seems to draw less from these later two than many other cultures, they are not completely absent: "Ask not what your country can do for you," President John F. Kennedy famously exhorted, "but what you can do for your country."

the oppressive collectivism of Fascism and Stalinism. Likewise, rational (in the broad sense of reasonable) projects in contemporary societies may be obstructed by NIMBY (not-in-my-backyard) or racist in-group sentiments and religious fundamentalism.

Should individualist ethics be entirely thrown over in favor of community and purity? Certainly not. Individual rights are important, even if they are not all-important. The point of this essay is not to reverse course, nor even that we need to seek to introduce somewhat more consideration of other ethical clusters into our social decision making. Rather, I want to make the empirical point that such clusters already function in social decision making. For example, many economists' allegiance to seeing behavior exclusively in terms of utility or profit maximization, in spite of all evidence to the contrary, is arguably motivated along these lines: Feelings of in-group professional loyalty and/or implicit beliefs in the purity of (Divine) Reason might go a long way in explaining such puzzling behavior. At the other pole of environmental discussions, philosopher Robert E. Goodin's revulsion towards pollution permits seems to be based in a purity ethic (Goodin, 2010, p. 241), as may be the positions of many who equate "nature" with "wilderness" (e.g., McKibben, 1989). Values clustered around community and purity have not received adequate attention within academic individualist-oriented economics and philosophy not because they don't already exist, but because Beta-induced blindness says they *should* not exist.

What does climate change *demand of us*? The phrasing of the subtitle of this essay was very deliberately chosen. Hans Jonas, after extensive discussions of Enlightenment Beta ethical axioms, "the idea of Man" (1984, p. 43), rational principles, Kant, and so on in his *Imperative of Responsibility*, ultimately claims that the type of ethics that we need comes from quite a different source:

> [A]ll proofs of validity for moral prescriptions are ultimately reduced to obtaining evidence of an 'ontological' ought…[W]hen asked for a single instance…where the coincidence of 'is' and 'ought' occurs, we can point at the most familiar sight: the newborn, whose mere breathing uncontradictably addresses an ought to the world around, namely, to take care of him. Look and you know. (Jonas, 1984, pp. 130–31)

That is, "the always acute, unequivocal, and choiceless responsibility which the newborn claims for himself" creates "the ought-to-do of the subject who, in virtue of his power, is called to its care" (Jonas, 1984, pp. 134, 93). Rather than simply grounding a formal responsibility or accountability for deeds, the newborn demands of us a substantive responsibility for care. The sight of the newborn is specific, emotional, and moves us in some sense out of ourselves. Its demand is grounded not in notions of independent agents, but in a recognition of the infant's profound aliveness and profound fragility. It is grounded in a visceral perception of the deep interdependence of life, and the totally inegalitarian distribution—between the parent and the newborn—of the power to act to support and sustain that life.

This insight does not, of course, immediately generalize to all situations of adults and children, or to the situation of generation and future ones, or situations of rich and poor. But perhaps it contains the seed for the recognition of common humanity and substantive responsibilities for care. It is not a notion of simple "altruism," either in the economists' usual sense (since the adults "preferences" are rather beside the point) or in the sense of selfless sacrifice (since the adult remains—and must, for the sake of the newborn, function as—an active individual). The necessary ethic for us in regard to future generations has more to do with Amartya Sen's "commitment" than with his "sympathy" (1977).[10]

But what of our relations to others of our current generation, with whom climate change demands that we cooperate? Here reciprocity among similarly situated people—as well as non-reciprocal care towards people with less power—is also involved. If we assume that people and nations are purely self-interested and prone to free riding, then of course the situation is hopeless. The costs climate change will inflict on the currently powerful are not enough to "incentivize" change. Calls for personal virtue and individual radical lifestyle change, on the other hand, while popular among the idealistic (and especially the young and idealistic) rely on an opposite assumption that individuals will act from their highest principles no matter how other similarly-situated people act. Yet empirical evidence demonstrates that many very concerned people, have not (yet, at least) become car-less, non-flying, vegetarian locavores, perhaps because we have noticed that such individual changes are more symbolic than substantive until larger social and structural issues are addressed. What is to be done?

Here some very simple broadening of economists' assumptions about human ethical motivations may be of service. Howard Margolis (1982) suggested that a model of humans as desiring to be "neither selfish nor exploited" better explains actual behavior than assumptions of either pure self-interest or pure sacrificial altruism. Business scholar J. Gregory Dees and economist Peter Cramton similarly have proposed a tripartite structure that delineates among opportunists (pure egoists), moral idealists (pure altruists), and what they call "pragmatists," or people who "are willing and able to constrain their self-seeking behavior for moral reasons, provided that they can be reasonably sure that others with whom they are interacting will do so as well" (1991, p. 146). Business ethicist Mary Gentile has, in practice, found that most people identify themselves along the "pragmatist" lines, but need practice in giving voice to their values (2010). Institutionalist economists have, of course, for generations now emphasized that societies shape individuals at the same time that individuals shape societies. Such literatures suggest that working with ethics as a question of concrete, active, trust-based and goal directed social behavior could take us down more helpful roads than discussions limited to private incentives or individual virtue.

Some evidence on how social values are created, and changed, already exists, and the evidence, again, does not bode well for theories of disembodied rational

[10] Perhaps more acceptance by scholars of climate change of such demands on us would also help create better ties between scholars and members of more traditional cultures or moderate religious groups. A haughty attitude of superior secularism, and out-of-hand dismissal of the sorts of rituals and practices that encourage communal and spiritual identities, does not win academics many friends.

agents. As Haidt writes, investigation into the shaping of moral judgments suggests that "[c]ultural knowledge is a complex web of explicit and implicit, sensory and propositional, affective, cognitive, and motoric knowledge" (2001, p. 827). Gigerenzer suggests that moral intuitions are a sort of unconscious "moral grammar," built up within particular social environments and having emotional goals, and taking the form of gut feelings or rules of thumb (2007, p. 185).[11]

Consider, for example, why soldiers practice marching in formation for hours, often chanting at the same time. I had always assumed this was merely a matter of practicing moving efficiently from Point A to Point B until this literature drew my attention to "motoric" knowledge and the bodily enculturation of moral values. Drawing on work by neuroscientist Andrew Newbury, Haidt points out that repetitive motor activities and chanting have been used throughout history to create "resonance patterns" among people that lead to feelings of group harmony and cohesion (2006, p. 237). Similarly, behavioral scientists, including economists, have found that the creation of apparently substantively meaningless group identifications among experiment subjects (e.g., assignment to a "team" that never works together) can create in-group feelings.

Can such use of embodied, affective, in-group-oriented rituals and perceptions be abused? Of course. Historically, the next step after creating military group cohesion has been to go attack some other group. Yet what we—we, as a global humanity—need in order to gain a sense of confidence and mutual trust is precisely some such heightened recognition of our common identity. The issue, again, is not whether such techniques will be used—advertisers have been exploiting them left and right for decades—but how they will be used. There is no safe alternative. Our choices are not between group loyalty and pure individual freedom, but about what kind of group loyalties our culture—and more specifically, our discipline—encourages.

8.4.2 More than "Conversation"

At a more structural level, if we can't count on the market to coordinate our actions in a morally appropriate direction, what can we trust? Perhaps the public sphere, considered as an ideal realm of deliberation?

---

[11] Exactly how specific environmental structures (e.g., default rules, incentives, framing factors, feedback or lack thereof, and peer pressure) can has been interestingly demonstrated in two recent explorations. Gigerenzer reports on the analysis of the judgments of a group of English magistrates. While perceiving themselves as making complex and rational decisions in the service of justice, the magistrates in actuality acted more in accord with a goal of not being blamed for bad releases of criminal suspects (Gigerenzer, 2007, p. 197). Kitcher, in a refreshing change from philosophies of science that treat science as a pure search for truth, takes into account the more personal goal of a scientist to be "the one who found out the truth" (2011, p. 238), and looks at the implications of this for that social project. A similar study of economists does not come to mind, though a brief study by Margolis suggests that economists are just as prone to the errors of logic that rational choice theorists disdain (Margolis, 1982).

A number of philosophers who encourage immediate, ethically grounded action on climate change base their arguments in the idea of an ideal human conversation or ideal participatory democracy in which all views are expressed. Philosopher of science Philip Kitcher has recently given cogent arguments, for example, about the inescapability of ethical questions, grounded in such a conversational narrative (2011).[12] Environmental philosopher Dale Jamieson similarly emphasizes participatory democracy (2010, p. 84). Economist Partha Dasgupta has suggested (in relation to global poverty) that there is a hard-and-fast dichotomy between the market sphere, in which "we should not worry about others" and the public sphere in which such worry and ethical concern is appropriate (2005, p. 247, 2007, p. 151). Dasgupta puts his hope in "well-ordered" democracies with civic education and rational voting rules that, as far as possible, properly aggregate individual preferences (2007, p. 152).

Is there not some sense, however, in which such an image of an ethics-creating process engaged in by cooperating, rational, adult conversationalists, in fact assumes its own result? What would it take, in the real world, to get adults sitting at a table (or, perhaps, squatting under a tree), unarmed, adequately nourished and reasonably healthy, speaking a common language, willing to put time into the effort, and respectful of others' contributions to the mutual conversation? As a more skeptical philosopher notes, "the homogenized—you might say sterilized—rational subject" who settles things through conversation and rational deliberation is apparently "not prey to ambivalence, anxiety, obsession, prejudice, hatred, or violence" (Meyers, 2010). Two elements that seem to me to be lacking in discussions centered around "conversation" are first, leadership, and second, habit and custom.

Our working together can also come through moral and political leadership—on scales from the very local, through communities, through religious and educational organizations, through companies,[13] and on up through states and nations and global fora. Leading means being willing to get out in front of the pack. Leading means working to create those shifts that will give ethical "pragmatists" the confidence to do the right thing. I was greatly surprised, in conversing a few years back with a

[12] Kitcher writes, for example, that "…our Paleolithic predecessors sat down together to decide on the precepts for governing their group life" (2011, p. 42). Relevant to the discussion of the previous section, Kitcher also seems to prioritize reason over emotion when thinking about human motivation. Kitcher assumes that his imagined contemporary human conversationalists, in their weighing of benefits and economic costs, are more moved by the idea of harm to future humans than by issues of species extinction, so that the moral focus should be on the former (2011, pp. 296–7). Yet it seems, empirically, that people are—for better or (mostly, from a humanitarian viewpoint) worse—often more moved by the plight of their pets, to whom they have emotional attachments, and by the plight of big-eyed animals that bring out protective feelings, than by human suffering abroad (especially chronic poverty). While it may be appealing, from the point of view of ethical principles, to disdain the human tendency to focus on "charismatic metafauna" such as baby seals and polar bears, from the point of view of ethical motivation it is not so clear that vividly describing the effects of climate change on Fido and Whiskers is a bad idea.

[13] The idea that companies are immune from ethical concerns because their nature is to maximize profits is a creation of economists—strongly preached by Milton Friedman, and weakly preached in all orthodox economics classes. It does not need to be believed (Nelson, forthcoming).

noted environmental philosopher, that while he had adopted rather radical lifestyle changes himself in response to climate change, he felt he had no obligation, or even right, to encourage others to do the same. In his role as resident ethicist in various working groups on climate change, he shied away from any intervention that might carry a whiff of prescription or exhortation—that is, from any role as a leader rather than as a "neutral" expert.

Can leadership be abused? No doubt. Hitler and Pol Pot immediately spring to mind, and there are countless other horrific examples. One can only be glad, however, that Gandhi, Martin Luther King, Harriet Beecher Stowe and others were not so overly scrupulous. Radical decentralization and (perhaps impossible) ideal democratic conversations is not the only alternative to bad leadership. Good leadership is also possible—and necessary.

Habits, customs, and other widely spread practices are also ways of generating and sustaining cooperation. Nobel Laureate Elinor Ostrom's work on governance of the commons, for example, points towards the role of relatively decentralized and informal rules, institutions, and trust-creating processes in supporting appropriate community behavior (1990). A recent book by Harvard scholar Elaine Scarry suggests that the urgency of a crisis need not be taken as a sign that it requires centralized, top-down action. Rapid response, she suggests, can also come from "practices that we dismiss as mere habit and protocol" (2011). The routes to change suggested by the creation of habits of household recycling, for example—or even the spread of the sometimes-ridiculed "bring your own shopping bag" practice—might, in this sense, hold more promise for action on climate change than their current actual impact on the problem (which is exceedingly small) would suggest.

Nicholas Stern writes that focusing on issues of "credibility, trust and mutual confidence" as well as on "how to foster change" are critical for moving forward on climate issues (2011, p. 10). While economists should not drop our more conventional efforts towards advising on national-level regulation and international agreements, such levels of action cannot be the whole story about learning to work together. Particularly when those avenues seem, as in the United States at present, to be largely blocked, as social scientists economists could also contribute to action by directing attention to these other avenues of change. At the very least, we could stop preaching their neglect, by including in our textbooks only self-interested individuals.

8.5 We Must Focus on Avoiding the Worst

In a mechanical, safe, rational, and certain world, we can strive to achieve the very best. If, conveniently, that world is also characterized by smoothly differentiable functions, small changes, and known probabilities of events, we can optimize using techniques of calculus. We can build mathematical models pointing the way to maximum efficiency, and forecast the future using our models and data from the past. Such Enlightenment Beta "early stage" (to quote Marshall, above) approaches, however, do not provide guidance for dealing with living complexities and potentially catastrophic change.

In his recent bestseller, *The Black Swan*, professor and trader Nassim Nicholas Taleb has taken the discipline of economics harshly (though also, in a dark way, amusingly) to task for this neglect (2010). Taleb convincingly argues that history is mainly created by large and fundamentally unpredictable events—Black Swans (e.g., inventions and revolutions)—rather than small events that follow appealing narratives of cause and effect. Just as every day that it gets fed confirms a turkey's narrative about the beneficence of human beings, so that it is not prepared for the Wednesday before Thanksgiving (40), we are deceived if we think we can predict the future. Mainstream economics' emphasis on mechanistic modeling and econometrics is, Taleb claims, therefore not just somewhat beside the point but actively harmful. By directing people's attention to optimization and efficiency, we have distracted them from true uncertainty.

The denial of Black Swans leads to the creation of fragile social and economic systems—systems that are designed to be "optimal" relative to what we know, but which are extremely vulnerable to what we do not know (321). The financial crisis of 2008 thus, Taleb writes, was actually not a Black Swan, but instead a somewhat predictable Grey Swan: "You know with near certainty that a plane flown by an incompetent pilot will eventually crash" (321).[14]

Taleb, along with economist Weitzman, is bringing to economic and popular attention the notion of "fat tails" in probability distributions. While most economic models that include uncertainty assume that the probability of rare events falls off quickly and smoothly, in a world with "fat tails" there may lurk a rare, never before-experienced event of huge consequence. The usual expected utility approach of adding up the values of outcomes multiplied by their associated probabilities falls apart in this case (Taleb, 2010; Weitzman, 2011; see also "dread risk" in Gigerenzer and Fiedler undated). This does not mean, however, that there is no rational way of responding. Rather, the rational response is to "invest in preparedness, not in prediction" (Taleb, 2010, p. 208). The rational response is to pay attention to the size of the consequences, not the size of the (unknowable) probabilities, and then try to "mitigate the consequences" (Taleb, p. 211).

Epistemic humility, mentioned earlier in this essay as a characteristic of the needed Enlightenment 2.0, is a thoroughly necessary and rational response to the existence of unpredictable worst cases. In regard to climate change, Taleb writes,

> The position I suggest should be based both on ignorance and on deference to the wisdom of Mother Nature, since she is older than us, hence wiser than us, and has been proven much smarter than scientists. We do not understand enough about Mother Nature to mess with her…we are facing nonlinearities and magnifications of errors…we need to be hyper-conservationists ecologically…the burden of proof is…on someone disrupting the old system. (Taleb, 2010, pp. 315–16)

[14] See also DeMartino (2011, pp. 144–153) for a discussion of the ethical implications of economists advocating "optimal" but (since much is unknown) potentially damaging structures.

Elsewhere he refers to "elephant matriarchs" (78) and "grandmothers" (332) as the keepers of long-time-frame, conservative, life-preserving wisdom (in contrast to the "institutionalized frauds" (210) of neoclassical economics). Redundancy, Taleb writes, is "the opposite of" optimization and efficiency, and is the key component of this wisdom (312).

Epistemic humility, however, is in very short supply in some areas of environmental economics and policy. Belief that massive geoengineering,[15] for example, would be the best first-line defense against climate change is a thoroughly Enlightenment Beta-inspired project: It attempts to solve a problem caused by our ignorance and hubris by adding more of the same. More crucially, in relation to current U.S. environmental policy, epistemic humility is in short supply at the helm of the White House Office of Information and Regulatory Affairs. Cass Sunstein, administrator of this office and noted contributor to legal philosophy, has recently derided the Precautionary Principle—alluded to at the end of the Taleb quote above—as rigid and unworkable (2002/2003, 2005). He seems to miss the point of this principle, which in spirit is an admonition to be humbly careful about messing around with complex natural systems that we do not really fully understand. Adhering to the idea that all principles must be logically crisp and clear, Sunstein reinterprets the Precautionary Principles as essentially another version of economists' Pareto Efficiency criterion: Because there are risks "on all sides of social situations," an admonition to do no harm to anyone (like an admonition to leave everyone at least as well off), he writes, "will be paralyzing, forbidding any imaginable step, including no step at all" (2002/2003, p. 32). He dismisses the tendency of people to focus on outcomes and neglect probabilities (which Taleb, Weitzman, and Gigerenzer argue can be a wise move in some cases) as simply an unfortunate psychological anomaly, and blithely assumes that unknown probabilities arise in regard to natural systems only in "special circumstances" (2005, p. 114).[16] Sunstein appears to believe we live in a fundamentally safe and predictable world.

Does this need for epistemic humility mean that, for ethical reasons, Neoclassically-trained economists need to give up our usual modes of analysis? I have, above, mentioned a defensive role for using such tools to counteract go-slow arguments framed in the same mode. I would also acknowledge that techniques such as cost-effectiveness analysis could play something of a role in the evaluation of specific alternative projects, once mitigation (and adaptation) efforts are underway. Yet I think the primary message of climate change—and Enlightenment 2.0—is that our profession requires a major shift.

---

[15] For an example of advocacy of this from within the U.S. Environmental Protection Agency, see Carlin (2008).

[16] Other economistic approaches are also apparent in his work—for example, in the idea that (a la Schelling) a loss of agriculture in wealthy countries would not hurt much because agricultural production makes up a small proportion of GDP (Sunstein, 2002/2003, p. 36), and in a pervasive framing of the issues in terms of cost–benefit individual freedom (Sunstein, 2005).

8.6 Concrete Steps

Let me suggest a few major themes that should be immediately incorporated in economists' work, in economists' roles as researchers, public intellectuals, teachers, consultants, reviewers of papers and grants, and so on:

- Be willing to take an ethical stand on climate change. There is no place to hide from this. Economists don't contain some kind of ethereal, neutral economist part that exists separately from our human bodies and human responsibility.
- Regard economics as being about provisioning—that is, the way societies organize themselves to provide for the sustaining and flourishing of life.[17] This avoids the dead ends inherent in notions centered around rational choice or markets—and also corresponds better to what outsiders believe they are paying us to help them with.
- Spread the world that economics is not just about self-interest and accumulating more goods. While this may mean breaking our old professional habits, it will, in fact, make economists seem more sane to outsiders. Behavioral economics, the economics of happiness, and the economics of interpersonal relations may be of some help here, since they raise questions about whether such pursuits necessarily lead to enhanced well-being.[18]
- Become more active in researching how—structurally, institutionally, culturally, and morally—people come to take action, work together, and avoid catastrophe. Instead of dreaming up ideal structures in our heads, could we get involved in the actual investigative study of structures of resilience and robustness?
- In regard to the environment, include conservative—in the sense of precautionary—viewpoints in our work and teaching. Adding "resource maintenance" to the usual list of main economic activities (i.e., production, distribution, and consumption) is a start.[19]
- Include a healthy respect for uncertainty and danger in our work—and respect for the aliveness that demands our care-giving response.

This list is not meant to be exhaustive or timeless. If nothing else, at sometime Enlightenment 3.0—should humans survive to see it—will require different perspectives and priorities.

---

[17] This definition has been used by Institutional, social, and feminist economists (e.g., Nelson, 1993).

[18] For example, Camerer, Loewenstein, et al. (2003), Kahneman (2003), Gui and Sugden (2005), Frey (2008), and Gui and Stanca (2010).

[19] This approach is used in teaching materials from the Global Development and Environment Institute (e.g., Goodwin, Nelson, et al., 2008).

8.7 Conclusion

The world we live in is profoundly unsafe, interdependent, and uncertain. Economics that neglects these facts—or, even worse, distracts us from them with stories about mechanism and predictability—does harm. It is high time for economics to catch up with both science and social needs, and become a positive force in dealing with climate change.

8.8 Coda

There is one quite obvious reason for the evident resistance to updating Enlightenment Beta that I have declined to expound on in the body of this essay. Feminist philosophers and economists have long noted the alignment between Enlightenment Beta ideals and dominant cultural understandings of masculinity (e.g., Keller, 1985; Nelson, 1995). It is both encouraging and irksome to see some realization of this coming out in some of the above-referenced literature, but with no acknowledgement of the work already done by feminist scholars.

Taleb's positive valuation of Mother Nature, grandmothers, and matriarchs and Gigerenzer's revaluing of stereotypically female "intuition" (2007, pp. 69–73) for both men and women are striking examples of some of the anti-macho aspects of Enlightenment 2.0. When Jonas sees critical ethical importance in a parent's response to a newborn, he briefly notes that this is most strongly experienced by "the childbearing part of humanity" (1984, p. 39)—in other words, women. Such recoveries of long-neglected parts of human experience are reminiscent of extensive feminist work on the moral philosophy and economics of care (e.g., Folbre, 2001; Meyers, 2010; Ruddick, 1989).

It is simply irksome, however, to see feminist scholarship ignored in places where it would be supremely relevant. For example, Haidt's critique of conventional notions of moral reasoning does not even mention Carol Gilligan's earlier influential critique and the resulting controversies (Gilligan, 1982; Jaffee & Hyde, 2000), and even recent volumes may still call on only male authors (e.g., Gardiner, Caney, et al., 2010) when prominent female and feminist authors—e.g., Chris Cuomo (2005), Nancy Tuana (Brown, Lemons, et al., 2006), and Karen Warren (2000)—could have been included.

The point is not that "women do it differently." Rather, having been excluded from full membership in Enlightenment Beta from the start, women have tended to be better positioned to notice the one-sided masculine-stereotyped gender of the ideals that it adopted. However, it is still the case that what a woman says is often not heard until a man repeats it. Or until a disaster occurs.[20]

[20] This includes even prominent women directing important U.S. economic offices: See the comments made by Sheila Bair, chair of the FDIC (in Scherer, 2010).

Acknowledgments Financial support for this project was received from Economists for Equity and the Environment.

References

Ackerman, F. (2009). *Can we afford the future? (The economics of a warming world)*. London: Zed Books.

Ackerman, F., & Finlayson, I. (2006). The economics of inaction on climate change: A sensitivity analysis. *Climate Policy, 6*(5), 509–526.

Ackerman, F., Munitz, C. (2011). *Climate damages in the FUND model: A disaggregated analysis. Economists for equity and the environment*. Working Paper.

Broome, J. (2006). *Valuing policies in response to climate change: Some ethical issues. Supporting research for the stern review on the economics of climate change*. http://www.hm-treasury.gov.uk/media/5/0/stern_review_supporting_technical_material_john_broome_261006.pdf

Broome, J. (2008). The ethics of climate change. *Scientific American, 298*(6), 97–102.

Brown, D., Lemons, J., et al. (2006). The importance of expressly integrating ethical analyses into climate change policy formation. *Climate Policy, 5*, 549–552.

Camerer, C. F., Loewenstein, G., et al. (Eds.). (2003). *Advances in behavioral economics*. Princeton, NJ: Princeton University Press.

Carlin, A. (2008). Why a different approach is required if global climate change is to be controlled efficiently or even at all. *William & Mary Environmental Law and Policy Review, 32*(3), 685–758.

Cuomo, C. (2005). Ethics and the eco/feminist self. In M. E. Zimmerman, J. B. Callicot, K. J. Warren, I. J. Klaver, & J. Clark (Eds.), *Environmental philosophy: From animal rights to radical ecology* (pp. 194–207). Upper Saddle River, NJ: Pearson Prentice Hall.

Damasio, A. R. (1994). *Descartes' error: Emotion, reason, and the human brain*. New York: G.P. Putnam's Sons.

Damasio, A. R. (1997). *Exploring the minded brain. The Tanner lectures on human values*. Salt Lake City: University of Utah

Dasgupta, P. (2005). What do economists analyze and why: Values or facts? *Economics and Philosophy, 21*, 221–278.

Dasgupta, P. (2007). *Economics: A very short introduction*. Oxford, NY: Oxford University Press.

DeCanio, S. J. (2003). *Economic models of climate change: A critique*. New York: Palgrave Macmillan.

Dees, J. G., & Cramton, P. C. (1991). Shrewd bargaining on the moral frontier: Toward a theory of morality in practice. *Business Ethics Quarterly, 1*(2), 135–167.

DeMartino, G. F. (2011). *The economist's oath: On the need for and content of professional economic ethics*. Oxford, NY: Oxford University Press.

Dietz, S., & Stern, N. (2008). Why economic analysis supports strong action on climate change: A response to the Stern review's critics. *Review of Environmental Economics and Policy, 2*(1), 94–113.

Dijksterhuis, A., Bos, M. W., et al. (2006). On making the right choice: The deliberation without-attention effect. *Science, 311*(5763), 1005–1007.

Drèze, J., & Sen, A. (1989). *Hunger and public action*. Oxford, UK: Clarendon.

Folbre, N. (2001). *The invisible heart: Economics and family values*. New York: The New Press.

Frank, R. H., Gilovich, T., et al. (1993). Does studying economics inhibit cooperation? *Journal of Economic Perspectives, 7*(2), 159–171.

Frey, B. S. (2008). *Happiness: A revolution in economics*. Cambridge, MA: MIT Press.

Gardiner, S. M., Caney, S., et al. (2010). *Climate ethics: Essential readings*. Oxford, NY: Oxford University Press.

Gentile, M. C. (2010). *Giving voice to values: How to speak your mind when you know what's right*. New Haven, CT: Yale University Press.
Gigerenzer, G. (2007). *Gut feelings: The intelligence of the unconscious*. New York: Penguin.
Gigerenzer, G., & Fiedler, K. (undated). *Minds in environments: The potential of an ecological approach to cognition*. Berlin, Germany: Max Planck Institute for Human Development.
Gilligan, C. (1982). *In a difference voice: Psychological theory and women's development*. Cambridge, MA: Harvard University Press.
Goodin, R. E. (2010). Selling environmental indulgences. In S. M. Gardiner, S. Caney, D. Jamieson, & H. Shue (Eds.), *Climate ethics: Essential readings* (pp. 231–246). Oxford, NY: Oxford University Press.
Goodwin, N., Nelson, J. A., et al. (2008). *Macroeconomics in context*. Armonk, NY: M.E. Sharpe.
Greene, J., & Haidt, J. (2002). How (and where) does moral judgment work? *Trends in Cognitive Sciences, 6*(12), 517–523.
Greene, J. D., Sommerville, R. B., et al. (2001). An fMRI investigation of emotional engagement in moral judgment. *Science, 293*, 2105–2108.
Gui, B., & Stanca, L. (2010). Happiness and relational goods: Well-being and interpersonal relations in the economic sphere. *International Review of Economics, 57*(2), 105–118.
Gui, B., & Sugden, R. (Eds.). (2005). *Economics and social interaction*. Cambridge, NY: Cambridge University Press.
Haidt, J. (2001). The emotional dog and its rational tail: A social intuitionist approach to moral judgment. *Psychological Review, 108*(4), 814–834.
Haidt, J. (2006). *The happiness hypothesis: Finding modern truth in ancient wisdom*. New York: Basic Books.
Howarth, R. B. (2003). Discounting and sustainability: Towards reconciliation. *International Journal of Sustainable Development, 6*(1), 87–97.
Howarth, R. B., & Norgaard, R. B. (1992). Environmental valuation under sustainable development. *American Economic Review, 82*(2), 473–477.
Iacoboni, M. (2008). *Mirroring people: The new science of how we connect with others*. New York: Farrar, Straus and Giroux.
Iyengar, S. S., & Lepper, M. R. (2000). When choice is demotivating: Can one desire too much of a good thing? *Journal of Personality and Social Psychology, 79*(6), 995–1006.
Jaffee, S., & Hyde, J. S. (2000). Gender differences in moral orientation: A meta-analysis. *Psychological Bulletin, 126*(5), 703–726.
Jamieson, D. (2010). Ethics, public policy, and global warming. In S. M. Gardiner, S. Caney, D. Jamieson, & H. Shue (Eds.), *Climate ethics: Essential readings* (pp. 77–86). Oxford, NY: Oxford University Press.
Jonas, H. (1984). *The imperative of responsibility: In search of ethics for the technological age*. Chicago: University of Chicago Press.
Kahneman, D. (2003). Maps of bounded rationality: Psychology for behavioral economics. *American Economic Review, 93*, 1449–1475.
Keller, E. F. (1985). *Reflections on gender and science*. New Haven, CT: Yale University Press.
Kitcher, P. (2011). *Science in a democratic society*. New York: Prometheus Books. Book Manuscript, forthcoming.
Lakoff, G. (2004). *Don't think of an elephant! Know your values and frame the debate*. White River Junction, VT: Chelsea Green.
Lakoff, G., & Johnson, M. (1999). *Philosophy in the flesh: The embodied mind and its challenge to western thought*. New York: Basic Books.
Margolis, H. (1982). *Selfishness, altruism, and rationality: A theory of social choice*. Chicago: University of Chicago Press.
Marshall, A. (1898). Distribution and exchange. *Economic Journal, 8*(29), 37–59.
McCloskey, D. N. (1985). *The rhetoric of economics*. Madison, WI: University of Wisconsin Press.
McKibben, B. (1989). *The end of nature*. New York: Random House.

Meyers, D. (2010). Feminist perspectives on the self. In E. N. Zalta (Ed.), *The Stanford encyclopedia of philosophy (electronic)*. http://plato.stanford.edu/archives/spr2010/entries/feminism-self

Nelson, J. A. (1993). The study of choice or the study of provisioning? Gender and the definition of economics. In M. Ferber & J. A. Nelson (Eds.), *Beyond economic man* (pp. 23–36). Chicago: University of Chicago Press.

Nelson, J. A. (1995). Feminism and economics. *Journal of Economic Perspectives, 9*(2), 131–148.

Nelson, J. A. (2005). Interpersonal relations and economics: Comments from a feminist perspective. In B. Gui & R. Sugden (Eds.), *Economics and social interaction* (pp. 250–261). Cambridge, NY: Cambridge University Press.

Nelson, J. A. (forthcoming). Does profit-seeking rule out love? Evidence (or not) from economics and law. *Washington University Journal of Law and Policy, 35*.

Ostrom, E. (1990). *Governing the commons: The evolution of institutions for collective action*. Cambridge, NY: Cambridge University Press.

Putnam, H. (2003). For ethics and economics without the dichotomies. *Review of Political Economy, 15*(3), 395–412.

Ruddick, S. (1989). *Maternal thinking: Toward a politics of peace*. Boston: Beacon Press.

Scarry, E. (2011). *Thinking in an emergency*. New York: W.W. Norton & Company.

Scherer, M. (2010). The new sheriffs of Wall Street. *Time, 175*, 22–30.

Sen, A. (1977). Rational fools: A critique of the behavioral foundations of economic theory. *Philosophy and Public Affairs, 6*, 317–344. Summer.

Stanton, E. (2011). Negishi welfare weights in integrated assessment models: The mathematics of global inequality. *Climatic Change, 107*(3), 417–432.

Stern, N. (2011). *How should we think about the economics of climate change? Lecture for the Leontief Prize*. Medford, OR: Global Development and Environment Institute. http://www.ase.tufts.edu/gdae/about_us/leontief/SternLecture.pdf.

Sunstein, C. R. (2002–2003). *The paralyzing principle. Regulation Winter*.

Sunstein, C. R. (2005). *Laws of fear: Beyond the precautionary principle*. New York: Cambridge University Press.

Taleb, N. N. (2010). *The black swan: The impact of the highly improbable*. New York: Random House.

The Onion. (2011). Republicans vote to repeal Obama-backed bill that would destroy asteroid headed for earth. *The Onion, 47*(5).

Warren, K. J. (2000). *Ecofeminist philosophy: A western perspective on what it is and why it matters*. Lanham, MD: Rowman & Littlefield Lanham.

Weitzman, M. L. (2009). On modeling and interpreting the economics of catastrophic climate change. *The Review of Economics and Statistics, 91*(1), 1–19.

Weitzman, M. L. (2010). *GHG targets as insurance against catastrophic climate damages*. Working paper. Harvard University.

Weitzman, M. L. (2011). *Fat-tailed uncertainty in the economics of catastrophic climate change. REEP symposium on fat tails*. Cambridge: Harvard University.

Williams, L. E., & Bargh, J. A. (2008). Experiencing physical warmth promotes interpersonal warmth. *Science, 322*, 606–607.

Chapter 9
Ethics and Experimental Economics

John Ifcher and Homa Zarghamee

Abstract A variety of ethical considerations in designing, conducting, and reporting both laboratory and field experiments in economics are reviewed. An important area of ethical concern in experimental economics stems from its use of human subjects. The standards used by Institutional Review Boards to sanction research using human subjects are expounded upon, with an emphasis on application to economics experiments. The authors draw from other experimental researchers and from their own experience to discuss issues related to the interaction of experimenter and subject—e.g., deception, informed consent, blindness, and monetary incentives—and issues related to the interaction of experimenter and consumer of research—e.g., the reporting of negative results, pilot data, or details of the experiment that may offer alternative interpretations of results.

Keywords Ethics • Experimental economics • Human subjects • Conducting experiments • Reporting results

On September 18, 2010, the New York Times featured a piece on two cousins, Thomas McLaughlin and Brandon Ryan, both in their early twenties, both battling the lethal skin cancer melanoma (Harmon, 2010). Thomas's initial diagnosis was much worse than his cousin's—so much so, that he was eligible to participate in a clinical trial for a new drug, PLX4032. He was assigned to the treatment group and

J. Ifcher (✉)
Department of Economics, Santa Clara University,
500 El Camino Real, Santa Clara, CA 95053, USA
e-mail: jifcher@scu.edu

H. Zarghamee
Department of Economics, Barnard College, Columbia University,
3009 Broadway, New York, NY 10027, USA
e-mail: hzargham@barnard.edu

E.A.M. Searing, D.R. Searing (eds.), *Practicing Professional Ethics in Economics and Public Policy*, DOI 10.1007/978-94-017-7306-5_9

saw miraculous rates of improvement; meanwhile, Brandon's health deteriorated with the progression of the melanoma and under the phenomenal physical stresses of chemotherapy. It therefore came as a mixed blessing when Brandon finally became sick enough to qualify for the next round of PLX4032's clinical trials. Any potential upside of this mixed blessing, however, was quickly dispatched upon news that he had been assigned not to the treatment group receiving PLX4032, but to the control group—the counterfactual, the group that the miracle-drug's rates of success would be compared to and in which his ineffectual chemotherapy would continue.

To maintain experimental tidiness (and, importantly, validity), assignment to the control group in clinical trials precludes any alternate routes of access to the drug being tested and does not allow patients to participate in future trials if they drop out. Much to the chagrin of Brandon, his family, and his doctors, Brandon was stuck in the control group with absolutely no access to the treatment, the treatment that was working wonders on his cousin. So successful was PLX4032 in its trials and so mild were its side effects (compared to chemotherapy) that even the most assuredly learned and devout followers of the experimental method—that is, much of the medical-research community itself—believed it unethical to block the control group from getting PLX4032 until the experiment's end. A raging ethical debate ensued in the research community that boiled down to whether the hard, scientific knowledge derived from completing the trials was, indeed, the greater good. In the end, Brandon succumbed to his illness and died at age 22. True, Thomas's fate would likely have been the same without the PLX4032 trials, but the fact remains that in the ethical calculus of such trials, for every Thomas there had to be a Brandon.

Compared to what medical researchers face, the ethical considerations of experimental economists may seem like child's play. At least a few experimentalists we know admit that, when first confronted with the pages-long application for approval to use human subjects in their research, they thought of it as an annoyance so pointless and mechanical that it must have been a bureaucratic mistake that their university required them to go through the process. Surely, they thought, such approval was really meant for researchers like the ones testing PLX4032; surely, sooner or later the university Institutional Review Board (IRB) would notice that experimental economists weren't working on issues of life and death and spare them the paperwork.

But to deny the importance of experimental economists' ethical considerations on the grounds of seemingly distant, if any, relation to issues of life and death is to deny the importance of economics research on the same grounds. Economic experiments—implemented from sterile university laboratories to the ministries of health and education in developing countries—test the theories and evaluate the social policies that shape the economic environment in which people live and the resulting choice-sets they confront. The findings can have profound impacts. For example, it was experimentally demonstrated that changing from an "opt-in" to an "opt-out" 401(k) pension program increased employee participation from about one-third to over 80 % (Madrian and Shea, 2001). Johnson and Goldstein (2003) studied organ-donation programs, where "opt-in" versus "opt-out" defaults have a profound impact on organ donation participation rates. Even in less policy-oriented contexts, any decent economist knows to, at a bare minimum, speculate upon the implications of her work: "why does it matter?"

The answer to this question lies in the cost-benefit analysis of conducting research. On the benefits side (and allowing for a little hyperbole), maybe it *alone* drives the researcher to spend her days, months, years deriving the proofs of her theorem, obtaining just the right data set with just the right measures and analyzing it from every possible angle. To the experimentalist studying the impact of X on Y, the right data set with the right measures may have to be one designed *with the research question in mind*. That is, the effect of interest may be impossible to tease out of observational data because of the difficulty of proving that the people to whom X happened and did not happen were otherwise identical. So she makes certain that the subjects assigned to X and not-X are assigned randomly and not on the basis of any observed or unobserved characteristics: this is critical to experimentalists' identification strategy (for demonstrating a causal link) and knowledge-generation, and its violation undermines the methodological benefits of the experimentation. The key point is that the experimenter conducts her research by *exerting control* over her subjects' environment and *manipulating* their choice sets—these are required to secure the benefit of a well-run experimental study. So it is incumbent upon her to add to the cost side of her cost-benefit analysis the effects of her control and manipulation and how these effects weigh against the answer to "why does it matter?" If this doesn't occur naturally, then certainly the benevolent social planner, also known as IRB, will help her internalize the externalities of her research method.

Below, we offer our thoughts on the ethics of economic experiments. Because we are economists and somewhere along the way our brains' hemispheric division became cost-benefit instead of left-right, we will continue to fall back on that framework in hashing out the impact of an experimenter's choices. We don't claim to be the originators of many of these thoughts. Despite being the last social science to adopt a code of ethics and despite this code of ethics having nothing to say about experimentation or human subjects (or really anything other than citing sources of funding and being up front about financial conflicts of interest in published work), a number of economists have written about the ethics of experiments, and our insights draw from their writing in addition to our own experiences. As in any cost-benefit analysis without common units of measurement, ours will not lead to decisive rules on how to run experiments, but hopefully it will provide food for the introspective experimenter's thought. A final obvious but important note: in the words of Karen A. Hegtvedt, "researchers do not have an inalienable right to pursue research with human subjects (Hegtvedt, 2007, p. 159)." My wanting to know the economic consequences of war—an undoubtedly important economic question—does not give me a carte blanche to start one. I may have to resign myself to accepting that, like a world without World War II, the proper experimental counterfactual is untenable. If a question cannot be answered without breaches of ethics, then the experiment shouldn't be conducted.

Let's first consider some of the actors affected by an economic experiment. The researcher (either with or without a non-research partner or sponsor) uses human subjects (either with or without their knowledge) to measure the causal effect of X on Y. The researcher herself stands to gain from this research, as do the targeted population of the research (e.g., any individual or institution trying to change its Y) and other researchers working on related themes (e.g., researchers studying the effects of X, researchers identifying the determinants of Y, researchers using experimental methods, etc.). The experimenter's research choices will impact these different actors in obvious and not-so-obvious ways. We will first consider the ethics of using human subjects and then the ethics of reporting and publishing results.

9.1 Ethics of Using Human Subjects

The most obvious group affected by experimentation is the pool of human subjects. In the lion's share of economics experiments, there are no real threats of the physical suffering and side effects that may be inflicted by biomedical experiments, nor is the psychological stress ever going to compare to what Brandon Ryan went through being denied PLX4032. That said, the direct benefits to the human subjects of economics experiments will never come close to those enjoyed by Brandon's cousin Thomas. The potential costs and benefits to human subjects in economics are usually much more subtle. Perhaps because of the subtleties, it is important to know the ethical standards used by IRBs to approve the use of human subjects. The common source of these standards is the Belmont Report, created in 1978 by the National Commission for the Protection of Human Subjects of Biomedical and Behavioral Research. The Belmont Report puts forth three guiding principles: respect for persons, beneficence, and justice. Respect for persons asks that the autonomy of individuals be respected, that they give informed consent to participate in the experiment, and that individuals with diminished autonomy be protected. Beneficence stresses the Hippocratic maxim to "do no harm"—that is, to maximize the benefits and minimize harm to human subjects. Justice requires that subjects be chosen non-exploitatively and that the benefits of the research be available to those burdened by it.

In the infamous Tuskegee syphilis study, the untreated syphilis-progression of 399 impoverished African American men was tracked for 40 years and compared to the health of 201 non-syphilitic men. The subjects, made to believe that they were receiving free government health care, were never told they were part of the study, that they had syphilis, or that they could be cured with penicillin. In fact, there are reports that the researchers blocked access to alternative treatments when they became available. It should come as no surprise that Tuskegee fails to meet any of the Belmont Report's three guiding principles…that, in fact, the Belmont Report was created in response to the whistle blown on Tuskegee. What may come as more of a surprise is that another controversial set of experiments, Stanley Milgram's Yale experiments (1963, 1965, 1974), does not categorically fail to follow the three guiding principles. Suspecting that the magnitude of Nazi violence was at least partially rooted in obedience to authority, Milgram tested the willingness of subjects to administer increasingly powerful electric shocks to confederates masquerading as subjects, whose (albeit fake and scripted) objections, pleas, and screams could be heard from an adjacent room, all under the guise of a laboratory experiment on memory and learning. After a certain voltage, the confederate would fall silent, suggesting that he may have passed out or died, and the experimenter would urge the subject to continue. Despite having been told up front that they were free to leave the experiment at any time without forfeiting the show-up fee, a whopping 65 % of subjects administered shocks up to the maximum voltage of 450 V.

Milgram took care to debrief his subjects at the end of the experiment, to follow up with them regularly, and to attempt to relieve them of any resultant guilt, lost self-esteem, or identity crisis. To many critics, this was hardly enough, but Milgram's student Alan C. Elms argues that, if anything, it was too much, that Milgram was under no ethical obligation to bolster subjects' false sense of self-esteem (Elms, 1972). In a rare case of real-time experimental education, the vast majority of subjects themselves were actually glad to have participated, many claiming to have learned an important lesson about themselves and human nature. So careful was Milgram that his protocol had to be only lightly tweaked (psychological prescreening, closer observation for signs of stress, one third the maximum voltage, and more immediate debriefing) by Jerry Burger to be repeated with full university IRB approval in 2009 (Burger, 2009). The real harm of the Milgram study is the psychological distress the subjects feel when they think they are seriously injuring the confederate. The real achievement of the study is showing that the psychological distress doesn't stop the subjects from taking the actions that would seriously physically injure the confederate. The interesting point is that it isn't the deception in Milgram's study that would make it unacceptable to a contemporary IRB, nor is it that the subjects suffered psychological distress: both of these are present in Burger's follow up. It's just a matter of degree. So even with the Belmont Report and IRBs, we don't get concrete ethical answers, just a framework for ethical thought.

Christopher B. Barrett and Michael R. Carter (2010) apply the framework, with equally ambiguous results, to Gugerty and Kremer (2008), an experimental study of the Rockefeller Effect:

> Taking its cue from John D. Rockefeller, who refused to give money to Alcoholics Anonymous on the grounds that the money would undercut the organization's effectiveness, the Gugerty and Kremer (2008) article explicitly sets out to determine whether grants of money to women's organizations in Kenya distorts them and leads to the exclusion of poorer women and their loss of benefits. Donor groups were providing grants to women's organizations on the presumption that they were doing good. Proving otherwise, and that the Rockefeller Effect is real, could of course be argued to bring real social benefit. However, the ethical complexities of undertaking research designed to potentially harm poor women are breathtaking. Standard human subjects rules require: (1) that any predictable harm be decisively outweighed by social gains; (2) that subjects be fully informed of the risks; and, (3) that compensation be paid to cover any damages incurred. It remains unclear whether these rules were met in the Gugerty and Kremer (2008) study, which is somewhat chilling given that the study indeed confirms that poor women were harmed by the injection of cash into randomly selected women's groups. (Barrett and Carter, 2010, p. 520)

9.1.1 Deception

Since the hypothesized, or at least expected, outcome of the Gugerty and Kremer (2008) study was a counterintuitive negative one, it may even be considered deceptive of the researchers to have withheld information about the Rockefeller Effect from the subjects. That said, the common practice of withholding the hypothesis being tested and the full breadth of the experiment is not generally considered to constitute deception. Rather, deception occurs when experimenters convey false or intentionally misleading information to subjects. The use of deception in economics experiments is essentially forbidden (by virtue of the impossibility of getting deception past journal referees), and, as a matter of course, the discipline's distaste for deception is often the first thing subjects are told in economics experiments.

Deception can benefit the researcher by increasing the range of questions she can answer. Its costs, to economists, are threefold. First, economics experiments are often designed around monetarily incentivized decisions. Deception in the context of financial rewards would quite simply constitute fraud. Second, it may exacerbate feelings of objectification in the subjects and call into question their ability to exercise autonomy in the experiment. Third, deception, especially when institutionalized as it has been in psychology, breaks down the potency of the monetary incentive in all experiments by calling its veracity into question or by supplanting it, if only partially, with other incentives—for example, the incentive to outsmart the experimenter or "spot-the-deception." In their 2001 compilation of the existing experimental evidence both for and against the use of deception, Ralph Hertwig and Andreas Ortmann (2001) recount the real anecdote of a subject's epileptic seizure going initially ignored by other subjects because they thought it was an experimental hoax (MacCoun and Kerr, 1987). More broadly, a researcher's choice to employ deception creates a negative externality for other researchers, present or future, who want to conduct behavioral research without it: the external validity of the subject pools' psychological state in the experiment will be reduced and the credibility of their research will be compromised. In the words of Hertwig and Ortmann, "participant's trust is a public good worth investing in (Hertwig and Ortmann, 2001, p. 398)."

9.1.2 Informed Consent and Blindness

Deception relates closely to informed consent, one of the cornerstones of the Belmont Report; too much deception may render informed consent moot, as the veracity of the information and what exactly subjects are consenting to is called into question. Given the paucity of deception in economics experiments, satisfying the right to informed consent is usually as simple as obtaining a signature from subjects approving the general nature of the study in which they will be involved and reassuring them of their freedom to abstain from any or all of it if they so choose. The situation becomes more complicated in natural field experiments in which subjects are not made aware of their involvement in a randomized experiment, either because the nature of the intervention is naturally occurring (e.g., manipulating the wording of a political contribution solicitation letter) or because of any of a slew of named "effects" that would cause subjects to change their behavior because they know they are in an experiment. The John Henry Effect occurs when subjects in the control group take actions to overcome the real or perceived disadvantage of their random assignment. Hawthorne Effects occur if subjects in either control or treatment suspect that the experiment's hypothesized results will be used in negative ways and hence modify their behavior to eschew the results. The Pygmalion Effect occurs when subjects' actions and perceptions respond not necessarily to the treatment itself, but to meet the expectations of the treatment's hypothesized effect. The likelihood of these possible effects—which are quite real given that human subjects, unlike plots of soil, are active agents—and the feasibility of addressing them with blinded studies must be weighed against violations or augmentations of informed consent.

The "effects" described above can occur when subjects are not blind to their own treatment versus control status. A related set of concerns can arise when the experimenter is not blind to subjects' treatment versus control status. As Gary Burtless notes, "Except among philosophers and research scientists, random assignment is often thought to be an unethical way to ration public resources (Burtless, 1995, p. 74)." Assuming that the experimenter herself—like, for example, Brandon Ryan's doctors—can, in the name of maintaining experimental validity, stomach the difficulties of withholding treatment from deserving or distressed members of the control group, policy partners and implementers may not. As Barrett and Carter note,

> [I]n our experience the unfairness and wastefulness implied by strict randomization in social experiments often sows the seeds of some implementers' breach of research design. Field partners less concerned with statistical purity than with practical development impact commonly deem it unethical to deny a control group the benefits of an intervention strongly believed to have salutary effects, or to knowingly treat one household instead of another when the latter is strongly believed likely to gain and the former not. Well-meaning field implementers thus quietly contravene the experimental design, compromising the internal validity of the research and reintroducing precisely the unobserved heterogeneity that randomization was meant to overcome (Barrett and Carter, 2010, p. 521).

Thus, when feasible, double blind experiments are best.

9.1.3 Monetary Incentivization

Our earlier discussion of "no deception" brought up another pillar of experimental economics: monetary incentives. Economists are notoriously suspicious of the Bradley Effect (in the 1982 California gubernatorial race, opinion polls favored the black candidate Tom Bradley, and his subsequent unexpected loss was understood as proverbial money not being put where the mouth is). Economists generally think talk is cheap: preferences cannot be credibly spoken of, they can only be revealed when there are stakes involved. So we have institutionalized the use of monetary incentives in our experiments to gain the benefit of credibility. One obvious cost is the financial one incurred by the experimenters; less spoken of are the ethics of monetary incentives. On the one hand, they provide compensation for any inconvenience, boredom, or harm that may arise in the experiment. On the other, monetary incentives may be seen as an instrument of coercion or exploitation. In order to recruit subjects and inform them of the benefits of participating, experimental economists usually advertise the opportunity to make money, publicizing both the minimum show-up fee, and the average and maximum payouts. Despite being ensured the show-up fee, subjects are often attracted by the extra money (beyond the show-up fee) that they may receive, and they may feel compelled to stay in the experiment or act in accordance with the experimenter's wishes in order to receive it. Remember that Milgram's participants were initially told that they could leave the experiment at any point they wished and still receive payment, but clearly they perceived otherwise later in the experiment. Interestingly, while greater experimental stakes are appealing to economists on the grounds of increased validity, they actually exacerbate the problems of coercion and exploitation. Consider a field experiment in a developing country where the stakes are equivalent to a household's monthly wages. While it can be argued that the high stakes make the subjects' choices that much more real and important, the high stakes may make the subjects feel compelled to do what they think the experimenter wants them to do, or to stay in an experiment against their better judgment instead of settling for the nominal show-up fee.

Another problem with monetary incentives is that they may reward bad behavior. Barrett and Carter report: "As but one prominent example involving widely respected scholars, Marianne Bertrand et al. (2007) randomized incentives for subjects in India who did not yet possess a driver's license, so as to induce them to bribe officials in order to receive a license without having successfully completed the required training and an obligatory driver safety examination. The very predictable consequence of such an experiment is that it imperils innocent non-subjects—let alone the subjects themselves—by putting unsafe drivers on the road illegally. This is irresponsible research design, yet the study was published in one of the profession's most prestigious journals (Barrett and Carter, 2010, pp. 519–520)." David T. Dearman and James E. Beard (2009) argue that principal-agent experiments, in which the agent earns more by trumping up her hidden costs, foster deceptive, unethical behavior. This is particularly troublesome in university labs, which are, like it or not, embedded in a learning environment and use students as subjects.

A related but much more subtle point raised by psychologists is that financial incentives may dampen intrinsic motivations. Protecting subjects from boredom may not be an ethical matter, but it may be of importance to the extent that the change in motivations may diverge with what would be observed of subjects outside the lab. It may also give rise to a culture of "professional subjects" who use experiments as a regular source of income without putting any real thought into the choices they make while there.

9.2 Ethics of Reporting

As much as we may want to believe that some mix of intellectual curiosity and wanting to help the world are the only motivation for our research, we all know that, at a practical level, our careers are built on the success of our research—and this success is often measured not by the conscientiousness with which our experiments were conducted, but by the publish ability of their results. Ethical scrupulousness in reporting results protects the public and scientific community from fraudulent results and a general loss of trust in research; in preserving this, the researcher should consider a host of questions.

First, has there been any violation of the exogeneity-assumption in random assignment? Such a violation could arise, as noted above, if a field implementer did not stick to the random assignment either by accident or for her own reasons. Or we may find out from exit surveys that randomization was not valid ex post. Experimentalists are divided about the proper response to ex post violations of randomization. We are personally of the opinion that ex post invalid randomization should be controlled for (Barrett and Carter fall on our side), but we have been advised by senior colleagues at conferences and in referee reports that anything but reliance upon ex ante randomization becomes too subjective (more on this below).

Second, to what extent do the results truly reflect treatment effects or behavioral responses to other features of the experiment? Again, unlike research with passive agents in which the treatment given is the treatment received, human subjects' behavioral responses may be to features of the experiment other than treatment features of which the experimenter may not be aware. For example, did the results from the second session of an experiment change because of the change in treatment or because it was getting too close to lunch? Much of this can be controlled with good experimental design, but researchers can sometimes become very cavalier about the soundness of their own work.

Third, if sponsored by a partner, to what extent is the experimenter biasing her methodology to obtain results that appeal to the partner? As noted above, the American Economics Association's Code of Ethics requires that funding and financial conflicts of interest be reported. Surely, reporting such a conflict of interest is important, but being conscious of it in the design and implementation process is equally important. Glenn Harrison and John List give the example of paired-audit field experiments:

> the Urban Institute makes no bones about its view that discrimination is a widespread problem and that paired-audit experiments are a critical way to address it…. There is nothing wrong with this apart from the fact that it is hard to imagine how volunteer auditors would not see things similarly. Indeed, Heckman (1998, p. 104) notes 'auditors are sometimes instructed on the problem of discrimination in American society prior to sampling firms, so they may have been coached to find what audit agencies wanted them to find.' The opportunity for unobservables to influence the outcome are potentially rampant in this case. (Harrison and List, 2004, pp. 1038–1039)

Lastly, are negative results being reported? And are the reported results in response to the original research question or coming from post hoc analysis? More specifically, negative results are often not as interesting to journals and referees as positive results, so they go unpublished. We have personally conducted costly experiments only to find out later that our colleagues have conducted the same ones years before with negative results. This may incentivize data-mining. For example, consider the analysis of pilot experiments. A pilot may only be called that ex post when results are not obtained. Or it may be dropped from analysis with the main experiment for no other reason than that it reduces statistical significance. Similarly, justifications may be made for dropping observations that likely would not have been dropped if statistical significance had been achieved in the first shot. Such practices surely confirm the suspicions of those who argue for reliance on ex ante randomization: everything else might just be a trick.

9.3 Conclusion

Economic experiments are replete with ethical considerations, both large and small. There exists a social welfare function accounting for the implications of any experiment for the researcher, the human subjects, the sponsors, the implementers, future researchers, the potential beneficiaries of the research, and the public at large. Experimental economists may fall short of precisely identifying the formal specification of this function, but remembering its existence is critical in a science often abstracted away from its social core.

References

Barrett, C. B., & Carter, M. R. (2010). The power and pitfalls of experiments in development economics: Some non-random reflections. *Applied Economic Perspectives and Policy, 32*(4), 515–548.

Bertrand, M., Djankov, S., Hanna, R., & Mullainathan, S. (2007). Obtaining a driver's license in India: An experimental approach to studying corruption. *Quarterly Journal of Economics, 122*(4), 1639–1676.

Burger, J. M. (2009). Replicating Milgram: Would people still obey today? *American Psychologist, 64*(1), 1–11.

Burtless, G. (1995). The case for randomized field trials in economic and policy research. *Journal of Economic Perspectives, 9*(2), 63–84.

Dearman, D. T., & Beard, J. E. (2009). Ethical issues in accounting and economics experimental research: Inducing strategic misrepresentation. *Ethics and Behavior, 19*(1), 51–59.

Elms, A. C. (1972). *Social psychology and social relevance*. Boston, MA: Little, Brown.

Gugerty, M. K., & Kremer, M. (2008). Outside funding and the dynamics of participation in community associations. *American Journal of Political Science, 52*(3), 585–602.

Harmon, A. (2010). New drugs stir debate on rules of clinical trials. *New York Times*, September 19, 2010. http://www.nytimes.com/2010/09/19/health/research/19trial.html?_r=1&emc=eta1

Harrison, G. W., & List, J. A. (2004). Field experiments. *Journal of Economic Literature, 42*(4), 1009–1055.

Heckman, J. J. (1998). Detecting discrimination. *Journal of Economic Perspectives, 12*(2), 101–116.

Hegtvedt, K. A. (2007). Ethics and experiments. In W. Murray & S. Jane (Eds.), *Laboratory experiments in the social sciences*. Amsterdam: Elsevier.

Hertwig, R., & Ortmann, A. (2001). Experimental practices in economics: A methodological challenge for psychologists? *Behavioral and Brain Sciences, 24*(3), 383–403.

Johnson, E. J., & Goldstein, D. (2003). Do defaults save lives? *Science, 302*(5649), 1338–1339.

MacCoun, R. J., & Kerr, N. L. (1987). Suspicion in the psychological laboratory: Kelman's prophecy revisited. *American Psychologist, 42*, 199.

Madrian, B., & Shea, D. (2001). The power of suggestion: Inertia in 401(k) participation and savings behavior. *Quarterly Journal of Economics, 116*, 1149–1187.

Milgram, S. (1963). Behavioral study of obedience. *Journal of Abnormal and Social Psychology, 67*, 371–378.

Milgram, S. (1965). Some conditions of obedience and disobedience to authority. *Human Relations, 18*, 57–76.

Milgram, S. (1974). *Obedience to authority: An experimental view*. New York: Harper & Row.

Nofsinger, J. (2009). Opt-in and opt-out pension design. *Psychology Today*, August 30, 2009. http://www.psychologytoday.com/blog/mind-my-money/200908/opt-in-and-opt-out-pension-design

Thaler, R. (2009). Opting in vs. opting out. *New York Times*, September 26, 2009. http://www.nytimes.com/2009/09/27/business/economy/27view.html

Chapter 10
Ethics and Health Policy

Howard Brody

Abstract A career in the ethics of health policy is not necessarily a straight line. Starting from an academic interest in medical ethics, and without any concerns specifically about policy, I have gradually expanded my horizons to include a number of policy questions. I'll recount here what led me to shift my interests into a policy direction, what immediate lessons I took away from that experience, and finally, what longer-term questions seem to remain.

Keywords Professional ethics • Bioethics • Medical ethics • Health policy • Conflict of interest

10.1 Initial Interest in Health Policy

By the mid-1990s I thought of myself as well situated to teach and write about ethical issues in medicine: I was an MD and family physician in an academic practice, held a Ph.D. in philosophy, and was therefore, I thought, reasonably versed in philosophical ethical theories. As a family physician, I became most interested in ethical issues that arose in the context of the relationship between the individual physician and the individual patient, with less concern for larger policy matters. Much of the interest within medical ethics then focused on issues at the end of life. Working in Michigan during the heyday of Jack Kevorkian, I was naturally led to think about the policy implications of the legalization of physician-assisted suicide, but beyond that I had no particular bent toward health policy.

Then an event occurred which "radicalized" my engagement with the ethical issues at the interface between medicine and the pharmaceutical industry. In the family medicine residency where I taught, I had been asked to speak with the incoming residents about contacts with drug sales people, and had once been involved in writing some policy guidelines for our program regarding drug industry relations.

H. Brody (✉)
The UTMB Health Institute for the Medical Humanities,
301 University Blvd, Primary Care Pavilion Ste 2.301, Galveston, TX 77555-1311, USA
e-mail: habrody@utmb.edu

E.A.M. Searing, D.R. Searing (eds.), *Practicing Professional Ethics in Economics and Public Policy*, DOI 10.1007/978-94-017-7306-5_10

I thought of this as a minor sidelight to my main concerns. Early in my career I had made a personal choice not to spend any time dealing with drug sales representatives. But I had no expectation that my colleagues would necessarily adopt such a stance; further, I considered it a personal preference rather than an *ethical* concern whether or not they did so.

The radicalization occurred when I read a detailed editorial in the *Journal of the American Medical Association* (*JAMA*) about a drug company's effort to suppress research findings unfavorable to sales of one of their products (Rennie 1997). The editorialist mentioned in passing how hard it had been for the journal to find any scientific reviewers for an article about the drug who were not receiving payments from that drug company. For the first time I realized that behavior that seemed ethically of minor significance on a case-by-case basis—a physician's deciding whether or not to accept money from a drug firm—might assume much greater significance when viewed in the larger, policy perspective. It was one thing for drug company money to influence, or to threaten to influence, any individual physician; it was another thing to influence so broad a cross-section of the medical profession that a journal could not conduct unbiased scientific peer review.

At just about the same period during the mid-1990s, the medical ethics literature began to fill with works about professionalism. While it took me a while to decide what to make of this new trend in the literature, I eventually came to see that "professionalism" might best be viewed as a reawakening of interest in virtue ethics as it applies to medicine and health care, after a period when virtue approaches had been largely neglected. Professionalism, like virtue, seemed not to be primarily about what ethical rules or principles the physician follows in making a decision, but about the physician's deeper, abiding moral character—what sort of person the physician is and is striving to become.

Taking a professionalism approach to the ethics of the relationship between medicine and the pharmaceutical industry, I came to believe that the major ideas in play were *conflict of interest* and *trust*. Professionalism requires the physician to place the interests of the patient first. When a physician accepts financial benefits from another party whose interests (selling more, and more expensive, drugs) may conflict with what's best for the patient, the concern is raised that the physician will be tempted to stray from the pathway of true professionalism. That state of possible temptation, whether or not in the end the physician actually abandons fidelity to the patient's interests, affects the trust that individual patients and the general public ought to feel toward the physician and toward the profession. The virtuous professional seeks not merely to be trusted, she seeks to in fact be *trustworthy*. Trustworthiness and (avoidable) conflicts of interest seem fundamentally opposed.

The negative impact on trust in medicine occurs at two levels. If practitioners take money and gifts from drug representatives, how much can they be trusted to prescribe the drug that's truly best for the patient, instead of the drug the reps are pushing? The higher and ultimately more important level is that of medical science itself. If serious practitioners rely on medical journals for the scientific evidence on which to base their prescribing, and if the scientists who perform and then write up the research studies take money from the drug industry, how much can either physicians or patients trust the integrity of the science published in those journals? There is also concern regarding what the journals may be leaving out due to industry influence; The *JAMA* editorial revealed how the drug firm's machinations had succeeded in delaying for 7 years the publication of evidence that a cheaper generic thyroid drug was just as good as an expensive brand-name drug (Rennie 1997).

To research and write about these matters required that I learn much more about the drug industry, pharmaceutical research, and the economics of pharmaceuticals than I ever imagined. After some 6 or 7 years of this research I felt I knew enough to write a book about the ethics of the medicine-pharmaceutical industry connection. I also realized that due to the rapidity with which this scene was changing, the book would be obsolete as soon as it was printed; and so I also assumed the role of blogger as a way to try to keep the contents of the book up to date. I did not immediately realize that by undertaking the blog, I had also moved from my more usual role of academic scholar into the new role of issue advocate.

10.2 Immediate Lessons from the Experience

My closer encounter with ethics and health policy seemed, in the short run, to teach me a number of lessons.

One of my bioethics colleagues, Judy Andre, wrote a nice paper entitled "Learning to See" (Andre 1992). She noted that almost all the literature in health care ethics was about how to make a good ethical decision once one recognized that one was faced with an ethical problem. By contrast, there was hardly any literature on how to recognize an ethical problem when one is faced with it. Andre provided compelling examples to suggest that much of what is unethical occurs not because of shoddy decision-making, but rather due to a failure of moral perception—we simply don't *see* what is happening around us as calling for an ethical response.

As one who had, before my "radicalization," not *seen* the full ethical dimensions of the problems of conflicts of interest, I could understand why, when I began my research into pharmaceutical policy matters, hardly any of my fellow bioethicists thought this set of issues worth addressing. Since then, a great deal more attention has been paid to ethics at the medicine-industry interface.

As I have already summarized, I came to see professionalism, and the public trust related to it, in a new light. When I was in medical and graduate school, the primary scholarship on the medical *profession* came from sociology, and was quite skeptical if not indeed cynical. This scholarship was a more thorough version of what George Bernard Shaw had opined: "all professions are conspiracies against the laity" (Shaw, 1911). Professionals wanted power over their work, and if professionals talked about ethics or trust, that was simply a means to securing and protecting a greater degree of power. In the most cynical view, power over one's work translated into being able to maximize one's income, and so all this huffing and puffing about ethics and trust was really about money.

When the bioethics literature started to turn to professionalism in the mid-1990s, I was initially skeptical, in line with that older sociological perspective. Once I saw the connection between professionalism and virtue, I came to see that there might be a positive, aspirational sense of professionalism-as-ethics that one could contrast with the profession-as-power message from sociology (though it is important to keep at least some of that skepticism always in the back of one's mind). Put crudely, the really cynical actors in this drama did not seem to me to be the people who were invoking professionalism and trust and denouncing conflicts of interest. The cynics seemed rather to be those in medicine who defended the status quo, and their privilege of taking as much in the way of free dinners and hefty consulting fees as the market would allow, under the facile assumption that they could do so without threatening any of the fragile public trust on which medical practice is based.

This suspicion about who the real cynics were led to another major insight. I realized that my study of ethics at the medicine-pharmaceutical industry interface was unlike any previous inquiry I had undertaken in bioethics. When studying, for example, the ethical debate over physician-assisted suicide, I found passion on both sides, and strong reasons were offered as to why assisted suicide was on the one hand an ethical abomination for physicians who had promised to heal and never to kill, and on the other a compassionate response to otherwise incurable suffering. But I found no reason to doubt that the arguments raised on either side were sincere and honest portrayals of the deepest value commitments of the participants.

By contrast, I discovered that as I approached the ethical issues related to the pharmaceutical industry, I could get nowhere until I had first peeled away layer after layer of what I could only regard as rationalization. Social science research of physicians' attitudes confirms the prevalence of these rationalizations. For example:

- "I'm a trained scientist; how can my opinion be swayed by a free pen or doughnut?"
- "When drug reps see physicians, it's not marketing, it's education."
- "Okay, I admit that my peers are often influenced when they listen to the drug reps, but personally, I'm never influenced."
- "If we didn't allow physicians with conflicts of interest to sit on government advisory boards or clinical guideline panels, we'd have to exclude the most knowledgeable experts in the field."

All these statements are demonstrably false, yet all are offered, with a straight face, by defenders of the old system of financial exchanges between the industry and the profession.

It became clear that it would never be sufficient simply to expose the ethical flaws in the old system that was rife with financial conflicts of interest. I would have to offer some policy solutions. This need taught me a further policy lesson—and incidentally became a fundamental framework for organizing the book that I eventually wrote. I came to see how inadequate it was to view any activity involving medicine and the pharmaceutical industry in isolation—contacts between physicians and drug representatives, continuing medical education funded by companies, direct-to-consumer advertising, industry-sponsored research, or whatever. From an initial policy perspective it was tempting to break down the ethical issues into these convenient categories and then to propose targeted reforms for each. I finally came to see that the reason the ethical concerns had reached the extent that they had was because of the close interconnections among all of these issues. Drug companies are among the most financially successful businesses of the last several decades because they have become adept at coordinating all of these disparate activities. Drug reps don't visit doctors pushing a new product unless at the same time direct-to-consumer ads on television have primed patients to "ask your doctor" about that product, which in turn means that 5 or 10 years earlier, marketing experts sat down at the same table with scientific researchers to determine what sort of scientific studies would best position a new product for maximum sales. This is not a conspiracy theory, it is simple fact. "Ethical" policy proposals that failed to take into account these multiple layers of interconnections simply would never address the real problems.

10.3 Larger Questions

My foray into ethics and health policy, via the issues raised by the pharmaceutical industry (as well as the medical device industry), has led me to see larger questions beyond any of those that first attracted me into this area.

Let's assume for now (see my blog if you don't believe this) that the ethical concerns at the interface between medicine and the pharmaceutical industry raise serious implications for public health (Brody 2007). But when people propose substantial reforms—recalling that only reforms that address the multilayered character of this interaction are likely to be adequate—they often hit a brick wall. The wall consists of what's "realistic" as a matter of public policy and politics. I was struck by how few people seem to be asking the next logical set of questions—is what's "realistic" an immutable fact, or have we been somehow lulled into accepting a view of reality that serves certain powerful interests?

I will shift examples here to mention another huge issue in health care ethics and policy—reform of the U.S. health care system. When President Obama tackled health care reform in 2009, it immediately became apparent that certain options were simply not on the table for discussion. Despite the clear advantages of a single-payer financing system, which demonstrably would reduce the Federal deficit over the next decade more than any alternative plan, there was never any serious consideration of that option. While so-called "ObamaCare" was widely attacked by its right-wing opponents as "socialist," it could just as accurately have been labeled "Save private, for-profit health insurance at all costs." Yet not only was none of this seriously debated, the political discourse proceeded as if no one even noticed that the debate was not happening.

When not doing my work as a philosopher-bioethicist, I indulge myself in a love of the Sherlock Holmes stories. One of Holmes's most famous comments had to do with the curious incident of the dog that did nothing in the night-time. Attempting to follow this example, I have always tried to figure out what clues are offered by what's not being talked about, as much as by what is. We philosophers tend to think that our tribe's great-granddaddy was Socrates, and when Socrates was at his best, he did something similar. He took words or concepts that everyone around him thought had obvious, noncontroversial meanings, and by asking hard questions, he got them to see that they really had no idea what these things meant after all. And he showed them that if they didn't know what these things meant, they couldn't reason clearly about them, which meant that they were hampered when they had to take effective practical action.

I became persuaded of a number of things when I wondered about the dogs that were not barking around various aspects of health policy. I became, quite belatedly, acquainted with a belief system that I think is best called *economism*, though many of my colleagues in history and the social sciences prefer to call it *neoliberalism*. *Economism*, an extreme faith in unregulated free markets, appeared to be the unquestioned system of belief that governs the world of American policy and politics (Brody 2011). When I next asked where *economism* came from, I started off on a convoluted historical journey, and was reminded again of another lesson I learned from bioethics—if you wonder where you are now, and where you're going, it might be a good idea first to track where you've been. I came to see that both historically and logically, *economism* had the important features of a couple of religious belief systems that had been influential in America and in England between around 1700 and 1850.

This analysis of *economism* had some interesting implications for anyone concerned about ethics and health policy, as well as for anyone who cares about American economic policy generally. The analysis shows that we have come to accept a certain view of the world as "reality," that is a *scientifically* (that is, economically) valid picture of how the world is and is supposed to be. Yet, both logically and historically, this view of the world resembles religious doctrine much more than it resembles anything like science. And yet, when people talk about pressing social problems, hardly anyone questions this common-sense picture of reality and the straitjacket it puts us in when we consider our options. This analysis led me to do some further work that I never would have imagined back in the 1990s—writing a book about *economism* and our failure to question it in the basic ways it calls for.

I am sure that there are many ethically responsible ways to approach issues in health policy. People who focus in on a narrow set of issues and keep working away at them over time no doubt produce much good. And I also have no doubt that there are excellent, and ethical, ways to address many pressing health issues from a market-based, for-profit vantage point, so long as one is clearheaded about both the potential and the limits of such an approach.

My own path, however, needed to cast the net of analysis ever wider. Doing good ethics, as many say, involves first getting all the facts. But it also, importantly, involves asking the right questions. Sometimes the right questions to ask are precisely the ones that others are not asking.

References

Andre, J. (1992). Learning to see: Moral growth during medical training. *Journal of Medical Ethics, 18*, 148–152.

Brody, H. (2007). *Hooked: Ethics, the medical profession, and the pharmaceutical industry*. Lanham, MD: Rowman and Littlefield. see also associated blog, brodyhooked.blogspot.com.

Brody, H. (2011). *The golden calf: Economism and American policy*. Amazon/CreateSpace; see also associated blog, theeconomismscam.blogspot.com.

Rennie, D. (1997). Thyroid storm. *Journal of the American Medical Association, 227*, 1238–1243.

Shaw, B. (1911). *The doctor's dilemma: Getting married, & the shewing-up of Blanco Posnet*. London, UK: Constable.

Chapter 11
Ethics and Human Resource Management

Elizabeth Scott

Abstract Human Resource practitioners face decisions involving ethics on a regular basis. The author provides examples from personal experience of three kinds of challenges: discerning what is right, fulfilling agency responsibilities, and avoiding conflicts of interest. She suggests ongoing reading, reflection, and education to build one's capacity for real-time decision-making. To assist in discerning what is right, she suggests considering others' perspectives, identifying unintended consequences, and engaging in continuing education. While the author identifies ways to navigate many ethical challenges within the role of HR professional, she recognizes that some may require a willingness to leave a job.

Keywords Values • Professional ethics • Human resources • Conflict of interest • Agency responsibility

When I was in college, my work-study job was in the University Libraries. I began on the Reserves Desk; then, one spring semester, a friend asked me whether I wanted to work in "Administration" over the summer, handling student hiring and payroll and assisting with the full-time workers' personnel matters. I agreed, not knowing that this job would constitute the beginning of a career path in Labor Relations and Human Resource Management.

My university library's staff was unionized. At first, all this meant to me was a code on the papers I was typing or filing. As the summer progressed, though, it became apparent that the union was considering going on strike for higher pay. The negotiator for the university would come into our office requesting information on

E. Scott (✉)
Department of Business Administration, Eastern Connecticut State University,
Webb Hall, Willimantic, CT 06226, USA
e-mail: scotte@easternct.edu

E.A.M. Searing, D.R. Searing (eds.), *Practicing Professional Ethics in Economics and Public Policy*, DOI 10.1007/978-94-017-7306-5_11

salary and benefits. I helped gather the information and heard some of the discussions, but was still only peripherally involved. When I went home at night, my housemate's boyfriend, who was a union worker at the library, often told me the union's side. Eventually, negotiations broke down and the unions went on strike. I came from a family that had always supported unions, so when I approached the library, I faced a difficult personal decision: Should I cross the picket line?

I was torn. I did not want to cross, but I also didn't want to miss work. I didn't know what to do. Though I liked the workers and thought they should receive a decent wage, I didn't know what the right thing was for me to do. It seemed to me that an economic strike should rise and fall on the workers' ability to command the wages they wanted in the existing labor market. I also reasoned that crossing the picket line would enable me to help the Administration staff put together further negotiating packages in order to resolve the strike. I felt a responsibility to report to work on time, because my employment contract was with the library, which had treated me very well. I was also very worried about how I would pay the summer rent or afford the fall tuition if I had no income. This college experience captures the three issues I faced over and over again in my career: Discerning what was right. Fulfilling agency responsibilities. Avoiding conflicts of interest. All three play crucial roles in the life of any professional, but especially in the careers of managers and leaders in human resources.

There are many cases in which there is almost no discernment involved in determining what is right because the wrong action never crosses my mind. While I might be annoyed by a difficult supervisor or tempted by a loosely-monitored coffee kitty, I don't spend half a second believing murder or theft would be right. More complex situations or ones where I have little information, however, present much greater challenges for discernment. An HR manager's job often requires quick decisions, not allowing time for information gathering or reflection. When the payroll supervisor comes in half an hour before payroll cutoff, asking whether we should release the checks even though a significant percentage of workers were paid incorrectly or hold the payroll until all the errors are corrected, the HR manager has little time to evaluate the effects on employees of having their checks delayed, the effects on employees of being overpaid and having to pay back the money, the effects on the payroll staff of having to work overtime to fix the problem immediately, the effects on the organization of having to recover the money, potential for negative publicity to affect the organization's mission, etc. In order to ensure that my decisions were ethically sound, I had to build my capacity to recognize and evaluate ethical issues quickly. This requires ongoing reading, reflection, and education.

11.1 Recognizing Ethical Issues

One of the best ways to become more able to recognize ethical issues is to spend time reading and reflecting. Organizations can become insular, so reading or listening to people from outside the organization is important, especially people with a variety of views. Joining the Society for Human Resource Management (SHRM) and the state's association of HR managers; reading journals, books, newspapers, and magazines; volunteering at a shelter for men who were homeless – these were just a few of the ways I made sure that I wasn't confined by listening only to my staff. I also encouraged my staff to identify all of the implications of decisions, sometimes assigning them to make the best possible argument they could against something we were planning to do.

Part of a regular practice of reflection requires considering others' perspectives, which is much easier to do if one actually listens to others' perspectives. For example, in the early 1980s when I was a Personnel Director, I established a policy requiring all employees who were not reporting to work to call and speak directly to their supervisor within half hour of the start of the work day. I was a 20-something single woman with no children and a good salary; I tended to discount excuses offered by our minimum wage employees who were charged with excessive absenteeism. One day, responding to a disciplinary action for failing to talk to a supervisor when she called in sick, an employee said to me, "You have to understand, I was sick. I don't have a phone or a car. I couldn't take my kids to day care. So I dressed them, dressed myself, and walked to the convenience store down the road. I called, and the person who answered the phone said my supervisor had gone to the snack bar and would be back in 20 min. I had a fever. One of my kids was coming down with it. I couldn't stand around in the store to call back in 20 min. I had to go home before I collapsed." I realized that I was making policy from my own perspective. In the days of landline-only, corded phones, I could roll over in bed in the morning and pick up my bedside phone to call in, and if the supervisor wasn't there, easily call back later. From this experience, though, I learned I needed to work harder to consider the perspectives of others. One can take time each day or week to read or listen to others' perspectives on a wide variety of issues, enabling quick decision-making under pressure. This may mean seeking out night-shift employees, outside salespeople, telecommuters, or others who are on the margins and finding ways to listen to them.

Similarly, considering the unintended consequences of an action is important to ensuring ethical decisions. HR managers sometimes have tunnel vision, focusing in on the expected outcome, not the unanticipated consequences. When I was relatively new to the job of an HR manager, there was high unemployment and we were swamped with applications for every single position. My tunnel vision was focused on finding the best applicants efficiently, and I developed the solution of making it difficult to apply for a job, reasoning that this would help us screen out people who were not hard workers. You may be able to think of the unintended consequence to this decision; I certainly discovered it over time. We were quite successful in screening out lazy people, but we were equally successful in screening out people who were so good that they had lots of options. People who would have been great employees didn't bother to apply, because the application process was difficult and onerous.

Reading and reflection are important to ethical decision making, but it's impossible to do an adequate job of decision-making without education. Critical thinking was perhaps the most important overall benefit of my education, but mathematical literacy and economic literacy came in a close second and third. The ability to look at a set of numbers and draw conclusions quickly was only possible because I worked hard at the basics of math and economics courses and kept my skills active. Computers and calculators can make some tasks faster, but interpretation of data still requires the ability to understand concepts like mean, mode, median, standard deviation, compound interest, and marginal cost. An understanding of history helps in perspective-taking and consideration of unintended consequences – knowing about bad outcomes in the past helps us avoid them in the future. For example, awareness of the civil rights movement made me look closely at the brochures our employee assistance program (EAP) provider was producing in the 1980s, to see that all of the pictures of managers were white men, all the pictures of employees were white women, and there were no minorities at all. I was able to put myself in the position of minority employees and applicants, to see the subtle message that they did not belong and consider the negative effect that might have on recruitment. I told the EAP staff they needed to produce booklets with broader representation of workers if they wanted to keep our business. They complied. I think my raising the question may have had an effect on the brochures they produced for other employers as well.

My liberal-arts education was invaluable in preparing me for the breadth of problems that faced me in Human Resource Management. My business education helped me with the specific details of problems faced by HR managers. While I didn't remember every detail of my courses and textbooks, they contributed to better decision making, because I was aware of what I did not know. They gave me the sense the check to see whether there was legislation that might apply to a policy under consideration and the ability to find the relevant resources. Courses in human resource management, organizational behavior, compensation management, labor relations, and other fields prepared me to make decisions that took into account the wisdom of all of these fields.

11.2 Balancing Roles

Beyond the knowledge and reflection needed to discern what is right in complex situations, implementing decisions in organizations often requires balancing ethical duties and roles. HR Managers have ethical duties as members of their profession and agency duties as employees of organizations. In many situations, the HR Manager's role is advisory, not a line decision-maker. However, disagreements over ethics are fundamentally different from disagreements over strategy. Strategic choices are bets on the future, based on an assessment of the present. Ethical choices are decisions to choose good over evil. The HR Manager's choice, when faced with a disagreement over ethics, is not simply to say, "I had my say, but was overruled," as might happen in a disagreement over strategy. If the organization chooses to do what the HR manager believes is evil and cannot be convinced otherwise, the HR manager's choices are limited.

One manager whose integrity has always impressed me was responsible for field personnel who occasionally transported clients as part of their job duties. This was the 1980s, when we understood very little about AIDS, but were very afraid of it. The manager approached me to help write a requirement that any organization asking us to transport clients with knowledge that the clients had AIDS notify us so we could notify our employees and arrange for them to take precautions. I disagreed, and for at least an hour, he listened intently to my counter-proposal – that our employees should take universal precautions – asking questions and arguing with me. At the end, though, he said, "You've convinced me. Write a policy and develop the training to go along with it." To me, this was an ethical issue, because I did not want to contribute to the stigmatizing and ostracizing of people with AIDS. I did not want all of our employees to receive the subtle message that people with AIDS should be singled out and avoided. I did not want to lull them into the false sense of security – that if they had not been told someone had AIDS, there was no reason to take precautions. And I did not want to put the other organizations in the position of violating their clients' privacy (this was before HIPPA). Fortunately, the manager was persuaded by my argument and did what I recommended.

My college experience, however, was less satisfying. I chose to cross the picket line of the library workers and report to my job. I continued to do all of the duties I had performed as a student worker. I felt comfortable with this decision, since I was not crossing the picket line to replace my friends in the union, just to do my own job. As the strike wore on, I was asked to perform additional duties now and then – driving the truck to deliver books from one library to another, for example – that I had done in the past when the regularly-assigned union worker was out sick or on vacation. This made me exceedingly uncomfortable, so much so that when I went for my annual physical at student health, the doctor asked what was causing me to be so stressed. I told her about the effect of crossing the picket line on foot every morning and then having to drive back across it in the library truck a few times a day, listening to the workers call me names or beg me to stop. A few days later, the Director of Libraries called me in to ask how I was dealing with the strike. I told him it made me very uncomfortable to be doing the work of the striking workers, even if it was only a part of my overall duties. He told me they wouldn't ask me to do it anymore. I'm convinced that the Student Health Services doctor took it upon herself to call the Director of Libraries – this was long before HIPPA and in the days when the University considered itself *in loco parentis*. I never dared ask. The experience gave me sympathy with workers who don't know how to speak up when they think they're sliding down a slippery slope towards behavior that violates their ethical standards. It also made me realize that it is important for managers to ask employees directly, rather than assuming that silence means agreement.

In another case, I was a board member for a volunteer organization that provided shelter to people who were homeless. This organization was housed in a church, which had recently embraced a policy of providing sanctuary to workers who had overstayed their visas because their home countries were not safe. I respected the long tradition of the Church in providing sanctuary, and had no problem sharing the space with the workers. Not long afterwards, the board asked my assistance as it sought to hire its first paid employee. I was happy to help, working on recruitment, interviewing, selection, and an employment paperwork package, including all the required forms. I can't remember the specifics, but somehow, someone decided to remove the I-9 form, which verifies eligibility to work, from the required paperwork. I was told it was done to be consistent with the church's sanctuary policy. Sadly, I wrote a letter of resignation from the board, explaining that as an HR professional, I could not participate in violating an employment law that I viewed as legitimate. Upon receipt of my letter, the board met and reconsidered its decision, reversed itself, and invited me back.

11.3 Being an Ethical Manager

These three examples are of cases where I believed the organization was asking me to engage in or be a part of activities I believed were wrong. Not just white-shoes-after-Labor-Day wrong, but violations of my moral values. There are instances when a person in my position might have to become a whistleblower, going to the authorities to challenge harmful behavior that an employer refused to correct. I never had to do that in my career, but I realized early on that being able to quit a job is an important component to being able to maintain one's ethical standards. I encourage all of my students to stay out of debt and to live on significantly less than they make, in order to create a financial cushion allowing them more freedom to quit when pressured to violate their own standards.

Personal conflicts of interest still arose in my career – both perceived and actual. The biggest challenge for a person in Human Resources is that one can never really have friends in the organization. I was often in the role of investigating complaints of discrimination or proposals for disciplinary actions. To be *perceived* as biased would make my job impossible, because people would not trust me enough to tell me anything or to rely on my recommendations. To *be* biased would be a violation of the ethics of our profession. In fact, I often explained to new members of the office that they would have to create a kind of barrier in their brains, between the knowledge they gained in the course of their work and the knowledge they gained in their everyday interactions. A retirement form adding a spouse or health insurance claim for an ultrasound might signal good news in the life of one of our employees, but greeting them in the hall with "Congratulations on your marriage/baby!" was a violation of our duty to maintain confidentiality.

Perception of bias is especially difficult for HR managers who are promoted or transferred from within the organization, because they already have friends. When I supervised the Employment unit, I used to go to lunch with the supervisors of Benefits and Classification most days. I was promoted to manager and continued to lunch with them until I heard grumblings that I supported them in employee disputes because they were my friends. I got a gym membership and left the lunch group.

Actual bias is sometimes hard to recognize in ourselves, precisely because we are biased. Believing one's friends and peers is a natural tendency. We learn about halo effects and other biases in our HR classes because we have to guard against them, devising systems to avoid letting our natural tendencies interfere with our obligations to treat all employees fairly and without bias. We also have a natural tendency to look out for ourselves. HR Managers develop compensation systems, they select insurance providers, they write attendance policies, and they propose all kinds of employee benefits. Since they are employees, they also have interests in the effects of these programs on themselves. Recognizing the potential for conflict is a necessary part of ethical human resource decision-making. If I don't recognize that I am predisposed to prefer a particular benefit or policy because it fits my life situation better, I can't perform my professional obligation to choose the best one for the organization. It may be that what is good for me is also good for the organization, but I have to be prepared to recommend the benefit that is better overall.

11.4 Concluding Thoughts

Jobs in Labor Relations and Human Resources Management are incredibly varied and interesting. They provide great opportunities to help employees and organizations. As any manager in the field will attest, no two workdays are alike, and it is a rare day one doesn't have to change plans midstream to address an unanticipated issue. Many of these are ethical issues or point to potential future ethical issues. Three challenges: discerning what is right, balancing professional and agency roles, and avoiding conflicts of interest face every Human Resource manager who seeks to be both effective and ethical. In each case, education, reflection, a good-faith effort, and a willingness to sacrifice for one's principles make it possible to navigate through the challenges.

Chapter 12
Ethics and Forensic Economics

John O. Ward

Abstract Forensic Economics has become a full-fledged field of economics over the past 35 Years, and the quality of forensic economic analysis is far superior to what existed in the 1980s. There are ethical and professional practice standards in the legal world involving conflicts of interest, due diligence, confidentiality and disclosure. I would like to think that the field has risen to the challenges presented by the legal system by internally producing those techniques and knowledge necessary to accurately calculate such damages and by adopting a code of professional practice and ethics.

Keywords Professional ethics • Forensic economics • Legal ethics • Conflict of interest

12.1 Introduction

Forensic economics is the application of economic principles and techniques of analysis to the calculation of economic damages in litigation.[1] Such damages might include a firm's lost profits or lost value of business or an individual's lost earnings resulting from injury due to the wrongful actions of another business or person. I was first introduced to forensic economics in the late 1970s while working as a professor and department chair at the University of Missouri-Kansas City. A local attorney asked me if I would calculate the economic loss suffered by the survivors of a man killed in an automobile collision. The request was accompanied with an offer to pay me $900 (a magnificent sum at the time) for a report on damages and testimony at a trial.

After collecting some basic information about the man's work history, the surviving family, tax returns and W-2's and fringe benefits I embarked on the task. I

[1] See, Robert Thornton and John Ward, "The Economist in Tort Litigation", *The Journal of Economic Perspectives,* spring 1999, V. 13, N. 2, pp. 101–112 for a survey paper on the economist in litigation.

J.O. Ward (✉)
John Ward Economics, 8340 Mission Road Ste 235, Prairie Village, KS 66206-1363, USA
e-mail: wardjo@umkc.edu

E.A.M. Searing, D.R. Searing (eds.), *Practicing Professional Ethics in Economics and Public Policy*, DOI 10.1007/978-94-017-7306-5_12

soon discovered that other than a few bar journal papers, there was little literature available on calculating such damages and that literature that did exist offered widely conflicting views on how to make such calculations. There were no organizations of forensic economists (FE's) or economists doing forensic economic work. I found that most economists doing forensic economic work were professors doing such work part-time. Because forensic economics was not viewed as an academic field of research, most economics departments gave little credit for forensic economic consulting and some actively discouraged such work as a drain on energy that should have been directed to academic research. There were several large consulting practices attached to major universities that did forensic economic work in high profile commercial disputes, but there was little communication between FE's around the nation in this pre-internet age. I also discovered that my economic training in microeconomic theory, human resource economics and labor economics did not address the task at hand. I talked to several associates at other universities who had done similar assignments and found they did not know much more than I knew about making such projections of economic damages. So, to complete my task, I tied together a present value calculation based on the decedent's base earnings, run to a social security age of retirement, current bond yields, a 10 year average growth rate in earnings based on a 10 year past period for all workers, reduced by a historical average rate of unemployment, reduced by annual probabilities of death and an assumed self-consumption rate of a third. This was not rocket science and unfortunately, at that time, the state of the art of forensic economics was rather simplistic. The attorney accepted my calculations and the case settled out of court. I was paid for my effort and I thought, "This is pretty easy". It wasn't easy and in subsequent cases I discovered that deposition examination, motions to exclude my testimony and trials were stressful and demanding and my academic credentials did not buy me any slack in cross examination. I also found that the first forensic economic assignment for most academic economists was their last assignment. This was not an academic arena! I had to discover the rules of the legal arena and the standards of professional practice necessary to be a forensic economist.

12.1.1 Ethics and Professional Practices

There are no codes of ethics or professional practice for economists in the academic world other than the general standards of avoiding plagiarism in research and inappropriate relationships with students and the later standard is loosely enforced. There are ethical and professional practice standards in the legal world involving conflicts of interest, due diligence, confidentiality and disclosure. As a FE I was being asked to perform independent and impartial calculations of damages, having reviewed often confidential information supplied by the plaintiff or defendant. In preparing my report I had to collect all relevant information concerning the lost earnings, services or profits being claimed. I had to be sure that sufficient factual foundation existed to make an assumption in my calculations. An economic expert is an agent of the court with special privileges to offer opinions to a jury that would assist them in arriving at an informed decision. In a deposition, I would be examined on any conflicts of interest that could affect my impartiality and independence including my prior work for the retaining attorney, prior cases I had done and methodologies used in those cases and the thoroughness of my investigation of the facts of the case. The opposing side might retain their own economists or CPA to review my work and my prior reports in other cases might be reviewed to find inconsistencies in methodology. The purposes of the deposition are to discover what the economic expert is going to say, and to disqualify the expert if possible. One lesson learned early on was that the issue at hand for the attorney is not necessarily the truth or a fair evaluation, it is winning the case maximizing damages or minimizing loss. The FE should not look to the attorney for direction on ethical issues. That is not to say that attorneys are unethical, but they are advocates for their client's interests.

Conflicts of interest include contingency payments to the FE, based on the outcome of the case, and other relationships and actions that would make the FE an advocate for the client have to top the lists of practices to avoid by a FE. The FE should strive to be neutral, using the same methodologies and assumptions in a case, whether retained by the plaintiff or defense. The attorney retaining the FE wants an opinion favorable to the interest of their client and there are a small number of "hired guns" who will produce a damage number favorable to their client. Growth rates of earnings, interest rates for discounting, work life expectancies and self-consumption rates can be selected that will significantly increase loss or reduce loss and it is important for the FE to maintain consistency in calculations, assumptions and methodologies, and due diligence in gathering the factual foundation for assumptions to avoid the appearance of bias and advocacy. While some attorneys may pressure the FE to alter assumptions to favor their client's damages, good attorneys appreciate the importance of independence in the expert's analysis and testimony. After all, a jury and a judge are the triers of fact in a case and one lesson learned over the years is that the judgment of both the judge and jury should never be underestimated. There are hired guns and if they are good enough they can fool a judge or jury much of the time, but not all of the time.

Two ethical FE's can have widely different opinions on damages in a specific case, although my experience is that such situations are rare. I don't see many instances of unethical practices among FE's or hired guns, but I do see incompetent work by FE's who have not kept up with the literature or have not performed due diligence in investigating the facts of the case. Does the market weed out bad FE's? It may, but it takes a long time to do so. Most cases never go to trial and many never go to deposition. Exposing incompetence is probably more important than exposing unethical practices in terms of enhancing the image of forensic economics. So, how do you expose incompetence? The best way is to develop a professional literature of peer reviewed research and to hold the FE's work to the light of that research.

In 1993, Federal Judges were assigned the role of gatekeepers in ruling whether experts and their testimony are admissible in the case *Daubert v. Merrell Dow Pharmaceuticals, inc.* The U.S. Supreme Court, in this case ruling, encouraged federal judges to become more active in determining the admissibility of scientific experts and the reliability of their testimony. Changes in the Federal Rules of Evidence have resulted in fuller disclosure of expert's reports, opinions, calculations, experience and credentials. These changes have been adopted by many State courts and while not out ruling incompetence, these changes have tended to weed out the incompetent FE.

Since *Daubert* and the changes in the Federal Rules of Evidence, the FE must now produce a report disclosing all materials and assumptions considered, a list of all cases resulting in testimony for the past 4 years and a listing of credentials.

The passage of time since my first case also saw the development of the personal computer, analytical software and the internet that has allowed the FE to quickly access government data sources on life expectancy, unemployment rates, disability rates, family expenditure data, earnings growth trends and a myriad of other data sources used in personal injury and commercial litigation. In the 1970s and 1980s my calculations involved the university library hard copy data sources, an HP 12c financial calculator, a pencil and a pad of paper. It was far more time consuming to do a report and it was much easier to commit an error in calculations. It was also more difficult to review and replicate the work of another FE when hired by the other side.

12.1.2 Personal Perspective

Doing my first case began a learning process for me that has lasted 35 years. Central to that learning process was my recognition of the importance of following standards of professional practice and ethics which evolved in the field of forensic economics over that span of time.

During the past 35 years my part-time forensic economic practice became a full-time activity after I took retirement from the university in 2003. My firm now has five economists and three support staff and provides litigation support in commercial disputes, securities analysis, employment law, personal injury and death cases.[2] We have worked with both plaintiff and defense attorneys in over 25 states in over 2500 cases. The field of forensic economics grew rapidly after 1977 as attorneys increased their use of economic experts in litigation and the field itself began to organize. The use of economists and financial experts in commercial litigation, employment law and personal injury torts grew significantly in the 1980s and spurred the development of a recognized field of forensic economics.

In 1986 I incorporated the National Association of Forensic Economists based on contacts with 80 other FE's around the country and we had our organizational

[2] Our web page is at www.johnwardeconomics.com. The name of NAFE was changed to the National Association of Forensic Economics in 1991 to recognize the membership of CPA's, vocational experts and finance experts.

meeting in New Orleans.[3] A year later we started the refereed *Journal of Forensic Economics* (*JFE*), published three times/year. I served as Editor of the *JFE* for 15 years and by 2001, NAFE had 850 members. Another organization, the American Academy of Economic and Financial Experts, and its refereed journal, *the Journal of Law and Economics*, began in 1991.[4] By 1991, NAFE was conducting meetings at the ASSA and the four major regional economics association meetings each year and in the next 12 years NAFE added an annual winter meeting and an International meeting held in Europe annually. Through these organization, their annual meetings, their internet list serves and their publications, a forensic economic literature grew rather dramatically.

As an organization NAFE debated whether to create a code of ethical practices from its inception. While surveys of NAFE members suggested that the majority of FE's followed ethical standards of transparency, replicability and impartiality in their work, there was a belief that a code of ethics would both enhance the image of forensic economics as a discipline and such a code would serve to enhance ethical standards of all members. A code was adopted in 1992 and it encouraged members to avoid conflicts of interest, produce replicable calculations, disclose opinions and be consistent in their assumptions and methodologies. But, the code had no enforcement mechanism and there were no requirements that members accept the code as a condition of membership. AAEFE adopted a similar ethics code in the early 1990s. The 2002, NAFE Statement of Ethical Principles and Principles of Professional Practice consisted of eight principals of practice addressing the avoidance of conflicts of interest, the promotion of due diligence in research and analysis, the promotion of full disclosure of methods used in analysis and an emphasis on the responsibility of the FE to maintain current knowledge in the field and to report abuses of ethics in NAFE forums. While the Statement of Ethical Procedures does not have an enforcement mechanism, its acceptance is a condition of membership in NAFE. It is also the only Ethics Code imposed as a condition for membership for any economic association.

12.1.3 Final Comments

Forensic Economics has become a full-fledged field of economics over the past 35 years and the quality of forensic economic analysis is far superior to what existed in the 1980s. The membership composition of NAFE also changed in the 1990s with fewer NAFE members being PhD's from academic institutions. Increasingly, new FE's are CPA's or have MA's or MBA's. Also, the membership is aging, with a significant number of members in their 60s and 70s. Members of NAFE and AAEFE have encouraged the participation of new entrants into the field and many

[3] The NAFE webpage is at www.NAFE.net

[4] The AAEFE web page is at www.aaefe.org

opportunities exist to enter the field. Our meetings coincide with all of the major academic meeting of economists and we encourage students and new PhD's to attend our sessions. The legal system has come to increasingly rely upon testimony by forensic economists on damages in complex commercial litigation, employment law and personal injury death litigation. I would like to think that the field has risen to the challenges presented by the legal system by internally producing those techniques and knowledge necessary to accurately calculate such damages and by adopting a code of professional practice and ethics. In a NAFE session at the 2012 ASSA meetings in Chicago, Judge Richard Posner, a prominent legal and economic scholar and federal Court Appellate Judge was asked a question about his view of the role of ethics in the field of forensic economics. His view, he responded, was to assume that the expert is an advocate for the client (the attorney) because that is who is paying the bill. I would hope that the field has progressed to the point where this is not the case and that the FE can act in an impartial and objective way, but I agree that this is a work in progress.

Chapter 13
Ethics and Nonprofits

Woods Bowman

Abstract Nonprofit organizations have a public mission. Therefore, their leaders and their workers are arguably held to higher ethical standards than the standards applicable to for-profit companies. Governments likewise have a public mission, but their records and meetings are open to public view, so they are more transparent than nonprofits. The opaqueness of nonprofits provides fertile ground for unethical behavior. Moreover, the need to solicit donations and the tax advantages associated with most nonprofits create entire classes of temptations that are unknown in the business sector and incidental to the government sector. This article first explores ethics within nonprofits and then the ethics of nonprofits themselves. Finally, it identifies three trends that are shaping ethical standards for the next generation of nonprofit leaders.

Keywords Ethics • Nonprofits • Not-for-profits • Transparency

13.1 Ethics Within Nonprofit Organizations

Thanks to the Ethics Resource Center, there are fairly reliable and comprehensive data on ethics in nonprofits. The quotations and statistics cited in this section are from its most recent report on nonprofits (Ethics Resource Center, 2008). The best news is that nonprofits generally have a strong ethics culture compared to business or government: 58 % of employees in nonprofits report a strong, or strong-leaning, ethics culture compared with 52 % in business and 50 % in government. The difference is statistically significant but not impressive. Furthermore a strong ethics culture in nonprofits is only one-fourth as prevalent as a culture "leaning" in that direction. Clearly there is more work to do, even at the top of the scale.

One would expect a stronger ethics culture to produce less misconduct but it does not; slightly more than half of employees in nonprofits observed misconduct in the

W. Bowman (✉) (deceased)
School of Public Service, DePaul University,
25 E. Jackson (Lewis) – Room 1250, Chicago, IL 60604, USA
e-mail: wbowman@depaul.edu

E.A.M. Searing, D.R. Searing (eds.), *Practicing Professional Ethics in Economics and Public Policy*, DOI 10.1007/978-94-017-7306-5_13

previous year and this is roughly on par with that observed in the other sectors. Although 60 % nonprofit employees who observed misconduct reported it, nearly 40 % of witnesses remained silent, due largely to feelings of futility or fear of retaliation. Several famous controlled psychological experiments clearly demonstrate that most people in a crowd will wait for someone else to take action – whether it is helping someone in distress or reporting a crime. Even if employees do not fear the kind of retaliation that is forbidden – discharge, demotion, stalled advancement, and reassignment – they may not want to "get involved" in other people's affairs. "It's not my job," they might say. Good ethics programs address this perverse psychology by providing training that sensitizes people to their personal responsibility in addition to the rules and regulations. In organizations with little to no ethics and compliance program, 68 % of employees observed two or more types of misconduct over the course of a year. This is significantly reduced in organizations with a well-implemented program to just 22 %.

On average nonprofits face severe risk from a handful of behaviors: conflicts of interest, lying to employees, misreporting hours worked, abusive behavior, and Internet abuse. Interestingly, financial fraud is observed more often in nonprofits, plausibly because their managers are untrained persons who do not appreciate the value of internal controls or know how to implement them. A reasonable conclusion is that the greater opportunities for fraud in nonprofits tend to cancel the effect of their stronger ethical cultures. Good management practices may not eliminate ethical dilemmas from an organization, but sloppy and careless management almost certainly cause them. Nonprofits that operate without written policies and rely heavily on untrained staff have an extra burden to carry in creating an ethical culture.

A culture of ethics need not compromise financial performance. In fact there is evidence that the converse is true: "There is a statistically significant link between a management attitude favoring strong controls that emphasize ethically and socially responsible behavior and favorable corporate performance, both financially and socially" (Verschoor, 1997). This statement was written with for-profit corporations in mind. Given that nonprofits are expected to put people before profits, we presume that nonprofits with a strong ethical culture do a better job of serving the public without experiencing adverse financial consequences.

The following are three actual mini-case studies related to fundraising, an activity that is nearly unique to the nonprofit sector. They are based on letters addressed to this author in his role as the Nonprofit Ethicist columnist for the *Nonprofit Quarterly*.

13.1.1 Case 1

Dilemma One writer wanted to know whether it was ethical to count time spent on grant writing by the Executive Director and other senior staff toward fundraising and whether a distinction should be made between prospecting and writing new grant proposals vs. closing a deal or writing repeat applications to existing funding sources.

Response On its face this is a technical question answered by the Financial Accounting Standards Board's Standard 117 and the American Institute of Certified Public Accountants' Statement of Position 98–2. However, the question recognizes the larger problem of public aversion to high overhead costs. Don't fudge the numbers to look good and lean to donors and "watchdog" groups. Don't guess. Keep the necessary records for measuring fundraising overhead. Nonprofits themselves need know what it really costs to raise money so they can manage effectively.

13.1.2 Case 2

Dilemma A fundraiser was in a difficult situation when her Executive Director suggested that the organization engage a donor's business for a major building contract. Unbeknownst to the fund raiser, the donor's business was already involved in pre-construction work, after having made a small donation.

Response There is a larger governance problem here. When current or prospective donors are involved, boards must take extra care to avoid even the appearance of impropriety. The fact that the Executive Director talked about giving Mister Moneybags the organization's construction business sounds as if the board is cut out of the process. If the board does not insist on bidding, it is not doing its job.

13.1.3 Case 3

Dilemma A fundraiser spent many hours discussing a multi-million dollar bequest. Because of the size of the gift, the national president was present at the closing. When the donor asked for assurances that his gift would be used for activities in his home state, the fundraiser readily agreed. As soon as they were out of the donor's hearing, the president berated the fundraiser for agreeing. The gift was targeted to quasi-endowment (unrestricted funds).

Response If the donor wanted something in particular done with his money, he or she should have been specific in the gift agreement. That it was not is a good example of sloppy management. The fundraiser should have pointed that out. If the president had no intention of honoring the donor's wishes, he should have said so.

13.2 Ethics of Nonprofit Organizations

Ethical organizations should be accountable to their stakeholders. Accountability involves being "answerable" and "responsible" (Levasseur & Philips, 2005). Answerability describes a family of relationships between a nonprofit organization and external entities, implying sanctions or other forms of redress. Responsibility is a felt sense of obligation (Gregory, 1995). "[R]esponsibility concerns the acceptance for actions. It involves both 'being held to 'account' via sanctions or other methods of redress and 'taking account' of stakeholders' needs and views in the first place and responding to these by revising practices and enhancing performance as necessary" (Levasseur & Philips, 2005, p. 214).

A sense of autonomy easily leads to a disregard for actively seeking input from stakeholders. Revealing a distressing lack of concern, "[o]ver 70 % of nonprofit board members believed that they were accountable only to their board or to no one" (Millesen, 2004, p. 10). Executive directors of *community-based* organizations in three low-income neighborhoods of Philadelphia defined the needs of their communities differently from the residents they served. "Nonprofit directors across neighborhoods held more similar views with each other than they did with residents of their own communities, even though the communities were quite different" (Kissane & Gingerich, 2004, p. 38). Though this study was limited to one city, there is no reason to believe that Philadelphia is unique.

Legally, nonprofits are answerable to state attorneys general and (if they are also tax-exempt) the U.S. Internal Revenue Service (IRS), but they ought to feel answerable to the people they serve and to the public as well. Nonprofit status, tax-exemption, and deductibility of charitable contributions are legal artifacts – privileges granted by the public's elected representatives to organizations run by law abiding and socially-minded individuals performing socially desirable activities. Most nonprofit organizations may not discern the general public as a major actor, let alone the dominant one, yet it is the ultimate source of every privilege they enjoy.

Given generally weak public supervision, nonprofits aspiring to be ethical organizations must shoulder greater responsibility. It behooves all nonprofit organizations, but public charities particularly, to have a "felt sense of obligation" toward their constituents and toward the public. One can observe an organization's sense of obligation in its actions. There are five markers which identify responsible organizations:

Marker 1 Responsible organizations are true to their missions. Nonprofits are increasingly relying on earned income and less on donations and grants. Consequently "missions of nonprofits engaged in commercial activity will grow more ambiguous through time. New demands on senior management to pay attention to both mission and profit, the adoption of new structures such as joint ventures that create mixed missions and messages for participating entities, and the tendency of senior management to look at the activities from the perspective of their contribution to revenues may create an environment in which nonprofits must work especially hard to keep their charitable mission in daily focus" (Tuckman, personal communication, as quoted in Weisbrod, 2004, p. 44).

This is not to say that nonprofits should avoid commercial ventures or modifying their missions, but they should do so deliberately after a process of soul-searching that respects their stakeholders' interests. Nonprofits should keep in mind that actions and methods that are acceptable in for-profit businesses may be grotesquely inappropriate for them to practice. Nonprofit hospitals across the country have recently come under heavy criticism for being overly aggressive in collecting debts from "charity" patients. Some of them even lost their property tax exemption as a result.

Marker 2 Responsible organizations act as if outcomes matter. Doing good requires doing the right thing, not just the easy thing. Feeding America (formerly America's Second Harvest), the preeminent food bank network in the United States, began as a way to channel surplus foodstuffs to hungry people. However, these items were typically nonperishable, which provided a diet that was high in carbohydrates and low in protein. As one of Feeding America's executives explained to me, it became concerned that it was not providing recipients with a balanced diet, so it began to supplement its gifts in kind with fruits, vegetables, and meats purchased in the open market.

Marker 3 Responsible organizations are candid. They do not wait for others to reveal suspected misbehavior. They police themselves and then share the results of their investigations with the public. In 2004 Oxfam International responded to a tsunami in Indonesia but temporarily suspended their operations when an internal audit uncovered "financial irregularities" (Strom, 2006). Oxfam could have conducted further investigations without suspending aid to avoid raising questions, but it took the more responsible course.

Marker 4 Responsible organizations are proactive. In 2005 the American Red Cross set up a coordination center at national headquarters a day before Hurricane Katrina made landfall – the first time it had mobilized in anticipation of a disaster. By contrast, the trustees of the J. Paul Getty Trust of Los Angeles, one of the world's richest private art institutions, appointed a committee to investigate charges of financial mismanagement and dealing in stolen antiquities 10 months after critical newspaper stories first appeared and then only after the California Attorney General began an investigation (Felch & Fields, 2005).

Marker 5 Responsible organizations learn from their mistakes, a practice which is also good management (Verhage, 2004). Formal evaluation facilitates organizational learning. "Under conditions of high upward accountability, organizational learning is more likely if staff perceive evaluation as central to their own work rather than as a task only for managers and outside experts" (Ebrahim, 2005, p. 75). On the other hand, learning can occur without formal evaluation. Learning behavior is easily recognized. It involves changing procedures and methods so that similar adverse outcomes are less likely to occur again.

13.3 Trends in Nonprofit Ethics

Ethics is an ever-evolving concept. What was acceptable behavior in one era may be discouraged and even punished in a later era. Four trends are emerging from the current landscape and are already shaping future ethical standards for nonprofits.

Trend 1 Small donors will demand that charities pay the same deference to their wishes and expectations that have always been accorded large donors. Do you remember the unprecedented public generosity following the tragedies of September 11, 2001? Donors presumed that the receiving charities would use their money to provide relief for families of victims. Many of them became angry upon learning that half of the donations to the American Red Cross (ARC) went for "investments in volunteer mobilization, chapter development for response to weapons of mass destruction, expanded blood security, and continuity of operations efforts" (Wetzstein, 2001). Three years later, Doctors Without Borders, responding to a tsunami that destroyed parts of Southeast Asia, set a new ethical standard when it ceased fundraising after only 3 days, once it determined that it had sufficient funds (Strom, 2007).

Trend 2 Courts will become less tolerant of sweeping generalizations and vaguely misleading statements made by charities in the course of fundraising. According to legal briefs, commercial solicitors working in Illinois for Telemarketing Associates told prospects that a "significant amount of each dollar donated would be paid over to VietNow," a charitable veterans assistance organization. In fact, the contract provided only 15 % for VietNow which in turn spent only 3 % of its $1.1 million share on charitable programs. The Attorney General of Illinois prosecuted Telemarketing Associates for fraud, though not VietNow (Madigan *v*Telemarketing Associates, Inc. 538 U.S. 600, 2003). The case went all the way to the U.S. Supreme Court, which had applied first amendment protections to the previous charitable solicitation cases, sent it back to the trial court for a hearing on the merits where the parties settled off the record. It may not sound like much of a victory for honesty in fundraising, but deception may be fraudulent, but it is certainly unethical.

Trend 3 As mentioned above, responsible organizations act as if outcomes matter, so it is good news that "the nonprofit community in the United States (and increasingly elsewhere) has begun to shift its attention from measuring outputs as indicators of progress to measuring outcomes" (Ebrahim, 2005, p. 68). To continue with the disaster relief example: outputs are things like meals served, bottles of water distributed, etc., while outcomes are measured in terms of the well-being of victims. Outcomes might be the proportion of displaced persons whom the agency housed, fed and assisted medically, or the average length of time that people lived in shelters before finding permanent replacement housing.

Trend 4 More regulation is a certainty. A minimal ethical standard is obedience to the law; if a law is unjust, then a direct challenge would be in order, but self-serving disobedience never is. The U.S. Senate Finance Committee recently considered, before rejecting, staff proposals requiring nonprofits to establish, approve and review program objectives and performance measurements, then report the results to the IRS on their 990 forms. The IRS is taking an increased interest in how nonprofits manage conflicts of interest. It now has a question about the existence of an organizational policy on the 990 Form and it provides a sample policy as an appendix to Form 1023 (Application for Recognition of Exemption). Since the IRS rarely does anything gratuitously, it seems likely that conflict of interest regulation will eventually find its way onto the public agenda.

13.4 Conclusion

In some ways, our nonprofit financial models are a set up for irresponsibility because they often have us paid by one stakeholder to provide service to another. This interrupts the direct line of accountability between a customer and provider. Nonprofit constituents often cannot vote a nonprofit leader out of office, nor can they necessarily stop using the service. Thus nonprofits have a greater power advantage relative to the people they serve than for-profit businesses have relative to their customers or politicians arguably have *vis a vis* constituents (O'Neill, 1992).

These are only some ways that nonprofit organizations are different from business and governments. The direct result is that nonprofits bear extra responsibilities. If they want to promote an ethical culture internally and behave ethically in their dealings with the rest of the world, nonprofits should relentlessly cultivate a "felt sense of responsibility" toward others. Competent management is an essential part of the picture because I firmly believe that sloppy and careless management almost certainly cause ethical dilemmas and encourage people to make wrong choices. Over the years, I have seen the strategic plans of many nonprofits and none mentioned ethics. This is sad because continuous self-evaluation is the best regulator of behavior.

References

Ebrahim, A. (2005). Accountability myopia: Losing sight of organizational learning. *Nonprofit and Voluntary Sector Quarterly, 34*(1), 56–87.

Ethics Resource Center. (2008). *National nonprofit ethics survey: An inside view of nonprofit sector ethics*. Arlington, VA: Author. The data are for 2007.

Felch, J., & Fields, R. (2005). New getty panel to examine operations. *Los Angeles Times*, October 30, A1.

Gregory, R. (1995). Accountability, responsibility and corruption: Managing the public production process. In J. Boston (Ed.), *The state under contract*. Wellington, New Zealand: Bridget Williams Books.

Kissane, R. J., & Gingerich, J. (2004). Do you see what I see? Nonprofit and resident perceptions of urban neighborhood problems. *Nonprofit and Voluntary Sector Quarterly, 33*(2), 311–333.

Levasseur, K., & Philips, S. D. (2005). Square pegs in round holes: Vertical and horizontal accountability in voluntary sector contracting. *The Philanthropist, 19*(3), 211–231.

Millesen, J. (2004). Who "Owns" your nonprofit. *Nonprofit Quarterly, 12*(4), 10–14.

O'Neill, M. (1992). Ethical dimensions of nonprofit administration. *Nonprofit Management and Leadership, 3*(2), 199–213.

Strom, S. (2006). Charity delays tsunami work as audit finds irregularities. *New York Times*, March 16, A4.

Strom, S. (2007). Nonprofit groups draw a line at some donors. *New York Times*, January 28, A17.

Verhage, J. (2004). Learning from the mistakes of some ... and the bravery of others. *Nonprofit Quarterly, 11*(2), 43–45.

Verschoor, C. C. (1997). Principles build profits. *Management Accounting, 79*(4), 42–46.

Weisbrod, B. A. (2004). Why nonprofits should get out of commercial ventures. *Stanford Social Innovation Review, 2*(3), 40–47.

Wetzstein, C. (2001). Red Cross relief efforts under fire. *Washington Times*, November 7, A1.

Chapter 14
Ethics and Professional Practice

Andrew I. Cohen

Abstract This chapter discusses what role ethics has in guiding professionals. The chapter criticizes a "lawgiver model" of ethics, in which ethics purports to be universal, authoritarian, and counterpreferential. The chapter sketches parts of a different model of ethics, one in which ethics is participatory and guides us. Ethics need not merely constrain us. Ethics can help economists (and other professionals) to figure out how to do the right thing. There may be more than one way to get this right. Figuring out how to do it is not something ethicists can facilitate without the lived experience and advice of those in the field. In formulating an ethics for economists, economists have to do a lot of the ethical work.

Keywords Professional ethics • Economic ethics • Duty • Virtue

14.1 Introduction

Ethics studies what we may do, what we ought to do, what we must do, and what we must not do. That might not be everything ethics does, but those four subjects are what many ethicists study much of the time. The last two subjects—what we must or must not do—often crowd out everything else. Perhaps this is what gives ethics a bad reputation: its conclusions often come to us in the form of commands and prohibitions. That can make ethics difficult.

Over the past 30–40 years, there has been an explosion of subfields in practical and applied ethics. Scholars now study and teach environmental ethics, journalistic ethics, business ethics, medical ethics, and more specialized areas such as nursing ethics, genetic ethics, nanoethics, neuroethics, computer ethics, and engineering ethics. In each case, people typically explore what specific insights traditional ethical theories might offer for particular practices. In each case, ethics often stands for a body of rules that prevent people from succumbing to temptation.

A.I. Cohen (✉)
Jean Beer Blumenfeld Center For Ethics, Department of Philosophy, Georgia State University, P.O. Box 3994, Atlanta, GA 30302-3994, USA
e-mail: aicohen@gsu.edu

E.A.M. Searing, D.R. Searing (eds.), *Practicing Professional Ethics in Economics and Public Policy*, DOI 10.1007/978-94-017-7306-5_14

A common understanding of economics is that it studies the production, distribution, and consumption of goods. Perhaps an ethics of economics can provide some guidance in what economists can study and how to present their conclusions. But given what ethics does, it may seem all it has to offer economists is another set of cautions, mandates, and stop signs.

My short reply is that this is not quite right. While it is true that sometimes, doing the right thing is hard, it is also true that sometimes, being ethical (and understanding what that entails) is rewarding in many ways. My discussion below has modest aims. I hope to show some problems with one way of thinking about professional ethics. I suggest some alternatives for a model of professional ethics and then point to what this might mean for economists.

14.2 The Lawmaker Model of Professional Ethics

When ethicists speak to professional groups, they often discuss the foundations of ethical principles. They sometimes add something about how virtuous persons might use those principles. Afterwards, someone often asks a question that sounds something like this: "Thank you for the presentation. That was all very interesting. But *we need to know what to do*. What do we have to do so we can get on with our jobs?"

Coming from people who are committed to a job and want to do it well, this query shows a polite concern with staying out of trouble. Perhaps this is how ethicists help professionals in other fields: they figure out what the ground rules are or ought to be, they pass the word, and then the professionals may go do their work. Understood in this way, the ethicists are a bit like Moses: they return from the mountaintop and deliver the tablets that say what the people must or must not do. Call this the *lawgiver model* for professional ethics.

There are several notable features of the lawgiver model. Here I highlight three. First, the ethicist identifies some laws that can and should apply to everyone. This captures the *universality* of ethical principles. Second, the ethicist is delivering the laws, which gives ethics (and the ethicist) an *authoritarian* quality. Third, ethics comes significantly if not entirely in the form of commands and prohibitions, which makes ethics *counterpreferential*. As I discuss below, each of these features shows serious drawbacks with the lawmaker model of professional ethics, but each also points to better alternatives.

14.2.1 The Universality of Ethics

On the lawmaker model of professional ethics, ethics applies to everyone—or at least everyone meeting certain criteria. In the case of Moses, the law applied to all the children of Israel. If basic ethical principles apply universally, then it is not clear what if anything is interesting or new about any specific code of professional ethics. After all, the law is the law, and there is nothing more to say. What else do we need to know besides the usual rules forbidding murder, theft, and lying?

Imagine the manufacturers of self-adhesive notes were to ask an ethicist what their professional code should be. Would there be anything especially novel that the ethicist can relate? "Do not murder CEOs of rival manufacturers of self-adhesive notes." But this is just an application of the usual rule: do not murder. "Do not misrepresent how many notes are in the package." But this is just an application of the rule: do not lie. "Do not manufacture self-adhesive note paper with pulp made from trees taken off land without the owner's permission." Here too, that is just an application of the rule forbidding theft. One might then complain that the silliness of the ethics of self-adhesive-note-manufacturing shows general problems with any sort of professional ethics.

This is too quick. There is often important content to professional ethics. Especially in new or changing fields, practitioners may be uncertain what they may or may not do. Consider, for instance, our growing understanding of genetics. Scientists know certain genes are linked to certain diseases and physical attributes. Researchers have designed tests to detect some of these. The ethical issues are complicated here. May geneticists assist people in determining whether they are at risk of producing offspring with certain diseases, or, perhaps more sharply, a particular sex? May prospective parents terminate pregnancies when the fetus has a gene that increases chances of mid-life onset breast cancer? May prospective parents *not* terminate pregnancies when testing shows the fetus has a gene linked to deafness, or muscular dystrophy, or Huntington's disease? Do insurance companies have a right to demand such tests of prospective clients?

Ethicists, doctors, scientists, lawmakers, and others have grappled with these issues. They continue to do so. Simply saying "do not murder" does not tell us whether one might be justified in terminating the pregnancy of a fetus that is prone to some debilitating genetic disorder—let alone terminating a pregnancy at all. It is also not clear whether the common ethical injunction "do no harm" forbids parents from gestating and birthing a child sure to be deaf. These controversies have occupied not only people working in genetic ethics but also scholars working in the field of disability studies. Many writers have strenuously resisted the idea that deafness is a disability. Some argue that selective abortion of children prone to deafness, or even giving hearing-impaired children cochlear implants, disrespects all deaf persons and might express an unjustified view that hearing must be part of any good life.

The point here is not to resolve these difficult questions. The point is that in many fields, there are distinct challenges and distinct norms of professional conduct. Appealing mechanically to basic ethical principles may not resolve what professionals may do, must do, should do, or must not do. That is why certain inquiries in professional ethics are hardly vacuous. There are ethical dilemmas, and we can make progress in framing them and taking steps toward resolving them.

Ethicists might then help people in a field to grapple with distinctive challenges. They can help clarify what the problems are and what alternative ways there are for resolving them consistent with the basic principles that apply to everyone. This suggests ethicists can help practitioners reach specific conclusions that might not apply to people in other fields. Economists and geneticists do different things. Of course, neither sort of professional should murder, but that is not the point. Some code of professional ethics may offer much guidance beyond the universality of basic ethical principles.

14.2.2 Ethics as Authoritarian

Consider how in the lawmaker model of professional ethics, the ethicist is asked to "deliver" the ethical rules. Moses, after all, went up the mountain for 40 days and came back with the commandments. Moses went up alone. He delivered the pronouncements alone. The children of Israel did not go up the mountain with him.

Consider how this might work for any code of professional ethics. Imagine—purely for argument's sake—that economists have no ethical compass. As persons, or, at least, as economists, they simply do not know how to do the right thing, how to avoid the wrong thing, and even what the right or wrong things are. In that case, perhaps the ethicist could helicopter in to rescue economists from being morally adrift. Of course, for the ethicist's rules to have any traction with economists, the ethicist would need to know (at least a little) economics and have a sense of what economists do for a living. Let us assume the ethicist acquires that. Afterwards, perhaps with a sense of *noblesse oblige*, the ethicist can drop off the tablets with the social scientists who will then shout their thanks as he ascends from the adoring crowd in his helicopter, off to rescue other guilds of savant professionals in need of moral guidance.

This authoritarian approach is inappropriate to formulating the structure and content of codes of professional ethics. People are not idiots. More precisely: it is simply not true that no one among a group of professionals has an ethical clue, and it is not true that the professionals have no consensus on what at least some of their areas of ethical concern are. They can achieve that consensus on what the problems are even if they do not know how to resolve them. More importantly, we do not have a Moses. Even if there were such a person, reasonable professionals might disagree on whether his deliverances ought to be accepted. Appeals to authority do not always help, especially when people disagree on who the authority is.

Another problem with the authoritarian approach comes with the image of the ethicist helicoptering in to deliver the truth. Having someone "deliver" the ethical rules is typically not the way to find rules appropriate for a group—let alone getting sufficient buy-in to achieve the basic ethical goals we typically share. Sometimes the people cannot simply sign for delivery. Sometimes they need to go up the mountain with Moses and participate in formulating the rules themselves.

An alternative approach would then be more participatory—more *democratic*—than the authoritarian lawmaker model. On this alternative, the ethicist does not necessarily deliver anything. At best, he can facilitate the experts in the field in figuring out among themselves what rules should apply to them. This is not something they merely need to discover, as if the truth is out there (up the mountain?) waiting to be delivered. Perhaps sometimes they need to invent it. Inventing the rules does not mean they can do it any old way; it may take great care to do it correctly while remaining sensitive to the distinct goals and challenges in their field. There are some ground rules that might constrain what they invent. Some of these might be facts about the natural world. Some of these might be norms of human psychology, culture, academe, or politics. Sometimes those norms need to be examined, but that task might be beyond the scope of the professionals' work. Perhaps the ethicist can, nevertheless, help people to understand some common ethical requirements. He can help the professionals figure out how to apply those principles to formulate specific rules appropriate to their craft. But the problems with the authoritarian model suggest that for economists (and likely for any sort of profession), members need first to identify what their ethical challenges are. Ethicists can help the economists to figure out how to begin to resolve them.

Ethicists can serve additional consultant functions by giving an outside perspective about professional norms. Sometimes there is a culture that blinds practitioners to defective norms and possibilities for improvement. But typically people within a profession are committed to living well and being good professionals. They have unique insight into the challenges they face and what norms make certain possibilities more feasible than others.

14.2.3 Ethics as Counterpreferential

Under the lawmaker model of professional ethics, the rules come to us as commandments. Professionals must do what the rules require and they must avoid what the rules forbid. That sounds like such a drag.

Consider the commandments Moses delivered. Among them were rules forbidding people from doing things they might like to do. After all, people sometimes want to bash in the heads of their rivals, take their stuff, lie to them, and sleep with someone else's spouse. But the commandments ruled all those things out. This suggests that rules often clash with what we might otherwise prefer to do.

Sometimes ethics seems to serve that role. It furnishes rules that tell us what we must do (even if we do not want to) and what we must not do (even if we want to anyway). Sometimes we prefer something (and do not merely desire it), but acting on that preference is forbidden. We can say: too bad for our preferences. We have to do what we have to do.

Codes of professional ethics may similarly serve a counterpreferential role. Here is where knowing the intricacies of a profession is crucial. It is important to understand a field's common temptations to shortcuts, cheats, likely complicities, and other ethical lapses. Some are common to other fields (such as massaging statistical results in econometrics until they produce something interesting). Others might be distinct to a particular field. The practitioners are often the ones to identify those. In economics, for instance, certain analyses may presuppose an evaluative framework (such as a standard of benefit, or a view of acceptable human motivation) that may raise distinct ethical questions. Philosophers can help explore those.

Philosophers and economists dispute whether ethics is ever counterpreferential (See, for instance, Hausman, 2011; Sen, 1977). I do not wish to address this dispute here. Even if ethics is not a source of counterpreferential reasons, surely it is sometimes *difficult*. But many things worth doing are hard. Indeed, economists might best satisfy the reasons that apply to them (such as improving how they can explain and predict economic phenomena) by codifying certain rules of professional inquiry and conduct. There might be many incompatible ways of doing this correctly. This is something economists need to figure out in light of the particular demands on them, and in light of the ethical challenges that face all of us as human beings.

Recall the characterization of ethics that started this chapter. Ethics studies not simply what we must or must not do. It also studies what we may or ought to do. This opens up more for ethics to do than admonish us. Ethics might also point the way toward lucrative possibilities. Independently of professional responsibilities, ethics can sometimes identify how certain character traits help persons to live life well. Our understanding of what this involves might change, and sometimes it might be mistaken. But the portrait of the good person need not be of someone beaten down by the demands of duty. She might do what she needs to do but also exploit opportunities to succeed in her life and her profession. How she does this is significantly a function of her insight, creativity, and lived experience. Likely her success, whatever shape it takes, must take stock of what people in her field do and what they hope to do.

Figuring out how to live well and succeed in a profession is something that requires a bit of experimentation. But the room for experiment should not obscure that certain things are settled. Sometimes codifying them can help people to notice opportunities for success instead of dwelling on how not to murder rivals today. There is more to life than nonperformance of nefarious deeds. What else there might be is sometimes not obvious. The ethicist can hardly helicopter in to deliver the answers. She might simply guide persons who are busy with living life. She might also guide practitioners busy with their careers who see the need to devise professional norms.

14.3 Preliminaries for Ethics for Economists

Economists often study the production and distribution of wealth. They sometimes study why some peoples are poorer than others. They can discuss correlations among stable norms of property rights, openness to trade, and relative prosperity. They can suggest losing the dictator, cultivating the infrastructure, reducing market restrictions. But ethics can come along and rattle us a bit, especially when it comes to poverty.

Some persons are abjectly poor. They suffer from easily preventable or curable diseases. Meanwhile, residents of the wealthy west vacation in tropical paradises, drive their private cars to climate-controlled restaurants to enjoy the finest food that they chew with orthodontically straightened teeth, and afterwards drive to a nearby coffee shop to buy a fancy coffee with money that might instead have rescued perhaps a dozen children in the developing world from dying of malnutrition. This juxtaposition bothers people. Some writers think it presents one of the greatest ethical challenges of our time (see, e.g., Singer, 2009). They argue that our reluctance to fix the problem is beside the (ethical) point. People are suffering, we can do something about it, so we need to get moving. Indeed, we need to do this *above all else*, since stopping easily preventable deaths is not trivial. On this view, fancy coffees clearly take second place to rescuing starving babies. Indeed, it might be so important that economists have no business being economists! They should just rescue starving babies (see, e.g., Singer, 1972).

Here is where the lessons can go the other way. Economists can contribute to our understanding of the proper scope and content of ethics. As development economists would stress, curing and preventing suffering from poverty is not just a matter of transferring resources. It is a matter of nurturing the local institutions that make the creation of wealth possible. When well-intentioned people from without attempt to rescue needy locals, they sometimes generate moral hazards, prop up or create defective institutions, and undermine local markets. However, as economists often note, allowing people to figure things out on their own helps them to create institutions responsive to local conditions and thus most likely to foster succeed. There may be more than one way to get it right. It may be a matter of understanding what can happen when people act on their self-interest within certain institutions. (I discuss this in Cohen, 2014.) So the work of economists is important. It gives economists and everyone else good reason to think that ethics permits (and perhaps requires) them to go about their business.

Consider one possible lesson from all this. Imagine, against the earlier assumption of this chapter, that economists are indeed basically good persons who are interested not just in succeeding in their profession but in living well. Economists often tell us that foisting rescue plans on people is counterproductive. They would often suggest grounding the helicopters filled with well-intentioned aid. There might similarly be good reason to warn off the Moses-ethicists in their helicopters. Figuring out how to live well (especially as a professional economist) is not something that can come on tablets from some exalted authority. It requires lived experience from within the profession.

When children ask us how to live well, we often point to examples of successful persons and failures. We provide some basic rules. And if we are honest, we admit that it is hard to live well. There are many ways to go wrong, and a bunch of ways to get it right.

Economists may want to know how to be good economists. Mature professionals from within their ranks might focus on various examples of success and failure and consider the traits common to each. Drawing on the advice of experts both from within and without their field, economists might then together formulate principles to offer suggestions and rules for coping with challenges and exploiting opportunities to their fullest.

Economists have to do a lot of the work. Ethicists can help shape continuing conversations about the content of the norms to bind and inspire their profession. How such norms function and how they are promulgated is something the economists will need to determine after careful deliberation. It is something that requires the input of mature members of the profession.

14.4 Closing Thoughts

The conclusions here are modest. There are important drawbacks to a lawgiver model of professional ethics, which has us treating an ethicist as someone who delivers the truth. That is rarely if ever the ethicist's role. Moreover, thinking of ethics as authoritarian and merely counter-preferential undermines the possibility that professional ethics can guide us and not merely constrain us. Ethicists can point to some basic rules, but following them is not all there is to living well and succeeding as a professional. Otherwise, ethics, career, and life itself is little more than a chore. Surely doing the right thing is more than that. Much remains for professional economists to figure out on their own and with others what they might do and how to do it best.

Since our concern here is not so much with living well but in figuring out what norms can guide members of a profession, it should be clear that the content of these norms is not something a philosopher can pronounce in any interesting way from the armchair. Philosophers can discuss why economists should not murder one another without knowing too much about economics. They can also discuss why economists should not fudge their data. Putting flesh on the bones of a particular set of rules is something economists must do with much patience, insight, and creativity. Ethicists might help them to clarify their disputes, distill the stakes, and formulate a coherent body of governing norms. They can do this once mature economists start to identify what it is to be a successful economist. This is why a lot of the hard work belongs to economists. They know what it is to be an economist.

Acknowledgments For comments and advice about earlier drafts, I am grateful to the editors of this volume.

References

Cohen, A. I. (2014). Famine relief and human virtue. In A. I. Cohen & C. H. Wellman (Eds.), *Contemporary debates in applied ethics* (2nd ed.). Malden, MA: Wiley-Blackwell.

Hausman, D. M. (2011). *Preference, value, choice, and welfare*. Cambridge: Cambridge University Press.

Sen, A. K. (1977). Rational fools: A critique of the behavioral foundations of economic theory. *Philosophy & Public Affairs, 6*, 317–344.

Singer, P. (1972). Famine, affluence, and morality. *Philosophy & Public Affairs, 1*, 229–243.

Singer, P. (2009). *The life you can save*. New York: Random House.

Chapter 15
Ethics and Public Policy

Judith Wagner DeCew

Abstract My work in ethics has focused on theoretical material from Aristotle on the good life, Mill on utilitarianism, Hume's emotivism and subjectivism, Kant's rationalism (including his account of the moral worth of an act and his categorical imperative about right acts), and W.D. Ross' intuitionism on what makes right acts right. I found all these very different views fascinating and wondered if one of the theories might truly be the correct one. In my studies of mathematics, I had been trained to find the correct answers, and from that perspective it was natural to have a similar expectation in my newer field of interest, ethics, which I characterize as an inquiry into and about ways of life and rules of conduct. I argue in this paper that often no one theory is correct, but ethical theory as a collective is essential for practical decision-making.

Keywords Ethics • Theory • Practice • Law • Decision making • Public policy

15.1 Introduction

I have been teaching and publishing in ethics, social and political philosophy, and philosophy of law for nearly 35 years. I was an undergraduate mathematics major, took a course in logic as a sophomore, and then fell in love with philosophy, particularly ethics, by my junior year. Like most other students, my first class in ethics focused on theoretical material from Aristotle on the good life, Mill on utilitarianism, Hume's emotivism and subjectivism, Kant's rationalism (including his account of the moral worth of an act and his categorical imperative about right acts), and W.D. Ross' intuitionism on what makes right acts right. I found all these very different views fascinating and wondered if one of the theories might truly be the correct one. In my studies of mathematics, I had been trained to find the correct answers, and from that perspective it was natural to have a similar expectation in my new field of interest, ethics, which I characterize as an inquiry into and about ways of life

J.W. DeCew (✉)
Department of Philosophy, Clark University, Worcester, MA 01610-1477, USA
e-mail: jdecew@clarku.edu

E.A.M. Searing, D.R. Searing (eds.), *Practicing Professional Ethics in Economics and Public Policy*, DOI 10.1007/978-94-017-7306-5_15

and rules of conduct. I argue that often no one theory is correct, but ethical theory as a collective is essential for practical decision-making.

We have probably all informally asked ourselves questions about the point or goal of life, how we ought to live, whether there is a fundamental principle at the root of all moral philosophy, and whether there is a single test for distinguishing right and wrong. Historically, moral philosophers have tried to give answers to these questions by proposing abstract theories, and their attempts have been classified as the core of what is called *theoretical normative ethics*. Unlike our own musings about these questions, moral philosophers have tried to give general or crucial guidelines rather than detailed advice for particular occasions. They have worked to set forth systematically first principles of morality that are consistent, often defending a true moral code, and they have tried to justify their accounts.

After taking and then teaching graduate courses in ethics and social and political philosophy, I soon was immersed in more practical ethical problems such as those concerning (1) when taking an action is the same or different from letting something happen through inaction; (2) when there appears to be an objective answer to an ethical question independent of one's mental states – attitudes, beliefs, or feelings of approval, and when one's feelings seem crucial to a moral decision, as Hume held; (3) arguments that favor absolutism, and the allure but difficulty of defending relativism; and (4) how to balance interests of an individual and individual rights against social benefit and public policy arguments.

However, as I wrote in the Introduction to *Theory and Practice* (Shapiro & DeCew, 1995):

> Since time immemorial, students of philosophy, politics, and law have disagreed over the relations between theoretical principles and everyday practice. Some have stressed the value of theory, arguing that it should be pursued for its own merits and that it is difficult, impossible, or misleading to apply its ideals to the real and imperfect world. Others have championed the importance of focus on practical problems in daily life and have urged that theory is not worthwhile unless it sheds light on how to resolve actual conflicts or real-world problems.

Aristotle and Kant made foundational contributions to this discussion, including Aristotle's (1941). famous distinction between *theoria* and *praxis* in *The Politics*. Both seemed to embrace a link between the two, and both are usually taken to be advocates of the traditional view in moral philosophy that the goal of moral theory is to resolve conflicts in moral decision making by giving clear guidance and systematizing moral thought to ultimately provide a principle or set of principles to overcome what at first appear to be irresolvable moral dilemmas. As Kurt Baier wrote, "when there are conflicts of interest, we always look for a 'higher' point of view, one from which such conflicts can be settled. …By the moral point of view we *mean* a point of view which furnishes a court of arbitration for conflicts of interest" (*The Moral Point of View*, NY: Random House 1965, 96). In contrast, over the last 35 years a group of contemporary pluralist philosophers including Ruth Barcan Marcus, Bas van Fraassen, Bernard Williams, Thomas Nagel and Stuart Hampshire have argued, to the contrary, that the inevitability of moral conflicts is data in the world, and that abstract and ideal theory is incompatible with conflicts, disagreements and divisions that exist in practice. On their view, moral theory often cannot provide comprehensive explanations, evaluations, or answers to practical and fundamental problems in real life. The debate over both the value and relation between theory and practice continues, and I am convinced that the relationship is more nuanced than either the traditional or pluralist views acknowledge.

15.2 Applying Ethics to Public Policy

I have come to understand and be a productive advocate for various public policy positions, such as codes of warfare, arguments against the combat exclusion and in favor of the role of women in the military, the feminist critique of privacy, issues concerning privacy and drug testing, as well as privacy and medical information and genetic research; in doing so, I have found that this requires a solid grounding in the theories that have influenced moral thinking through the ages as well as the contemporary moral evaluations of these theories. At its best, philosophical analysis depends on achieving a thoughtful and fair understanding of major rival positions, whether or not one ultimately endorses them. In the process one also needs to engage in critical evaluation of the theories and theoretical attempts to set out fundamental concepts in ethics and morality.

Many will agree that there is not one single theory of morality or conception of ethics that allows us to settle all moral and public policy controversies. However, looking for insights in what different philosophers have said about what morality is can help us in crucial ways to evaluate how best to go about making moral decisions, how we can live life in as moral a way as possible, and what conflicts and fundamental disagreements in morality help us learn about the people and world around us. If we can identify some important visions from historical and contemporary moral philosophers and combine these with moral ideals that we find compelling, we will have made worthwhile progress. One must understand the weaknesses of utilitarian accounts and theories of individual rights, the difficulties of defending relativism, the advantages of objectivism in ethics as well as the contributions of emotivist and subjectivist approaches, before relying completely, or even in part, on such arguments. A major reason is that using practical examples from applied ethics is one way of testing various theories against our thoughtful and informed intuitions. At the same time real life examples are messy and complicated and not usually easily compartmentalized into analysis by a single theory or set of principles, and thus examining and working through ethical practice emphasizes the need for theory. In decision making in politics, economics or elsewhere in real life, a focus on only one or a couple strands of thought would be hasty. Pitfalls to avoid are dogmatism and emphasis on one perspective. In economic discussions, for example, it is not uncommon to find that efficiency arguments often dominate and win. But there are usually competing normative issues to consider that permeate a particular real life problem. It seems far better to expect a decision to be complex, to contain features or ramifications that are difficult to uncover, and that may rely on concerns one had not anticipated. Life is messy – expect that messiness to arise in real life decisions, and recognize the ethical themes and implications relevant to a decision.

Contemporary moral philosophers often present applied cases which may at first seem oversimplified to a new reader. But the oversimplification, though real, is usually presented in order to highlight a particular moral distinction. For instance, consider Phillipa Foot's famous trolley examples: a runaway trolley with no brakes can head down a track with five workers on it or alternatively down a track where only one person is going to be hit. The obvious utilitarian response is that the engineer should head down the track with one, as it is better to kill one individual than five – the numbers do seem to count. In contrast, consider her other example of a rescue team on a deserted island. Imagine one person needing a rescue on the East side, and five on the West, and a driver who has not enough time to get to both sides to rescue all six. It is better to save the five than the one on her view. However if the *only* way the driver can get to rescue the five is to run over and kill the one on the narrow path along the way, then Foot argues that it is impermissible to kill one in order to save five lives – here it is not just the numbers that count. Some have disagreed with Foot here (e.g. John Taurek), but many have accepted her famous distinction between the morality of killing and letting die. Her examples may seem oversimplified, but her ethical point is not. It is in the real world that there may be a tangle of moral issues and distinctions like this – in debates over active and passive euthanasia for instance – that need to be addressed to generate a public policy recommendation for some practical field.

15.3 Theory Versus Practice

My first understanding of this important distinction between using theory (e.g. utilitarianism vs. Foot's examples) and practice (practical applications and decision making in the world of public policy) came during an exhilarating year of study on a fellowship during the 1980s at Harvard Law School. The initial impetus for this study was my positive response to a request to teach a course in Philosophy of Law, which I found totally absorbing but actually mostly a disaster – on the first attempt I realized I knew almost nothing about the theory or practice of law. I could barely keep ahead of the students and am sure I missed major points in the readings. My experience is not merely applicable to Philosophy of Law and legal ethics, but can be generalized. Anyone teaching or doing research in engineering ethics, business ethics, environmental ethics, and so on, would do well to have a firm grounding in both fields. I have, for instance, hired part-time instructors to teach Environmental Ethics, and when students feel they are getting an overdose of environmental studies without ethics or an overdose of ethical theory independent of environmental concerns they complain – legitimately I believe.

I was also moved to learn more about the law and legal arguments because my teaching and scholarship had clarified for me that for many of our major moral issues, such as capital punishment, euthanasia, abortion affirmative action, and more, it was the courts making the actual decisions for us. It seemed obvious that I had better learn more about their reasoning and constraints on these major public policy problems. Unfortunately, Harvard no longer has this Liberal Arts Fellowship in Law program allowing professionals with advanced degrees in the humanities and social sciences to study law for a year (without enrolling to get a J.D. degree) to learn more about the law and legal research to take it back to their own disciplines to use in their teaching and research with credibility. But other law schools might be willing to allow a similar opportunity, and I would recommend it to anyone working in theory or practice in a field where legal decisions are crucial. The experience was profound for me because it altered my teaching and scholarship in a huge way: nearly all my teaching and research is now interdisciplinary and legal cases and discussions are now a routine part of my teaching and publications. I have learned that in addition to a mountain of ethical arguments, judges often add in practical appeals to administrability (the ability to administer and enforce decisions), political appeals to deference to the legislature and the role of courts and judges in a democracy, economic arguments, as well as concerns about whether a particular decision will cause a flood of litigation, and more. These are hardly arguments that play a prominent role in ethical theory.

One might be tempted to think, therefore, that since theory is distinct from practice, practitioners need not study moral theory. However the combination of work in law and ethics makes manifest the many ways in which theory and practice are intertwined. Legal decisions may highlight concerns about individual rights, duties and obligations, social benefit, responsibility, guilt, mental state, free will, causation, autonomy, paternalism, privacy, self-defense, and a whole host of issues that dominate philosophical discussions, especially those in ethical and social and political theory. In the context of legal and practical decision making, these issues gain importance and complexity. In addition, it is not uncommon to find that arguments on the majority and minority side of a case appear to checkmate each other: there are often utilitarian arguments on each side, individual rights arguments on each side, legal precedents on each side, economic arguments on each side, justice and fairness arguments on each side, and judges must determine which are most compelling and deserve the most weight.

15.4 Examples from Case Law

Consider, for example, a pair of legal cases that illustrate how real life dilemmas reflect the importance of ethical theory concerns and moral reasoning. These cases focus on causation and responsibility. In *Palsgraf v. The L.I. Railroad Co.* (New York Court of Appeals, 1928), an employee of the railroad saw a passenger attempting to board a train as it began moving forward. Hoping to help the passenger, the employee rushed over to give him a hand to get on the train before it was too late. The passenger was holding a brown bag, and in the process of helping him, the train employee dislodged the package, which dropped. The bag contained fireworks, and when it fell it set off an explosion which rocked the wooden train platform, rattling a metal scale on a wooden overhang further down on the platform, which then fell onto and hurt Mrs. Palsgraf. A real life story and obviously far more complex than most examples one finds in the literature on ethical theory.

Up until this time the legal standard on causation had been a reasonably straightforward principle that whoever causes the damage must pay reparation, and it seemed obvious the outcome would be some compensation for Mrs. Palsgraf for her injuries. But no, in a famous opinion by Justice Cardozo, the court in a close decision changed the course of public policy, arguing that while there was a clear and direct causal chain from the action to the injury, that the causation was not proximate or close enough, that the railway employee could not have foreseen that fireworks were in the package and thus could not have foreseen the damage, and that he displayed no negligence. Mrs. Palsgraf did not recover any compensation. Even though the employee did push the passenger enough to set in motion the harm to Mrs. Palsgraf and could have acted otherwise, leading to his moral responsibility on some accounts, he was not legally liable. One might think the moral of the story is that ethical theory is irrelevant. But to the contrary, the case led to consideration of an individual's right to recover, the responsibility of the railroad company and its employees, the role of the mental state of the employee who did intend to push the passenger onto the train but did not intend any harm, concerns over forseeability and negligence, and perhaps most importantly the public policy concern about what precedent would be set for society by a decision either in favor of or against Mrs. Palsgraf.

Pair the *Palsgraf* case with a later one, *Summers v. Tice* (Supreme Court of California, 1948). Summers, Tice and a friend have gone quail hunting. The three begin as a group, but spread out and Summers urges the others to stay in a straight line together as they walk. Disobeying his own instructions, Summers moves ahead so that the 3 hunters form a triangle, with Summers 75 yards in front and in an unobstructed view of the others. Tice flushes out a quail which flies above Summers, and both other hunters shoot at the quail. Summers is injured by bird shot in the right eye and face, and yet because both other hunters had identical shotguns and ammunition there was no way to tell if one had shot Summers twice or each had shot him once. This time the context was also complicated and the situation was the opposite of *Palsgraf*. No direct causal chain could be identified to determine who – one or the other or both of the shooters – caused the damage to Summers, and the court again ignored the previous dictum that whoever causes the harm must pay, but in a different direction. The court decided both hunters should pay damages to Summers, in a proportion they could negotiate. So without direct evidence of who caused the harm, Summers' claim to a right for damages was upheld, the danger was said to be foreseeable and both hunters were deemed negligent for shooting in Summers' direction. Yet, the decision still seems both legally and morally problematic. Fault was ambiguous, Summers certainly added contributory negligence by disregarding his own caution to stay in line as he moved ahead where he was more likely to be hit, and it is not difficult to question whether the other hunters' rights were violated in the name of providing the best public policy for society. The simple rule that whoever causes the harm must pay was insufficient in both cases. So the legal cases move on as new and unexpected complications arise, but fundamental moral issues remain as judges work to find the best legal outcomes.

Consider one more example from case law, since that is my interdisciplinary area of expertise. Another famous case, *Henningsen v. Bloomflield Motors* (Supreme Court of New Jersey, 1960), demonstrates different ways in which moral arguments often dominate legal practice and decision making. The Henningsens bought a car manufactured by Chrysler from Bloomfield Motors and then Mrs. Henningsen suffered harm in an accident caused by defective parts. The car advertisements proclaimed the safety of Bloomfield Motors' cars, and the Henningsens signed a contract with Bloomfield Motors with an explicit clause that the seller and manufacturer would not be held liable for defects in the cars they sold. Overruling the traditional understanding of a single principle *caveat emptor* – let the buyer beware – the court acknowledged the importance of freedom of contract, and acknowledged that ignorance is no defense if one has signed a contract, yet upheld the Henningsen's claim for damages for the injuries. Not only the traditional understanding of *caveat emptor* but also the traditional priority of contracts entered into freely and with full consent, as well as the letter of the law would normally have left the Henningsens with no redress.

What swayed this court otherwise? First, they cited the advertising assuring safe cars. Second, they pointed out that the contract signed by the Henningsens was a uniform one, used by all manufacturers in the American Automobile Association, and thus it was the same contract they would have had to sign to buy a car from any motor company and manufacturer – in effect creating a monopoly and thus an unfair contract. Third, they defended the Henningsen's right to compensation for the harm caused to them. Fourth, they argued that as the use of cars was becoming more common and essential in everyday life, law needed to keep up with evolving technology and the understanding of *caveat emptor* could not be upheld for a complex product like an automobile, which a buyer could not possibly assess properly for safety. Fifth, they defended the view that public safety was paramount, and the best public policy to assure the safety of cars would place the burden of liability for defective cars on the manufacturers and sellers. Sixth, they argued that the interests of the consumers with little bargaining power needed to be protected. For the judges, context was important, along with the rights and protection of consumers with less power than the large companies involved, as well as the best public policies of fair contracts, safe cars, and preservation of public safety in general. Together these arguments were used to override traditional respect for freedom of contract and the principle of *caveat emptor*. In this case, the Henningsen's rights arguments aligned with the multiple utilitarian defenses of the court's decision. Some have argued that the court took the side of the arguments displaying fairness and justice. Others have felt that the judges were most persuaded by the public policy arguments, while still others have charged they were exhibiting extreme judicial activism for defending a decision inimical to the traditional prominence given to freedom of contract and the written law. But the multiplicity of perspectives and arguments addressed and balanced by the decision maker is the key: focusing on a single one or two of them would hardly be adequate for such a difficult and complex decision, especially one which overrules the prior path of law in product liability cases.

15.5 Complex, But Necessary

Although I have described some famous legal cases to illustrate my views, I think the points can be generalized. If a policy maker is attempting to assess whether and what anti-pollution restrictions to impose on an individual or a privately owned corporation, there are going to be issues of individual property rights to use and enjoy one's property as one wishes and, in contrast, there will also be utilitarian and public policy issues about the benefit to society in minimizing pollution for the environment. There will likely be concerns about an individual property owner's ability to be autonomous as a decision-maker opposed to arguments favoring governmental paternalism to demand proper environmental controls. There will be economic issues about the costs imposed on the property owner, and the extent to which social benefit should mandate financial assistance for the property owner. There will be practical issues about the ease or difficulty of installing anti-pollution controls, as well as issues of protecting the integrity of the land as well as the environment.

In my essays on the combat exclusion and the role of women in the military, I criticized then Chief Justice Rehnquist's majority opinion in the U. S. Supreme Court's 1981 decision in *Rostler v. Goldberg*, which has perpetuated inequality for women in the military. I identified a wealth of arguments on each side. In favor of excluding women from combat roles there were early paternalistic and protectionist views about women's roles, concerns about the physical disadvantages of women, questions about the purported psychological differences between men and women, the relevance of women's biological roles in pregnancy and child rearing, purported problems of team spirit and bonding among women, issues of fraternization, how the role of women can denigrate the effectiveness of the power of the armed forces, and an overall malevolent interpretation that women are inferior. There was no mention of skills women had attained in engineering, aeronautics, as pilots and so on. Arguments against the combat exclusion may be fewer but are powerful, stressing equal rights and equal opportunity for women, fairness and justice, the need for women to face combat to be promoted, the changing meaning of "combat" over time, the importance of clarifying whose perspective is relevant in evaluating the qualifications of women, and the social benefit of including well trained women with special talents in a military changing with new technology. The arguments favoring the combat exclusion repeatedly ignore the perspective of women, rely on stereotypical and paternalistic views of their needs and abilities, assuming there is no difficulty with the status quo of the military, and ensuring that women and men cannot and will not be deemed similar enough to be treated alike. With women barred from combat, their absence leads to a culture that breeds sexism and domination and leads to increased harassment and abuse. The example illustrates a situation where either failing to recognize or ignoring or omitting nearly all the ethical arguments on one side led to a biased decision violating individual rights and weakening the social benefit of a military enhanced by the inclusion of all the best talent our nation has to offer.

What I hope my students take away from a case when we study it in class is not only the different theories of law and judicial-decision making at work (which I have not been able to discuss here), but also the multiplicity of ethical considerations and arguments on both sides of a case, going beyond the practical arguments that are relevant. In the *Henningsen* case, for example, no single argument won the day; no single theory seemed to override all the others. In this case the Henningsen's rights arguments fell on the same side as most of the utilitarian arguments defending maximal benefit to society. But surely if the two were competing then, despite Ronald Dworkin's strong view that individual rights arguments should nearly always trump utilitarian arguments, it is worth our while to understand the merit of both types of arguments, while also being mindful of the weaknesses of utilitarian claims which can easily overwhelm individual rights claims in pursuit of the ends without adequate consideration of the means. Having a grasp of traditional moral theories and contemporary commentaries on these views gives one the tools to assess the value and weight of these multiple arguments in complex cases, without feeling obliged to rest one's case on a single theory or approach. The intricate and complex and sometimes overlapping arguments arising in real life and practical cases for decision makers have roots in alternative ethical theories and moral visions. The best philosophical and analytical reasoning takes John Stuart Mill's advice to assess each moral approach in its best light, considering all the possible angles and arguments, understanding which arguments are ethical ones and which are practical or prudential ones, and not being blinded by a single perspective or point of view. Some decisions may seem to be clear cut; more often, decision making is more complicated and the best answer is unclear. But not recognizing the relevance of the ethical theory concerns behind the arguments, and their strengths and weaknesses, leaves one open to misunderstanding, lack of depth in one's reasoning, and quick, efficient solutions that may overlook crucial considerations of justice and morality.

References

Aristotle. (1941). The politics. In R. McKeon (Ed.), *The basic works of Aristotle* (B. Jowett, trans.). New York: Random House.

Shapiro, I., & DeCew, J. W. (1995). *Nomos XXXVII: Theory and Practice*. New York: New York University Press.

Chapter 16
Ethics and Social Justice

Drucilla K. Barker

Abstract Economists often operate as though they had perfect knowledge and their expert knowledge, couched in difficult and abstruse mathematics, was infallible. In the material world of uncertainty, risk, reward and, all too often, impoverishment, the consequences of bad policy decisions are not just theoretical mistakes on paper; but rather, they create harms for many people. Thus a meaningful code of ethics is necessary. Developing a meaningful code of ethics may be difficult if economists must remain within the mainstream paradigm; however, there are many alternative economic approaches that may or may not use the methods and tools of the mainstream. All of them have ethics at their core in the sense of respect and care for other persons and the environment. The prudential principle, the principle of informed consent, and autonomy are embedded in their methodologies and approaches. In developing a code of ethics for economics, we should look to other heterodox schools and related disciplines where such codes have a long and successful record.

Keywords Globalization • Expert knowledge • Consent • Prudential principle

I begin this brief essay by sharing a personal anecdote. At the end of my first year in my Ph.D. program in economics I was asked by to teach a summer school course at a nearby university. The title of the course was "Problems in the World Economy." Needing money badly, like all graduate students, I accepted. But as I began preparing I realized that I knew next to nothing about the problems in the world economy. I did, however, have a wealth of information about two rational economics agents in an Edgeworth box, both with initial endowments and stable preferences. An Edgeworth box, for those of you who are not initiates into the arcana of the economics profession, is simply a fancy type of graph. At any rate, I wanted out of that box. But being a novice I simply assumed that my professors felt that I wasn't yet ready for more advanced knowledge. So I thought, maybe next year they will teach us the real things, the important things that would enable me to make better sense of the

D.K. Barker (✉)
Department of Anthropology, University of South Carolina,
Gambrel 408, Columbia, SC 29208, USA
e-mail: barkerdk@mailbox.sc.edu

E.A.M. Searing, D.R. Searing (eds.), *Practicing Professional Ethics in Economics and Public Policy*, DOI 10.1007/978-94-017-7306-5_16

world. Why are some people rich and others poor? Why does much of the global South remain mired in desperate poverty? Why do poor women suffer disproportionately from the ill effects of globalization? And most importantly, how can we, as economists with specialized knowledge, use our training to ameliorate some of these inequities? Sadly, I did not receive satisfactory answers in graduate school.

16.1 Why Economics Needs a Code of Ethics

That was in the early 1980s. Today's economic systems are even less well suited to being described in terms of an Edgeworth box. Globalization, the flows of people, labor, capital, and technologies across countries, cultures and economies, is the dominant characteristic of the economy today. It is a market-driven and multidimensional process characterized by rapidly expanding markets that transcend national boundaries and are increasingly independent of geographical distance. Nearly instantaneous electronic communication has facilitated the mobility of financial capital and the emergence of the transnational corporations. Transnational corporations are able to relocate their low-skill production operations in areas characterized by low-wages and business friendly political regimes. Two significant changes occur as a result of economic globalization: changes in the international division of labor, including the feminization of labor, and a decrease in the power of nation states to regulate and tax market activities. These changes have been accompanied by a neo-liberal rhetoric that champions free markets and free trade, and rationalizes the dismantling of protective labor legislation, health and safety standards, and welfare services. These changes raise a host of significant ethical issues.

I am in agreement with George DeMartino (2005) who argues that the mutual interdependence among countries today requires economists to carefully engage "with a range of ethical matters for which they are, by virtue of their training, largely unprepared" (185). Nonetheless, their pronouncements wield enormous influence in international organizations such as the World Bank, the International Monetary Fund (IMF), and the World Trade Organization (WTO). These organizations exist outside democratic processes and the policies formulated by these organizations affect the lives of people all over the world. He observes that "the consequence of the convergence of the ethical unpreparedness of the economics profession with its increased influence in the world has been economic policy prescriptions of dubious ethical content" (2009, p. 185).

Unfortunately, economists often operate as though they had perfect knowledge and their expert knowledge, couched in difficult and abstruse mathematics, was infallible. It is not. Mathematical theories live in Edgeworth boxes. The rest of us live in the material world of uncertainty, risk, reward and, all too often, impoverishment. The consequences of bad policy decisions are not just theoretical mistakes on paper; but rather, they create harms for actual people. Moreover, the people who bear the unfortunate consequences of public policies based on the recommendations of the expert knowledge of economics have absolutely no say in these decisions. Since the financial meltdown in 2008, there has been much hand wringing and ink spilled over the need for a code of ethics for the economics profession. The writing comes from a wide variety of economists ranging from mainstream economists (both on the left and the right), feminist economists, radical political economists, and various other heterodox economists. In response the American Economic Association (AEA) adopted a disclosure policy that simply requires authors who publish in AEA journals disclose financial support and other benefits such as consultant fees, consultant fees, grants, retainers and so forth (Epstein, G., & Carrick-Hagenbarth, J., 2011, American Economic Association, n.d.). I agree that this sort of disclosure is absolutely necessary; however, it does not go far enough. Most professional codes of ethics include the obligation to avoid conflicts of interest. Economics needs a code of ethics similar to the ones put for by the American Anthropology Association and the American Sociological Association, which address more of the complexities that are inherent in social science work.

A code of ethics based not only on disclosure, but also on the prudential principle and the principle of prior informed consent would go far in reforming the field of economics. The prudential principle is based on the understanding that professional practices may harm others and professionals have an ethical obligation "to avoid causing harm when it is possible to so and ameliorate its impact when it is not" (DeMartino, 2011, p. 124). The principle of prior informed consent entails on obligation on the part of the professional, whenever possible, to obtains the consent of the people and populations who will be affected by their practices.

Both principles are difficult to put into practice. Consider prior informed consent. It is troubling even in one to one encounters if asymmetries of knowledge and information are present. Economists are professionals and the asymmetries between the expert knowledge of the economist and the understanding of peasants who are driven off the land to work in export-production factories or middle-class families in the developed world who find their life savings destroyed by policy decisions make informed consent difficult. However, as DeMartino (2011) argues, there are precedents to fall back on. A patient badly injured in an automobile accident cannot give informed consent. So the job of the health care professional is to act on behalf of the patient and attempt to ascertain what he or she would have wanted. Economists are in a similar position. We have to speak and work on behalf of populations whose lives will be deeply affected by our work. In these cases the issue is even more complex because we must ask, who is authorized to speak "for the people." Where did their authority come from? Anthropologists frequently encounter this question in working with indigenous peoples. Is the consent of the elders enough? In what sense does it reflect the consent of the rest of the body? In economics the problem is that different groups will be affected differently by economic interventions (this could also be the case in anthropology). Any policy intervention will create both winners and losers. How to adjudicate between competing interests is a complex matter that goes far beyond a simple cost-benefit analysis problem.

Similarly, the prudential principle is not without problems. Most policy interventions create the potential for harm, regardless of whether they are or are not successful. Doing nothing is often not the answer either. Consider the structural adjustment policies (SAPs) imposed on the developing world in the 1980s. SAPs are austerity programs implemented in indebted countries as a condition of receiving the additional loans necessary to meet debt obligations and avoid default. They were premised on the notion that countries could return to economic health and repair their economies if they reduced the size and influence of government on economic activity and opened their markets to international economic forces. These policies created enormous hardships for the poor, and women bore a disproportionate share of the burden. Doing nothing was not an option either. Policy changes were needed in what were then called the Third World countries. Borrowed funds were often wasted by politically powerful and corrupt elites. Some development projects were ill-conceived. Third World rulers were encouraged to spend billions on weapons, and billions more ended up in the Swiss bank accounts of arms merchants, politicians, and drug dealers (Barker & Feiner, 2004). So although doing nothing was not an option, SAPs were not the right policy prescription. Moreover, evidence shows that economists were well aware of the harms their interventions would cause (DeMartino, 2011). They justified them on the grounds that they would be short lived. In the long-run the economies would return to prosperity. I cannot help but think of the aphorism by the great economist, John Maynard Keynes, "in the long-run we are all dead" (Keynes, 1923, p. 80).

I will take the charitable view that many, perhaps most, economists are committed to using their expert knowledge to promote the "social good." The question at issue is, what is the social good? What policies will work to achieve it? Who are the winners and who are the losers? For feminist economists, the social good requires gender equity and the alleviation of the extreme poverty and hardship the plague poor people all over the world. However, we often find ourselves constrained by the demands of our profession which aspires to be a science on par with physics and the other natural sciences: objective, rigorous, and value neutral. Thus the value judgments implied by feminists or other groups dedicated to social justice are often eschewed by the mainstream of the profession. When I was a graduate student the worst insult that could be thrown at you was, "that's not economics, that's sociology."

16.2 Economics as Social Engineering

De Martino (2011) argues that although economists celebrate the free market as the best way to allocate global resources, it is economists who influence the decisions of bankers, financiers, and development policy makers that often decisively influence economic outcomes. Economists are in a sense social engineers whose interventions create incentives, rewards, costs, and risk. Their interventions into the global economy have enormous, often disastrous, consequences on the lives of people who have absolutely no say in the matter.

> …when economists act, they act on others in consequential ways. There is a gap between subjects and objects of economic practice—between those who design economic interventions and those whom the interventions target…Economist's influence is not an unintended by-product of their work: it is rather the whole point. Economists hope to make interven-

tions that improve the functioning of the economy and public policy and that enhance the quality of life. (2011, pp. 105–106, emphasis in the original)

Now of course economists work in a world of imperfect information, and economic interventions affect different groups of people in different ways. Policies that may, in theory, help in the aggregate, often benefit some groups and harm others. Those who are harmed are rarely compensated. I would also add, that there are some harms that by their very nature cannot be compensated. For example, the building of a hydroelectric dam that enhances economic growth while at the same time displaces entire communities both physically and culturally can probably never be compensated. What is the value of culture? Should it be considered a commodity that can be bought and sold? Thinking through these conundrums requires a code of ethics in the sense of a set of general principles to guide to sorting out ethical complexities.

Returning to the financial crises that have troubled the global economy since the 1980s: the Third World debt crisis of the 1980s, the Asian financial crisis in the mid 1990s, the financial crisis of 2007, and most recently the Euro crisis of 2009. In all these cases the "solutions" imposed by the IMF and other international financial institutions were to provide the "bailout" funds to soothe the fears of the transnational investors. Although each of these crises are different, the unintended consequences of the solutions on the lives of ordinary people, especially the poor who constitute the majority of people in the world, are generally awful. Austerity measures do not save money. They shift costs and risk from the monetized sector to the non-monetized private sector of households and communities. The poor are left to pay for the excess of the rich. Moreover, the poverty, hardship, and deprivations caused by these measures fall disproportionately on the shoulders of women and children because women comprise a disproportionate share of the poor. Women have to work longer hours to earn the same income, have to do more household labor because public supports are gone, and have to stretch already meager budgets even further (Barker & Feiner, 2004). If the situation were not so dire, I would have laughed when then Prime Minister of Greece, George Papandreou, took a salary cut in order to set a good example to the rest of the country, an announcement that came while approximately 25,000 rioters took to the streets of Thessaloniki to protest austerity measures (Nikolas, 2011). There is a world of difference in the effects of a salary cut when you are making the prime minister's salary than when you are in already dire economic straits.

Mainstream economists have long argued that deregulation and liberalization of global finance would result in great economic efficiency and growth in both the developed and developing world. Alan Greenspan, former head of the United States Federal Reserve and disciple of the libertarian author, Ayn Rand, believed that the self-interest of financial institutions was sufficient to protect the shareholder's assets and stimulate economic prosperity. Consider his remarks in 1999 to the Futures Industry Association: "The product and asset price signals enable entrepreneurs to finely allocate real capital facilities to produce those goods and services most valued by consumers, a process that has undoubtedly improved national productivity growth and standards of living" (Greenspan, 1999, n.p.). In other words, in a "free market," prices send the appropriate signals and direct resources to their most highly valued uses. Government regulation only interferes with this market mechanism. History has certainly proved him wrong.

Thinking about my list of crises above and the reactions to them by conservatives and liberals alike, one thing becomes clear. Large scale questioning of free market orthodoxy and calls for a code of ethics only began in the mainstream when the crisis hit home: the developed world. The hardship and deprivation of people in developing nations were certainly taken into account by many (including mainstream economists like George Stiglitz and James Tobin), but the cracks in orthodox economics and mainstream calls for reform began in earnest during the great recession of 2007. That is when "we" were the ones enduring the harm. As professionals, we should reflect on why local demonstrations of economic failings have raised questions of orthodoxy which, when asked by other people in the global south, were treated with silence.

What difference would a code of ethics have made? I am really not sure within the confines of mainstream economics. I think the answer lies in working outside the prevailing orthodoxy. There are alternative ways of conceptualizing what economics is and how to engage in more humane economic practices; one of the most useful approaches is that of feminist economics.

16.3 Rethinking Economics from a Feminist Point of View

Feminist economics puts ethics in the center. For example, the feminist economist Julie A. Nelson (2006, see also Chap. 8) suggests thinking about economics not as the science that examines how societies allocate scarce resources among competing goods, but as the study of provisioning. In other words, the study of how societies manage land, labor and capital in order to meet their material, cultural and emotional needs. This approach to economics would necessarily be ethical because it would take into consideration the respect and care for others that human beings should demonstrate. Part of this ethical commitment is to take into consideration the important role that social reproduction—food preparation, cleaning, cooking, caring for children and the elderly—plays in meeting human needs.

The capabilities approach, pioneered by Amartya Sen (1985) is another approach that has ethics at its core. Capabilities are the means by which individuals, families, and societies achieve the things they need in order to enhance or maintain their well-being. The capabilities approach does not explain poverty, inequality, or well-being, but rather provides a normative framework to conceptualize and evaluate them (Robeyns, 2009). The questions are, do people have the freedoms and opportunities to lead the life they want to lead and be the people they want to be?

This approach is the foundation for the United Nations Development Programme and the development of the Human Development Index (HDI) as well as the Gender Inequality Index (GII). Included in the HDI are life expectancy, education, and living standards. (UNDP 2013). Reproductive freedom, empowerment, and labor force participation comprise the GII.

The diverse economies framework is another important step toward an ethical economics. This approach, pioneered by JK Gibson-Graham (2008), asks researchers to work toward creating environmental sustainable and socially just economies. The diverse economies framework broadens the conception of the economy to include alternative markets where considerations other than supply and demand influence the terms of exchange, as well as non-market exchanges and transactions. Some examples include unpaid household labor, consumer, worker, and producer co-ops, and the social economy, comprised of voluntary organizations, foundations and non-profits. What diverse economies have in common is that they put social objectives ahead of profits.

A recent example of a social economy can be found in Greece, a country deeply mired in debt and subject to strict austerity measures. The Vio.Me. factory, which produces building materials like mortars, plasters, tile and so forth, in Thessaloniki, Greece had been abandoned by its owners and the workers had not been paid in May 2011. On February 12, 2013, the workers reopened the factory as a worker's cooperative. This does not solve all their problems; they have high production costs and no access to credit. Opening the factory was made possible by the participation of various movements in raising funds and awareness. The workers are committed to producing products in ways that are non-toxic and ecological (Vio.Me. 2013).

Finally in my book, co-authored with Susan F. Feiner, we suggest five ways of evaluating economic systems (Barker & Feiner, 2004):

1. Is the economic system fair? What is a fair share of society's output? Under what conditions are some people entitled to more than enough for the enjoyment of life, liberty, and the pursuit of happiness? Is it ever acceptable for others to suffer lifelong malnutrition or live without basic medical care, education, and shelter?
2. Does the economic system provide an enhanced quality of life over time? An enhanced quality of life is more than just growth in per capita goods and services. Rather it refers to human well-being in Sen's sense of the word.
3. Does the economic system provide economic security? Economic security means something about the ability to care for one's self, family, and community.
4. Does the economic system waste human and nonhuman resources? If there are millions of people who want to work, but who are unable to find jobs, human resources are being wasted. Similarly, if a factory can produce 100 widgets per day, but is only producing 50, then the productive capacity of machines is wasted. And if while producing widgets, firms pour toxic wastes into rivers and spew gasses that cause acid rain into the air, then natural resources are wasted.
5. Does the economic system provide sufficient opportunities for meaningful work? Meaningful work includes not only monetary compensations but also opportunities for advancement, some degree of autonomy, the chance to exercise judgment, interactions with coworkers, and an environment that is free from harassment and intimidation.

We wrote this book quite a few years ago and today I cannot help but be struck by how much we really have in common with Sen's capabilities approach. It is a happy revelation.

16.4 Conclusion

Unfortunately, economists often operate as though they had perfect knowledge and their expert knowledge, couched in difficult and abstruse mathematics, was infallible. It is not. Mathematical theories live in Edgeworth boxes. The rest of us live in the material world of uncertainty, risk, reward and, all too often, impoverishment. The consequences of bad policy decisions are not just theoretical mistakes on paper; but rather, they create harms for actual people. Moreover, the people who bear the unfortunate consequences of public policies based on the recommendations of the expert knowledge of economics have absolutely no say in these decisions.

Developing a meaningful code of ethics may be difficult if economists must remain within the mainstream paradigm; however, there are many alternative approaches that may or may not use the methods and tools of the mainstream. . All of them have ethics at their core in the sense of respect and care for other persons and the environment. The prudential principle, the principle of informed consent, and autonomy are embedded in their methodologies and approaches. In developing a code of ethics for economics, we should look to other heterodox schools and related disciplines where such codes have a long and successful record.

References

American Economic Association (n.d.). AEAweb: The American Economic Association. Retrieved August 25, 2013, from http://www.aeaweb.org/

Barker, D. K., & Feiner, S. F. (2004). *Liberating economics: Feminist perspectives on families, work, and globalization*. Ann Arbor, MI: University of Michigan Press.

DeMartino, G. (2005). A professional ethics code for economists. *Challenge, 48*(4), 88–104.

DeMartino, G. (2009). Globalization. In Jan Peil & Irene van Staveren (Eds.), *Handbook of Economics and Ethics*. Cheltenham U. K. and Northhampton MA, USA, Edward Elgar.

DeMartino, G. (2011). *The economist's oath: On the need for and content of professional economic ethics*. Oxford, UK: Oxford University Press.

Economist. (2011, January 8). Dismal ethics; Economics focus. *The Economist (US)*.

Epstein, G. (2010, December 20). Ethics and credibility at the American Economics Association. *Triple crisis: Global perspectives on finance, development, and the environment*. http://triplecrisis.com/ethics-and-credibility-at-the-american-economics-association/

Epstein, G., & Carrick-Hagenbarth, J. (2011, January 3). Open letter to the American Economic Association. http://www.peri.umass.edu/fileadmin/pdf/other_publication_types/AEA_letter_Jan3b.pdf. Retrieved October 8, 2015. Retrieved February 24, 2013. This letter was signed by 300 economists.

Gibson-Graham, J. (2008). Diverse economies: Performative practices for 'other worlds'. *Progress in Human Geography, 32*(5), 613–632. doi:10.1177/0309132508090821. JK Gibson Graham is the pen name of Katherine Gibson and the late Julie Graham.

Greenspan, A. (1999, March 19). FRB: Speech, Greenspan – Financial derivatives – March 19, 1999. FRB: Speech, Greenspan – Financial Derivatives – March 19, 1999. Retrieved February 20, 2013, from http://www.federalreserve.gov/boarddocs/speeches/1999/19990319.htm

Human Development Reports – United Nations Development Programme (UNDP). (2013). Human Development Reports (HDR) and United Nations Development Programme (UNDP). Retrieved February 24, 2014, from http://hdr.undp.org/en/

Keynes, J. M. (1923). *A tract on monetary reform*. London: Macmillan.

Nelson, J. A. (2006). *Economics for humans*. Chicago: University of Chicago Press.

Nikolas, K. (2011, September 12). Greek Prime Minister to take symbolic pay cut as taxes rise again. Greek Prime Minister to take symbolic pay cut as taxes rise again. Retrieved February 18, 2013, from http://digitaljournal.com/article/311428

Robbins, L. (1938). Interpersonal comparisons of utility: A comment. *The Economic Journal, 48*(192), 635–641. Retrieved February 24, 2013, from http://www.jstor.org/stable/2225051?origin=JSTOR-pdf.

Robeyns, I. (2009). Capability approach. In J. Peil & I. V. Staveren (Eds.), *Handbook of economics and ethics* (pp. 39–46). Cheltenham, UK: Edward Elgar.

Sen, A. (1985). *Commodities and capabilities*. Amsterdam: North-Holland.

Vio.Me. (2013, February 12). The machines of self-management have been switched on! Vio. Me. – Occupy, resist, produce! Retrieved February 24, 2013, from http://www.viome.org/

Chapter 17
Where Ethics Was, Is, and Should Be

Elizabeth A.M. Searing and Donald R. Searing

Abstract The role of ethics in economics and public policy has been discussed since ancient Greece. Today, however, the field should take several steps in order to bring ethics back into the foreground of our professional practice. First, there should be a universally-recognized acknowledgment of the role of ethics in the practice, and pedagogy dedicated to the training of academics and professionals of practice should reflect this importance. Second, leaders and institutions within the field should take seriously the need for not only a committee or code, but also the incorporation of professional ethics into the common discourse. Finally, research in practical and professional ethics should continue and expand into a rigorous subfield of the broader ethical discussion.

Keywords Ethics • Professional ethics • Economics • Public policy

I remember the first time that I (Elizabeth) saw *Inside Job*. I was the President of the Graduate Student Association for the Economics Department, and we had decided to attend the local campus showing as a group. Part of the reason was because we all had heard the rumors and were interested in seeing what all the fuss was about; part of it was because, in case it deserved discussion or ridicule, at least we could band together and talk it out with someone more sympathetic to the job than the average student.

I will admit – I was very interested in what the movie had to say. I had been an undergraduate economics major before graduating to pursue both entrepreneurship and parenthood; through that, I always knew I would come back and finish my education in the hopes of becoming an academic. That decade between undergraduate and graduate school had some important lessons on small business ownership, property ownership, and day-to-day details I think that every person should possess

E.A.M. Searing, PhD (✉)
Assistant Professor, Department of Public Administration and Policy, Rockefeller College of Public Affairs and Policy, University at Albany – State University of New York, 305 Milne Hall, 135 Western Avenue, Albany, New York, USA
e-mail: esearing@albany.edu

D.R. Searing, PhD
CEO and Principal Scientist, Syncere Systems, Altamont, NY, USA
e-mail: dsearing@synceresystems.com

E.A.M. Searing, D.R. Searing (eds.), *Practicing Professional Ethics in Economics and Public Policy*, DOI 10.1007/978-94-017-7306-5_17

before attempting a terminal degree. As I found myself back in the academic world, the graphs in the books meant less compared to how I could integrate those lessons into actual breathable policy. Watching the economies of Iceland, then Russia, then the U.S. enter national calamity was enlightening, both mechanically and in the behaviors and reactions of the people affected. I had the privilege of knowing and working with scholars from all around the globe, including ones with first-hand accounts of hyperinflation, currency black markets, subsistence farming, political coups, and war. And all of these on top of my own experiences. Economics was no longer about the lines on the page; all I could see and hear was the people they represented.

I transitioned to the study of the economics of nonprofits and social enterprises in public policy both to be closer to what I considered the most pressing problems and because, as a field, the fight to include such normative elements as ethics was so much more advanced. As I did, I noticed how similar not only the policy sciences were, but the social sciences at large. Macroeconomics relied a great deal on findings in social psychology, while taxation especially was developing the hybrid field of behavioral finance. Anyone responsible for conducting interviews of any kind needed a fundamental understanding of human psychology, and public policy was a hot mess of almost everything depending on the question being posed. But in the publications and program offerings of the many fields, it was economics that had the largest silence regarding professional ethics, and this reminded me of a similar audience not traditionally linked with economics: engineering.

I had been involved in the engineering ethics program at Texas A & M University (though not as much as my co-author, who was the founding teaching assistant in the program). Again, it was a heavily mathematical field that placed great faith in the objectivity of the science, with practitioners often forgetting the human elements that framed, analyzed, and solved the problems. Over the last few decades, however, there had been great strides made in the acceptance of a field of engineering ethics that was similar to other types of professional ethics, but had unique features and often employed unique teaching methodologies that were much more natural for an engineering mind to embrace than tomes on abstract philosophy. So much of the problem with the acceptance of ethics in engineering was simply a communication issue between the fields coupled with acknowledgment of the role of being a human operator. What if it was a similar situation with economics and policy science? Could a text which presents the material in a more natural format be as useful to economics and policy science as it was for engineers?

17.1 Where Ethics Was

Questions regarding the ethics of and in resource allocation have been around since ancient Greece; Xenophon's text *Oeconomicus* has been used as often as a historical reference on feminism as it has the first official text on economics (Gini, 1993; Xenophon, 2008). Discussions of poverty and the obligations of those with wealth exist in religious texts, in addition to topics such as taxation and usury (Mosher,

2007). Much of this original work, however, regarded personal decision-making by the respective household figure. This applied whether you were the ancient Greek running a home or the medieval king looking after "his" subjects: these were decisions made on a very individual basis amongst interior allocation possibilities.

The advent of mercantilism, however, shifted the brunt of economic focus and writing to the competition between nation-states and off of the interior allocation of resources. This is not to say that competition and self-interest did not exist before now, only that such competition was not the focus of the scholarly work and, thus, the field as a science. This further developed as economies became more complex, needing tools and dedicated professionals to manage not only the coffers of the state, but also the needs of the workers, the landowners, the merchants, and the hosts of subclasses that continued to develop as the processes of manufacturing goods became more intricate. When political systems began to reject more authoritarian rule in favor of either less-authoritarian or democratic institutions, accountability to the perceived fairness of the distribution of resources became more important. Heading into the twentieth century, a schism was forming between those who considered their jobs to be the management of business and economic concerns and those who were concerned with the externalities or casualties of such systems. This became extremely pronounced during the Victorian era and women's suffrage movements. Unlike the Greek approach to economics, where the field of economics was a question of determining distribution of household resources, the Victorian female-dominated home extended outside the walls to humanitarian causes created by the inequitable distribution of wealth in the male-dominated world of business. Economics had excluded itself from the more problematic elements of its own science along gender boundaries.

As the twentieth century wore on and economics became more heavily mathematized and sophisticated, both the art and the training of professionals began to focus more on the technical elements and less on the empirical application of such. At the same time, outspoken capitalist advocates of the ethical implications of economics such as Amartya Sen and Deirdre McCloskey began to draw more serious attention. The last 30 years has seen a large number of quality books penned which dedicate themselves to justifying the use of ethics and morality in economics and public policy. Those are books, which we highly encourage reading, have and continue to fight the good battle on *why* ethics is important. This text takes the next logical step to answer the question of *how*.

17.2 Where Ethics Is

In the current state of the world, things have changed. We can't give all of the credit to *Inside Job* – though that was the final straw that gave the ethics movement enough public traction to force action, the momentum would not have continued had it not been for the continued struggles of various portions of the global economy to reboot. So long as stimulus plans and quantitative easing are in the news, it will be a fresh reminder of the situation that finally made it to the headlines. The first question becomes, then, whether the mental association between the Fed's quarterly meetings and the ethically-laden role of economists in economics remains as the years go on. Is this a phase? Will the public eye move back over to elected politicians or reality television? Further development of ethical awareness in economics does not hinge on the existence of a policy window, but it rarely hurts to have the public eye trained on the problem.

The second question regards what we have done already as a profession. Decades of calls for a code of ethics from the unofficial flagship professional organization in economics have resulted in a Disclosure Policy that was desperately needed.

But this still leaves a gaping hole for all of our activities in economics and public policy that is not an extension of research ethics. The AEA patterned their Disclosure Policy after that of the National Bureaus of Economic Research (NBER), which is an esteemed nonprofit institution that serves as a research organizer and promoter (National Bureau of Economic Research, 2014). Importantly, however, there are differences between the organizations. First, the NBER exists solely to promote research. Though a list of job openings is available on the NBER website, there are no coordinated services such as the Job Openings for Economists (JOE) or the Job Market Scramble (American Economics Association, 2014). There are also no public meetings – such affairs are invitation-only. There are no public interest committees such as the Committee on the Status of Women in the Economic Profession (CSWEP) and the Committee for Economic Education. In short, the AEA has made itself a fine example of a professional society, regardless of whether they are performing licensing. It is therefore perplexing that they would contend that a code of ethics is unnecessary, where similar organizations such as the American Society for Public Administration (ASPA) and the American Statistical Association (ASA) that address similar audiences with similar content have recognized the need (American Society for Public Administration, 2012; Wong, 1999).

17.3 Where Ethics Should Be

As a profession (and as professionals), we are not where we need to be in terms of professional ethics. It has taken decades for economics to entertain the subject seriously on a national level, and the approaches taken by public policy are widely varied. In a time where the Congressional approval rating is 12 % with varying, yet dismal results for other elements of government (Newport, 2013), regaining the public trust in our competence should be additional incentive to pull ourselves into conversations and subcommittees and put together some central tenets. For professional ethics to play a serious role in public policy, four elements need to be brought together.

17.3.1 A More Unified Approach to Teaching Professional Ethics in Economics and Public Policy

As mentioned previously, there is a wide variety of approaches to professional ethics taken in graduate programs. Though few places would denigrate it when asked, many universities offer only mandated ethical trainings. Those that do offer more can do so via standalone modules, seminar courses, full courses, or integration into other classwork on civic or organizational leadership. This variety also means that there is a lack of common content: there are no central authors, solid concepts, decision methodologies, etc., for people from different programs or fields to communicate about common dilemmas in. The result is a group of professions that lack the ability to communicate regarding ethical concepts in a uniform way. Do we see usage of this text as a potential step toward a resolution? We hope so. However, it is only a small piece.

17.3.2 Espousal of This Need by Leaders and Organizations

The development of a common ethical language will be assisted greatly if the leaders in the field share not only their beliefs that ethics is important, but also their own personal stories. From the beginning conversations regarding the writing of this book, the inclusion of the casual perspectives from leaders in a host of different policy fields has always been one of the centerpieces. There is always a stack of books that need to be read on every professional's desk – the ones that actually get read are the ones that are recommended by friends or that you feel a personal connection to. From a purely Darwinian perspective, we need to see that those who have made it to the top of their field have been able to do so while incorporating a sense of professional ethics. Show that the field prizes ethical behavior because, as every undergraduate in an economics course knows, people respond to incentives. From a more personal perspective, it is crucial to know, when faced with an ethical dilemma, that we are not alone in dealing with it.

17.3.3 Continued Research into Professional Ethics

One of the elements that this book should have made obvious is that ethics is not a static thing. Each situation we face is fluid, and though we have a growing portfolio of past decisions to guide our way, there is seldom an obvious right and wrong answer. Therefore, professional ethics should grow beyond the ad hoc subcommittee stage that is has often been relegated to and recognized as its own subfield in the economic and policy sciences. Just as in econometrics and program evaluation, there are competing methodologies, case studies, and applications that need exploration and explanation. Research in the area of ethics should be lauded in the same way that other elements of our craft are, especially since it will go just as far in increasing the worth of our policy proclamations as an advancement in one of the more mathematical branches of the science.

This also applies to the already-established professional ethics field at large. The Association for Practical and Professional Ethics has sections dedicated to several fields, including business and one forming in social work (Association for Practical and Professional Ethics, 2013); however, there are no sections dedicated to the social, policy, or administrative sciences aside from research ethics. Though such committees are formed based on grassroots support and initiative from members, the presence and marketing of such opportunities to the existing graduate programs would open eyes and doors to those who may not know there is a forum to bring such discussions to.

17.3.4 An Internalized Need to Behave in a Professionally Ethical Way

Finally, economists and public policy experts need to internalize the role of ethics in the day-to-day performance of their tasks. As has been remarked upon, having a written code of ethics will only go so far in the practice of ethics in the workplace. However, the legitimization of professional ethics as an essential portion of training creates the internal demand to follow such codes. This validation of ethics as something it is okay to talk about and conduct research on will come about slowly, in response to the behavior of exemplars, the field at large, the general public, and fellow scientists and experts. It is the ultimate irony that we spend our days worrying about maximizing a highly subjective and normative concept such as utility, but are afraid to discuss similar things such as ethics out loud in a code or oath.

17.4 Final Thoughts

W.W.G.D. (What Would Greenspan Do)? Of the many unflattering things suggested by *Inside Job*, the possibility that Alan Greenspan acted unethically was the most curious. Mr. Greenspan noted, now famously, that he might have been wrong about how he dealt with the subprime mortgage crisis; further, he admitted that he only expected to be right about his decisions at the Federal Reserve only 70 % of the time (Nasiripour & McCarthy, 2010). To many, this was an unacceptable number for someone who was advising the federal government on economic policy. But was it unethical?

- Is it unethical to be wrong, especially in a predictive science?
- How often do you need to be wrong, or for what reasons, to be considered unethical?

- Is hubris unethical, and was it a factor at play here?
- Would better communication about the goals of the Federal Reserve system help the perception of ethicalness? Would better communication about the predictive nature of economics and policy science help the perception of ethicalness?
- If Greenspan had been in a different predictive science, such as forecasting the weather instead of the economy, how do the standards and expectations change?
- Do our answers differ if we ask whether a particular act on a particular day was unethical versus the act of, say, inflation targeting?
- If we assume for a moment that Greenspan had acted unethically, what would an ethical Alan Greenspan have done differently?
- Would these questions be easier to address if there were clearer definitions and metrics for what constitutes professionally ethical behavior in the field?

The only question we can answer definitively is the final one: *yes*.

We hope it inspires you to continue learning about ethics. Many of us count ourselves among a particular subfield, a good number of which are represented in Sect. 17.3. Seek out the professional organizations for your fields and for the fields of the journals you read – from political economy to program evaluation, there are very likely ethical codes or guidelines to give you additional information and clarity regarding ethical practice. To make this exploration easier, we have included many of these organizations in Appendix B. The included list contains both subfields and other, related fields in the social and policy sciences. The main link should lead directly to the code of ethics, and many organizations have additional resources available from that page.

This book will not make you ethical. Placing this on the table next to your written statement at a congressional hearing will not recuse you. It will not keep you from facing a department chair who pressures you to phantom publish; an employer who promotes based on gender to correct an existing imbalance; the sustainability of an infrastructure project in an area where localized solutions may serve more, but employ less; or what to tell the television cameras when the angry and eloquent protester finishes speaking at your press conference, listens to the applause, and all eyes turn to you.

This book will not make you ethical. But it will show you, with the right tools, methods, and diligence, how you can be and why, as a profession, it is crucial that we are.

Discussion Questions

1. Using the decision methodology and ethical tests from the text, test the hypothesis that Alan Greenspan was professionally unethical in his response to the subprime mortgage crisis. Does your answer change if you had evaluated an individual decision within the policy process before the crisis, such as the lowering of the discount rate to 1.25 % in January of 2002?
2. Does your answer change to the above question if you look at the legal descriptions and motives of interest rate targeting as a practice? How much overlap should there be between individual decisions and abstract decisions?

References

American Economics Association. (2014). About JOE. Retrieved January 2, 2014, from http://www.aeaweb.org/joe/about.php

American Society for Public Administration. (2012, March [2013]). Code of ethics. Retrieved January 2, 2014, from http://www.aspanet.org/public/ASPA/Resources/Code_of_Ethics/ASPA/Resources/Code_of_Ethics/Code_of_Ethics1.aspx?hkey=acd40318-a945-4ffc-ba7b-18e037b1a858

Association for Practical and Professional Ethics. (2013). APPE special interest sections. Retrieved January 2, 2014, from http://appe.indiana.edu/programs-and-resources/special-interest-sections/

Gini, A. (1993). The manly intellect of his wife: Xenophon, "Oeconomicus" Ch. 7. *The Classical World* (pp. 483–486).

Mosher, L. A. (2007). A certain sympathy of scriptures: Biblical and Quranic – by Kenneth Cragg. *The Muslim World, 97*(3), 521–524.

Nasiripour, S., & McCarthy, R. (2010, June 7). Greenspan testifies to financial crisis commission, blames Fannie, Freddie for subprime crisis. *Huffington Post.*

National Bureau of Economic Research. (2014). About NBER. Retrieved January 2, 2014, from http://www.nber.org/info.html

Newport, F. (2013). Congress job approval drops to all-time low for 2013: Gallup.

Wong, B. (1999, August 19 [2011]). Ethical guidelines for statistical practice. Retrieved January 2, 2014, from http://www.amstat.org/committees/ethics/

Xenophon. (2008). *The economist* (H. G. Dakyns, Trans.): Project Gutenberg.

Appendix 1: Ethical Analysis Workbook

Framing the Situation (See Chap. 4)

Facts

The table of facts below is an accurate reflection of the objectively-known, incontrovertible facts surrounding the situation being analyzed.

#	Fact	Source
1		
2		
3		
4		
5		
6		
7		
8		
9		
10		

E.A.M. Searing, D.R. Searing (eds.), *Practicing Professional Ethics in Economics and Public Policy*, DOI 10.1007/978-94-017-7306-5

Factual Issues

The table of factual issues below is a list of the known bits of information that are factual in nature but are controversial or unsubstantiated. A good example of this type of issue is an unknown future effect of a given action. Your goal should be to resolve these issues through additional research and turn them into facts, or through making an educated assumption of its resolution.

#	Factual issue	Assumed resolution
1		
2		
3		
4		
5		
6		
7		
8		
9		
10		

Concepts

The table of concepts below is a list of the concepts and their definitions that bear on the situation at hand. This section is used to clearly define these concepts so that someone reading your analysis understands the concepts and definitions being used in your later analyses.

#	Concept	Definition
1		
2		
3		

#	Concept	Definition
4		
5		
6		
7		
8		
9		
10		

Conceptual Issues

The table of conceptual issues below is a list of the concepts that bear on the situation at hand that have ambiguous or controversial definitions. This section is used to state the definitions assumed in the rest of the analyses. They are stated here to clearly outline any controversial definitions separate from their use within the moral analyses.

#	Conceptual issue	Assumed definition
1		
2		
3		
4		
5		
6		
7		
8		
9		
10		

Morals/Values

The table of morals below is a list of the values that will be brought to bear on the situation at hand in the subsequent analyses. This is a good location to clearly elucidate the pieces of a code of ethics (especially a professional code of ethics) that will be brought to bear in this analysis. For example, in most engineering codes, it clearly states that the public's health, safety, and welfare are the paramount virtues and this section of the document would be where you would outline the values that will be used in the analyses.

#	Moral/value	Source
1		
2		
3		
4		
5		
6		
7		
8		
9		
10		

Moral/Value Issues

The table of moral/value issues below is a list of the values that while being followed by the decision-maker in the situation are controversial in nature. These are moral conundrums whose interpretations and proposed answers can change the outcome of the analyses.

#	Moral/value issue	Assumed rule/resolution
1		
2		

#	Moral/value issue	Assumed rule/resolution
3		
4		
5		
6		
7		
8		
9		
10		

Ethical Analysis (See Chap. 5)

Now that you have framed your decision with the information you know from your initial analysis, you are ready to start the ethical analysis phase of your decision-making process. First, define your hypothesis with a null reflecting a status quo of unethical behavior for the proposed action; also, specify an alternative hypothesis of appropriate scope for the situation. Second, you will define your audiences (i.e., those affected by the action being proposed in the hypothesis). Third, you will process some set of the analyses, basing your evaluations and observations on the data resolved and stated in your framing. Fourth, you will interpret the results of the analyses and select the most ethical course of action.

Generate the Hypotheses

There are two hypotheses: the null hypothesis, which is the assumption of an unethical status quo or assumed course of action, and the alternative hypothesis.

The Null Hypothesis

The Alternative Hypotheses

Determine the Audiences

The audiences of any given hypothesis set are all of the entities with moral standing that are affected by the proposed hypotheses. Depending on your moral philosophy these can either be limited to people only or to other living creatures or to large scale systems like the environment. Who you include is really a reflection of your answer to the moral issue surrounding who has moral agency (i.e., someone or something that is free to make their own moral decisions and be affected by them) and who has moral patiency (i.e., someone or something that is not at the level of autonomy to be considered a moral agent, but yet can still be affected by the decisions made around them).

Audience	Description

Visualization: Expected Reciprocity Analysis

Use the table below to organize the analysis results for each audience being considered. Be sure to base your analysis on the data from your frame so you have a solid argument.

Audience	Audience Analysis

Conclusion

Visualization: New York Times Analysis

Imagine the proposed action will be announced in all its glory/infamy in the New York Times tomorrow. Generate the headline and analyze how you would feel if it was published in the paper for all of your friends and acquaintances to see. Be sure to base your analysis on the data from your frame so you have a solid argument.

Proposed Headline

Analysis for Headline

Conclusion

Visualization: Anticipatory Self-Appraisal Analysis

Use the table below to detail your vision of yourself after you have performed the hypothesized action. Be sure to base your analysis on the data from your frame so you have a solid argument.

Analysis

Conclusion

Visualization: Aggregate Application Analysis (Categorical Imperative)

Use the tables below to develop your proposed universal rule and to capture its analysis. Be sure to base your analysis on the data from your frame so you have a solid argument.

Proposed Universal Rule

Analysis for Rule

Conclusion

Virtue Analysis

Use the tables below to describe your desired virtues or admired exemplars and your analyses related to each of the hypotheses as it relates to the virtue or exemplar.

Virtues / Exemplars

Analysis

Conclusion

Utilitarianism: Act Utilitarian Analysis

Use the matrix below to help detail out the effects of the hypothesized action on the audiences identified earlier. We find the use of '+' and '–' symbols a way to easily document the increase or reduction in utility for an audience, with '++' being a greater increase than '+' for example. Be sure to base your analysis on the data from your frame and the audiences identified earlier so you have a solid argument.

	Null hypothesis	Discussion	Alternate hypothesis	Discussion
Audience #1				
Audience #2				
Audience #3				
…				
Audience #N				

Conclusion

Utilitarianism: Rule Utilitarian Analysis

Use the matrix below to help detail out the effects of the universalization of the hypothesized action. Be sure to base your analysis on the data from your frame and the audiences identified earlier so you have a solid argument.

The Null Hypothesis Rule

The Null Hypothesis Rule Analysis

The Alternative Hypothesis Rule

The Alternative Hypothesis Rule Analysis

Conclusion

Utilitarianism: Cost-Benefit Analysis

Use the matrix below to help detail out the effects of the hypothesized action on the audiences identified earlier. Be sure to use a consistent currency and remember to be consistent in the evaluation of the costs and benefits in terms of their likelihoods and expected values. Also, if you are time discounting or using any other parameter involving ambiguity or risk, be sure to note this. Base your analysis on the data from your frame and the audiences identified earlier so you have a solid argument.

	Null hypothesis	Discussion	Alternate hypothesis	Discussion
Audience #1	$		$	
Audience #2	$		$	
Audience #3	$		$	
...	$		$	
Audience #N	$		$	

Conclusion

Respect for Persons: Rights-Based Analysis

The rights-based analysis processes how the proposed actions affect each of the audiences in terms of the actual or possible violation of their rights expressed in tiers. The Tiers to use are:

- Tier 1- Basic Rights- Life, bodily and mental integrity, freedom from torture
- Tier 2- Maintenance Rights- Maintenance of position, livelihood, emotional state
- Tier 3- Advancement Rights- Ability to advance or grow, achieve goals.

We have found that the table below can be used effectively by putting a 1, 2 or 3 in the grid for each violation, and you can subscript it with a 'p' or 'a' for whether it represents a possible or actual violation respectively. Be sure to base your analysis on the data from your frame and the audiences identified earlier so you have a solid argument.

	Null hypothesis	Discussion	Alternate hypothesis	Discussion
Audience #1				
Audience #2				
Audience #3				
…				
Audience #N				

Conclusion

Respect for Persons: Pareto Efficiency Analysis

The pareto efficiency analysis processes how the proposed actions affect each of the audiences in terms of the actual or possible benefit or harm the audience might face with the enactment of the proposed action. In this analysis, you will compare the change in benefits or harms with the enactment of the alternative hypothesis as compared to the null hypothesis. Ideally, your action will only provide benefits or no change for all audiences in order to satisfy the principle. Be sure to base your analysis on the data from your frame and the audiences identified earlier so you have a solid argument.

	Effects of the null hypothesis	Effects of the alternate hypothesis	Change
Audience #1			
Audience #2			
Audience #3			
…			
Audience #N			

Conclusion

Overall Conclusion (See Chap. 6)

The overall conclusion should take into account the conclusions drawn from the analyses performed. Ideally, you should have performed at least one test from each of the types of tests; Visualization, Virtue, Utilitarianism, and Respect for Persons. It is also a good idea to ensure you have used at least one situational (i.e., act-based) and one universal analysis to give you a well-rounded, well-reasoned overall analysis.

Concluding Judgment

The table below can be used for you to look at the results of all of the analyses you have performed in one location to do your final comparison and judgment either by collecting the conclusions from the analyses and solving by summation by observation or through the use of a line-drawing (casuistic) analysis.

Analysis		Conclusion reached
Visualization analyses		
	Expected reciprocity	
	New York times	
	Anticipatory self-appraisal	
	Aggregate application (categorical imperative)	
Virtue analysis		
Utilitarian analyses		
	Act utilitarian analysis	
	Rule utilitarian analysis	
	Cost-benefit analysis	

Analysis		Conclusion reached
Respect for persons analyses		
	Rights-based analysis	
	Pareto-efficiency analysis	
		+0 –

The table above can be used either as a summary table or as a line-drawing tool for helping you decide the final judgment. If you want to use the table for line-drawing, you would represent the conclusion from each of the tests as a point somewhere in the horizontal width of the grid cell according to the poles indicated at the bottom of the table (left-hand side represents absolutely morally permissible action, whereas the right-hand side represents the absolutely morally forbidden action).

Final Conclusion

After all of your framing, analysis, and judgment, you should be able to determine whether you have sufficient evidence to reject the null that the proposed course of action is unethical. If you fail to reject the null, ask yourself where the crucial issues in the process for the proposed course of action are. These will guide you in a redesign of a potential ethical solution to the situation at hand.

Final Conclusion

Discussion or Formulation of New Hypothesis

Appendix 2: Professional Codes of Ethics for the Social Sciences

Anthropology

American Anthropological Association
Main: http://www.aaanet.org/issues/policy-advocacy/code-of-ethics.cfm
Ad.Res.: http://www.aaanet.org/profdev/ethics/

Association of Social Anthropologists of the UK and Commonwealth
Main: http://www.theasa.org/ethics/guidelines.shtml
Ad.Res.: http://www.theasa.org/ethics.shtml

Communications

International Communication Association
Main: http://www.icahdq.org/about_ica/ethics.asp

National Communication Association:
Main: http://www.natcom.org/uploadedFiles/About_NCA/Leadership_and_Governance/Public_Policy_Platform/PDF-PolicyPlatform-NCA_Credo_for_Ethical_Communication.pdf
Ad.Res.: http://www.natcom.org/Tertiary.aspx?id=2119

Criminology

American Society of Criminology
No code of ethics adopted

E.A.M. Searing, D.R. Searing (eds.), *Practicing Professional Ethics in Economics and Public Policy*, DOI 10.1007/978-94-017-7306-5

British Society of Criminology
Main: http://www.natcom.org/uploadedFiles/About_NCA/Leadership_and_Governance/Public_Policy_Platform/PDF-PolicyPlatform-NCA_Credo_for_Ethical_Communication.pdf

Economics

American Academy of Economic and Financial Experts
Main: http://www.aaefe.org/en/ethics-statement

American Economic Association
No formal code of ethics adopted
Disclosure policy: http://www.aeaweb.org/aea_journals/AEA_Disclosure_Policy.pdf

National Association of Forensic Economics
Main: http://nafe.net/about-nafe/nafes-ethics-statement.html

International Economic Development Council
Main: http://www.iedconline.org/web-pages/inside-iedc/iedc-code-of-ethics/

Education

National Education Association
Main: http://www.nea.org/home/30442.htm

American Educational Research Association
Main: http://www.aera.net/Portals/38/docs/About_AERA/CodeOfEthics(1).pdf
Ad.Res.: http://www.aera.net/AboutAERA/AERARulesPolicies/CodeofEthics/tabid/10200/Default.aspx

Environment

National Association of Environmental Professionals
Main: http://www.naep.org/code-of-ethics

National Registry of Environmental Professionals
Main: https://www.nrep.org/ethics.php

History

American Historical Association
Main: http://www.historians.org/about-aha-and-membership/governance/policies-and-documents/statement-on-standards-of-professional-conduct

Human Resource Management

Society for Human Resource Management
Main: http://www.shrm.org/TemplatesTools/Samples/Policies/Pages/InternationalCodeofConductPolicy.aspx

International Relations

International Studies Association
Main: http://www.isanet.org/ISA/Governance/PolicyandProcedures/tabid/216/ID/9/ISA-Code-of-Conduct.aspx

Law

American Bar Association
Main: http://www.americanbar.org/groups/professional_responsibility/publications/model_rules_of_professional_conduct/model_rules_of_professional_conduct_table_of_contents.html

Linguistics

Linguistic Society of America
Main: http://www.linguisticsociety.org/files/Ethics_Statement.pdf

Politics

American Political Science Association
Main: http://www.apsanet.org/content_9350.cfm

Public Administration

American Society of Public Administration
Main: http://www.aspanet.org/public/ASPA/Resources/Code_of_Ethics/ASPA/Resources/Code_of_Ethics/Code_of_Ethics1.aspx?hkey=acd40318-a945-4ffc-ba7b-18e037b1a858

Psychology

American Psychological Association
Main: http://www.apa.org/ethics/code/index.aspx

Public Finance

Government Finance Officers Association
Main: http://www.gfoa.org/index.php?option=com_content&task=view&id=98&Itemid=108

Public Management

Academy of Management
Main: http://aom.org/uploadedFiles/About_AOM/Governance/AOM_Code_of_Ethics.pdf
Ad res: http://aom.org/About-AOM/Ethics.aspx

American Academy of Certified Public Managers
Main: http://www.cpmacademy.org/operations/Code_of_Ethics.pdf

International City/County Management Association
Main: http://www.gfoa.org/index.php?option=com_content&task=view&id=98&Itemid=108

Social Psychology

Society for Personality and Social Psychology
Main: http://www.spsp.org/?page=Ethicspolicy

Social Work

National Association of Social Workers
Main: http://www.socialworkers.org/pubs/code/default.asp

Sociology

American Sociological Association
Main: http://www.asanet.org/about/ethics.cfm

International Sociological Association
Main: http://www.isa-sociology.org/about/isa_code_of_ethics.htm

Statistics

American Statistical Association
Main: http://www.amstat.org/about/ethicalguidelines.cfm

Women's Studies

National Women's Studies Association
Main: http://www.nwsa.org/content.asp?pl=19&contentid=46

Index

E.A.M. Searing, D.R. Searing (eds.), *Practicing Professional Ethics in Economics and Public Policy*, DOI 10.1007/978-94-017-7306-5

V

W